Evolution

EVOLUTION
Genesis and Revelations

WITH READINGS FROM EMPEDOCLES TO WILSON

C. LEON HARRIS

STATE UNIVERSITY OF NEW YORK PRESS
ALBANY

To my father and mother, and to all my other ancestors, whatever their species

Published by
State University of New York Press, Albany

© 1981 State University of New York

All rights reserved

Printed in the United States of America

For information, address State University of New York
Press, State University Plaza, Albany, N.Y., 12246

Library of Congress Cataloging in Publication Data

Harris, C. Leon, 1943—
Evolution, genesis and revelations.

Bibliography: p.
Includes index.
1. Evolution—History. 2. Science—History.
3. Science—Philosophy. I. Title.
B818.H37   575^1.009   81-2555
ISBN 0-87395-486-6   AACR2
ISBN 0-87395-487-4 (pbk.)

Contents

Figures

Tables

Acknowledgments

Writing a book about the cultural influences on scientists has made me keenly aware of how much this book is a product of those around me. To my wife, Mary Jane, I am especially grateful for creating an environment nourishing to the mind. I am also grateful to her and to the following persons for reading parts of the manuscript, and for information, stimulating discussion, and encouragement: Malcolm and Anne Coe, Frank N. Egerton, Duane T. Gish, Mercedes Monjian, Anita Morreale, Paul Roman, Paul B. Siegel, and E. O. Wilson. The administration of the State University College of Arts and Science at Plattsburgh, New York and my colleagues in the Department of Biological Sciences made possible a sabbatic leave without which this book would not have been possible. For their cheerful assistance in obtaining books and articles I thank the staffs of the Feinberg Library of Plattsburgh State University College, the Harvard University Libraries, and the Earl Gregg Swem Library of the College of William and Mary in Virginia. Finally, I am as grateful to Dianna Seymour for typing the manuscript as she must be that it is finished at last.

Introduction

Since Copernicus there has been a growing awareness of the insignificant but propitious place of the Earth in space, but only since the first lunar voyage have we really been able to see ourselves clinging to this green island in the black void. This revelation has come too quickly and too recently for us to reliably judge its effect upon us, but future historians will mark it as a turning point in man's attitude toward himself.

In the same way that artificial satellites have given us a new awareness of our place in space, evolutionary thinking has given us an awareness of our place in time. Unfortunately the evolutionary portrait of man is not as easily analyzed as a photograph from the moon; instead of satellites we must rely on scientific knowledge, history, and philosophy for the necessary perspective. This places a great burden on anyone who would gain a comprehensive appreciation of evolution and its implications. The bibliography at the end of this book represents only a fraction of the literature on evolution. Because of this enormous volume of information no one until now has been rash enough to attempt a synthesis of the factual, historical, and philosophical aspects of evolution for the student and intelligent nonscientist. Evolution has had to be dismembered to be managed, and the reader is usually left with the task of piecing together scientific evidence, history, and philosophy into their original oneness.

Not only evolution but all of science has been hacked out of its historical and philosophical context. Too often science is presented as naked fact obtained in a laboratory sealed against the outside world. Consequently, science and scientists are often perceived as alien or hostile to the rest of humanity. This is likely to be the case until scientists begin to do a better job of portraying themselves realistically. Until then most people will continue to think of the scientist either as amoral automaton or as media crusader, depending whether their image of the scientist comes from the late movie or from Johnny Carson.

Students glean another image of scientists from the historical and philosophical tidbits included in textbooks. According to this model a Great Scientist is someone who managed to be born and to die on two different dates, and who doggedly turned the crank of *the* scientific method until a

1

true theory popped out. Surprisingly, some of our students want to become scientists in spite of such a model. Not surprisingly, many of them will perpetuate the myth of the scientist who lives in a cultural vacuum.

I hope to provide the reader with a more realistic picture of science, as illustrated by evolution. Readers should experience the development of evolutionism as an adventure, and know as people the major figures in this adventure. The only direct link we can have with them is through their writings; therefore I have organized the book around selections from the major writings on the origin of species. This strategy provides some sense of the writers' personalities and avoids the errors frequently found in secondary historical sources. A historical introduction precedes each group of selections. The historical facts included are narrowly selected to emphasize the factors which, in my opinion, influenced the authors. Each chapter closes with an essay on the philosophical basis or implication of each development in our knowledge of the origin of species. These essays are intended to be provocative.

EVOLUTION: WHAT IS IT?

One of the difficulties in thinking about evolution is that the word itself has evolved. Lately the word "evolution" has been extended to encompass the origin of life and even the transformation of inorganic matter as solar systems develop. This book does not deal with such a general evolutionary scheme, but only with special evolution, defined as follows: Evolution is a change in the genetic composition of a population which may gradually lead to a transformation of the population from one species to another. By genetic composition I mean the proportions of individuals carrying particular genetic traits: the gene frequencies. Evolution seldom involves a single mutation arising suddenly at an opportune time, but a gradual change in the frequency of several genes already present in the population. By population I mean the members which are interbreeding within a group. All of the members of a population are of the same species since, by definition, members of two different species are unable to interbreed under natural circumstances. By this definition it also follows that two populations originally of the same species may diverge into two different species if the changes in genetic compositions accumulate to the degree that the two populations could no longer interbreed with each other. It is important to note, however, that evolution is a gradual process, and may not result in the formation of new species.

If the preceding paragraph makes any sense, you understand enough to follow the rest of this book. Other concepts will usually be introduced in the same order that they arose historically, so the reader with little background in biology has the advantage of reviewing the history of evolution with an eye untainted by modern assumptions. However, for those who prefer tainted eyes, good introductions to evolution may be found in recent general biology texts and in encyclopedias. Those who are like me—irreversibly trained in modern biology—have nothing to lose by consulting advanced texts on evolution, such as the recent and authoritative volume by Dobzhansky et al. (1977).

One idea which occurs early in this book is the synthetic or neo-Darwinian theory of evolution. This is currently the most widely accepted explanation of why and how evolution took place. Unfortunately it is so well established that many evolutionists speak as if evolution and the neo-Darwinian theory of evolution are the same thing. They convolute the two in the phrase "the theory of evolution." In nonscientific parlance a theory is little more than a wild guess, so many people infer that even evolutionists consider it open to doubt whether evolution took place. Those who realize that a theory is a proposed explanation for a phenomenon are still left to wonder whether *the* theory of evolution is Lamarck's, Darwin's, the neo-Darwinian, the neutralist, or some other theory. It will save considerable confusion if the reader bears in mind the difference between evolution and theories which are proposed to account for it. In this book evolution will be treated as a fact regardless of whether any of the proposed theories are correct, just as gravity is a fact even though Newton's Law of Universal Gravitation is inadequate. I shall always use the term "evolution" to mean the process of evolution, and "theory of evolution" to mean a proposed explanation for evolution. May my typing finger wither and drop off if I use the phrase "*the* theory of evolution."

The synthetic or neo-Darwinian theory is a modification of Darwin's classical theory which synthesizes Darwin's idea of natural selection with modern genetics. This theory can be summarized in two statements: (1) There is natural selection for organisms expressing genetic traits which contribute to their survival, and (2) genes undergo mutations which are not directed by the environment or the organism itself. The idea of natural selection is analogous to artificial selection in which a breeder selects the most desired plants or animals for propagation. According to this concept, organisms are selected by nature according to their ability to leave viable offspring. Since those offspring are more likely to inherit the genes which contributed to the fitness of their parents, their offspring will also be more likely to leave viable offspring, and so on. In this way the proportion of individuals bearing those genes in the population will steadily increase. One might assume that populations would eventually become genetically homogeneous; but mutations are constantly occurring at random. The neo-Darwinian theory differs from many others in assuming that mutations are not willed or selectively induced by the organism or the environment. Thus if new conditions would make a particular mutation advantageous for a population, that mutation must already have arisen by chance in order to be naturally selected. The two fundamental ideas of the neo-Darwinian theory will be covered more thoroughly later in this book.

GENESIS: THE HISTORY OF EVOLUTIONISM

This book is as much about the evolution of science as it is about the science of evolution. What are the origins of scientific ideas, and why are some ideas accepted and some rejected? To use the neo-Darwinian metaphor, what historical factors have selected some mutants of scientific thought and allowed others to perish? The answer cannot be simply that some ideas are right and some are wrong, because many good theories were once ignored, and many presently useful theories are known to be not entirely correct. Only by considering the historical context of an idea—its environment—can we judge its fitness.

There was a time when historians of science could be satisfied just to get the names and dates correct and to show who was right and who was wrong. Several useful histories of evolutionism, such as those by Clodd (1897), Fothergill (1952), More (1925), Osborn (1929), and Radl (1930) are of this type. The approach these authors took was acceptable when science was regarded as the progressive accumulation of experimental data which eventually added up to a theory, or as a game in which the earliest correct theory won the prize. Most historians of science now realize that presently accepted theories are not the proper standard by which past theories can be judged. The histories of evolutionism that commemorated the centennial of the *Origin of Species,* such as those by Eiseley (1958), Glass et al. (1959), and Greene (1959) reflect the awareness that theories are shaped or selected by their social environment. This trend has continued in the past twenty years, mostly in journals not read by a wide audience.

REVELATIONS: EVOLUTION AND PHILOSOPHY

How do we get nature to reveal itself to us, and what does nature reveal about man and his place in nature? These questions ought to be the concern of biologists as well as philosophers, but life scientists (once called natural historians) have traditionally been content to describe phenomena rather than to probe ultimate causes. This may simply reflect my prejudice as a onetime physicist (formerly called natural philosopher), or it could be an impression obtained from the fact that most books on the philosophy of science deal only with physics. Happily there seems to be a growing interest n the philosophy of biology, as illustrated by such recent books as those by

Ayala and Dobzhansky (1974), Beckner (1959), Breck and Yourgrau (1972), Grene and Mendelsohn (1976), Hull (1974), Munson (1971), Rensch (1971), Ruse (1973), and Simon (1971). There are still many biologists who believe that philosophy makes no difference so long as they get the right answer to biological questions, but it seems to me that philosophy is the only assurance we have that science can provide right answers. How do we know that experimentation is a valid approach? Few scientists thought so before the Renaissance. What is the correct scientific method: the inductive method of Bacon, or the deductive method of Descartes? Most biologists would answer that the deductive (or hypothetico-deductive) method is correct, but that method was considered slipshod in Darwin's time. What is a scientific theory, anyway? One must go outside science, to philosophy, for answers to these questions.

In addition to these epistemological concerns, the philosophy of biology includes a continuing evaluation of man's place in nature. Evolution implies that we are animals, but are we *only* animals? Is man unique, not only on Earth, but in the universe? What do we owe to our fellow creatures? Where are we heading in evolution; can we and should we alter our course? The answers to these questions require not only scientific knowledge of man's origins, but philosophical understanding as well.

1

Prescientific Concepts of the Origin of Species: Genesis

People have probably always wondered where they came from. How we and other species originated is not simply a riddle for modern science and idle minds; the answer influences the way we treat other men and other species. How humane we are depends on whether we regard life as a whim of the gods, believe other species were created for man's pleasure, or think all species are equally a part of nature. Ideas of the origin of species depend in turn on moral and ethical codes, since an idea would not be accepted if it were not consistent with those codes. This holds true not only for religious concepts of origins, such as those found in Genesis, but also for the Darwinian concept. The relationship between science and society is reciprocal.

This book is about the interaction of culture with the development of the concept of evolution. We begin with a look at prescientific societies. By a prescientific society I mean one which does not accept the minimum conceptual requirement for science, which is *the belief that natural phenomena result consistently from causes which can be understood by man.* This is not an all-or-none requirement for science; cultures are scientific to the degree that they accept natural causality. Even prescientific people could recognize that the harvest follows the planting, but rather than infer a cause-and-effect relationship, they may have seen this as two aspects of the same thing. Do we harvest because we plant, or do we plant because we harvest? At the other extreme, even members of the most scientifically advanced societies have their cherished superstitions.

The term "prescientific" is not meant to be derogatory. Man has gotten along well—some would say better—without science for most of his history. Most of us believe that scientific thinking, or what we call ordinary logic, is "natural" because we happen to live in a culture permeated by the assumption of cause and effect, measurements of time, space, and mass, and the other trappings of science. Our acceptance of science is undoubtedly conditioned by the "goods" which result from its application, but we could well revert to prescientific thinking if the goods start to be cancelled out by such "bads" as radiation and pollution.

Science is only one of many approaches to an understanding of nature; many people, including scientists, also employ art, religion, mysticism, and other ways. Accepting one approach does not necessitate the rejection of others. Prescientific cultures were more likely to seek answers in religion and mysticism; in many cases those answers were more useful to them than scientific answers would have been. It is not literally true that women originated from the rib of a man, but this belief expressed the dependence of woman on man which was assumed by ancient Semites.[1]

It is seldom easy to interpret prescientific ideas, especially since many of them rely on assumptions not current in Western cultures. For example, we have a tendency to categorize concepts into dualities—cause and effect, matter and spirit, true and false—which is not found in prescientific thought. Like cause and effect, matter and spirit are considered two aspects of the same thing in many prescientific cultures. We in the West think of spirit (if we think of it at all) as something which occupies the same space as matter but with little influence upon it. We attempt to explain all phenomena, including life and mind, by material processes if possible. One often finds just the opposite inclination in prescientific thinking: a tendency to explain the behavior of nonliving objects as mental or spiritual phenomena.

Equally artificial to prescientific cultures is the distinction between truth and falsity. Sentences which are neither true nor false (or both), such as "The sentence you are reading is false," are only amusing paradoxes to us. We do not see them as evidence that there is something fundamentally wrong with the categories of true and false. Yet our exclusion of a middle state between true and false is merely a convention inherited from the Greeks. To many prescientific minds there was nothing odd about a statement being somewhere in between true and false.[2]

One can easily appreciate the difficulty of understanding prescientific ideas by trying to read a scientific article without assuming that there is a difference between cause and effect, matter and spirit, or true and false. This difficulty makes generalizations about prescientific cultures perilous, but it does appear that most prescientific cultures conceive of a small universe enlivened by numerous gods and spirits. All nature is animated by a spirit, even "inanimate" objects. The gods live among us or they commute easily from their abodes to Earth. The heavens and the heavenly bodies are a few miles away at most. The gods are either animals with human traits or humans with animalistic tendencies. Man originated as a plan, accident, or sport which the gods soon found cause to regret. It is a cozy world in contrast to our nightmare fall through infinite space and time, with no gods close enough or interested enough to reach out for us.[3]

THE EVOLUTION OF GENESIS

Genesis includes two of the most detailed and best preserved examples of prescientific thought on the origin of species. These creation stories are repeated here for that reason, but also because many of the evolutionists to be discussed later have been influenced through piety or fear by the acceptance of Genesis into the dominant religion of the West. To a great extent this influence is still felt in the United States, even though biblical scholars and most theologians are agreed that the significance of Genesis must be sought at a level more profound than the literal. Two centuries of biblical research and archeology indicate that Genesis was compiled by extraordinary but fallible men who would probably have been shocked to learn that some people centuries after them would regard them as stenographers of God's words.

Scholarly doubts regarding the literal authority of Genesis began in 1753 when Jean Astruc noted that two names were used in Genesis to indicate God: Elohim and JHVH (pronounced Yahweh). Astruc's suggestion led to the present recognition of at least five individuals or groups who contributed to Genesis and the other four books of the Pentateuch: J^1 and J^2, who referred to God as JHVH; E, who used the name Elohim for God; D, who wrote Deuteronomy; and P, whose editing and additions brought the Pentateuch to the approximate state which we now know.[4] We are concerned primarily with the authors of the two creation myths, J^1, J^2, and P. J^1 and J^2 wrote the simple, folksy stories of the Garden of Eden, Noah's Ark, and the Tower of Babel. They describe JHVH (usually translated Lord) as being not much more than human: he crashes about in the Garden (Gen. 3:8), is fooled by Adam and Eve (Gen. 3:9), considers it just to punish all men for the sins of Adam and Eve (Gen.3:16, 17), is jealous of his position as an immortal (Gen. 3:22), and admits his error in creating man (Gen. 6:6). P's God, Elohim, seems better cast in the role of the Almighty. He creates species simply by commanding them to be, rather than by planting and molding out of clay. There is logic behind his daily creations in the first chapter of Genesis, in contrast to the trial-and-error attempts by JHVH to find a suitable partner for Adam. Because of this logic, P is thought to have been a priest or a committee of priests. In order to understand the two creation stories in Genesis we need to understand the motivations of J^1, J^2, and P. Were they just telling good stories, or were they motivated by events in their times?

J^1 and J^2 tell us nothing about themselves. We know they lived around 1000 and 900 B. C., respectively, because their style appears in the Second Book of

Samuel describing events with which they were familiar. J[1] apparently began this book to protest the transfer by King David of the seat of government and religion from Hebron to Jerusalem, in about 1000 B. C.[5] By referring to JHVH's command to David to rule at Hebron (2 Sam. 2:1), and by writing in the Pentateuch of the founding of the nation of Israel and of the Exodus, J[1] seems to have been accusing David of departing from JHVH's plan for the Jews.

J[2] completed this narrative in response to an even greater crisis—a split between the northern tribes (called Israel) and the southern tribes (Judah). J[2], dismayed by this further thwarting of JHVH's plan, attempted to reunite Israel and Judah by emphasizing their common heritage. This was no simple task, because the northerners had long been isolated from the south by geography and diverging tradition. The northern tribes did not share with the southerners the tradition of having entered Canaan from the south with Moses; they believed they had come from the east across the Jordan River. While Judah felt that its covenant with JHVH had been established at Kedesh during the Exodus, as described by J[1], Israel held Sinai to be the source of its relation with JHVH. These differences were further compli- · cated by the adoption of local customs and even religions from the Canaanites. Following the conquest of Canaan the demands of mutual defense had masked the differences between north and south under a weak alliance ruled by the Judges and then the Kings. However, this alliance was finally undermined by the heavy taxation to support the extravagant projects of King Solomon. Finally, in 936 B. C., Israel seized the occasion of Solomon's death as a time to secede.

In appealing to Israel to reunite with Judah J[2] could not simply repeat the writings of J[1], with his southern perspective. J[2] therefore modified the J[1] account of the Exodus to make it appear that Moses detoured first to Sinai and then to the east of the Jordan River. (See Fig. 1.) In this way the traditional origins of both the north and the south could be combined in a single Exodus, even though the impression was created that Moses wasn't quite sure where he was going. In addition, J[2] added to J[1]'s writing folklore which the northerners had absorbed from the Canaanites. By weaving into this history the myths of Eden, the Flood, and the Tower of Babel, J[2] apparently hoped to convince Israel that all Jews had a covenant with JHVH, and that the rift between them thwarted their destiny.[6]

J[2] did not succeed. The split and occasional war continued for two centuries. During this time a wealthy class in Israel accumulated large tracts of land, and many of the once-independent Jews became serfs, then slaves in their Promised Land.[7] Such conditions do not inspire patriotism, and the Assyrians easily conquered Israel in 721 B. C. The Assyrians themselves were eclipsed by the Babylonians, who then absorbed not only Israel but Judah as well. In 586 B. C. Judah declared its independence, an act of bravado which

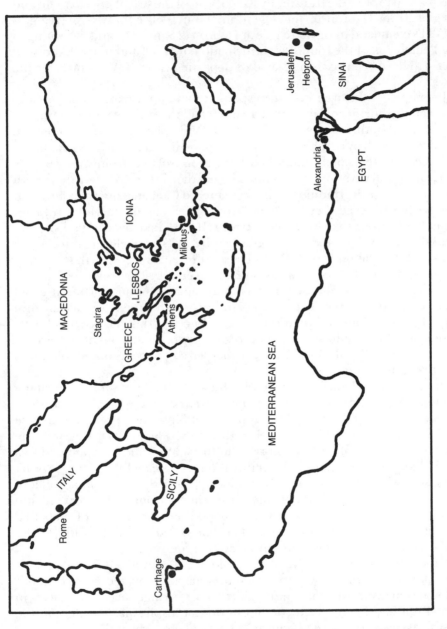

Figure 1. Outline map of the eastern Mediterranean showing principal places mentioned in the first two chapters.

Babylonia rewarded by destroying Jerusalem and carrying off virtually the entire population to Babylon.

The fifty-year Babylonian captivity proved to be the impetus for reunification of Israel and Judah. The Jews functioned in Babylonian society without losing their cultural and religious identity, and Babylon served as a neutral ground on which differences between Israel and Judah were resolved. Thus, when the Persians under Cyrus conquered Babylonia in 539 B. C. for the purpose (Cyrus claimed) of restoring the gods deposed by Babylonia, the Jews were prepared to make good use of the opportunity (Isa. 44:28). They reconquered Palestine from those who had settled there in their absence, and rebuilt the Temple at Jerusalem as the center of a united Israel. Israel's history remains relatively uneventful thereafter until the rise of Alexander's empire.

Rebuilding Israel after the Captivity required the reconstruction of history. P's task was to sift through the writings of J^1 and J^2 (which had been combined with those of E) to provide a coherent social bond, based on the plan of JHVH-Elohim for the Jews. P eliminated most of the obvious contradictions and deviations from the religious forms established in Babylon and prefaced J^2's Eden myth with another creation story based on the *Enuma elish,*[8] which was then popular in Babylon. The result of P's work is the following account of the creation by Elohim (God) in the first week (Gen. 1:1–2:4), which is followed by what appears to be the elaboration of the creation of animals and humans by JHVH-Elohim (Lord God) (Gen. 2:4–25).

Chapter 1

[*First story of creation.*] 1 In the beginning, when God created the heavens and the earth, 2 the earth was a formless wasteland, and darkness covered the abyss, while a mighty wind swept over the waters.

3 Then God said, "Let there be light," and there was light. 4 God saw how good the light was. God then separated the light from the darkness. 5 God called the light "day," and the darkness he called "night." Thus evening came, and morning followed—the first day.

6 Then God said, "Let there be a dome in the middle of the waters, to separate one body of water from the other." And so it happened: 7 God

made the dome, and it separated the water above the dome from the water below it. 8 God called the dome "the sky." Evening came, and morning followed—the second day.

9 Then God said, "Let the water under the sky be gathered into a single basin, so that the dry land may appear." And so it happened: the water under the sky was gathered into its basin, and the dry land appeared. 10 God called the dry land "the earth," and the basin of the water he called "the sea." God saw how good it was. 11 Then God said, "Let the earth bring forth vegetation: every kind of plant that bears seed and every kind of fruit tree on earth that bears fruit with its seed in it." And so it happened: 12 the earth brought forth every kind of plant that bears seed and every kind of fruit tree on earth that bears fruit with its seed in it. God saw how good it was. 13 Evening came, and morning followed—the third day.

14 Then God said: "Let there be lights in the dome of the sky, to separate day from night. Let them mark the fixed times, the days and the years, 15 and serve as luminaries in the dome of the sky, to shed light upon the earth." And so it happened: 16 God made the two great lights, the greater one to govern the day, and the lesser one to govern the night; and he made the stars. 17 God set them in the dome of the sky, to shed light upon the earth, 18 to govern the day and the night, and to separate the light from the darkness. God saw how good it was. 19 Evening came, and morning followed—the fourth day.

20 Then God said, "Let the water teem with an abundance of living creatures, and on the earth let birds fly beneath the dome of the sky." And so it happened: 21 God created the great sea monsters and all kinds of swimming creatures with which the water teems, and all kinds of winged birds. God saw how good it was, 22 and God blessed them, saying, "Be fertile, multiply, and fill the water of the seas; and let the birds multiply on the earth." 23 Evening came, and morning followed—the fifth day.

24 Then God said, "Let the earth bring forth all kinds of living creatures: cattle, creeping things, and wild animals of all kinds." And so it happened: 25 God made all kinds of wild animals, all kinds of cattle, and all kinds of creeping things of the earth. God saw how good it was. 26 Then God said: "Let us make man in our image, after our likeness. Let them have dominion over the fish of the sea, the birds of the air, and the cattle, and over all the wild animals and all the creatures that crawl on the ground."

27 God created man in his image;

> in the divine image he created him;
> male and female he created them.

28 God blessed them, saying: "Be fertile and multiply; fill the earth and subdue it. Have dominion over the fish of the sea, the birds of the air, and all the living things that move on the earth." 29 God also said: "See, I give you every seed-bearing plant all over the earth and every tree that has seed-bearing fruit on it to be your food, 30 and to all the animals of the land, all the birds of the air, and all the living creatures that crawl on the ground, I give all the green plants for food." And so it happened. 31 God looked at everything he had made, and he found it very good. Evening came, and morning followed—the sixth day.

Chapter 2

1 Thus the heavens and the earth and all their array were completed. 2 Since on the seventh day God was finished with the work he had been doing, he rested on the seventh day from all the work he had undertaken. 3 So God blessed the seventh day and made it holy, because on it he rested from all the work he had done in creation.

4 Such is the story of the heavens and the earth at their creation. [*Second story of creation*.] At the time when the Lord God made the earth and the heavens—5 while as yet there was no field shrub on earth and no grass of the field had sprouted, for the Lord God had sent no rain upon the earth and there was no man to till the soil, 6 but a stream was welling up out of the earth and was watering all the surface of the ground—7 the Lord God formed man out of the clay of the ground and blew into his nostrils the breath of life, and so man became a living being.

8 Then the Lord God planted a garden in Eden, in the east, and he placed there the man whom he had formed. 9 Out of the ground the Lord God made various trees grow that were delightful to look at and good for food, with the tree of life in the middle of the garden and the tree of the knowledge of good and bad.

10 A river rises in Eden to water the garden; beyond there it divides and becomes four branches. 11 The name of the first is the Pishon; it is the one that winds through the whole land of Havilah, where there is gold. 12 The gold of that land is excellent; bdellium and lapis lazuli are also there. 13 The name of the second river is the Gihon; it is the one that winds all through the land of Cush. 14 The name of the third river is the Tigris; it is the one that flows east of Asshur. The fourth river is the Euphrates.

15 The Lord God then took the man and settled him in the garden of Eden, to cultivate and care for it. 16 The Lord God gave man this order: "You are free to eat from any of the trees of the garden 17 except the tree of knowledge of good and bad. From that tree you shall not eat; the moment you eat from it you are surely doomed to die."

18 The Lord God said: "It is not good for the man to be alone. I will make a suitable partner for him." 19 So the Lord God formed out of the ground various wild animals and various birds of the air, and he brought them to the man to see what he would call them; whatever the man called each of them would be its name. 20 The man gave names to all the cattle, all the birds of the air, and all the wild animals; but none proved to be the suitable partner for the man.

21 So the Lord God cast a deep sleep on the man, and while he was asleep, he took out one of his ribs and closed up its place with flesh. 22 The Lord God then built up into a woman the rib that he had taken from the man. When he brought her to the man, 23 the man said:

> "This one, at last, is bone of my bones
>   and flesh of my flesh;
> This one shall be called 'woman,'
>   for out of 'her man' this one has been taken."

24 That is why a man leaves his father and mother and clings to his wife, and the two of them become one body.

25 The man and his wife were both naked, yet they felt no shame.

FUNDAMENTALISTS VERSUS EVOLUTION: THE ORIGIN OF SPECIOUS ARGUMENTS

Even though the diverse and profane origins of Genesis have been known to scholars for 200 years, Protestant clergymen were not always trusted with this knowledge during their training, and many who were found reasons for not sharing it with laymen. Consequently, a large number of people still regard the Bible as a literal transcription of the word of God. Because evolution means a gradual transformation of new species from old, the conflict with the fundamentalist[9] belief in the miraculous creation of "kinds" was inevitable. Darwin's *Origin of Species* aroused intense religious opposition led by Bishop Wilberforce. Darwin, who remained aloof from the fracas, fortunately had as his "bulldog" Thomas Henry Huxley, who in 1860 seems to have stunned the opposition into silence by preferring an ape over Bishop Wilberforce as a desirable ancestor.

In the United States the public was diverted by the buildup of hostilities between North and South, so the evolution debate simmered until 1925, when the state of Tennessee saw fit to prosecute Thomas Scopes for the crime of teaching evolution in a public school. In defending Scopes, Clarence Darrow made a monkey of William Jennings Bryan, the leader of an antievolution crusade and prosecutor at the trial. The victory of evolution over fundamentalism was a hollow one, however. Even as America was laughing at the Scopes fiasco, pious legislators were passing laws to keep schoolchildren from learning their ancestry and timid book publishers and school officials were completing the de-Darwinizing of biology. As recently as 1968 it was possible for an American teacher to be prosecuted and fired for teaching evolution—the First Amendment, separation of church and state, and academic freedom notwithstanding.[10]

Most Christians have made their peace with Darwin, and fundamentalism was thought to be mostly a relic of America's more innocent past. Evolutionists were therefore surprised when the corpse of antievolution arose in a new shroud beginning in the early 1970s. Fundamentalists adopted the tactic of portraying creation as a scientific theory and evolution as a dogma of the religion of "humanism." (See Morris, 1977a.) In a burlesque of civil rights arguments, they demanded equal time for the teaching of creation in public schools. (They did not, however, demand equal time for the teaching of evolution in religion courses.) The California Board of Education nearly adopted their scheme in 1970, and several state legislators and many school boards continue to take it seriously, even though the courts have rejected it. The idea of equal time for alternative theories is seductive to fair-minded people, but if creation is not scientifically supported it has no more right to equal time than the stork theory of childbirth.[11]

Evolutionists have generally responded to antievolutionist attacks simply by asserting once more that evolution is the only scientifically accepted explanation of the origin of species. This has played into the hands of fundamentalists who claim that evolution is only a dogma held by an elite core of arrogant authoritarians. People who resent control of their lives by experts are all too willing to believe such claims (Nelkin, 1977a). With few exceptions (such as Aulie, 1972; Callaghan, 1980; Cloud, 1977; J. A. Moore, 1975), evolutionists have not provided the public with the evidence against creation as an alternative to evolution. This seems an appropriate occasion to depart from that polite custom, even though it risks offending my friends who are nonmilitant fundamentalists.

Is the Bible Literally True?

There are apparently no creationists who are not fundamentalists first. Thus the case for creation and against evolution rests largely on the claim that the Bible is without factual error. Fundamentalists believe that man and other "kinds" of life were created suddenly and separately some 6,000 years ago,[12] but there is no reason to accept this if there are factual errors elsewhere in the Bible. (Of course we may disregard errors such as that which caused a seventeenth-century Bible to read, "Thou shalt commit adultery.")

Errors in the two creation accounts in Genesis will be dealt with at the end of this chapter. For now let us begin with Cain's story in Genesis 4:12–17. Whom did Cain marry (4:17), since in the Bible only he and his parents, Adam and Eve, exist at the time he married? When the Lord condemned Cain to be a "restless wanderer on the earth," why did Cain fear that "anyone" would slay him (Gen. 4:14, 15)? How did Cain escape the curse and settle in Nod (Gen. 4:16), and who populated his city of Enoch (Gen. 4:17)?

How could Jabal have been "the ancestor of all who dwell in tents and keep cattle" (Gen. 4:20) when only Noah's family survived the Flood (Gen. 7:21)? (See also Gen. 4:21, 22.) What are we to make of Gen. 6:1–4: "The sons of heaven had intercourse with the daughters of man, who bore them sons"? Who were these sons of heaven if not figments of mythology?[13]

Is not Leviticus 11:5–6 in error when it states that hares and rock badgers chew the cud? Doesn't the Bible betray further zoological confusion in stating in Jon. 2:1 that a fish swallowed Jonah, and in Matt. 12:40 that it was a whale?

Could "the Lord" have been "a satan" when he provoked David to take a census? (Compare 2 Sam. 24:1 with 1 Chron. 21:1.)

How came Joseph to have two fathers (Matt. 1:16; Luke 3:23), and Jesus to have two different genealogies? Was it not an error that made Luke (3:35–36) delete from his genealogy a generation which is recorded in Gen. 11:13 and 1 Chron. 1:18?

Were there two autopsies of Judas, one finding that he hanged himself (Matt. 27:5) and another that he died from a fall (Acts 1:16–18)? (Or did the fall perhaps occur when the rope broke?)

Did God inspire three different versions of the dying words of Jesus? (Compare Matt. 27:47 and Mark 15:34 with Luke 24:46 and with John 19:30.)

But enough. The recitation of factual shortcomings in the Bible is of concern only to fundamentalists. It will only bore those who search the Bible for something deeper than fact.

Fundamentalist Arguments against Evolution

Fundamentalists usually offer only two choices—Genesis or evolution. Having convinced themselves that evolution is false, they are then satisfied that Genesis must be true, even in the absence of proof.[14] We would commit the same error if we believed that the contradictions within the Bible leave no alternative but evolution. Evolutionists need to be challenged by rational questions from informed skeptics; the stagnation of science follows shortly after its theories are thought to be proved.[15] Let us therefore examine the arguments of fundamentalists.

The volume of antievolutionist writings shrinks considerably if we observe the distinction between evolution and theories of evolution, since much of this literature really consists of biologists' criticisms of natural selection passed off as criticism of evolution. Evolution is one of the few things almost all biologists can agree on, so it is especially disturbing for them to find themselves conscripted into battle against evolutionism on the basis of their doubts about natural selection. In an effort to keep this from happening to me in a 1975 article on the neo-Darwinian theory, I took the precaution of stating in the opening paragraph that the paper does not support "the arguments of anti-evolutionists, since evolution is a fact regardless of whether the neo-Darwinian theory is correct. . . ." Imagine my surprise upon reading that I was admitting that "evolution is really no more scientific than is creation" (Gish, mimeographed manuscript), and that I was denying the claim "that creation is mere religious dogma while evolution is a scientifically testable theory" (Gish, 1976, p. ii). Whether deliberate or not, this is playing rather loosely with the Ninth Commandment.[16]

When doubts about natural selection are eliminated, antievolutionists' arguments are of three major kinds: 1) *moral* arguments based on the moral consequences of accepting evolution; 2) *design* arguments based on the appearance of design in biological adaptations; and 3) *scientific* arguments about the evidence for and against evolution.

Morality

The teaching of evolution promotes (in alphabetical order) abortion, corruption, drug addiction, environmental problems, genocide, greed, immorality, lust, militarism, racism, and streaking. It fosters both Nazism and Marxism. And it has led to the assassination of President Kennedy. (The fatal shots were fired from a building in which evolutionist school books were stored!)[17] At least this would be so if fundamentalist critics of evolution are to be believed. At times these fundamentalists seem unsure whether it was Eve or Darwin who first discovered sin. No matter what the current fashion in immorality, they can almost always show that evolutionism is the cause.

In the late 1920s, however, there were several notable instances when fundamentalists could not blame Darwin for lapses in morality; one fundamentalist leader was convicted of stealing govenment liquor, another killed an unarmed Catholic, and a third emerged from a love nest claiming she had been kidnapped by a gang of gamblers, dope peddlers, and evolutionists. And since Darwin was clever enough to be born in the nineteenth century, he escapes blame for the racism and militarism of the Holy Crusades, the corruption of the church which led to Protestantism, and the killing and torture of Christians by Christians in the Counter-Reformation. It is debatable whether terrorism in Northern Ireland or the activities of the Lebanese Christian Militia are simply a continuation of these sacred traditions or the product of Darwin's teachings. I personally doubt that evolutionism is capable of inspiring as much meanness and evil—or as much greatness and goodness—as Christianity.[18]

Design

The concept of design is as old as the making of tools, but probably no older. In Western cultures the legacy of Aristotle and the ubiquity of our contrivances make design inescapable. It is therefore not surprising that we think we see design in the adaptations of living organisms to the conditions of life. Even evolutionists find themselves thinking teleologically: as if organs served a *purpose* and not simply a *function*. Many evolutionists believe personally that even though adaptations occur by natural processes they were ultimately designed by the god who dictates the laws of nature. This is the concept of theistic evolution. It would be impossible to disprove supernatural guidance in evolution, although it can be shown to be unnecessary for a scientific explanation. Theistic evolution is therefore an alternative to purely mechanistic and materialistic evolution.

The special creation posited by fundamentalists differs from theistic evolution. It postulates the sudden appearance of species already designed to survive, while evolutionism—theistic or otherwise—postulates the slow acquisition of adaptations, leading to gradual changes and the emergence of new species. Fundamentalists often distill the design argument into the question "Can there be a watch without a Watchmaker?"[19] But does it follow that the "Watchmaker" must be the Judeo-Christian God, and not simply nature, or perhaps a totem in some remote African village? Hume raised that question two centuries ago, and no satisfactory answer has been provided except by revelation. Hume raised two additional weaknesses of the design argument: 1) The argument implicitly assumes that God would design things in about the same way man would; otherwise we would not be able to perceive the design. This amounts to creating God in our own image. 2) In order to determine whether an object is designed we need to compare it with something not designed. But fundamentalists tell us that the entire universe is designed by God.[20]

There is still another logical flaw in the design argument. The concept of design belongs to the realm of the artificial. We recognize that an object was designed by man if its appearance or functioning suggests that it was made with a purpose in mind. But is it logically valid to apply the same reasoning to natural objects? Two examples may make this clearer. Before the invention of the compass many sailors must have thanked God for designing the North Star to guide them (even though it is off by 1° and is no help in the southern hemisphere). But can we believe today that this star was positioned for the good of inhabitants of an insignificant planet 470 light years (4.3×10^{15} kilometers) away? If the agnostic Clarence Darrow had died from a stroke just after defending Scopes many fundamentalists would have rejoiced in this marvelous exhibit of God's design. As it was, William Jennings Bryan was the one who died. Both of these examples raise doubts about man's competence as a judge of God's or nature's works.

Fundamentalists often represent the choice as one between God's design and random evolution. How can any adaptation emerge from a process which depends on chance? The fact is that evolutionists never claim that evolution is solely reliant on chance; this is obvious in the term "natural *selection.*" The evolutionists' watchmaker is the biological parent(s), unconsciously "designing" its offspring according to its genetic instructions. Occasionally a slightly improved "watch" occurs because of a random change in the genetic instructions, and natural selection tends to favor that model.

Scientific

Unlike arguments based on morality and design, scientific arguments are those which have direct bearing on the question whether evolution occurred. Evolutionists could benefit from logically valid challenges to their present concepts; unfortunately most fundamentalists' arguments against evolution prove nothing except their ignorance of science. For example, a Jehovah's Witness publication states that Siamese twins are mutant. (Anon., 1967, Ch. 6). The author of *Awake!* for 22 October 1973 (p. 24) apparently sees no difference between evolution and embryonic development. A booklet for the International Christian Crusade (Anon. 1970) states that Darwinism denies altruism (p. 93), and that there is no known source of new genes (p. 46). (Darwin [1859, Ch. 4] recognized the occurrence of altruism, and any good evolution text deals with both altruism and new genes.) In some cases Anonymous has been overtaken by events, as when he stated that no new species has been produced experimentally (1970, p. 35), and that all reptiles are "cold-blooded" (p. 12). His ink was hardly dry when Dobzhansky and Pavlovsky (1971) reported the production of a new incipient species of fruit fly: one which produced viable offspring when mated with its own type, but not when mated with the species from which it was derived. Recent research on dinosaur fossils indicates that many dinosaurs were "warm-blooded" (Bakker, 1975; Ostrom, 1978).[21]

Not all antievolutionist literature is this silly. There are several organizations of Bible-oriented scientists who are interested in the relation of evolution to Scripture. Among these are the American Scientific Affiliation (which does not take a stand against evolution), the Evolution Protest Movement (British), the Creation Science Research Center, the Institute for Creation Research, and the Creation Research Society (Nelkin, 1977a, Ch. 5.) The last of these, the CRS, is perhaps the most active, with more than 600 voting members, all with graduate degrees in science. The CRS is unique among organizations with scientific pretensions in its insistence upon homogeneity of thought among its members. Every applicant for membership must attest to his orthodoxy on the following doctrines: 1) "The Bible is the Word of God, and . . . all of its assertions are historically and scientifically true in all of the original autographs. . . .This means that the account of origins in Genesis is a factual presentation of simple historical truths." 2) "All basic types of living things, including man, were made by direct creative acts of God during Creation Week as described by Genesis." 3) "The great Flood described by Genesis . . . was an historical event. . . ." 4) "Finally, we are an organization of Christian men of science. . . ."

According to Gish (1975), the CRS

was established primarily for research in all fields of science *designed to demonstrate* that the scientific evidence related to origins can be correlated and explained much more satisfactorily by the concept of special creation and a universal catastrophic flood than the concepts of evolution and uniformitarian geology. [Note: Uniformitarian geology is based on the assumption that the Earth's crust was shaped in the past by the same forces operating today. Emphasis added.]

In other words, the purpose of CRS research is to prove a preconceived theory rather than to test it objectively.

In spite of their peculiar philosophy of science, contributors to the *CRS Quarterly* and to other creation-science journals can be expected to represent the best arguments for creation and against evolution. The major areas of argument are geology, genetics, taxonomy, and thermodynamics.

Geology. One of the most frequently cited geological arguments for creation is the allegedly sudden appearance of numerous fossilized animals in Cambrian strata. (See Table 1 for an outline of the geological time scale.) Presumably, we are supposed to infer that creation took place at the dawn of the Cambrian period. However, fossils of microorganisms, jellyfish, worms, and possibly sponges have been discovered in Precambrian strata (Schopf, 1975, 1978). Even if there were no evidence of life prior to the Cambrian period, the fossil record cannot be reconciled with a brief period during which every kind of organism was created. The earliest Cambrian fossils include only marine invertebrates; none of the kinds mentioned in Genesis is represented. Fish, great sea monsters, birds, creeping animals, beasts, and men began littering the countryside with their remains much later. (See Table 1.)

Moreover, measurements of Cambrian fossils by several methods based on the rate of formation of isotopes by nuclear decay indicate an age of about 600,000,000 years for the Cambrian fossils, not the 6,000 years allowed by Genesis. Creationists (for example Morris, 1974, Ch. 6) have pointed out

Outline of the geological time scale

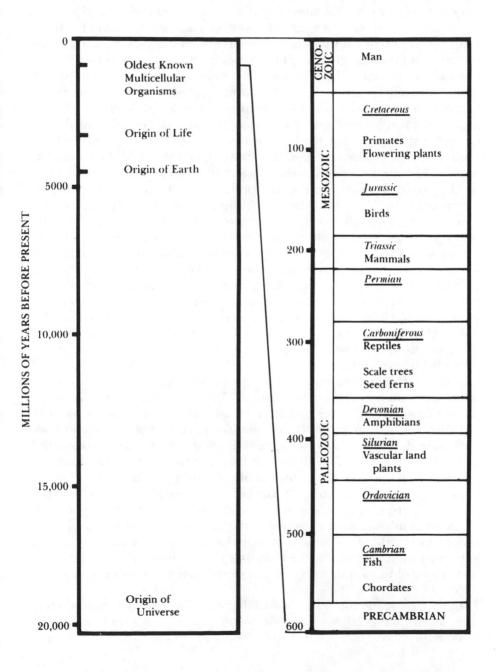

possible errors in these techniques, but they neglect to mention that the errors could not add up to the 10,000,000% error needed to make 6,000-year-old rocks appear to be 100,000 times as old. The required error is so large that a clock that inaccurate would gain ten years every hour![22]

Creationists also make a great fuss over the gaps which exist in the fossil record. They point out that with evolution one would expect a continuous sequence of gradually changing fossil types, rather than the sudden transitions actually found. They discount the explanation that fossilization is a fortuitous event requiring the sudden covering of organisms in mud or sand before the carcass is destroyed by scavengers. Nor do they mention that the gaps in the fossil record are equally inconsistent with Genesis, unless God created a species, waited for it to become extinct and form fossils, then created another species for the next stratum, and so on, all in less than a week! Some fundamentalists who are less fundamental than others have tried to avoid this problem and the problem of the Earth's great age by interpreting the "days" of Creation as arbitrarily long periods. Even so, the sequence of fossils is all wrong. According to Genesis the first birds should be found in deeper strata than the first reptiles ("creeping things"). The assumption of very long "days" would also create ecological problems for the first plants and animals. For example, how could plants which require insects for pollination have avoided extinction between the third and fourth "day"?

What one would expect from a literal reading of Genesis is the intermingling of all fossil types, since all species coexisted since the sixth day of the Earth. Humans and trilobites would have lived at the same time.[23] Instead the most primitive fossils are generally found in the deepest strata, as predicted by evolution.

Genetics. "Creationists maintain that it is extremely doubtful if a truly beneficial mutation ever occurs" (Gish, 1975). But if beneficial mutations are so rare how have the races of man, each adapted in numerous ways to its environment, developed in the few thousand years since Adam and Eve? How have the races of all species arisen from the limited stock aboard the Ark? Gish (1978, pp. 143–146) suggests that racial features such as skin color resulted from the "natural sorting out of preexisting genetic traits." That is, among the eight human survivors of the Flood were all the genes for every future racial trait, and as their descendants dispersed and became isolated, whatever combination of these genes they carried gave rise to distinctive racial types, without the benefit of mutations. This might be a reasonable explanation if it were not for the short time allowed by fundamentalists. The production of races at such a rapid rate would have been noticeable to early historians.[24]

Taxonomy. Creationists once claimed that each species was a separate creation. Then man's ability to alter domestic species by selection became so obvious that creationists had to redefine the biblical "kinds" as genera, families, or undefined taxa (Gish, 1978, pp. 30–40; Morris, 1977b, p. 29). Thus the formation of new species need never contradict their preconceptions. Creationists admit to variations within the originally created kinds, but invoke some magical limit to keep one kind from becoming another kind. (See Gish, 1975.)

Creationists may feel confident that no living man will ever witness evolution from one "kind" to another in his lifetime. Yet the fossil evidence clearly shows such evolution. The best-known evidence is in the famous fossils of *Archeopteryx*, a winged, feathered animal with a skeleton almost identical to that of some dinosaurs (Ostrom, 1978). The relationship of birds to dinosaurs is even more plain since the recent discovery that some dinosaurs were "warm-blooded," like birds but unlike present reptiles. Most creationists simply deny the evidence that *Archeopteryx* is a missing link between reptiles and birds. (See Gish, 1978 for example.) They insist that *Archeopteryx* was just another bird and pass over the vestiges of its reptilian ancestry.

Taxonomists once had to rely exclusively upon similarities in the structures of organisms in classification. By studying corresponding anatomical structures in various species the taxonomist could often determine their kinship. The similarities of structures among related species could be explained by assuming evolutionary descent of related species from a common ancestor, but it is also possible to assume that similarities of structure in different species are only apparent and not real, or that it pleased God to create species with these similarities. Linnaeus, the founder of modern taxonomy, was a creationist, so it cannot be said that evolution is immediately deducible from taxonomy. Today taxonomists have more exact techniques which are not subject to the same objections as the classical methods. These techniques involve comparisons of the structure of proteins which serve the same functions in different species (Dickerson, 1972; Dobzhansky et al., 1977, Ch. 9). These techniques are entirely objective and not merely a matter of individual opinion. Creationists would be expected to predict that the protein structures would not depend on the taxonomic relationship of species but on the conditions of life, since God designed the proteins to serve the needs of each individual kind of organism. Yet, to pick just one example, in diving mammals (whales, seals, porpoises) the structure of hemoglobin, so vital for oxygen transport, is quite similar to that of cows and very different from that of another diving vertebrate (frog) (Dobzhansky et al., 1977, p. 304). This is the result expected from evolution. There would have been little time for mutations to accumulate in the time since diving mammals and cows diverged from a common ancestor, but much more time since diving mammals and frogs diverged from their common ancestor.

While on the subject of molecular biology we could mention that the same genetic code of DNA is used to produce the proteins of every species so far studied. As far as we know one genetic code should work as well as another, so a creationist should have predicted that some species would have different genetic codes from other species, since all species would have been created independently. That all species have the same genetic code is consistent with the evolutionary postulate that all present species have descended from one original species.

Thermodynamics and probability. Creationists repeatedly assert that evolution would violate the Second Law of Thermodynamics. (Special creation would violate most laws of physics, but it is an admittedly supernatural process anyway.) Roughly, the Second Law of Thermodynamics states that in an isolated system (one which cannot exchange matter or energy with the outside) any conversion of energy from one form to another must cause some of the energy to become unavailable for further use. This will be accompanied by an increase in the total disorder, or entropy, of the system. One example of a process forbidden by the Second Law of Thermodynamics would be the spontaneous movement of all steel objects to one corner of a satellite, since this would cause a decrease in entropy. (This is a farfetched example; isolated systems don't occur on every street corner.) If the satellite entered a magnetic field which could penetrate the shell the system would no longer be isolated, and the steel objects could well move to one corner. Note that the movement of the steel objects to one corner increases the orderliness but not necessarily the organization or adaptedness of the satellite—especially if those objects are things like control knobs! As Wicken (1979) points out, the Second Law says nothing about organization or adaptedness.

The basis for creationists' objections to evolution is that it implies the emergence of more highly ordered species, having lower entropy. There are at least three flaws fatal to the argument. First it is not obvious that later organisms, such as humans, are more highly ordered than their evolutionary antecedents (Lewontin, 1968, p. 204; Williams, 1966, pp. 38–47). For example, how shall we compare the order of a human with that of a bacterium? One could argue that the bacterium must be more ordered since it manages to survive so simply. Shall we estimate the amount of order on the basis of body size? Then whales and dinosaurs are more highly ordered than humans. Estimates of orderliness based on the amount of genetic information per cell are also of no help, unless we accept that squids and certain amphibians are more highly ordered than man. My prejudice is to consider myself a member of the most orderly species on Earth, but I doubt that I could convince a honey bee of that.

Second, evolution does not occur in an isolated system but on Earth, where solar energy drives all of the processes of life. This has been pointed out numerous times, even by critics of evolution (Bube, 1971, pp. 185, 186; Cloud, 1977; Cramer, 1971), but creationists usually ignore the objection. Morris (1976) acknowledges the objection and meets it head-on with a novel approach which could revolutionize science. He simply rewrites the Second Law of Thermodynamics to make it apply to systems like the Earth which are not isolated. According to him "the Second Law really applies only to *open* systems, since there is no such thing as a truly isolated system." By the same logic the formula πr^2 = area of a circle really applies only to squares since there is no such thing as a perfect circle. (If only we could in like manner solve our energy shortage by repealing the First Law of Thermodynamics so that energy need not be conserved.)

Third, the argument that the Second Law of Thermodynamics forbids evolution could also be used to prove that organisms cannot grow, since an adult has a lower entropy than an infant. Again we do not have an isolated system, but even if an organism were in an isolated system the Second Law requires only that the *total* entropy increase, not necessarily the entropy of the body. We can demonstrate this in a thought experiment. Imagine a healthy three-year-old placed into a closed, insulated box with a day's supply of food, water, and oxygen to sustain growth. Now imagine the scene when the box is opened at the end of the day! The baby has decreased its own entropy by growing, but the heat, carbon dioxide, and waste all represent a greater increase in entropy. By the same token unsuccessful mutants, dead organisms, and extinct species represent an increase in entropy which is probably greater than any decrease in entropy associated with evolution.

The argument against evolution based on probability applies only to the origin of life, which is beyond the scope of this book. Nevertheless it may be worthwhile to deal with it. Creationists argue that life could not have arisen without an intelligent creator since the probability of randomly moving atoms arranging themselves into a living cell is vanishingly small. (See Morris, 1974, pp. 59–69, for example.) That such arguments can be misleading is easily demonstrated by estimating the probability that you, of all people, should be reading these words, out of all the words in English, at this very time. That probability is so small that it would seem impossible that you should have been reading those words unless God made you. Every event can likewise be shown to be impossible. Thus either God must be controlling everything, or there is something wrong with trying to prove an event impossible after it has already happened. The criticism of evolution based on probability also falters in its assumption that atoms and molecules move purely at random. Actually they interact with each other and with the environment, and in a sufficiently rich mixture it has been shown experimentally that more complex molecules can arise from simpler ones. In any case it is infinitely more probable that living things could arise from random matter than that it could arise from nothing.[25]

Predictions from Creation Compared with Those from Evolution

A measure of the success of a theory is its ability to make correct predictions. If the predictions are false the theory is false. It is often stated—sometimes by evolutionists—that evolution is of no predictive value. This is true if one is only interested in the evolutionary fate of a particular population. However, we have already indicated several general predictions which can help us decide whether evolution or creation is the more satisfactory explanation of the origin of species. These predictions are summarized in Table 2.

TABLE 2. PREDICTIONS OF CREATION COMPARED WITH THOSE OF EVOLUTION

Evolution	Creation
In general, new fossils will be found in their respective geological strata. (For example, no fossil mammals will be found in Cambrian deposits.)	New fossil species may occur in any stratum since all species were created at about the same time.
Newly discovered species will be similar in anatomy to related species. (For example, no mammal will be discovered with five limbs.)	New species may be found with great innovations in anatomy if God felt it necessary to improve the design.
Similarities of proteins will be greatest among closely related species.	Protein structure will depend on the conditions of life for each kind of organism, not on taxonomy.
Every newly studied species will be found to have the same genetic code.	Some species will have a different genetic code.

Teaching Biology Creatively

We have undoubtedly not heard the last of fundamentalists' demands to get evolution out and Genesis into the classroom. It may even happen someday that a majority of the Supreme Court will be smitten with senility at the time when they are considering a legal challenge to the teaching of evolution. One could then imagine the following scenario in a biology class.

Teacher: Now that we have studied the origin of species as revealed by Genesis are there any questions?
Student: How could there have been evenings and mornings and days and nights three times before there was a sun?
Another Student: And how come astronauts don't crash through the dome around the Earth and cause a flood?
Teacher: I'm afraid I can't answer those questions. Why don't you ask your astronomy teacher? Are there any biology questions?
Student: What were the great sea monsters mentioned in Genesis 1:21?
Teacher: The King James Version of the Bible translates that as whales. I can't imagine what else they could be.

Student: But isn't it true that whales are air-breathing mammals which probably originated on land?

Teacher: Yes, it appears so.

Student: Then how come they were created on the day before the other land animals were created?

Teacher: Well, maybe . . . I don't know. I guess it wasn't a whale after all.

Student: My dog ate grass once and got sick.

Teacher: Let's keep to the point, please.

Student: But sir, it says in Genesis 1:30 that God gave "all the animals of the land . . . all the green plants for food," and I was wondering how come dogs can't eat grass.

Another Student: Yeah, and what about ticks and mosquitoes?

Teacher: Quiet, all of you! Let me remind you that we are talking about the Holy Bible, and a lot of smart people—preachers, lawyers, politicians, and even some scientists—assure us that Genesis has the answer to where species originated. So let's be serious.

Student: Could we make a man in a lab? I'll bring the clay.

Teacher: Don't be silly. Doesn't anyone have a serious question?

Student: Can you describe how Adam's rib was converted into Eve?

Teacher: Now that's better. It was probably a simple trick of genetic engineering, like cloning. Some of Adam's genes in his bone marrow were turned on or off to give the various skin, nerve, muscle, and other cells to make Eve.

Student: But a big woman from a little rib?

Teacher: She grew.

Student: But wouldn't she have been a man if she got Adam's genes?

Teacher: Good point. Uh . . . remind me to mention that when we get to the section on genetics.

Student: Genesis 2:5–9 says that plants were not made until after Adam because there was no one to till the ground. Didn't God create any wild plants?

Teacher: Of course. If you had read Genesis 1:11–12 you would have known that on the third day God created "every kind of plant that bears seed and every kind of fruit tree on earth."

Student: But man wasn't created until the sixth day according to the first chapter of Genesis. Isn't that a contradict. . .?

Teacher: Next question.

Student: Were birds created on the fifth day, before man, as Genesis 1:20–23 says, or after Adam, as it says in Genesis 2:19?

Teaher: Gee, kids, I'd love to go on answering your wonderful questions, but I have a terrible headache. Class dismissed.

TABLE 3. MAJOR EVENTS AND PEOPLE OF ANCIENT GREECE AND ROME

Year B.C.	Science/Philosophy	Arts	Politics & War
600			
	Thales	Homeric	
	Anaximander	tradition	Babylonian Captivity
		already old	(586-538)
			Cyrus subjugates Ionia
	Pythagoras		
			Roman Republic
			founded
500			
			Persian War (477-468)
	Empedocles (500-430?)		
	Eleatics	Parthenon	Golden Age of Pericles
	Sophists	Sophocles	(463-431)
	Socrates (469-399)	Aristophanes	Peloponnesian War
	Hippocrates	Euripides	Tyranny of Thirty
			(404)
400			
	Plato (427?-347)		
	Academy (386)		
	Democritus (460?-362?)		Philip II (382-336)
			Philip defeats Greece
			(338)
	Aristotle (384-322)		Alexander (356-323)
	Lyceum (334)		Alexandria (332)
300			
	Euclid		
	Epicurus (342?-270)		
	Archimedes (287-212)		
200			
			Rome conquers
			Macedonia
100			
	Lucretius (99?-55?)	Cicero	Spartacus
			Julius Caesar (100-44)
			Caesar crosses Rubicon
			(49)
		Horace	Antony and Cleopatra
			(died 30 BC)
		Virgil	Jesus (4 BC-30 AD)
1			

2

The Origin of Science: Ancient Greece

Around the ninth century B.C., while J[1] and J[2] were trying to reunite the Hebrews, a new culture, as important to us as that of the Hebrews, arose in the eastern Mediterranean. Fortunately we are not required to trace the migrations of the Achaeans, Ionians, Dorians, and Aeolians southward, over the Greek peninsula and the neighboring shores and islands. (See Fig. 1 in previous chapter.) Let us only note that by the sixth century B.C. they were aware of themselves as Hellenes, sharing a common language, religion, and form of government, but with many local variations.

The language was Greek, of course. That the Greeks spoke Greek was fortunate for two reasons. Unlike many ancient languages Greek has written vowels, which encourages literacy. (In contrast, Hebrew had no vowel symbols until the seventh century A.D. Even if you were familiar with the spoken word Yahweh, would you recognize JHVH?) Secondly, Greek is rich in nuance, largely because its alphabet is not ideogrammatic. That is, words are not patterned after the objects they represent, as in Egyptian heiroglyphs or Chinese. Thus it is easier to get away from concrete thoughts, to create new meanings. Perhaps for that reason the early Greek scientists often wrote in verse. On the other hand, Greek scientists were handicapped by a number system which had no zero and which used the letters of the alphabet to represent numbers. This was certainly more confusing than the system we borrowed from the Arabs (which they borrowed from India); perhaps it was as bad as Roman numerals. The operation $o - \kappa\epsilon = \mu\epsilon$ is no easier for us than LXX-XXV = VL.

The religion of Greece centered around a vast pantheon. The closest comparison we can make today is to a government bureaucracy, with the important difference that only a few bureaucrats now try to manage nature as the Greek gods and goddesses did. Zeus, the chief god, looked after the sky; Poseidon had responsibility for the sea; Hephaestus was in charge of fire, and so on. There were enough gods to go around for every town and for each household. Homer, in the *Iliad* and the *Odyssey,* relates time and again how the fates of men became entangled with the schemes of the gods. On the other hand, the fates of the gods also depended on man: when Athens was attacked, Athena was literally threatened.

Government in Greece was centered around the city-state—the *polis*. The polis consisted of a town and its environs, with a population of no more than several thousand. This political fragmentation was dictated by the geographic fragmentation imposed by mountains and sea. This arrangement contributed to the greatness of Greece, but also made that greatness short-lived. Jealousy among competing poleis made wars inevitable (for example the Peloponnesian War) and often prevented alliances against outside invaders such as the Macedonians. But in intervals of peace the competition could be healthy. The small size of each city-state dictated that it had to import many goods, and along with them many ideas. The small population made it possible for each citizen to participate knowledgeably in public affairs. Thus was born democracy; an ideal of the polis which we try to apply to the metropolis and megalopolis.[1]

All the Greeks had much the same language, religion, and government, but in the sixth century B.C. something peculiar to the shores of Ionia (present-day Turkey) gave rise to a new and bizarre notion. A number of Ionians became obsessed with the heresy that nature is not simply a whim of the gods, but that natural phenomena consistently follow particular causes which men can understand. There is no record of the idea prior to that time, and mankind was apparently cured of the fixation afterward, until it broke out again in the European Renaissance. Now, of course, this epidemic of science has infected us all.[2]

THE PRE-SOCRATIC PHILOSOPHER-SCIENTISTS

The first known scientist was Thales, who flourished around 600 B.C. Augustine (*City of God* VIII. 2) says Thales was an author, but nothing of his has survived. As with many early scientists, all we know of him is what Aristotle, Herodotus, Diogenes Laertius, and others said, often centuries later. There is evidence that Thales travelled to Egypt and returned with geometry. In the hands of the Greeks geometry became much more than the surveying tricks of the Egyptians. (Geometry literally means "earth-measurement.") Pythagoras, particularly, was to be impressed with the idea that the gods were geometers, if, indeed, they were not numbers. In addition to introducing geometry, Thales may also have been the first to pose a question which was to preoccupy all of the Greek philosopher-scientists: What is the primary element of which all things are made? It is not surprising that a resident of the chief Greek seaport (Miletus) decided that water must be the primary element. (See Burnet, 1957, pp. 40–50.) Thales would undoubtedly be amused by our physicists' search for quarks.

Anaximander (flourished around 580 B.C. was also a resident of Miletus and may have learned science directly from Thales. He is of interest to us here because of his speculation on the origin of man, which has sometimes been interpreted as evolutionary. Anaximander's reputation as an evolutionist rests on the following opinions attributed to him by other ancients:[3]

1. Living creatures arose from the moist element as it was evaporated by the sea. Man was like another animal, namely a fish, in the beginning.

2. Further, he [Anaximander] says that originally man was born from animals of another species. His reason is that while other animals quickly find food by themselves, man alone required a lengthy period of suckling. Hence, had he been originally as he is now, he would never have survived.

3. He [Anaximander] declares that at first human beings arose in the insides of fishes, and after having been reared like sharks, and become capable of protecting themselves, they were finally cast ashore and took to land.

Thus, Anaximander suggests that man originated from a previous species, namely a fish. But if this is considered evolution, then the honor of being the first evolutionist must surely go to the nameless primitive who first spun a tale of one species being transformed into another. Far from proving that Anaximander was an evolutionist, these quotations prove that he was not. The problem he wished to solve was how the first human, as an infant without human parents, could have survived. That problem would not occur to an evolutionist, because the first human would have had parents similar enough to him to provide nourishment. Clearly Anaximander believed that the first human arose suddenly (from the sea, naturally), not by gradual evolution.

Although Anaximander does not deserve the title of First Evolutionist, he should be credited with an equally important innovation. That is the notion that naked reason is better than ignorance cloaked in priestly garb. Even on the touchy question of the origin of man he did not resort to a supernatural explanation, but attempted to apply his understanding of present causes to past phenomena. In short, Anaximander was the first to suggest a scientific explanation for the origin of a species.

Of the other Ionian philosopher-scientists we need say little since they left no writings pertaining to the origin of species. They interest us primarily as carriers of science to Athens and to other areas of Hellas following the subjugation of Ionia by Persia, which began in 546 B.C. under Cyrus.[4] Let us leave Ionia, as the Ionians did.

We skip a hundred years and a thousand kilometers to Sicily. In that time and place lived Empedocles, who, like Anaximander, is sometimes said to have been an evolutionist. Empedocles was something of a character; were he alive today he would have to be either a rock star or a resident of a back ward of a mental institution. He was a powerful aristocrat who claimed to have been a god in a previous life, and dressed accordingly in bronze sandals and purple robes. He was a faith healer and evangelist for his own religion. He must also have had a dual personality, for he is said to have declined a dictatorship in order to lead a simple life. Aristotle credited him with the invention of rhetoric, and Cicero praised his poetry. Empedocles is said to have died in the crater of Aetna.[5]

Of the 2,000 verses which Empedocles wrote *On Nature,* only a few fragments survive. The case for Empedocles as an evolutionist is based on six of them (see selections in this chapter), plus a few comments by Aristotle. According to this evidence Empedocles taught that the two great forces of nature were Love (or Friendship) and Hate (Strife).[6] During a "reign of Love" parts of animals arose from the Earth through the attraction of the four elements (fire, air, earth, and water), and these parts combined randomly with each other. A large number of monsters, such as cattle with human faces, would have been produced in this way. According to Aristotle (*Physics* II. 8), Empedocles said these monsters would not have survived. However, a few lucky individuals with the correct number and arrangement of parts would have survived, and these were the originals of the species alive now. Clearly this is not the evolution of one species from another.

Empedocles' unearned reputation as an evolutionist is largely due to his clear statement of the survival of the fittest in the citation by Aristotle. Empedocles seems to have been the first to appreciate the constructive power inherent in the elimination of the unfit. But we must remember the difference between natural selection as a cause of evolution and evolution itself. Empedocles knew the answer to what causes evolution, but he did not know the question.

Meanwhile the Persians were attempting to spread their empire into the Greek peninsula. To meet this threat Athens formed an alliance in 477 B.C. in which it provided ships and troops for the defense of other city-states for a price. Following the defeat of the Persians in 468, this arrangement continued. (Some of the allies attempted to break away, but were made offers by Athens which they could not refuse.) In effect there was an Athenian Empire. With a strong fleet to enforce peace and promote trade, money flowed into Athens. For the brief period of 463 to 431, under the democracy of Pericles, Athens enjoyed a Golden Age which is still the envy of Western man. Dramatists, sculptors, and philosophers were attracted from all over Hellas by the patronage of Pericles. Grand as its achievements were, however, Athens was still a small town, and its citizens had that smallness of spirit which periodically prunes off those who grow too far above the ordinary. Anaxagoras had to flee after suggesting that the sun was not a god but only a ball of fire. Pericles himself was pulled down, charged with starting war, squandering public funds on arts and science, and turning his home into a brothel. And gentle Socrates paid with his life for allegedly "refusing to recognize the gods recognized by the state . . . introducing new divinities [and] corrupting the youth."

This was not a golden age for science. For more than a century after Thales, philosopher-scientists had explored nearly every combination of primary elements, ideal geometry, and the other obsessions of the pre-Socratics. Then the Eleatics added a new twist: all was one and unchanging. Thus motion was an illusion, and one could not rely upon the senses. Although the Eleatics respected reason, the paradoxes they used in their arguments made others doubt it. Then came the Sophists, who argued that one can never know anything except the real. They doubted the power of abstract reasoning and made a mockery of it by their ability to defend any side of an argument. With the Eleatics arguing that things are not what they seem, and the Sophists arguing that things are *only* what they seem, science was undermined as its very foundation. With either philosophy one must doubt man's ability to understand the causes of natural phenomena.[7]

In addition, political conditions following the Golden Age were unfavorable to science. From 431 to 404 Athens and Sparta seemed bent on suicide in the Peloponnesian War. That war had no definite conclusion, but ended largely because the forests which had covered Greece were stripped (to this day), and no more warships could be built. In Athens, during the last year of the war, democracy was interrupted by a violent Tyranny of the Thirty. In such times of grave problems the claim that science is an unaffordable luxury must have been as familiar to the Athenians as it is to us. (When have there not been grave problems?) Without advanced technology, supporters of science could not even claim that knowledge of the atom and such might end war or otherwise materially benefit mankind. Thus, as Aristotle notes,[8] "in Socrates' time . . . philosophers gave up the study of Nature and turned to the practical subject of 'goodness' and to political science."

SOCRATES (469–399)

Socrates turned away from science to contemplate his soul. This is reflected in his disregard for appearance and money, and in his patient bearing of abuse from his wife Xanthippe.[9] For Socrates the important questions related to absolute equality, beauty, goodness, justice, and holiness. The answers were not to be found in nature, but within one's self. Many pre-Socratics had tried to explain human behavior on the basis of the behavior of the elements—not even distinguishing among body, mind, and soul—but Socrates saw no value in this approach. While waiting to drink the fatal hemlock he explains to his pupils that there must be an immortal, nonmaterial soul directing his body: "for I am inclined to think that these muscles and bones of mine would have gone off long ago to Megara or

Boeotia—by the dog, they would, if they had been moved only by their own idea of what was best. . . ."[10] The soul, he maintained, exists fully formed from birth, and learning is but remembering what the soul has always known. This innate knowledge could be drawn out by the method of dialectic—the Socratic method of asking questions which lead to an inevitable conclusion. For Socrates the soul was primary and eternal. Since the body was only its temporary vessel, he showed little interest in how it originated.

PLATO (428–348)

From age twenty Plato was torn between the philosophy of Socrates and a career in politics. His family was one of the most influential of Athens (like many aristocrats, his father traced his ancestry to a god), and Plato's achievements in music, mathematics, rhetoric, poetry, wrestling, and warfare would have made him a formidable candidate. The mantle of Pericles would have rested easily on his broad shoulders, but it was no longer the Golden Age. For the first twenty-four years of Plato's life Athens was entangled in the Peloponnesian War, and then Plato's own relatives plotted the Tyranny of the Thirty. Plato was offered a share of the spoils of the Thirty, but he declined because of their violence and schemes against Socrates. Democracy was soon restored, but the condemnation of Socrates convinced Plato that he had no future in governing such people as the Athenians. (Ironically, an older Plato decided that imprisonment and death were appropriate sentences for heretics. See his *Laws,* Book X.)

Following the execution of Socrates, Plato made a tour of the Mediterranean. We can imagine him wandering dejectedly, much of his family and his beloved teacher now dead. Perhaps it was then that Plato made plans to carry on the teachings of Socrates, and if unable actually to rule, at least to advise others how to. He visited Italy and Sicily, where he found the political turmoil and "laborious prosecution of debauchery" repulsive. He attempted, with some personal risk, to deter the rulers of Syracuse from despotism. Upon returning to Athens in 387 Plato founded his Academy, which survived as a leading university of Greece for nine centuries.[11]

Like Socrates, Plato was primarily interested in absolute goodness and abstract principles underlying reality. As he explained in the famous parable of the cave (*Republic* VII), what we perceive as reality is like a shadow of the absolute. Real chairs, triangles, and animals are only imperfect copies of perfect abstractions. Plato believed that studying these imperfect copies could only lead to imperfect knowledge, just as studying real triangles can only result in inaccurate geometry. In fact, Plato took geometry as the model for all reasoning. Above the door of the Academy was inscribed "Let no one without geometry enter here." Plato hoped that the same reasoning which allowed one to imagine a tangent touching a circle at only one infinitesimal point would also allow one to contemplate the absolute. Undoubtedly Plato was still somewhat under the spell of the Pythagoreans, who had made mathematics a religion encompassing music, art, and astronomy. Socrates, in contrast, had considered mathematics as only a useful technique of measurement.

Plato's one scientific dialogue (actually more of a monologue) is put into the mouth of Timaeus; it is not clear whether all the views expressed are Plato's. Perhaps he intended it to be that way to avoid charges of impiety. Timaeus describes how the creator, a god not otherwise identified, made the world out of chaos by shaping the four elements, using the abstract ideal universe as a model. The creator then made the lesser gods (which correspond to the element fire), and delegated to them the task of creating birds (corresponding to air), aquatic animals (water), and terrestrial animals (earth). These gods first created men (male humans), who were, naturally, flawed copies of the ideal of the species. The body was composed of tiny triangles, which, as their corners begin to wear down, fit increasingly badly, resulting in disease and aging. Timaeus says there are three types of soul in man: The highest resides in the head and is unique to man. A second soul is the source of courage; it resides in the chest and is shared by animals. The lowest soul is responsible for maintaining life; it resides in the abdomen and is shared even by plants. Men could live well or badly, according to which soul was dominant.

Women and other species of animals arose through reincarnation. When a man died the soul of him "who lived well during his appointed time was to return and dwell in his native star, . . . but if he failed in attaining this, at the second birth he would pass into a woman . . . and if . . . he did not desist from evil, he would continually be changed into some brute. . . ." Women came from cowardly and unrighteous men.[12] "Flighty" men became birds. Men who never used the higher soul became terrestrial animals. The most ignorant became "fishes and oysters." (See selection in this chapter.)

This description of the origin of species may sound just as mythical as the ones discussed in the previous chapter. (In fact, the *Timaeus* was translated into Latin in 350 A.D. because it was thought to be a religious work [C. U. M. Smith, 1976, p. 60].) Unlike Genesis, however, the *Timaeus* makes as much—or as little—sense without the gods. To the degree that physical causes and effects are invoked, it is scientific work.[13]

ARISTOTLE (384–322)

We have explored two main streams of Greek philosophy: the materialist stream of the pre-Socratics, and the idealist stream of Socrates and Plato.

Now we come to the confluence of these currents with Aristotle. As Plato's star pupil from 367 to 347, Aristotle absorbed the belief in abstract principles governing nature. Yet Aristotle's idealism was tempered by a curiosity about the real world and especially about life. Perhaps this reflected the influence of his father, who was a physician. Unlike Plato, Aristotle did not wish to make an end run around nature to get to the ideal: "For though there are animals which have no attractiveness for the senses, yet for the eye of science, for the student who is naturally of a philosophic spirit and can discern the causes of things, Nature which fashioned them provides joys which cannot be measured." (*Parts of Animals* I. 5. A. M. Peck translation.)

Aristotle's refusal to follow Plato's footsteps precisely may have created some friction between the two. For some reason Aristotle was not chosen to be Plato's successor as head of the Academy. Instead Aristotle and other former students of Plato founded their own school in the northwest of what is now Turkey. Their patron was the tyrant Hermias the eunuch, who gave a town to the school, and his adopted daughter to Aristotle. Shortly after-wards the Persians crucified Hermias for plotting with Philip II of Macedo-nia against them. Aristotle fled a short distance to the islands of Lesbos, where he studied marine biology, and where the death of his wife left him a widower with a daughter. Because of his connection with Hermias, and because Aristotle's father had been a physician to Philip's father, Aristotle was summoned in 343 to be one of the tutors to Philip's son, Alexander. During the time that Aristotle served in Philip's court, Philip expanded his dominion southward. Athens was absorbed in 338, but there was little disruption in the intellectual life, for Philip hoped to unite the Hellenes, not merely to subdue them. When Philip was assassinated in 336 that goal fell to Alexander, then age twenty and not yet "the Great." Aristotle returned to Athens, wealthy enough to establish his new school and confident that he would be spared the fate of Socrates as long as Alexander ruled. Aristotle's Lyceum was well equipped with the best library in Europe, maps, and a zoological garden. There, adorned in rings and bright robes, he lectured to eager and competent students. Aristotle's career at the Lyceum ended in 323 with the death of Alexander following a successful wine-drinking contest. Athenians lost no time in manifesting their hostility toward those with Macedonian ties. They charged Aristotle with impiety for composing a hymn to his father-in-law and for refusing to worship the old gods. Aristotle died within a year after fleeing. His parting words were said to have been "I will not let the Athenians offend twice against Philosophy."[14]

The surviving works of Aristotle fill more than 1,400 pages of fine print (Hutchins, 1952, vols. 8, 9), and they are only the fraction left after the Goths sacked Rome (410 A.D.) and Christians burned the libraries at Alexandria (392) and Constantinople (1204). Diogenes Laertius lists more than 350 books by Aristotle! This is a bit much for one mortal, even allowing that

Alexander the Great had a thousand men collecting specimens and information for him, as Pliny claimed. Whoever made his observations showed great skill as an observer, pushing the unaided eye to its limit. Yet many of the errors in Aristotle's works, such as the belief that insects are generated spontaneously and the charming tale of salamanders putting out fires, could have been corrected by the most elementary experiments. (See selection in this chapter.) Probably many of the writings attributed to Aristotle were actually compiled by students as projects, but those students clearly took their inspiration from Aristotle, for there is remarkable coherence and lack of contradiction in the writing.

Aristotle's interests included physics, logic, meteorology, metaphysics, the soul, memory, dreams, politics, rhetoric, drama, and various aspects of biology. As we shall see in the next chapter, this encompassing breadth and unity, rediscovered so soon after the Dark Ages, would dazzle many Europeans into regarding Aristotle's work as a second Bible. So tangled are the threads uniting Aristotle's writings that one cannot question his *Metaphysics* without doubting his biology. The *Parts of Animals,* for example, is not simply a book on anatomy, but a description of the ultimate causes of life. His *History of Animals* may seem to be a collection of animal lore—from the trivial (on lice) to the weighty (copulation by elephants)—but for Aristotle this is the evidence of design and purpose in nature. Repeatedly he tells us, "Nature does nothing in vain."

Aristotle's insistence on design and purpose in nature leads to other inevitable conclusions. A problem with design (in addition to those which were discussed in the previous chapter) is that all earthly things are changing (unless the Eleatics were correct). But why should an ideally designed object change? Aristotle responded by arguing, with Plato, that real objects are imperfect, and the changes we see are their movements toward a final, perfect state. But this too presents a problem, because Aristotle was a good enough physicist to know that motion does not originate spontaneously within an object. It was therefore necessary for him to postulate an unmoved or Prime Mover, which was the source of all other motions. (See *On the Heavens.*) In the Middle Ages the Prime Mover was equated with the Judeo-Christian God, but Aristotle wrote of it only as a divine, rotating sphere surrounding the universe, with the Earth at its center.

The unmoved mover presented Aristotle with another problem. The four earthly elements which had been agreed upon by Aristotle's time were all corruptible and moved only briefly in straight lines. (See Fig. 2.)
But Aristotle knew from ancient astronomical data that the stars and planets had not departed from their apparently circular orbits, so they could not be composed of air, fire, earth, or water. He therefore proposed a fifth (quintessential) element, *ether,* whose natural motion was circular, as the material of the celestial realm. The unmoved mover transmitted its circular motion

FIGURE 2. Natural motion and qualities of the four elements. Fire is hot and dry and tends to rise; earth is cold and wet and tends to fall, etc.

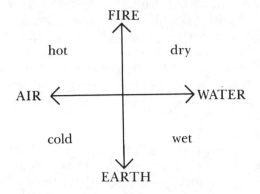

through the ether, stars, and planets to the moon, which then transmitted it to the Earth and its inhabitants.

The motions induced in living and nonliving things on Earth were the result of *final causes* driving them to fulfill their destinies. Thus the final cause of the egg is the chicken. Aristotle also recognized a *material cause;* whether the egg contains more or less fire, for example, could determine the health of the chick. There were also an *efficient cause* (the hen) and a *formal cause* (the egg-ness of the egg). Another pervasive theme of Aristotle is *psyche*—what the translators have chosen to call "soul." As explained in *On the Soul,* Aristotle regarded each living thing as a unique entity with a *psyche,* and not just a collection of atoms and organs. He expanded the number of aspects of soul from the three of *Timaeus* to five: there was a nutritive part which even plants had; the sensory, locomotive, and appetitive parts which certain animals had in addition to the nutritive part; and the intellectual part, which only humans had. The souls of modern man have been relieved of the duties assigned to the *psyche* by Aristotle. Biologists now attribute those functions to physiology.[15]

Aristotle's vision of life was very different from our evolutionary, ecological, clockwork view. He saw each organism as aspiring to the ideal of its own species, not as evolving toward some other species. To him ecological competition resulted from the less-than-perfect state of nature; to us the struggle for existence *is* nature. Individual organisms were moved by their psyches, which were driven by the Prime Mover; they were not simply reading the DNA script or obeying the commands of the hypothalamus. Yet Aristotle is often accused of having a modern conception of evolution. As with Anaximander and Empedocles, this error results from careless reading of what Aristotle actually said, especially in four passages.

The first passage was quoted by Darwin in a footnote in his "Historical Sketch," which he included in later editions of *Origin of Species*. In the quotation Aristotle is actually rejecting Empedocles' idea of natural selection, but Darwin was apparently told just the opposite. Darwin's footnote reads:

Aristotle in his Physicae Auscultationes (*Physics*, II. 8), after remarking that rain does not fall in order to make the corn grow, any more than it falls to spoil the farmer's corn when threshed out of doors, applies the same argument to organization; and adds (as translated by Mr. Clair Grece, who first pointed out the passage to me), 'So what hinders the different parts (of the body) from having this merely accidental relation in nature? as the teeth, for example, grow by necessity, the front ones sharp, adapted for dividing, and the grinders flat, and serving for masticating the food; since they were not made for the sake of this, but it was the result of accident. And in like manner as to the other parts in which there appears to exist an adaptation to an end. Wheresoever, therefore, all things together (that is all the parts of one whole) happened like as if they were made for the sake of something, these were preserved, having been appropriately constituted by an internal spontaneity; and whatsoever things were not thus constituted, perished, and still perish.' We here see the principle of natural selection shadowed forth, but how little Aristotle fully comprehended the principle, is shown by his remarks on the formation of teeth.

That Aristotle was actually rejecting the idea of natural selection is seen by his words immediately following those quoted by Darwin: " . . . as Empedocles says his man-faced ox-progeny did. Such are the arguments (and others of the kind) which may cause difficulty on this point. Yet it is impossible that this should be the true view."

The second cause of Aristotle's reputation as an evolutionist is William Ogle's translation of Aristotle's word for formation or development as "evolution." (Aristotle's word was none other than *genesis*.) Ogle's translation reads:

The best course appears to be that we should follow the method already mentioned, and begin with the phenomena presented by each group of animals, and, when this is done, proceed afterwards to state the causes of these phenomena, and to deal with their evolution. For elsewhere, as for instance in house building, this is the true sequence. The plan of the house, or the house, has this and that form; and because it has this and that form, therefore is its construction carried out in this or that manner. For the process of evolution is for the sake of the thing finally evolved, and not this for the sake of the process. (*Parts of Animals* I. 1)

At the time of Ogle's translation (1882) the word "evolution" was used in a general sense to mean gradual change, and in a biological sense to mean embryonic development (Bowler, 1975; Gould, 1977, Ch. 3; T. H. Huxley, 1896, Ch. 6). Darwin himself rarely applied the term to the origin of species, and since Aristotle was apparently referring to embryonic development in this passage, Ogle's translation was justified at the time. The fault lies not with Ogle but with those who apply current meanings to old words.

Osborn (1929, p. 87) considered Aristotle an evolutionist on the basis of a passage which occurs shortly after the one quoted above by Darwin. The translation he cites reads: "Further still, it is necessary that germs should have been first produced, and not immediately animals; and that soft mass which first subsisted was the germ." In other translations, and in the context, it is clear that "germ" is the seed from which individual plants and animals arise, not the primordial cell from which all organisms evolved.

Finally, many biologists and historians (for example Nordenskiold, 1929, p. 37, and Sarton, 1927, p. 128) have been misled by the following words: "Nature proceeds little by little from things lifeless to animal life in such a way that it is impossible to determine the exact line of demarcation, nor on which side thereof an intermediate form should lie" (*History of Animals* VIII. 1. D'Arcy Wentworth Thompson translation).[16] The troublesome word here is "proceeds," which implies progression in time. From the rest of the paragraph, however, it is clear that Aristotle is noting the difficulty of distinguishing between similar species. This was a remarkable observation in itself, but hardly sufficient to infer evolution.

So what were Aristotle's views on the origin of species? In the first place he was not quite sure they had an origin, but if they did it would have been no different from the origin of individuals through embryonic development.

> Hence one might suppose, in connection with the origin of men and quadrupeds, that if they were really "earth-born" as some say, they came into being in one of two ways; that either it was by the formation of a scolex (larva) at first or else it was out of eggs. . . . It is plain then, that, if there really was any such beginning of the generation of all animals, it is reasonable to suppose it to have been one of these two, scolex or egg. (*Generation of Animals* III. 11. A. Platt translation)

In the case of certain invertebrates, eels, and certain fish Aristotle is more confident—they arose and still arise spontaneously from filth. Intestinal worms and flies are generated in feces, some fish and eels come from mud and sand, and so on. (See the selection in this chapter and *History of Animals* VI. 15, 16.) The idea of spontaneous generation did not originate with Aristotle; nor did it die with him. It took twenty centuries for a Francesco Redi to do the experiments, which Aristotle could easily have done, to disprove spontaneous generation of insects. The idea of spontaneous generation, in fact, survived until Pasteur's experiments little more than a century ago (Farley, 1977).

EPICURUS (342?–270)

Science did not die with Aristotle; the work of his student, Theophrastus, in botany rivaled that of Aristotle in zoology, and the achievements of Euclid and Archimedes are still admired. But the best science was no longer done in Athens, but in Alexandria. Alexander had founded this city in 332, and its Museum and Library were the center for knowledge for many years under the first few Ptolemys. Alexander's conquest of Persia and his completion of Hellenization from India to Egypt broke down linguistic and political barriers to the spread of science. Alexander's impact can be judged from the fact that Jewish scholars had to have the Pentateuch translated into Greek in order to read it. (This is why our oldest biblical text, the Septuagint, is in Greek, and why the first book of the Bible has a Greek title.) Scholars, physicians, priests, philosophers, and scientists were drawn to Alexandria as they had once been to Athens. Imagine the lunch-time conversation with Euclid the geometer, and perhaps a priest from Jerusalem, a Persian sage, and a student from the Lyceum. Oh, for a time machine and a tape recorder! By law any new books brought into Alexandria had to be submitted for translation and publication by the Library. Eventually the Library accumulated hundreds of thousands of books. This was a major feat considering that books were hand-copied on long rolls of papyrus. Such scrolls were expensive and scarce, and only the best writings would have been worth the effort. How different from our inexpensive books which can be turned out virtually overnight—and forgotten just as quickly.[17]

As the center of learning migrated to Alexandria, Athenians seem to have sought consolation from the Cynics, Skeptics, Stoics, and Epicureans. Only the Epicureans concern us here, because Epicurus apparently expounded on the origin of species. None of his writings on the subject remains, but his other views were so faithfully plagiarized by Lucretius that we can assume the same for his ideas on origins. We may thus postpone a discussion of them until we get to Lucretius, but it is of present interest to learn the circumstances which led Epicurus to such speculations. Epicurus was apparently as impressed by the social and political chaos of the times as Aristotle was by the orderliness of nature. He saw in the randomly moving atoms proposed by Democritus (460?–362?) a picture in miniature of the state of the world.[18] Epicurus modified Democritus's ideas by postulating that atoms occasionally swerve spontaneously, thus giving rise to man's free will. This swerve allowed Epicurus to dispense with Aristotle's Prime Mover, with its attention concentrated on Earth. As far as Epicurus was concerned, the gods did not bother about the problems of man, so there was no reason for men to. The Earth and its troubles vanish in infinite space. Though under a sentence of death, all men may find tranquility in contemplating the benign indifference of the universe.[19]

LUCRETIUS (99?–55?)

While Athens was in its senescence, Rome was in the throes of labor, giving birth to a new empire. Its victory over Carthage in the Punic Wars (264–146) had left Rome virtually unopposed in its control over the Mediterranean. Macedonia, then only a fragment of Alexander's empire, tried but failed to organize resistance. Many Greeks first welcomed Roman conquest in 197 as being at least a change from the Macedonians. They later had reason to change their minds after witnessing Roman methods for dealing with Greek desires for independence. Rome continued its expansion into Europe under Julius Caesar (100–44), but at the same time that Rome was demonstrating its ability to rule others, it seemed unable to rule itself. Although nominally a republic since 509 B. C., Rome became essentially an anarchy by the first century B. C., following a series of civil wars, revolts, and reigns of terror. The revolt of Spartacus (73 B. C.) and the crucifixion of 6,000 of his followers give some idea of those brutal times. Finally, in 49, Caesar crossed the Rubicon, captured Rome, and restored order at the price of liberty. The rest of Rome's history will wait until the next chapter.

Titus Lucretius Carus had the misfortune to live during the terrible times leading up to Caesar's dictatorship. Little is known about him, possibly because of the deliberate policy of suppressing Epicurean writings under the Caesars and later emperors. Rome wanted its subjects to believe that the gods were on their side; Lucretius dared to suggest that the gods did not even notice our little planet, much less worry over who was trying to conquer it. The one semblance of a fact regarding Lucretius is the doubtful statement by Saint Jerome, writing four centuries afterwards, that Lucretius went insane from an aphrodisiac and eventually killed himself. Perhaps Lucretius did seek peace in the arms of Venus, as he sought it in the writings of Epicurus. Like many Roman artists and philosophers of the time, Lucretius was not especially original, but he displayed excellent judgment in choosing what to copy. Parts of his poem *De Rerum Natura (On the Nature of Things)* are quite similar to letters by Epicurus explaining his philosophy. (For these letters see Diogenes Laertius, 1950, vol. 2, pp. 565–659.) Although Lucretius was himself an elegant poet, the idea of writing in verse may have been borrowed from Empedocles. Empedocles may also have been the source of Lucretius's ideas on natural selection, which appear in the last selection of this chapter. The major difference between Empedocles and Lucretius is that the latter has the Earth bringing forth entire organisms, not just parts. According to Lucretius, men originated from wombs attached to trees! This and other of Lucretius's ideas may seem fanciful, but his motive was clearly to dispel religious superstitions by proposing natural explanations for the origin of species and other phenomena. In that sense, he was a scientific writer.[20]

Empedocles: Six fragments. From K. Freeman, *Ancilla to the Pre-Socratic Philosophers.* Harvard University Press, Cambridge, 1956, pp. 58, 59. By permission.

57. On it *(Earth)* many foreheads without necks sprang forth, and arms wandered unattached, bereft of shoulders, and eyes strayed about alone, needing brows.

58. Limbs wandered alone.

59. But as the one divinity became more and more mingled with the other *(i. e. Love and Hate),* these things fell together as each chanced, and many other things in addition to these were continuously produced.

60. Creatures with rolling gait and innumerable hands.

61. Many creatures were created with a face and breast on both sides; offspring of cattle with the fronts of men, and again there arose offspring of men with heads of cattle; and *(creatures made of elements)* mixed in part from men, in part of female sex, furnished with hairy limbs.

62. Come now, hear how the Fire as it was separated sent up the night-produced shoots of men and much-lamenting women; for my tale is not wide of the mark nor ill-informed. At first, undifferentiated shapes of earth arose, having a share of both elements Water and Heat. These the Fire sent up, wishing to reach its like, but they did not yet exhibit a lovely body with limbs, nor the voice and organ such as is proper to men.

Selection from Plato, *Timaeus.* Translated by B. Jowett.

Thus our original design of discoursing about the universe down to the creation of man is nearly completed. A brief mention may be made of the generation of other animals, so far as the subject admits of brevity; in this manner our argument will best attain a due proportion. On the subject of animals, then, the following remarks may be offered. Of the men who came into the world, those who were cowards or led unrighteous lives may with reason be supposed to have changed into the nature of women in the second generation. And this was the reason why at that time the gods created in us the desire of sexual intercourse, contriving in man one animated substance, and in woman another, which they formed respectively in the following manner. The outlet for drink by which liquids pass through the lung under the kidneys and into the bladder, which receives and then by the pressure of the air emits them, was so fashioned by them as to penetrate also into the body of the marrow, which passes from the head along the neck and through the back, and which in the preceding discourse we have named the seed. And the seed having life, and becoming endowed with respiration, produces in that part in which it respires a lively desire of emission, and thus creates in us the love of procreation. Wherefore also in men the organ of generation becoming rebellious and masterful, like an animal disobedient to reason, and maddened with the sting of lust, seeks to gain absolute sway; and the same is the case with the so-called womb or matrix of women; the animal within them is desirous of procreating children, and when remaining unfruitful long beyond its proper time, gets discontented and angry, and wandering in every direction through the body, closes up the passages of the breath, and, by obstructing respiration, drives them to extremity, causing all varieties of disease, until at length the desire and love of the man and the woman, bringing them together and as it were plucking the fruit from the tree, sow in the womb, as in a field, animals unseen by reason of their smallness and without form; these again are separated and matured within; they are then finally brought out into the light, and thus the generation of animals is completed.

Thus were created women and the female sex in general. But the race of birds was created out of innocent light-minded men, who, although their minds were directed toward heaven, imagined, in their simplicity, that the clearest demonstration of the things above was to be obtained by sight; these were remodelled and transformed into birds, and they grew feathers instead of hair. The race of wild pedestrian animals, again, came from those who had no philosophy in any of their thoughts, and never considered at all about the nature of the heavens, because they had ceased to use the courses of the head, but followed the guidance of those parts of the soul which are in the breast. In consequence of these habits of theirs they had their front-legs and their heads resting upon the earth to which they were drawn by natural affinity; and the crowns of their heads were elongated and of all sorts of shapes, into which the courses of the soul were crushed by reason of disuse. And this was the reason why they were created quadrupeds and polypods: God gave the more senseless of them the more support that they might be more attracted to the earth. And the most foolish of them, who trail their bodies entirely upon the ground and have no longer any need of feet, he made without feet to crawl upon the earth. The fourth class were the inhabitants of the water: these were made out of the most entirely senseless and ignorant of all, whom the transformers did not think any longer worthy of pure respiration, because they possessed a soul which was made impure by all sorts of transgression; and instead of the subtle and pure medium of air, they gave them the deep and muddy sea to be their element of respiration; and hence arose the race of fishes and oysters, and other aquatic animals, which have received the most remote habitations as a punishment of their outlandish ignorance. These are the laws by which animals pass into one another, now, as ever, changing as they lose or gain wisdom and folly.

Aristotle, *History of Animals,* Book V, Chapter 19. Translated by D. W. Thompson

With regard to insects, that the male is less than the female and that he mounts upon her back, and how he performs the act of copulation and the circumstance that he gives over reluctantly, all this has already been set forth, in most cases of insect copulation this process is speedily followed up by parturition.

All insects engender grubs, with the exception of a species of butterfly; and the female of this species lays a hard egg, resembling the seed of the cnecus, with a juice inside it. But from the grub, the young animal does not grow out of a mere portion of it, as a young animal grows from a portion only of an egg, but the grub entire grows and the animal becomes differentiated out of it.

And of insects some are derived from insect congeners, as the venom-spider and the common-spider from the venom-spider and the common-spider, and so with the attelabus or locust, the acris or grasshopper, and the tettix or cicada. Other insects are not derived from living parentage, but are generated spontaneously: some out of dew falling on leaves, ordinarily in spring-time, but not seldom in winter when there has been a stretch of fair weather and southerly winds; others grow in decaying mud or dung; others in timber, green or dry; some in the hair of animals; some in the flesh of animals; some in excrements: and some from excrement after it has been voided, and some from excrement yet within the living animal, like the helminthes or intestinal worms. And of these intestinal worms there are three species: one named the flat-worm, another the round worm, and the third the ascarid. These intestinal worms do not in any case propagate their kind. The flat-worm, however, in an exceptional way, clings fast to the gut, and lays a thing like a melon-seed, by observing which indication the physician concludes that his patient is troubled with the worm.

The so-called psyche or butterfly is generated from caterpillars which grow on green leaves, chiefly leaves of the raphanus, which some call crambe or cabbage. At first it is less than a grain of millet; it then grows into a small grub; and in three days it is a tiny caterpillar. After this it grows on and on, and becomes quiescent and changes its shape, and is now called a chrysalis. The outer shell is hard, and the chrysalis moves if you touch it. It attaches itself by cobweb-like filaments, and is unfurnished with mouth or any other apparent organ. After a little while the outer covering bursts asunder, and out flies the winged creature that we call the psyche or butterfly. At first, when it is a caterpillar, it feeds and ejects excrement; but when it turns into the chrysalis it neither feeds not ejects excrement.

The same remarks are applicable to all such insects as are developed out of the grub, both such grubs as are derived from the copulation of living animals and such as are generated without copulation on the part of parents. For the grub of the bee, the anthrena, and the wasp, whilst it is young, takes food and voids excrement; but when it has passed from the grub shape to its defined form and become what is termed a "nympha", it ceases to take food and to void excrement, and remains tightly wrapped up and motionless until it has reached its full size, when it breaks the formation with which the cell is closed, and issues forth. The insects named the hypera and the penia are derived from similar caterpillars, which move in an undulatory way, progressing with one part and then pulling up the hinder parts by a bend of the body. The developed insect in each case takes its peculiar colour from the parent caterpillar.

From one particular large grub, which has as it were horns, and in other respects differs from grubs in general, there comes, by a metamorphosis of the grub, first a caterpillar, then the cocoon, then the *necydalus;* and the creature passes through all these transformations within six months. A class of women unwind and reel off the cocoons of these creatures, and afterwards weave a fabric with the threads thus unwound; a Coan woman of the name of Pamphila, daughter of Plateus, being credited with the first invention of the fabric. After the same fashion the carabus or stag-beetle comes from the grubs that live in dry wood: at first the grub is motionless, but after a while the shell bursts and the stag-beetle issues forth.

From the cabbage is engendered the cabbage-worm, and from the leek the prasocuris or leekbane; this creature is also winged. From the flat animalcule that skims over the surface of rivers comes the oestrus or gadfly; and this accounts for the fact that gadflies most abound in the neighbourhood of waters on whose surface these animalcules are observed. From a certain small, black and hairy caterpillar comes first a wingless glow-worm; and this creature again suffers a metamorphosis, and transforms into a winged insect named the bostrychus (or hair-curl).

Gnats grow from ascarids; and ascarids are engenderd in the slime of wells, or in the places where there is a deposit left by the draining off of water. This slime decays, and first turns white, then black, and finally blood-red; and at this stage there originate in it, as it were, little tiny bits of red weed, which at first wriggle about all clinging together, and finally break loose and swim in the water, and are hereupon known as ascarids. After a few days they stand straight up on the water motionless and hard, and by and by the husk breaks off and the gnat are seen sitting upon it, until the sun's heat or a puff of wind sets them in motion, when they fly away.

With all grubs and all animals that break out from the grub state, generation is due primarily to the heat of the sun or to wind.

Ascarids are more likely to be found, and grow with unusual rapidity, in places where there is a deposit of a mixed and heterogeneous kind, as in kitchens and in ploughed fields, for the contents of such places are disposed to rapid putrefaction. In autumn, also, owing to the drying up of moisture, they grow in unusual numbers.

The tick is generated from couch-grass. The cockchafer comes from a grub that is generated in the dung of the cow or the ass. The cantharus or scarabeus rolls a piece of dung into a ball, lies hidden within it during the winter, and gives birth therein to small grubs, from which grubs come new canthari. Certain winged insects also come from the grubs that are found in pulse, in the same fashion as in the cases described.

Flies grow from grubs in the dung that farmers have gathered up into heaps: for those who are engaged in this work assiduously gather up the compost, and this they technically term "working-up" the manure. The grub is exceedingly minute to begin with; first—even at this stage—it assumes a reddish colour, and then from a quiescent state it takes on the power of motion, as though born to it; it then becomes a small motionless grub; it then moves again, and again relapses into immobility; it then comes out a perfect fly, and moves away under the influence of the sun's heat or of a puff of air. The myops or horse-fly is engendered in timber. The orsodacna or bud-bane is a transformed grub; and this grub is engendered in cabbage-stalks. The cantharis comes from the caterpillars that are found on fig-trees or pear-trees or fir-trees—for on all these grubs are engendered—and also from caterpillars found on the dog-rose; and the cantharis takes eagerly to ill-scented substances, from the fact of its having been engendered in ill-scented woods. The conops comes from a grub that is engendered in the slime of vinegar.

And, by the way, living animals are found in substances that are usually supposed to be incapable of putrefaction; for instance, worms are found in long-lying snow; and snow of this description gets reddish in colour, and the grub that is engendered in it is red, as might have been expected, and it is also hairy. The grubs found in the snows of Media are large and white; and all such grubs are little disposed to motion. In Cyprus, in places where copper-ore is smelted, with heaps of the ore piled on day after day, an animal is engendered in the fire, somewhat larger than a bluebottle fly, furnished with wings, which can hop or crawl through the fire. And the grubs and these latter animals perish when you keep the one away from the fire and the other from the snow. Now the salamander is a clear case in point, to show us that animals do actually exist that fire cannot destroy; for this creature, so the story goes, not only walks through the fire but puts it out in doing so.

On the river Hypanis in the Cimmerian Bosphorus, about the time of the summer solstice, there are brought down towards the sea by the stream what look like little sacks rather bigger than grapes, out of which at their bursting issues a winged quadruped. The insect lives and flies about until the evening, but as the sun goes down it pines away, and dies at sunset having lived just one day, from which circumstance it is called the ephemeron.

As a rule, insects that come from caterpillars and grubs are held at first by filaments resembling the threads of a spider's web.

Such is the mode of generation of the insects above enumerated.

Lucretius, *On the Nature of Things,* Book V, ll. 783–877. Translated by
C. E. Bennett. Walter J. Black, Roslyn, N. Y., 1946.

In the beginning, earth did bring to being
Herbage of every kind and verdure bright
Upon the hills and over every plain,
Till all the flowery meadows were agleam
With vesture green, and mongst the various trees
A mighty contest arose, as each did strive
To rise aloft with every rein let loose
Through the soft airs. And e'en as down and hair
And bristles first are formed upon the limbs

Of fourfoot creatures and the bodies too
Of strong-winged fowls, so then the new-born earth
First reared her shrubs and herbage; then in turn
In order due did bring to birth the tribes
Of mortal creatures, risen in many ways
By means diverse. For ne'er could living beings
Have fallen from heaven, nor beasts that roam the earth
Have issued from the briny pools. With right
It followeth then that earth hath won the name
Of Mother, since from earth have all things sprung.
And even now we see full many a breed
Of living creatures rise from out the earth
Begot by rains and by the genial warmth
The sun doth shed. Hence we may marvel less
If then in larger numbers and endowed
With ampler bulk were creatures brought to birth
And reached their prime, since earth and air were new.
First, then, the winged tribes and every breed
Of flying fowl did leave their eggs, safe hatched
By springlike warmth, as now, in summer's heat,
Locusts will fain put off their polished shells
In quest of life and living. Then it was
That earth did first give birth to mortal beings.
For all the fields did teem with gentle warmth
And moisture. Hence, where there was at hand
Appropriate place, there grew up wombs, attached
By roots to earth; and when, at time fulfilled,
The tiny creatures' growing age, in flight
From moisture and in search of air, had burst
Their prison, so would nature turn toward each
The pores of earth, and from wide-opened veins
Constrain them to exude a sap most like
To milk, as even now, when she hath borne
A child, each woman's breasts are filled forthwith
With sweet new milk, since thitherward are turned
All the rich humors of her nourishment.
Earth gave these little ones their food, the warmth
A garment, and the soft thick-tufted grass
A downy bed. But since the world was young,
No bitter cold it roused, nor heat o'er fierce,
Nor winds of violent might. For evenly
Do all things wax and reach their full-grown strength.

Wherefore once more I do aver that earth
Hath justly won, and justly doth she keep
The name of Mother, since 'twas she herself
Did in her own fixt time create the race
Of men, and every breed of beast that here
And yon among the mighty mountain tops
Doth hold wild revel; and the flying fowl
Likewise that dwell in air, in all their range
Of forms and hues diverse. But since at length
She needs must reach some end of bearing, so
Did she give o'er, e'en as a woman, worn
With length of lingering years. For time doth change
The mold of all the world, and one estate
Upon another needs must overtake
All things that be, nor aught doth long abide
Like to itself, but all things shift their place;
Yea, nature altereth all, and doth constrain
Each one to change its form. For one doth wane
And, worn with age, doth pine, then somewhat else
Doth rise to take its place and issue forth
From whilom place of scorn. So then did time
Bring change to all the nature of the world,
And one estate upon another seize
Upon the earth, that so what once it bore
It can no longer compass, and can bear
What ne'er it brought to birth in days of old.

And in those days did earth essay to frame
Full many a monster, born with visage strange
And limbs awry, the woman-man, midway
Between the two, yet neither, and apart
From both; and some there were bereft of feet,
Or wanting hands in turn, and some were found
Dumb without mouths, or featureless and blind,
Or chained through all their frame by limbs that clung
One to another, so that power they lacked
To compass aught, or move toward any side,
Or flee from danger, or to gain whate'er
Their needs required. And other monsters, too,
And creatures strange would she create, but all
In vain, since that their nature did forbid
Increase, nor could they reach the envied bloom
Of age, nor gather sustenance, nor join

In Venus' arts; for many a requisite
We see must be fulfilled in living things
Ere they avail to propagate their kind
By generation: first, they must have food,
And then the means whereby from out their frames
Birth-giving seeds may issue, cast abroad
From the appropriate members, so that male
And female may be joined, and each possess
The means whereby to exchange their mutual joys.

And in those far-off days full many a race
Of living things must needs have perished, nay,
Nor aught of offspring could beget and thus
Preserve its kind; for whatsoe'er we see
To breathe the vital air of heaven, 'tis craft,
Or courage, yea, or fleetness that since first
Their life began hath guarded and preserved
Their several breeds. And many too there be
Which by their use commended to our care
Live on, entrusted to our guardianship.
First, to the ravening race of lions, that breed
Of savage beasts, 'tis valor hath vouchsafed
A sure protection; in the fox 'tis craft,
The stag, the swiftness of his flying feet;
But otherwise the lightly slumbering minds
Of faithful-hearted dogs, and all the breeds
That spring from seed of burden-bearing beasts
And fleecy flocks withal, and horned herds;
All these, good Memmius, are nursed by care
Of human kind. For eagerly, I ween,
Have they escaped their savage enemies
And sought the quietude and plenteous store
Of sustenance ourselves are pleased to grant
As wage for service rendered. But those breeds
Whereunto none of these advantages
Hath nature granted, so that of themselves
They cannot live, nor render unto us
Some useful service, in return wherefor
We might permit their kind to feed and dwell
Beneath our safe defense, these, thou mayst know,
Did fall a prey and spoil to others, each
Chained by the fateful trammels of its being,
Till nature brought their kind at length to doom.

THE CREATION OF SCIENCE: INSTRUCTIONS FOR THE POST-SCIENTIFIC AGE

A note to contemporary readers. I have described in this chapter the first generation of science in Greece and Rome. We are now in the second generation of science, which began in the Renaissance. Probably you assume this second generation will continue forever. Aristotle must have felt the same way about his generation of science. Perhaps we should withhold our optimism until modern science has survived at least as long as the interval from Thales to Lucretius. The political and social causes of the decline of Greek science are insignificant compared to the potential consequences of nuclear proliferation and massive retaliation, which technically sane people are now planning in the guise of "nuclear diplomacy." Only a dull wit can fail to imagine the dawn—or dusk—of a new Dark Age as the result of energy shortages, famine, pollution, and so on. The survivors in such catastrophes are not likely to look smilingly upon science to rescue them from a situation which it got them into. Undoubtedly such a turn of events would initiate a Post-Scientific Age. It is not good to dwell upon such a prospect; once we start believing the prophecy that science and civilization are doomed, that prophecy becomes self-fulfilling. Yet I think it would be useful to a Galileo of the Post-Scientific Age to leave some guidance to help him start the third generation of science. As a contemporary reader, you might also find it useful for delaying the coming of the Post-Scientific Age.

Dear Reader of the Post-Scientific Age:
    I cannot imagine the circumstances which have brought you and this book together. That you are reading it at all can only mean that many more worthy books of science have been lost or destroyed. Were they lost in some holocaust of our devising? Were they destroyed as evil or heretical? Or did they simply vanish through neglect? Are you reading these words in secret, dreading a knock on the door that will consign you and this book to the flames? Or have you simply stumbled upon it in the dust of some abandoned cellar?
    Whatever the circumstances you are apparently interested enough to have read this far. Our theories are probably comical or disturbing to you, but perhaps our way of thinking of nature as being the result of causes and effects seems worthwhile. You may, in fact, be considering a rebirth of scientific thinking. Rather than have you puzzle out an approach yourself, I will reveal to you four of the prerequisites to the establishment of science. I will not guarantee that fulfilling these conditions will automatically create a new age of science, but there is no chance that you will succeed without them.
    1. *Create a climate of religious tolerance.* (Well, I never claimed you would have an easy task.) It does happen occasionally that the majority will tolerate a minority with bizarre opinions which conflict with their religious views. In

Miletus I suppose the mortals who ordained themselves the protectors of the gods did not realize the threat implicit in Thales' idea that nature obeys set rules. By the time science began to spread to other shores the Persians had created more serious problems for the defenders of the Greek pantheon than those posed by the Ionian scientists. The execution of Socrates, the suppression of Lucretius, and the activities of my contemporary antievolutionists may serve to warn you how rare such tolerance is. You will be fortunate if you achieve the degree of religious freedom enjoyed in the recent past by those in the United States and a few other Western countries.

There is a strategy that may help you avoid becoming a martyr for science: pretend that science is irrelevant, or better yet, supportive of whatever the prevailing dogmas may be. This may be how Plato avoided becoming a second Socrates. Apparently some of the astronomers in my own time have learned this lesson. In announcing new evidence that the universe began with a "Big Bang" they proclaimed it as support for Genesis and passed over the fact that it is equally consistent with the creation myths of dozens of other religions. If they had found evidence for an eternal, evolving universe they surely would not have proclaimed it as support for Buddhism or Taoism.

In addition to religious intolerance you may also be faced with an intolerance for all "useless" knowledge. Your fellow men will want science to cure their diseases, make their lives easier, and help kill their enemies. They will not want you exercising your mind on such questions as the origins of species, especially if your findings cast doubt on their belief that they were divinely created in the image of God. You may tell them, however, that every material benefit of science began with some scientist puttering around out of curiosity. Let your motto be "Knowledge for the hell of it."

2. *Do not let science become a religion.* An essential difference between science and religion in their purest forms is that science forms communities, and religions form hierarchies. Scientists talk and listen to each other; followers of a religion listen to those above and talk to those below them. The strengths of the scientific community are the same as those in a population which benefits from hybrid vigor and natural selection, except that one deals with ideas and the other with genes. What is wanted in both cases is an absence of inbreeding and an elimination of the unfit. Religious hierarchies, on the other hand, depend upon the stability of the pyramid, with the gods and their interpreters at the top, supported by an expanding base of followers.

There seems to be an inherent tendency for all humans to seek the stability of the pyramid, and scientists are no different. There are some, like Plato, who wish to be at the top of a pyramid. Others are elevated against their will, like Aristotle in the late Middle Ages. Modern science has resisted that tendency well so far, unless one includes Freud, Jung, Pavlov, and some other psychologists. Newton, Darwin, and Einstein are the most revered figures of modern science, yet any real scientist would be delighted to discover a new error in their work, because he knows that science marches fastest over the corpses of dead theories.

3. *Be prosperous.* History is devoid of poor economies which produced great science. Miletus was a rich seaport; Athens thrived on slavery and the income for its mercenary forces. Following the Renaissance the growth of science was proportional to the growth of the economies of Italy, Britain, France, and Germany. The reasons for the dependence on wealth are not hard to understand, though they vary with the type of science practiced. Greek science was cheap because it was entirely theoretical, but even Aristotle had to eat. He could not have been a scientist without Hermias and Alexander. (It is true that Socrates disdained money, but then he could afford to.) Not only did the upper economic stratum of Greece have to support science, but the lower stratum had to be comfortable enough to tolerate men who, as far as they could tell, did nothing to earn a living. Even if scientists could live entirely on their salary as teachers, there had to be enough wealth and leisure so that students could be spared from supporting themselves and their families.

As science became more experimental in the Renaissance it became more expensive. The first modern scientists supported the building of telescopes, laboratories, and such out of their own pockets, or, more often, out of the pockets of rich patrons. This is a situation you should avoid, since it excludes those who are not servile to the rich. How many Newtons were wasted because they were poor or honest? Following our Second World War the governments of the United States and many other countries began to support scientific teaching and research through tax-funded grants. This arrangement has the advantage of rewarding merit (so much so that many scientists and university administrators act as if getting the money is more important than doing the research), but it has the disadvantage that the support waxes and wanes with the public's generosity, the mood of legislators, and the state of the economy.

4. *Start a war.* Unless humans have evolved greatly since my time this will be the easiest part of your task. In fact, it is difficult for me to prove that science advances most rapidly in time of war because of the scarcity of peaceful times with which to make comparisons. This requirement for science is closely linked to the requirement for prosperity, as the examples of Athens and our Second World War illustrate. It is therefore rather important that you not lose the war or let it debilitate your economy. The best kind of war for the purpose is a cold war, such as existed between the United States and Russia in the 1950s and 1960s. (In case you are not familiar with the term, a cold war is something like you and your neighbor pointing guns at one another's children, and each of you daring the other to shoot first.) During a cold war one can justify virtually any activity by claiming that one's

opponent is doing it better. The formula developed in the United States was to announce that "we are losing the (fill in the blank) Race." For example, an announcement that "we are losing the Chess Race" would result in thousands of Americans patriotically discovering that they had a consuming passion for the game. It helps if you really are losing the race. In 1957, after the Russians launched Sputnik, the first artificial Earth satellite, all sorts of money was provided for scientific research and education to help us win the Space Race. The relation to the cold war was manifest in the fact that much of the money was provided under a National Defense Education Act and by various military agencies. Unfortunately many of the things a progressive society ought to do anyway, it will do only when it perceives itself threatened.

Now that the good old days of the cold war are over, this kind of support for science has slackened. If I were a cynic I might wish that the Russians would accomplish the biological equivalent of Sputnik—perhaps the synthesis of life. You might consider advancing science in your own country by introducing it first to your enemies. Lots of luck.

TABLE 4. MAJOR EVENTS AND PEOPLE OF THE FIRST 13 CENTURIES A.D.

Year A.D.	*Science/Philosophy*	*Arts*	*Politics & War*
1			
	Pliny (23-79)		Diaspora (70)
		Plutarch	
100			
	Ptolemy (100?-178?)		
	Galen (130?-200?)		
200			
	Plotinus (205-270)		
300			
			Council of Nicaea (325)
400			
	Augustine (354-430)		Sack of Rome (410)
			End of Western Empire (476)
500			
	Boethius (475?-524)	Cathedral of St. Sophia	
600			
	Isidore, Bishop of Seville (560?-636?)	Beowulf	Mohammed (570-632)
700			
	Venerable Bede (673-735)	Gregorian Chant (600-1100)	Battle of Tours (732)

Year A.D.	Science / Philosophy	Arts	Politics & War
800			
			Charlemagne (768-814)
	School of Salerno (848)		
900			
		St. Mark's, Venice	
1000			
	Avicenna (980-1037)		
	University of Cordova	Song of Roland	Battle of Hastings (1066)
	Oxford University		Crusades (1095-1291)
1100			
	University of Paris	Omar Khayyam	
	Adelard of Bath	El Cid	
	Averroes (1126-1198)	Notre Dame	Jenghis Khan (1162-1227)
1200			
	Albertus Magnus (1193-1280)		Frederick II (1194-1250)
	Thomas Aquinas (1225-1274)		Magna Carta (1215)
	Roger Bacon (1214-1292)	Alhambra	
1300			

3

The Infanticide of Science:
Rome and the Middle Ages

Non-Westerners and native Americans who do not distinguish between the natural and supernatural must be puzzled by the modern Westerner's attempt to parcel out nature and his own mind into the realms of science and religion. Even Plato, Aristotle, and Epicurus would be surprised that instead of an integral mode of thought we have the rational and spiritual modes which we consider independent of one another. How can we explain to them, and to ourselves, the internal conflicts arising out of this schism of thought? Why have men been willing to kill and die in boundary disputes between science and religion? To find the answer we must go to the source—ancient Rome.

We need not be detained by the familiar tales of Julius Caesar, Antony and Cleopatra, and Rome at the height of its glory in the first Century A.D. What is important for our story is the way Rome imported Greek science, the way Christianity bloomed in the midst of bloody thorns, and the eventual juxtaposition of the two systems of thought. Rich Romans acquired Greek arts and philosophy the way they acquired slaves: by buying them and by breaking their spirit. Greek philosophers and artists were brought to Rome in chains to amuse, teach, and glorify their masters. Vast libraries were purchased from Alexandria, mainly to create an impressive interior decor. Roman gentlemen commissioned statues of themselves which, beside the works of the Golden Age, reveal the vacuousness which the Greek sculptors must have seen in their masters. The only Roman scientists worth mentioning—Lucretius, Ptolemy (100?–178?), and Galen (130?–200?)—were more Greek than Roman. Lucretius imported his ideas from Athens, Ptolemy followed the Greek tradition at Alexandria, and Galen was from Pergamum, 100 kilometers east of Lesbos. We would charitably like to think that the Romans were sincerely trying to learn from the Greeks, but realistically we recognize the impulse of every Caesar, Napoleon, and Hitler to pretend to be civilized by surrounding himself with the plunder of a superior civilization.

One reason why Rome was not receptive to science was its devotion to the gods, who paralleled in many respects the Greek gods. As if the Roman pantheon were not already crowded, even more gods were continually being introduced from abroad by tradesmen, soldiers, and missionaries. Augustus and later emperors took advantage of the Roman enthusiasm for worship by declaring themselves to be gods, after the fashion of the Egyptian pharaohs.[1] These emperor-gods were easily accommodated by most Romans (even if they often betrayed an ungodly susceptibility to poison). There was one major exception: converts to the fledgling religion called Christianity refused to burn candles before the image of the emperor. Probably the initial reaction of Augustus was to send out spies and search through records to find out what this new religion was all about. We can imagine—and almost sympathize with—his perplexity when the report came back that the instigators of this cult were followers of an obscure carpenter's son who was executed like a common criminal. "Why should these Christians prefer a provincial rabble-rouser who was crucified by his own people, to me, with the power of life and death over thousands? Am I not more divine with my wealth and splendor than this man who offered only sacrifice to the poor, forgiveness of one's enemies, and silly promises of an afterlife for believers?" To the emperors the Christian disregard for their divinity and for law and order must have been not only an impertinence but a real threat to the declining empire. Ordinary non-Christians began to think that their troubles were punishments from the gods offended by the Christian "atheists," and they undoubtedly were not amused by prophecies of the destruction of the "mother of harlots" (Rev. 17, 18). Eventually the Roman demands for law and order, and their enthusiasm for a good show, resulted in Christians being burned at the stake, crucified, and fed to the lions. In 64 Nero avenged the burning of Rome by martyring Peter, Paul, and numerous other Christians, whom he accused of the arson. Yet Christianity continued to spread throughout the empire. That so many could find in the words of Jesus the strength to survive such ordeals was—and perhaps still is—the most compelling argument for Christianity. The intensity of persecution varied over three centuries, reaching maniacal vigor between 303 and 311. Churches and sacred books were burned, secret worship was punishable by death, and Christians were deprived of any protection of the law. Finally Galerius on his deathbed put an end to this madness with an edict which reveals political and perhaps humanistic enlightenment:

Among the important cares which have occupied our mind for the utility and preservation of the empire, it was our intention to correct and re-establish all things according to the ancient laws and public discipline of the Romans. We were particularly desirous of reclaiming into the way of reason and nature the deluded Christians who had renounced the religion and ceremonies instituted by their fathers. . . . The edicts which we have published to enforce the worship of the Gods having exposed many of the Christians to danger and distress, many having suffered death, and many more, who still persist in their impious folly, being left destitute of *any* public exercise of religion, we are disposed to extend to those unhappy men the effects of our wonted clemency. We permit them, therefore, freely to profess their private opinions, and to assemble in their conventicles without fear or molestation, provided always that they preserve due respect to the established laws and government.[2]

By this time the empire had been through two centuries of decline.[3] The empire was falling apart, and the Emperor Constantine (280?–337) saw in Christianity one last hope for reuniting it. But first he had to reunite the Christians. Christianity had come a long way from Nazareth. Bishops were becoming wealthy, priests vied for promotion, and all but a hard core of monastics seemed to have remained pagans in spirit. The bishops had made liberal use of syncretism, adopting the rites and beliefs of established religions, in order to gain a wider acceptance. The adoration of a virgin mother of God, the Eucharist and holy water were borrowed from the Alexandrian cult of the Serapis-Isis-Horus trinity. The idea of Jesus as a blood sacrifice, Sunday as the sabbath, and December 25 as a holy day were adopted to placate Roman soldiers who believed mainly in Mithraism (Legge, 1964, vol. 1, pp. 85–88, vol. 2, pp. 259–261). The church was dangerously split over the nature of Jesus: Was he one with the Father and the Holy Ghost, or was he a creation of God? In order to settle this and other questions Constantine (although he was not even a Christian then) summoned all the bishops to Nicaea in 325 for the first ecumenical council. The outcome of the vote, embodied in the Nicene Creed, was that the one God was a Trinity: Father, Son, and Holy Ghost. That settled, Constantine declared Christianity to be the official Roman religion, although he granted complete freedom to other religions as well.[4] At the time Christians must have regarded this decision as a decisive victory of Christianity over the Roman Empire. I wonder what Jesus would have thought.

Constantine's hope of revitalizing the Roman Empire under a single religion failed. The decline accelerated under the added burden of invasions by northern and eastern nomads whom the historians call Huns, Vandals, and Goths. The invaders themselves were not particular about such nice racial distinctions. They intermarried among themselves and among the citizens of the empire, further lessening the distinction of being a Roman citizen. In 330 Constantine moved his capitol to the more defensible site of Constantinople, which allowed the Eastern (Byzantine) Empire to survive for another eleven centuries. The Western Empire, however, fell after the Goths sacked Rome in 410. The last Roman Emperor died in 476, leaving the Pope to carry on as best he could.[5]

AUGUSTINE AND THE DARK AGES

At this point Saint Augustine (354–430) enters naturally into an account of the convergence of Greek science and Christianity. The young Aurelius Augustine would hardly have seemed a suitable candidate for sainthood. More deserving of the honor was his mother, Saint Monica, whose attempts to convert him to Christianity he found less compelling than the lure of the flesh. "Give me chastity," he prayed, "only not yet" (*Confessions* VII. 17). Moreover, Christianity had several rivals in Augustine's hills of northern Africa, and he was too serious to accept any religion simply on the recommendation of his mother or the empire. At age seventeen Augustine travelled 200 kilometers east to Carthage, where he studied and then taught rhetoric. He took a mistress to whom he was faithful for fifteen years, and he became a Manichean for nine years. Manicheanism was a religion imported from Persia via Alexandria, and its Oriental mysticism and Greek rationalism were probably an appealing combination for Augustine. In 383 he sailed to Rome to teach rhetoric. There he spent a miserable year being ill, feeling humiliated as a provincial who could not even read Greek, and being cheated out of his fees by students. He then taught in Milan for four years and became first a Neoplatonist and then, finally a Christian. He was baptized in 387 and then returned to his home to establish a commune—the parent of the Augustinian order. In 391 Augustine was called to nearby Hippo and accepted increasingly heavy burdens of preaching, administration, and writing, ultimately as bishop. He died in Hippo during the third month of a siege by Vandals. Augustine's two major works were written in Hippo; the *Confessions* around 400, and *The City of God* between 413 and 426. The latter book grew out of correspondence with two Roman officials who wanted to know why Christians and their property were respected by the Goths when they sacked Rome. Augustine responded by contrasting the evil city of Rome with the hypothetical city of God, which would be worthy of preservation. *The City of God* became the most influential work in the Western world prior to Thomas Aquinas, and is still one of the cornerstones of Catholic theology. Through it later Popes and emperors found justification for the Holy Roman Empire, and Plato found a new audience.[6]

The origin of the universe was a pivotal question in Augustine's development. In the declining empire there was ample evidence that evil exists, and it was hard to see how it could have arisen in a world created by an absolutely good God. Augustine at first accepted the Manichean explanation that the dualities of Good and Evil, Light and Dark, God and Satan had existed from the beginning. Like most Manicheans Augustine probably considered Genesis too naïve for serious consideration. (These doubts had nothing to do with evolution, of course.) Eventually Augustine became acquainted with the works of Greek philosopher-scientists, and found their ability to predict astronomical events proof of the superiority of Greek thought to Manicheanism (*Confessions* V. 3–6). Further study of the Greeks led him to Neoplatonism, a school founded by Plotinus (205–270), who had taught in Alexandria and Rome (*Confessions* VII. 13). Since Augustine could not read Greek he concentrated on the Latin translation of *Timaeus*. This dialogue provided a neat solution to the problem of evil which was compatible with the literal Genesis. He deduced that the creations of the first days of Genesis consisted only of the Platonic ideas of earth, sea, plants, man, etc. Thereafter the universe brought forth the actual imperfect copies of these ideals.[7]

Augustine later relegated Plato to a supporting role in his philosophy. In *City of God* VII he briefly reviews the history of Ionian and Athenian philosophy and finds Plato most nearly compatible with Christianity. He equates the creator in *Timaeus* with the Judeo-Christian God, and even suggests that Plato may have been familiar with the Scriptures (*City of God* VIII. 11). Yet he does not hesitate to reject Timaeus's idea of reincarnation (*City of God* XII. 20, 26), or the physical explanation for lust (XII. 7). In the selection in this chapter Augustine rejects a fundamentalist interpretation of Genesis, compares the lesser gods of *Timaeus* with angels, and asserts that God is the creator of all things.[8]

For six centuries after Augustine Greek science remained buried in one of the deeper fissures of the Roman brain.[9] It has often been asked why science was so neglected in the Dark Ages. Such a question presumes that men of that period should have been different from the majority of people before or after them, even as society was falling apart around them. The Goths were still occupying Italy until the sixth century. The Vandals in North Africa and the Visigoths in Spain were replaced by Moslems, who also took over the remnants of the Persian and Hellenized world as far east as India, closing trade routes and seaports.

Normans and Vikings caused similar disruptions in the north. Cities were often decimated by disease, when filthiness was often considered next to godliness, sanitation was nonexistent, and the idea of quarantining infected tradesmen and soldiers would have been regarded as futile against the spread of disease by demons (White, 1896, vol. 2, Ch. 14). The collapse of Rome abandoned Europe to barbarism, leaving the weak to seek protection from the strong under disadvantageous terms. Feudalism gave rise to a rigid class system and then to hereditary aristocracy. Latin degenerated into various dialects—the roots of our Romance languages. Priests and missionaries, often the only ones who could read law, were often called upon to judge in civil as well as ecclesiastical trials. Priests and feudal lords quickly saw the advantages of symbiosis, as shamans and chieftains have always done.

By the eighth century the Kingdom of the Franks had crystallized to encompass most of Western Europe. It looked to the Pope in Rome to confer upon it some sort of legitimacy, and the Pope in turn saw an alliance with the Franks as a means of getting out from under the shadow of Constantinople. Thus in 800 Pope Leo III (by some authority revealed only to him) crowned Charlemagne and hailed him Caesar and Augustus, thereby founding the Holy Roman Empire. In the tenth century, however, the Kingdom of the Franks broke up and the papacy was reduced to such a state that a woman was able to imprison the legitimate Pope and replace him with her illegitimate son as the spiritual descendant of Saint Peter. At the close of the Dark Ages Europe was like a jigsaw puzzle made of silly putty.

THOMAS AQUINAS AND THE LATE MIDDLE AGES

The idea of the Holy Roman Empire provided a nucleus around which Europe began to pull itself together in the eleventh century. The Italians reopened shipping in the Mediterranean, and feudalism proved capable of maintaining order. An important cause as well as an effect of a rising awareness of the empire were the Crusades. The First Holy Crusade was launched by the Pope in 1095 in response to the capture of Jerusalem and the destruction of holy places by the Turks. Tens of thousands of Europeans answered the call. Undoubtedly most of them were motivated by sincere religious passion, but organizers of the Crusade were not unaware of the potential for expanding trade and finally doing something about Constantinople. The First Crusade was a smashing success; Turkish blood flowed in the streets, and a good time was had by all. In fact the Crusade was so successful that a Second Crusade was held fifty years later, then a third one, and a fourth one, and . . . Between 1095 and 1291 there were a total of eight Holy Crusades, which became more and more disastrous and less and less holy. Enthusiasm wore thin as European casualties reached the tens of thousands, the political motives of the organizers became apparent, and financing became oppressive. Money for the Crusades was raised by means of the tithe (a ten percent mandatory tax to the church) and by selling dispensations and relics. So many pieces of the True Cross were sold that one must wonder whether the cross had taken root at Calvary and continued to grow for a thousand years. The Crusades did in the late Middle Ages what Viet Nam and Watergate did more recently; they stimulated a healthy suspicion of the motives and competence of leaders and encouraged a broadening of the mind. Largely through the Crusades many Christians had their minds opened to different cultures, including their Moslem neighbors.

They began to recognize them not merely as infidels but as intellectual links to bygone days of glory. Wherever Islam had conquered, it preserved and encouraged the educational institutions and libraries; for, as Mohammed had said, "He who travels in search of knowledge, travels along Allah's path to paradise." Thanks to Augustine, Plato had been a major influence prior to the twelfth century. However, because of the teaching of the Arab Scholars Avicenna (980–1037) and Averroes (1126–1198), Aristotle began to dominate Christendom (F. E. Peters, 1968).

One of the first, and certainly the most interesting of the early converts to Arabic science was the Holy Roman Emperor Frederick II (1194–1250). Frederick had been made king of Sicily at age four, orphaned at age five, and then placed in the care of the Pope, who let the young king roam the streets of Palermo. In those streets Frederick obtained a most liberal education which equipped him with a knowledge of nine languages and a tolerance for human imperfections. At age twenty-one he was made Holy Roman Emperor, but only after promising the Pope that he would lead a Crusade. He delayed so long in keeping this promise that the Pope excommunicated him temporarily—if that is possible. Finally in 1228 Frederick led the Sixth Crusade, but his Moslem opponent was so impressed by this urbane European who could speak Arabic that he conceded the objectives of the Crusade without a fight. Thereafter Frederick devoted much of his life in southern Italy to philosophy and science, and took a hand in running the University of Naples, which he had founded as one of the few universities free of religious domination. He surrounded himself with Jewish and Moslem scholars, maintained a zoo, and wrote an important book on falconry. It was even said (mostly by his many enemies) that he performed such experiments as raising a child in silence to see what language he eventually would speak, and sealing a man in a barrel in an attempt to collect a specimen of the soul. (Unfortunately no record remains of the results.) Frederick encouraged the translation of Aristotle into Latin, but, ahead of his time as usual, he was critical of Aristotle for his reliance on anecdotes.[10]

Thomas Aquinas (1225–1274) grew up in the liberal climate surrounding Frederick II in southern Italy. In 1239 Thomas became a student at the University of Naples. It was there that he first became acquainted with the teachings of Aristotle and with the Dominicans. He joined the latter order in 1244, but was delayed for a year from taking vows when his family kidnapped and attempted to "deprogram" him. They failed even after sending into his room a beautiful woman to convince him of certain privations of the religious life (Petitot, 1966, p. 41). From 1248 to 1252 Thomas studied with the Dominicans at Cologne under Albertus Magnus, who, along with other so-called Schoolmen, was attempting to reconcile Aristotle and Christianity.[11] In the next seven years he studied at the University of Paris, where he must have had further exposure to Aristotle through the Averroists there. He was then called to Italy as a preacher and teacher. There he induced

William of Moerbeke to make the first translations of Aristotle directly from Greek. Before this the only Latin translations of Aristotle were based on Arabic translations of Syriac translations of the Greek, and Thomas apparently had held back from embracing Aristotelianism because of their unreliability. As soon as he had the new translations he joined with Albertus Magnus and the Scholastics in trying to make Aristotle agree with Christianity. His major contribution to the task was *Summa Theologica,* which he began in 1267. Between 1269 and 1272 Thomas held the Dominican chair in theology at the University of Paris, and was caught in a violent dispute between Averroists in the Faculty of Arts and Augustinian anti-Aristotelians in the Faculty of Theology. He was able to moderate the Averroist position that God does not enter into natural phenomena, and successfully defended the philosophy of Aristotle to the theologicans. Now that the Thomistic philosophy has become orthodox we are apt to underestimate the courage this must have taken. The debate was not simply a professorial discussion over tea; Thomas was undoubtedly in physical danger (Petitot, 1966, p. 70). Also the Parisian clergy and the Inquisition in 1210, and the Pope in 1263 had condemned attempts to harmonize Aristotle and Catholicism, just as orthodox Judaism had condemned similar attempts by Maimonides (1135–1204), and Islam had condemned the efforts of Averroes. Thomas had convinced the Pope that Scholasticism was not heretical, but that did not satisfy the ultraconservative Parisian clergy. In 1277 the bishop of Paris in effect posthumously excommunicated Thomas for adhering to certain Aristotelian propositions (Grant, 1974, pp. 42–50). Of course Thomas was ultimately victorious. As we shall see in the next chapter, it eventually became heretical to contradict Aristotle. In 1272 Thomas returned to Italy. (As a Dominican, by the way, Thomas had to make all of these journeys on foot!) There he had a religious experience which made his scholarly work seem to him like "straw." He died shortly afterwards.

Every Westerner is to some degree an Aristotelian thanks to *Summa Theologica.* Unfortunately much of the work laid a poor foundation for the redevelopment of Greek science because of Thomas's tendency to use Aristotle's logic to pick nits. For example, in the "Treatise on Angels" (First Part, Questions 50–64), Thomas determines whether angels can move instantly, know each other and the future, have free will, and love God more than themselves, and whether demons are naturally wicked and sorrowful. (He did not answer the question which has bothered me for thirty years: If Superman and God got into a fight, who would win?) Scholasticism, using this kind of reasoning as a model, eventually brought Aristotle into disrepute.

The following selections from *Summa Theologica* on the fifth and sixth day of Creation are typical of Thomas's attempts to make God into an Aristotelian or Aristotle into a prophet. Believing that both the Bible and Aristotle must be true, he goes through bizarre logical contortions to make them agree. He accepts without question the first chapter of Genesis and Aristotle's four elements, spontaneous generation, and the classification of causes. (The efficient cause is here translated as "active principle.") Thomas's rank as a biologist is revealed by his belief that seals are fish. If Aristotle had been infallable Thomas would have achieved for all time his goal of reuniting the rational mind and the spiritual soul of man, but that hope was doomed by the very science which he helped restore.[12]

Augustine, from *The City of God,* Book XII. Translated by M. Dods.[13] By permission.

CH. 23. Of the nature of the human soul created in the image of God

God, then, made man in His own image. For He created for him a soul endowed with reason and intelligence, so that he might excel all the creatures of earth, air, and sea, which were not so gifted. And when He had formed the man out of the dust of the earth, and had willed that his soul should be such as I have said—whether He had already made it, and now by breathing imparted it to man, or rather made it by breathing, so that that breath which God made by breathing (for what else is "to breathe" than to make breath?) is the soul—He made also a wife for him, to aid him in the work of generating his kind, and her He formed of a bone taken out of the man's side, working in a divine manner. For we are not to conceive of this work in a carnal fashion, as if God wrought as we commonly see artisians, who use their hands and material furnished to them that by their artistic skill they may fashion some material object. God's hand is God's power; and He, working invisibly, effects visible results. But this seems fabulous rather than true to men, who measure by customary and everyday works the power and wisdom of God, whereby He understands and produces without seeds even seeds themselves; and because they cannot understand the things which at the beginning were created, they are sceptical regarding them—as if the very things which they do know about human propagation, conceptions and births, would seem less incredible if told to those who had no experience of them; though these very things, too, are attributed by many rather to physical and natural causes than to the work of the divine mind.

CH. 24. Whether the angels can be said to be the creators of any, even the least creature

But in this book we have nothing to do with those who do not believe that the divine mind made or cares for this world. As for those who believe their own Plato, that all mortal animals—among whom man holds the pre-eminent place, and is near to the gods themselves—were created not by that most high God Who made the world, but by other lesser gods created by the Supreme, and exercising a delegated power under His control—if only those persons be delivered from the superstition which prompts them to seek a plausible reason for paying divine honors and sacrificing to those gods as their creators, they will easily be disentangled also from this their error. For it is blasphemy to believe or to say (even before it can be understood) that any other than God is creator of any nature, be it never so small and mortal. And as for the angels, whom those Platonists prefer to call gods, although they do, so far as they are permitted and commissioned, aid in the production of the things around us, yet not on that account are we to call them creators, any more than we call gardeners the creators of fruits and trees.

CH. 25. That God alone is the creator of every kind of creature, whatever its nature or form

For whereas there is one form which is given from without to every bodily substance—such as the form which is constructed by potters and smiths, and that class of artists who paint and fashion forms like the body of animals—but another and internal form which is not itself constructed, but, as the efficient cause, produces not only the natural bodily forms, but even the life itself of the living creatures, and which proceeds from the secret and hidden choice of an intelligent and living nature—let that first-mentioned form be attributed to every artificer, but this latter to one only, God, the Creator and Originator Who made the world itself and the angels, without the help of world or angels. For the same divine and, so to speak, creative energy, which cannot be made, but makes, and which gave to the earth and sky their round-ness—this same divine, effective, and creative energy gave their roundness to the eye and to the apple; and the other natural objects which we anywhere see, received also their form, not from without, but from the secret and profound might of the Creator, Who said, "Do not I fill heaven and earth?"[a] and Whose wisdom it is that "reacheth from one end to another mightily; and sweetly doth she order all things."[b] Wherefore I know not what kind of aid the angels, themselves created first, afforded to the Creator in making other things. I cannot ascribe to them what perhaps they cannot do, neither ought I to deny them such faculty as they have. But, by their leave, I attribute the creating and originating work which gave being to all natures to God, to Whom they themselves thankfully ascribe their existence. We do not call gar-deners the creators of their fruits, for we read, "Neither is he that planteth anything, neither he that watereth, but God that giveth the increase."ᶜ Nay, not even the earth itself do we call a creator, though she seems to be the prolific mother of all things which she aids in germinating and bursting forth from the seed, and which she keeps rooted in her own breast; for we likewise read, "God giveth it a body, as it hath pleased Him, and to every seed his own body."ᵈ We ought not even to call a woman the creatress of her own offspring; for He rather is its creator Who said to His servant, "Before I formed thee in the womb, I knew thee."ᵉ And although the various mental emotions of a pregnant woman do produce in the fruit of her womb similar qualities—as Jacob with his peeled wands caused piebald sheep to be produced—yet the mother as little creates her offspring as she created herself. Whatever bodily or seminal causes, then, may be used for the production of things, either by the cooperation of angels, men, or the lower animals, or by sexual generation; and whatever power the desires and mental emotions of the mother have to produce in the tender and plastic foetus corresponding lineaments and colours; yet the natures themselves, which are thus variously affected, are the production of none but the most high God. It is His occult power which pervades all things, and is present in all without being contaminated, which gives being to all that is, and modifies and limits its existence; so that without Him it would not be thus, or thus, nor would have any being at all. If, then, in regard to that outward form which the workman's hand imposes on his work, we do not say that Rome and Alexandria were built by masons and architects, but by the kings by whose will, plan, and resources they were built, so that the one has Romulus, the other Alexander, for its founder; with how much greater reason ought we to say that God alone is the Author of all natures, since He neither uses for His work any material which was not made by Him, nor any workmen who were not also made by Him, and since, if He were, so to speak, to withdraw from created things His creative power, they would straightway relapse into the nothingness in which they were before they were created? "Before," I mean, in respect of eternity, not of time. For what other creator could there be of time, than He who created those things whose movements make time?

Thomas Aquinas, from *Summa Theologica,* the First Part. Translated by Fathers of the English Dominican Province.

QUESTION LXXI. Of the Work of the Fifth Day (In One Article)
    We must next consider the work of the fifth day.
    It would seem that this work is not fittingly described.

Objection 1. For the waters produce that which the power of water is adequate to produce. But the power of water does not suffice for the production of every kind of fishes and birds since we find that many are generated from seed. Therefore the words, *Let the waters bring forth the creeping creature having life, and the fowl that may fly over the earth,* do not fittingly describe this work.

Obj. 2. Further, fishes and birds are not produced from water only, but earth seems to predominate over water in their composition, as is shown by the fact that their bodies tend naturally to the earth and rest upon it. It is not, then, fittingly said that fishes and birds are produced from water.

Obj. 3. Further, fishes move in the waters, and birds in the air. If, then, fishes are produced from the waters, birds ought to be produced from the air, and not from the waters.

Obj. 4. Further, not all fishes creep through the waters, for some, as seals, have feet and walk on land. Therefore the production of fishes is not sufficiently described by the words, *Let the waters bring forth the creeping creature having life.*

Obj. 5. Further, land animals are more perfect than birds and fishes, which appears from the fact that they have more distinct limbs, and generation of a higher order. For they bring forth animals, whereas birds and fishes bring forth eggs. But the more perfect has precedence in the order of nature. Therefore fishes and birds ought not to have been produced on the fifth day, before the land animals.

On the contrary, The authority of Scripture suffices.

I answer that, As said above (Q. LXX, A. 1), the order of the work of adornment corresponds to the order of the work of distinction. Hence, as among the three days assigned to the work of distinction, the middle, or second, day is devoted to the work of the distinction of water, which is the intermediate body, so in the three days of the work of adornment, the middle day, which is the fifth, is assigned to the adornment of the intermediate body, by the production of birds and fishes. As, then, Moses makes mention of the lights and the light on the fourth day, to show that the fourth day corresponds to the first day on which he had said that the light was made, so on this fifth day he mentions the water and the firmament of heaven to show that the fifth day corresponds to the second. It must, however, be observed that Augustine differs from other writers in his opinion about the production of fishes and birds, as he differs about the production of plants. For while others say that fishes and birds were produced on the fifth day actually, he holds that the nature of the waters produced them on that day potentially.

Reply Obj. 1. It was laid down by Avicenna that animals of all kinds can be generated by various minglings of the elements, and naturally, without any kind of seed. This, however, seems wrong, since nature produces its effects by determinate means, and, consequently, those things that are naturally generated from seed cannot be generated naturally in any other way. It ought, then, rather to be said that in the natural generation of all animals that are generated from seed, the active principle lies in the formative power of the seed, but that in the case of animals generated from putrefaction, the formative power is the influence of the heavenly bodies. The material principle, however, in the generation of either kind of animals is either some element, or something compounded of the elements. But at the first beginning of things the active principle was the Word of God, which produced animals from material elements, either in act, as some holy writers say, or virtually, as Augustine teaches. Not as though the power possessed by water or earth of producing all animals resides in the earth and water themselves, as Avicenna held, but in the power originally given to the elements of producing them from elemental matter by the power of seed or the influence of the stars.

Reply Obj. 2. The bodies of birds and fishes may be considered from two points of view. If considered in themselves, it will be evident that the earthly element must predominate, since the element that is least active, namely, the earth, must be the most abundant in quantity in order that the mingling may be duly tempered in the body of the animal. But if considered as by nature constituted to move with certain specific motions, thus they have some special affinity with bodies in which they move; and hence the words in which their generation is described.

Reply Obj. 3. The air, as not being so apparent to the senses, is not enumerated by itself, but with other things: partly with the water, because the lower region of the air is thickened by watery exhalations; partly with the heaven as to the higher regions. But birds move in the lower part of the air, and so are said to fly *beneath the firmament,* even if the firmament be taken to mean the region of clouds. Hence the production of birds is ascribed to the water.

Reply Obj. 4. Nature passes from one extreme to another through the medium. And therefore there are creatures of intermediate type between the animals of the air and those of the water, having something in common with both. And they are reckoned as belonging to that class to which they are most allied, through the characters possessed in common with that class, rather than with the other. But in order to include among fishes all such intermediate forms as have special characters like theirs, the words, *Let the waters bring forth the creeping creature having life,* are followed by these: *God created great whales,* etc.

Reply Obj. 5. The order in which the production of these animals is given has reference to the order of those bodies which they are set to adorn, rather than to the superiority of the animals themselves. Moreover, in generation also the more perfect is reached through the less perfect.

QUESTION LXXII. Of the Work of the Sixth Day (In One Article)

We must now consider the work of the sixth day.

It would seem that this work is not fittingly described.

Objection 1. For as birds and fishes have a living soul, so also have land animals. But these animals are not themselves living souls. Therefore the words, *Let the earth bring forth the living creature,* should rather have been, *Let the earth bring forth the living fourfooted creatures.*

Obj. 2. Further, a genus ought not to be divided against its species. But beasts and cattle are quadrupeds. Therefore quadrupeds ought not to be enumerated as a class with beasts and cattle.

Obj. 3. Further, as other animals belong to a determinate genus and species, so also does man. But in the making of man nothing is said of his genus or species, and therefore nothing ought to have been said about them in the production of other animals, whereas it is said "according to its genus" or "in its species."

Obj. 4. Further, land animals are more like man, whom God is recorded to have blessed, than are birds and fishes. But as birds and fishes are said to be blessed, this should have been said, with much more reason, of the other animals as well.

Obj. 5. Further, certain animals are generated from putrefaction, which is a kind of corruption. But corruption is not appropriate to the first founding of the world. Therefore such animals should not have been produced at that time.

Obj. 6. Further, certain animals are poisonous, and injurious to man. But there ought to have been nothing injurious to man before man sinned. Therefore such animals ought not to have been made by God at all, since He is the Author of good, or at least not until man had sinned.

On the contrary, The authority of Scripture suffices.

I answer that, As on the fifth day the intermediate body, namely the water, is adorned, and thus that day corresponds to the second day; so the sixth day, on which the lowest body, or the earth, is adorned by the production of land animals, corresponds to the third day. Hence the earth is mentioned in both places. And here again Augustine says (*Gen. ad lit.* V) that the production was potential, and other holy writers that it was actual.

Reply Obj. 1. The different grades of life which are found in different living creatures can be discovered from the various ways in which the Scripture speaks of them, as Basil says (*Hom. VIII in Hexaëm.*). The life of plants, for instance, is very imperfect and difficult to discern, and hence, in speaking of their production, nothing is said of their life, but only their generation is mentioned, since only in generation is a vital act observed in them. For the powers of nutrition and growth are subordinate to the generative life, as will be shown later on (Q. LXXVIII, A. 2). But amongst animals, those that live on land are, generally speaking, more perfect than birds and fishes, not because the fish is devoid of memory, as Basil upholds *(ibid.)* and Augustine rejects *(Gen. ad lit. III),* but because their limbs are more distinct and their generation of a higher order, (yet some imperfect animals, such as bees and ants, are more acute in certain ways). Scripture, therefore, does not call fishes *living creatures,* but *creeping creatures having life;* but it does call land animals *living creatures* on account of their perfect life, and seems to imply that fishes are merely bodies having in them something of a soul, whilst land animals, from the higher perfection of their life, are, as it were, living souls with bodies subject to them. But the life of man, as being the most perfect grade, is not said to be produced, like the life of other animals, by the earth or water, but immediately by God.

Reply Obj. 2. By *cattle,* domestic animals are signified, which in any way are of service to man, but by *beasts,* wild animals such as bears and lions are designated. By *creeping things* those animals are meant which either have no feet and cannot rise from the earth, as serpents, or those whose feet are too short to lift them far from the ground, as the lizard and tortoise. But since certain animals, as deer and goats, seem to fall under none of these classes, the word *quadrupeds* is added. Or perhaps the word *quadruped* is used first as being the genus, to which animals are added as species, for even some reptiles, such as lizards and tortoises, are four-footed.

Reply Obj. 3. In other animals, and in plants, mention is made of genus and species to denote the generation of like from like. But it was unnecessary to do so in the case of man, as what had already been said of other creatures might be understood of him. Again, animals and plants may be said to be produced according to their kinds to signify their remoteness from the Divine likeness, whereas man is said to be made *to the image and likeness of God.*

Reply Obj. 4. The blessing of God gives power to multiply by generation, and, having been mentioned in the preceding account of the making of birds and fishes, could be understood of the beasts of the earth without requiring to be repeated. The blessing, however, is repeated in the case of man, since in him generation of children has a special relation to the filling up of the number of the elect, and "to prevent anyone from saying that there was any sin whatever in the act of begetting children." As to plants, "since they experience neither desire of propagation, nor sensation in generating, they are deemed unworthy of the words of the blessing."[14]

Reply Obj. 5. Since the generation of one thing is the corruption of another, it was not incompatible with the first formation of things that from the corruption of the less perfect the more perfect should be generated. Hence animals generated from the corruption of inanimate things, or of plants, may have been generated then. But those generated from corruption of animals could not have been produced then otherwise than potentially.

Reply Obj. 6. In the words of Augustine (*Super. Gen. contr. Manich.* I): "If an unskilled person enters the workshop of an artificer he sees in it many appliances of which he does not understand the use, and which, if he is a foolish fellow, he considers unnecessary. Moreover, should he carelessly fall into the fire, or wound himself with a sharp-edged tool, he is under the impression that many of the things there are hurtful; the craftsman, however, knowing their use, laughs at his folly. And thus some people presume to find fault with many things in this world, through not seeing the reasons for their existence. For though not required for the furnishing of our house, these things are necessary for the perfection of the universe." And, since man before he sinned would have used the things of this world comformably to the order designed, poisonous animals would not have injured him.

CLOSE ENCOUNTERS OF THE ABSURD KIND

The Middle Ages often bring to mind visions of the air darkened by the smoke of burning witches and heretics, and of minds equally clouded by superstition. Undoubtedly this is an exaggerated impression. I sometimes wonder, in fact, whether the fear, hatred, and superstition which inspired the witch-hunts and the Inquisition of the Middle Ages are still with us in the Scientific Age. By the Middle Ages only a few hundred generations had passed since humanity had removed itself from the natural state, and only about thirty generations separate us from our medieval ancestors. Biological evolution cannot keep pace with such rapid cultural changes. We should not expect that abandoning the nature in which we evolved could be accomplished without leaving some sort of mismatch of brain and environment. Cutting the umbilical cord linking us to nature may have left a behavioral navel which civilization has not entirely healed—a raw and bloody place in the mind, where primal fears and taboos fester and erupt, or only tickle and itch. Perhaps parts of our brains which produced drives and beliefs necessary for survival in the natural state gave rise to the dark and ugly horrors of medieval times, and to the speculations of Thomas Aquinas on the personalities of demons and angels. Perhaps they now produce the behavioral aberrations which shock and amuse us daily.[15]

The anti-Communist reaction of the late 1940s and 1950s in the United States has often been compared to a witch-hunt. Since many readers are too young to remember that period, it might be useful to recall it briefly to see how far we have come since the Middle Ages. Russia's take-over of Eastern Europe after World War II, their success in breaking the American monopoly on the atomic bomb, our "loss" of China to Communism, and the frustrations over Korea convinced many Americans that Communism had virtually supernatural powers. Rational people spoke of being "infected" by associating with Communists or by reading their propaganda. (Perhaps it is progress that the medieval idea of demonic possession was replaced by a germ theory of politics.) Attempts to prevent the spread of Communism took on the form of a quarantine: carriers were labelled "pinko," "Communist sympathizer," "fellow traveller," or (to avoid libel) "controversial." In small minds these labels became magnified to "red," "Communist," and "active agent in the Communist conspiracy." Just as medieval clergymen adopted the devil's own ingenuity in torturing demons from the bodies of witches and heretics, many of those elected to protect us from tyranny became tyrants. The House Committee on Unamerican Activities and Joseph McCarthy's Senate Subcommittee on Internal Security forced hundreds to confess legal acts and to implicate others. Those who did not recant and "name names" were jailed for contempt of Congress (which would have been fair enough if having contempt for such people were a crime). Those who invoked the right not to incriminate themselves became known as "Fifth-Amendment Communists." Merely being subpoenaed to testify threatened the loss of a job, but at least these modern Inquisitors did not extract confessions under *physical* torture.

Scientists came under particular scrutiny, for, as every science fiction movie showed, they had the "secret formula" which would enable the Communists to destroy us. Teachers were also closely examined regarding their beliefs and associations, because of their power over tender young minds. The Board of Regents of the University of Washington (which included such paragons as Dave Beck, who later distinguished himself as the corrupt president of the Teamsters) led the way in purging faculties of those who could not or would not sign loyalty oaths. Under the infamous Feinberg Law the loyalty of every New York State teacher was made the subject of an annual report, and teachers had to submit lists of organizations to which they belonged. This law was justified on the grounds that the "dissemination of propaganda may be and frequently is sufficiently subtle to escape detection in the classroom," as the New York legislature found out by some occult process. Perhaps the legislators reasoned that if they, in their childlike innocence, could detect undetectable propaganda, then schoolchildren also could, and under its spell might hand over the country to Stalin. In the Middle Ages, also, children were considered the most gifted at discovering witches.[16]

Naturally movie and television writers and actors were especially talented at subliminal propaganda, so a secret blacklist was instituted in the entertainment industry to prevent the transmission of the Communist infection via the media. Such dangerous characters as Will Geer, a "Fifth-Amendment Communist" most recently known as Grandpa on the Waltons, were thus prevented from turning their audiences into raving Communists.

What was said by a ninth-century archbishop could apply to America in the 1950s: "The wretched world lies now under the tyranny of foolishness; things are believed by Christians of such absurdity as no one ever could aforetime induce the heathen to believe."[17]

The retarded pace of cultural evolution since the Middle Ages is also revealed in ways that are less nasty than the preceding example. I have in mind the increasing fascination with alleged visits to Earth by extraterrestrial forms of life, beginning with the first sightings of "flying saucers" in the late 1940s. At present, claims of close encounters with humanlike beings from other planets are taken seriously even by sober newsmen, and segments of the publishing and entertainment industry thrive by nourishing our hopes or fears that human destiny will be changed by such an encounter. In the Middle Ages the only extraterrestrials conceivable were angels and demons. These beings filled the emotional gap separating man from God, provided an explanation for strange phenomena, explained the existence of evil in a world fashioned by perfect goodness, and held out hope for supernatural assistance. I believe the same needs are met by the beings from other planets who are supposedly taking such an interest in us. Now that we realize that we are not the center of God's universe we feel a certain loneliness when contemplating the emptiness separating us from our nearest intelligent neighbors. Belief in encounters with extraterrestrials assures us that "we are not alone." There is a certain nostalgia for a future when we shall be united with others who (we hope) will be much like ourselves. Also, as in the Middle Ages, there still remain many mysterious phenomena of nature, and we tend to think that if even our advanced state of science cannot explain such things as unidentified flying objects, then the only explanation must be that they are visitors from another planet. (This reminds me of an argument between two chickadees which I overheard while refilling the bird feeder. "O.K.," one chickadee said to the other, "If he's not from another planet, where does he get all the sunflower seed?")

It may not be simply a coincidence that the anti-Communist witch-hunt and sightings of UFOs began at about the same time. Perhaps there was too much evil to attribute only to the Communists, and many Americans thought that they must have recruited outside assistance to take over the world. This might explain why early encounters took the form of "dogfights" between "flying saucers" and military jets, and why there were rumors that the government was covering up evidence of a massive invasion. (Where demons are involved, no one is above suspicion.) Intelligent forms of life in Hollywood apparently sensed the American yearning for demons in modern dress, and satisfied that yearning with such immortal works as *It Came from Outer Space* (1953), *Earth vs. the Flying Saucers* (1956), *Invasion of the Saucer Men* (1957), *The Brain Eaters* (1958), and *Invasion of the Star Creatures* (1959). Apparently Viet Nam, Watergate, and our ecological follies have taught us that there are already demons enough on Earth (if not within each of us). There now seems to be a general desire for wise and kind visitors from Krypton or wherever, who will restore truth, justice, and the American way. We are too sophisticated to believe in angels fluttering about, so we have traded in their wings for spaceships.[18]

This revelation came to me at the climax of *Close Encounters of the Third Kind*. The first part of this film was a stunning buildup to an invited landing on Earth by a huge craft from another planet. Finally the craft sets down on the specially prepared field, surrounded by scientists and technicians looking expectantly at the hatch. Slowly it opens. The first to emerge are humans from Earth—specimens collected over the past few centuries. The hatch remains open for agonizing minutes as we wait to see what evolution has wrought elsewhere. Flashing through my mind are previous encounters on the Late Late Show, which I had experienced as my scorched and sleepless brain sought relief from too much scientific reality. Which of those beings, I wonder, has returned after a quarter of a century? Is it the infamous green slime, come to give back the energy it stole to sustain its life? Is it a mass of eyes and legs, looking like it was constructed of parts left over from the creation of spiders and crustaceans? Or is it an invisible mind, the ultimate in evolution, and the salvation of uninspired special-effects designers in Hollywood? For a moment my EEG goes flat. And then . . . there they are. Dimly at first against the glare of the interior lights. Slowly their forms come into focus. Oh, no! Horrible! They have only one head! It can't be! They have two arms, and walk on two legs! And there are five fingers on each hand! Ghastly! Now I can see two eyes in the front of the head, and a mouth below! Hideous! They are, in short, your average white, middle-class humanoids! They could move into my neighborhood without depressing property values. They are even rather sexy, with their long eyelashes and coy smiles, although I'm not sure I would want my sister to marry one. But what has happened to the unearthly beasts of the Late Late Show? What awful mutation has changed them to this?

And then it occurred to me. What had evolved was not intelligent life on another planet, but popular culture on our own planet. Our demons of the 1950s are gathering dust in Hollywood prop rooms because we no longer need them to explain our situation. We want angels now to save us from that situation, and we want them in our image. It is too hard to look a giant blob in all of its eyes at once with equanimity, and it is pointless to smile at a thing that has no mouth. Our angels have to resemble us even if it means violating the elementary principles of evolution.

What principles of evolution? you may ask. After all, aren't there at least a million galaxies, each with perhaps hundreds of thousands of millions of solar systems where humanlike life could have evolved to a level sufficient to enable a visit to us? Well, not quite. First we must confine ourselves to our own galaxy, since any form of life outside it would be at least 10,000 light years away. Thus, even if intelligent beings from another galaxy found us interesting 10,000 years before we took up farming around 10,000 B. C., they would have had to travel at the speed of light to have arrived by now. (It would have taken at least 10,000 years for information to arrive there from Earth, and an equal amount of time for them to get here.) Thus we are limited to the 200,000,000,000 solar systems in our own Milky Way, which one might consider sufficient since it is several times the number of hamburgers sold by a certain fast-food chain. We know little about planets in other solar systems, but let us guess that one out of every 200 of them has a planet with conditions sufficiently Earth-like to give rise to life as we know it. That leaves about a thousand million such planets.[19]

What is the expected number of these that could have evolved by now into technologically advanced cultures, composed of beings appearing more-or-less human? We cannot be precise, but a consideration of the evolution of man on Earth gives some idea of the improbability of its being repeated elsewhere. Let us concede that vertebrates like fish could arise on one-tenth of the thousand million planets. Our fishy ancestors just happened to have two eyes above a nose above a single mouth, without which no self-respecting extraterrestrial would show his face on Earth. I can imagine a hundred reasonable alternatives to this arrangement, so we reduce the number of likely planets to one percent. One lucky population of fish was able to survive on land and evolve into an amphibian species when bodies of fresh water dried up some 350 million years ago.[20] If that geological event had not occurred there might not have been the selection pressure to force vertebrates to become terrestrial. Let us assume the probability of such an event is about one in ten, leaving 100,000 candidate planets. Our amphibian ancestors decided that four was a good number of limbs, even though no limbs suffice for many animals, and ten or more are required to satisfy others. We therefore reduce to one-tenth the probability that on another planet life as we know it will evolve into intelligent beings having four limbs. Around 300 million years ago one species of amphibian evolved into the reptiles, and about 100 million years later a population of reptiles evolved into mammals. Somewhere along the way they settled on five digits at the end of each limb, even though any number from zero to ten might have served as well, considering the diverse ways in which various species use them. The number of the candidate planets on which the same number of digits will be selected would be about 1,000.

On Earth around seventy million years ago some mammals adopted tree-living habits, giving rise to the primate order, which now includes lemurs, monkeys, apes, and humans. Falling out of trees tended to select against a weak grip, so the opposable thumb arose. Similar considerations encouraged the movement of the eyes to the front of the head for depth perception, and an enlargement of the sensory and motor areas of the brain for eye-hand coordination. The ability to detect fruit favored the evolution of color vision, an unusual feature among mammals, but one which *Close Encounters of the Third Kind* takes for granted.[21] We can estimate the probability of this combination of primate features as one in a hundred. The number of planets capable of producing humanlike visitors has now shrunk to ten.

Now comes a truly unlikely series of events. In Europe, the Near East, and eastern Africa the forest habitat of primates began to change into grassland because of some climatic change about twenty million years ago. This forced many primates to spend increasing amounts of time on the ground, thus favoring an upright posture to allow them to see over the grass. Other changes followed inexorably. With no fruit in the grasses these hominids turned to hunting. However, most prey were either swifter or larger than they, so they were forced to hunt in groups, leading to social cooperation and eventually to language. The hands and large brains, now free from the chore of locomotion, began to be employed in the production of tools, starting a few million years ago. The ability to communicate and to manipulate the environment demanded an ever-expanding brain to handle more sensory information, and the fossils indeed reveal an astounding mushrooming of the brain compared to the rest of the body (Gould, 1977, Ch. 22; Pilbeam and Gould, 1974).[22] Thus a change in climate occurring at a time and place where there were primates to adapt to it gave rise to essential features required of our interstellar angels: upright posture, social organization, language, use of tools, and great intelligence. The ten remaining planets must be reduced by a factor equal to the likelihood of such an event being repeated. Let us generously call it one in ten, leaving only one planet in our galaxy likely to be inhabited by a humanlike form of intelligent life. Presumably we're it. There is no other planet from which angels will come to save us from ourselves.[23]

Because I have been deliberately conservative in estimating these probabilities, the expected number of planets harboring pseudo-humans is actually much less than one. This means that even on a planet identical to Earth it is unlikely that humans would arise again. In fact, we would probably not happen again if the Earth were turned back three thousand million years and given a second chance. Evolution relies on the natural selection of spontaneous mutations, and it is unlikely that the same combinations of mutations would occur again at the right times. Some other form of intelligent life might occur, but it wouldn't be us. For once science suggests that there really is something special about man.

We have seen that humanlike extraterrestrial visitors are unlikely. (So unlikely are they that anyone claiming to have met little green men or other extraterrestrial humanoids can reliably be considered a crank.) It is much more likely that nonhuman (inhuman?) forms of intelligent life could come calling some day. What form they will take is unimaginable, since it will not be like anything on Earth. You can easily satisfy yourself that it is unimaginable by trying to draw a picture of such a being. It looks like a composite of mundane forms of life, doesn't it? This is a good exercise for preparing oneself for the coming culture shock. Considering the misunderstandings between cultures in our own species, some sort of preparation is advised. Producers of science fiction films might begin by portraying an extraterrestrial intelligence which is not Caucasian. With many whites objecting to the bussing of blacks into their neighborhoods, I shudder to think of the reaction when blacks, greens, or blues are rocketed to our planet.

TABLE 5. MAJOR EVENTS AND PEOPLE OF THE RENAISSANCE

Year	Science/Philosophy	Arts	Politics & War
1300			
	Marco Polo (1254-1324)	Dante	
		Giotto	
	William of Occam (1300?-1349)		
		Petrarch	Black Death
			Wycliffe (1320-1384)
		Chaucer	
			Huss (1370?-1415)

Year	Science / Philosophy	Arts	Politics & War
1400			
			Great Schism (1378-1417)
		Donatello	
	Gutenberg (1395?-1468)		Fall of Constantinople (1453)
		Botticelli	
	Columbus (1446?-1506)		
1500			
	Leonardo da Vinci (1452-1519)		
		Raphael	Martin Luther (1483-1546)
		Thomas More	King Henry VIII
		Rabelais	(r. 1509-1546)
		Michelangelo	Magellan's voyage
	Copernicus (1473-1543)	St. Peter's (1505-1626)	(1519-1522)
	Vesalius (1514-1564)		Jean Calvin
	Servetus (1511-1553)		(1509-1564)
		Titian	Queen Elizabeth
	Montaigne (1533-1592)		(r. 1558-1603)
	Bruno (1548?-1600)	El Greco	Defeat of Spanish
	Gilbert (1540-1603)		Armada (1588)
	Fabricius (1533?-1619)	Cervantes	Sir W. Raleigh (1552?-1618)
1600			
	Kepler (1571-1630)	Shakespeare	Jamestown (1607-)
	Bacon (1561-1626)	King James Bible	
	Harvey (1578-1657)	John Donne	Pilgrims land (1620)
	Descartes (1596-1650)	Rubens	English Civil War
	Harvard College (1636-)		(1643-1649)
	Galileo (1564-1642)	Rembrandt	Thirty Years War
	Hobbes (1588-1679)		(1618-1648)
	Pascal (1623-1662)	Milton	English Commonwealth
	Redi (1626-1698)	Bunyon	(1649-1660)
	Leeuwenhoek (1632-1723)		King Louis XIV
	Newton (1642-1726)		(r. 1643-1715)
	Leibniz (1646-1716)		
	Locke (1632-1704)		
1700			

4

Born Again:
The Revival of Science in the Renaissance

A few alert readers may have noticed something about this book which distinguishes it from all other histories of evolutionism: we have covered three chapters without encountering any evolutionists. With trepidation I confess that you will have to wait four more centuries before meeting any. However, the next chapter will bring with it enough evolutionists to reward your patience. But first it is necessary to consider the rebirth of science which made an appreciation of evolution possible.[1]

When we left Thomas Aquinas, Catholicism had reached a detente with the Schoolmen, who were striving to become clones of Aristotle. At first the church permitted Scholasticism in spite of itself, then allowed it as an outlet for the energies of renegade students and clerics, and finally absorbed it into doctrine. The Thomistic synthesis ended in the Renaissance when men discovered that the study of nature is even more exciting than the study of Aristotle. Probably Augustine would have diagnosed the scientific Renaissance as an infectious "disease of curiosity," which drives men to "search out the hidden powers of nature . . . wherein men desire nothing but to know" (*Confessions* X.55). In reality the causes of the rebirth of science were many and more complex than that.[2]

We can only touch upon the most obvious religious factors leading to the rejection of authority in favor of reason. One major religious factor was the Great Schism from 1378 to 1417, when Christendom was split between the traditional Pope in Rome and another claimant to the papacy who resided at Avignon, with the blessing of the French. Pope and Anti-Pope excommunicated each other's followers for two damned generations. With the church in disarray, forerunners of the Reformation such as John Wycliffe (1320–1384) and John Huss (1370?–1415) dared to question doctrine on such matters as Purgatory and transubstantiation, and to demand the moral reform of clergymen. Such liberal trends were temporarily discouraged when the council which ended the Great Schism ordered Wycliffe's bones dug up and scattered and Huss burned alive. Of course these measures were ultimately no more effective than those of Nero had been, especially after the printing of inexpensive Bibles made it possible for masses of people to compare the teachings of the church with those of the Scriptures. Beginning early in the sixteenth century under Martin Luther (1483–1546) and Jean Calvin (1509–1564), Protestantism encroached increasingly upon the Catholic monopoly on Christianity. At the same time monarchs, having inherited the power of the old feudal lords, became restless at having to share that power with the Pope. Many kings desired a home-grown church which would be easily controlled, and they also coveted the tithes and wealth of the Catholic churches. Individual monarchs, such as Henry VIII, also had personal reasons for breaking with Catholicism. Here and there a king may even have been motivated by sincere religious convictions. The liberation of the kings from the Pope did not, however, bestow religious liberty upon the kings' subjects. In most of Europe people had only the choice of converting to the monarch's religion or of leaving the country. Many chose the latter, and some were desperate enough to undertake the hazardous voyage to the New World, where the struggle for religious freedom continues on more equitable terms. Other Christians remained in their native lands to fight wars of spiritual liberation, such as the Thirty Years War (1618–1648) and the English Civil War (1643–1649)

Challenges to the authority of the church on religious matters were quickly followed by challenges on scientific matters. The elaborate edifice of Aristotelian doctrine was challenged in 1543, when Nicolaus Copernicus (1473–1543) published *De Revolutionibus Orbium Coelestium,* which proposed that the sun was the center of the universe. This model overthrew the entire Aristotelian world view, for if the Earth was not the center of the universe then the idea of sublunar imperfection and supralunar perfection made no sense. Nor did the supposed natural motions of the four elements fit with the heliocentric model, for that model implied that the center of motion of these elements would be revolving with the Earth.[3] Copernicus avoided a confrontation with the church by quietly dying at the time of the book's publication. Later astronomers were not so fortunate. Giordano Bruno (1548?–1600) was burned at the stake for suggesting that there might be other inhabited planets, and Galileo Galilei (1564–1642) at age seventy was threatened with torture, forced to recant "the heresy of the movement of the Earth," and kept under house arrest until he died. But the telescope had already doomed Aristotle, along with the church's infallibility in matters scientific. Galileo's discovery of sunspots, Jupiter's moons, and the phases of Venus positively disproved the idea of unchanging planets moving around the Earth in perfect circles. The gulf separating science and religion became once more as wide as it had been before Thomas.

As if uncovered by the lifting of a great rock, philosophers began to scurry out into the Renaissance light, condemning Aristotle as "the god of scholastic knowledge" who "corrupted natural philosophy by logic" and "paltry Greek argumentation."[4] For a brief period it must have seemed as though man, aware that he was hurtling through space, was about to lose his balance, like a bicyclist suddenly conscious of his precarious situation. Nature, as in King Lear, had suddenly lost its reason. John Donne expressed it in 1611:

> And new Philosophy calls all in doubt,
> The Element of fire is quite put out;
> The Sun is lost, and th'earth, and no man's wit
> Can well direct him where to looke for it.
> And freely men confesse that this world's spent,
> When in the Planets, and the Firmament
> They seeke so many new; then see that this
> Is crumbled out againe to his Atomies.
> 'Tis all in pieces, all cohaerance gone;
> All just supply, and all Relation.
>   "The First Anniversary," 11. 205–214

Even Blaise Pascal (1623–1662), who savaged Aristotelian logic with his study of the vacuum, seems to have suffered a loss of nerve when he wrote: "When I consider the short duration of my life, swallowed up in the eternity before and after, the little space which I fill, and even can see, engulfed in the infinite immensity of spaces of which I am ignorant and which know me not, I am frightened. . . ." (*Pensées* 205).[5]

Man had sailed to the brink of thought, and looking out at the uncharted seas some feared "Here monsters be." Others sought to chart new routes to truth and mystery over nature. In a remarkably short time philosophers established the four cardinal points of science: induction, deduction, mathematics, and experimentation. Mathematics was seldom used in biology before Mendel, but the inductive approach of Francis Bacon, the deductive approach of René Descartes, and the experimental approach used by Francesco Redi were all crucial in the development of evolutionary thought.

FRANCIS BACON (1561–1626)

Bacon was the son of the Chancellor and Lord Keeper of the Seal, and seems to have been steered into a public life for which he was philosophically unsuited. He entered Cambridge at age twelve, and even at that impressionable age he was able (he says) to see that Aristotle's logic was unproductive of useful knowledge. After three years he left Cambridge without a degree and was sent to Paris for practical education in politics. In 1579 his father died, and Bacon returned to England to find that as youngest son he had inherited too little to live on. As a practical necessity he studied law and then went about climbing the ladder of patronage and political influence. Historians are still undecided whether Bacon was merely an eager statesman or a cheap politician.

Bacon became a member of Parliament and then scored a success with Queen Elizabeth by drawing up charges of treason against his former friend and benefactor, the Earl of Essex. Bacon's influence with Parliament was later exploited by James I, first in the role of Solicitor (1607), then as Attorney General (1613), Lord Keeper of the Seal (1617), and Chancellor (1618). By 1621 he had been named Baron Verulam and Viscount St. Albans. All of this seems to have been an honor without profit. Bacon was never able to live within his means, and had even been briefly jailed as a debtor in 1598. In 1621 Bacon was accused in Parliament of supplementing his income by taking bribes to influence cases under his jurisdiction. (The accusers were probably less concerned with ethics than the fact that they had lost both their money and their cases.) Bacon confessed to the common practice of receiving "gifts," and was stripped of public office. In these days when our scruples have been honed to a fine edge by political scandal, we are apt to accept Bacon's confession at face value. It is clear, however, that the charges—true or false—were aimed primarily at the king. Similar charges could have been brought against most of Bacon's accusers. It is possible that Bacon saw the futility of defense and tried to protect the Crown by cutting the controversy short with a confession. After his conviction Bacon devoted the remaining years of his life to science. His death was brought on by exposure while stuffing a bird with snow to see if it would preserve the meat.

Bacon's public career confounds historians who believe that great philosophers are simply the products of their times. Alexander Pope called him "the wisest, brightest, meanest of mankind." It is incredible that in the midst of such political turmoil Bacon could have created works which are models of clear thinking and expression. Bacon's earliest well-known work, the elegant *Essays* (1597), included "Colours of Good and Evil," which launched his lifelong project to build a new foundation for science to replace the rubble of Aristotelianism. *Advancement of Learning* (1605) was largely a critical review of philosophers of the past. *New Atlantis,* written between 1614 and 1617, described the utopia which Bacon hoped would result once the application of his method of science had allowed "mankind to regain their rights over nature assigned to them by the gift of God." In *Novum Organum* (1620) Bacon revealed the new method, based on experimentation and induction. Bacon also wrote numerous other published and unpublished works. (As if this were not enough, many people still believe Bacon wrote some of Shakespeare's plays.)

Opinions of Bacon's work have varied over the centuries. King James compared the *Novum Organum* to the peace of God, which passes all understanding. William Harvey, who was Bacon's physician, quipped that Bacon "writes philosophy like a lord chancellor."[6] Later generations had a higher opinion. Until quite recently induction was regarded by most English-speaking biologists as *the* scientific method. Bacon's influence is still felt in the popular stereotype of the scientist objectively collecting facts from which he induces true theories.

The first selection from *Novum Organum* is part of the description of Bacon's inductive method. This method begins with the compiling of three tables: the first is a table of similar manifestations of the phenomenon being studied; the second consists of examples similar to those in the first table which do not manifest the phenomenon; the third lists examples of cases in which the phenomenon varies in degree. From these tables Bacon hoped to be able to correlate the phenomenon being studied with others and thereby to deduce the essential properties of the phenomenon. Bacon illustrates his method by a study of heat. In the end he concludes that heat is a form of constrained motion—which would have been a remarkable conclusion if he had meant molecular motion. The tedium of Bacon's method may explain why he never produced a valuable scientific theory.[7]

RENÉ DESCARTES (1596–1650)

Descartes, born into the French lesser nobility, inherited enough to relieve him of concerns about a livelihood. Undisturbed by conflicts like those which surrounded Bacon, his life reveals a single-minded determination to find a sure method of reasoning. This determination grew out of his early schooling from age ten to nineteen under the Jesuits, who were then engaged in the futile effort to salvage Scholasticism by trying to fit the new discoveries into an Aristotelian scheme. As Descartes tells us in *Discourse on Method* (Part I), his education impressed him chiefly in the fact that after two thousand years of philosophy there was still no agreed-upon method of thought. Like Plato, however, he was "delighted with Mathematics because of the certainty of its demonstrations and the evidence of its reasoning." After taking a degree in law in 1616, Descartes resolved to "seek no other science than that which could be found in myself, or at least in the great book of the world." For the next twelve years he was a wandering gentleman-soldier, a profession which provided both the time for introspection and an exposure to the world. While fighting the Spanish in Holland he met another man whose interest in mathematical physics stimulated his first great achievement, the Cartesian coordinate system. This mathematical tool permits the application of algebra to solve geometrical problems. In 1619, while in an overheated room in Germany, Descartes had a revelation that mathematics was only one result of a general method of deduction which could be applied to all branches of learning to produce conclusions as certain as those of mathematics.

By 1628, when he settled in Holland, Descartes had worked out details of his method in the form of twenty-one *Rules for the Direction of Mind,* but these were not published until 1701. Like Bacon, Descartes hoped that the application of his method would "render ourselves the masters and possessors of nature." In 1633 Descartes started to publish a mechanistic theory of physiology and behavior in his *Treatise on the World,* but thought better of it after hearing of Galileo's trial. In 1637 Descartes summarized both the *Rules* and the *Treatise* in *Discourse on Method.*[8] In Part IV of the *Discourse* Descartes describes how he began his method by doubting everything, even his own existence. From the very act of doubting he made the famous deduction "I think, therefore I am," and from there deduced the existence of God and the world. This chain of deductions was further elaborated in *Meditations,* published in 1641. *Principles of Philosophy* followed in 1644 and *Passions of the Soul* in 1650. Shortly after the publication of *Meditations* Descartes's peace was shattered by a dispute at the University of Utrecht between a Cartesian professor and a theologian who hated Catholics, foreigners, and philosophers, and who therefore had a threefold hatred for Descartes. The major charge, that Descartes promoted atheism, must have grieved this devout Catholic. In 1642 the Senate of Utrecht forbade the teaching of Cartesian philosophy, "first because it is new, next because it turns our youth away from the old, wholesome philosophy, and finally because it teaches various false and absurd opinions." After further trouble erupted at the University of Leyden, Descartes went to Sweden in 1649 to become tutor to Queen Christina. Unfortunately the queen preferred to philosophize at the absurd hour of five o'clock in the morning, and Descartes contracted a fatal respiratory infection while returning from a lesson.[9]

Besides the catch phrase *cogito ergo sum* and the Cartesian coordinate system, Descartes's influence is still felt in the idea that the body is a kind of machine directed by an immaterial mind or soul. This "Cartesian dualism" is a radical departure from Aristotle, who conceived of several types of soul as the efficient causes of various phenomena of life. Instead of being distributed throughout the body, as Aristotle believed, the soul according to Descartes resides in the pineal gland in the brain, and controls muscle contractions by a valvelike direction of liquid pressure. Descartes argued that nonhumans lack souls and are thus nothing but machines. (Thomas Aquinas had argued on the contrary that "life is not an operation" [*Summa Theologica* I. Q. 18. Art. 2]. Descartes likened the animal body to "*automata* or moving machines" such as the powered puppets he could have seen in Paris.[10]

We are primarily concerned here with another major contribution of Descartes—deduction. Of course Descartes could not consider deduction itself an original creation, since the Scholastics, following Aristotle's *Prior*

Analytics, had used deduction in the form of the syllogism. The syllogism is a method by which two premises, the major and the minor, lead unerringly to a true deduction, so long as the premises are true. The classic example of the syllogism is:

> All men are mortal.
> Socrates is a man.
> Therefore, Socrates is mortal.

If the first two statements are true, then the third must also be. However, the major premise cannot be assumed true unless the conclusion of the syllogism is already known: one cannot assert that all men are mortal without already assuming that the man Socrates is mortal. Thus the syllogism is incapable of producing new knowledge. To avoid this difficulty Descartes directs us in the selection below to reject all universal generalizations which are suspect, and to begin our deductions from particular facts or from intuition (insight). Like Bacon, Descartes did not present a detailed method, but only a general approach, which he illustrated elsewhere in his treatises on *Dioptrics, Meteors,* and *Geometry.*

FRANCESCO REDI (1626–1698)

Redi was certainly not the first to use or advocate scientific experiments. Aristotle had made a rare bow to experience in his passage on the behavior of honeybees (*On the Generation of Animals* III.10), when he remarked that "credit must be given rather to observation than to theories, and to theories only if what they affirm agrees with the observed facts." Galen performed experiments to demonstrate the function of the urinary bladder (*On the Natural Faculties* I. 13), and even Augustine (*City of God* XXI. 4) proved experimentally that the flesh of peacocks does not spoil(!?). However, for most of the ancients and for the Schoolmen the real world was an inferior teacher compared to the ideal, abstract world of thought. Robert Grosseteste (1168?–1253), Albertus Magnus (1193–1280), and Roger Bacon (1214?–1292) cried alone in the medieval wilderness for the use of experience to generate premises and to test the conclusions of syllogisms. Modern experimentation began in 1600 with William Gilbert's (1540–1603) study of magnetism, and in 1605 with Francis Bacon's advocacy of experimentation. Harvey was the first to apply the method to an important biological question by demonstrating the circulation of blood in 1628. Thus Redi's experiments on spontaneous generation in 1668 came rather late. I have chosen to discuss them here because they relate to the origin of species, and because Redi was the first to use controls: preparations identical to the experimental preparations except for the one factor being tested.[11]

Francesco Redi was the son of a physician to the powerful Medici family in

Florence. In 1647 he graduated in philosophy and medicine from the University of Pisa, then entered the Collegio Medico of Florence, and later became personal physician to the Grand Dukes of Tuscany. As a true Renaissance man in the "Athens of Italy" he was not only a physician and scientist but also a linguist and poet. Redi was undoubtedly impressed by the experiments of Galileo. His own first experiments were on the properties of snake venom, which he described in a publication dated 1664. At that time venom was the subject of numerous superstitions, such as the belief that the anger of the viper imparted the toxic properties to the venom. Redi demonstrated that the effects of the poison had nothing to do with the disposition of the snake (Thorndike, 1958, vol. 8, pp. 20–30). In 1668 Redi published *Esperienze Intorno alla Generazione degli Insetti,* from which the selection in this chapter is taken. Redi amply demonstrated that insects thought to have arisen spontaneously from decaying meat were in fact the result of eggs deposited by adult flies. In 1684 he pioneered the field of parasitology by classifying intestinal worms and studying their life cycles. This study was apparently motivated by the common belief, going back to Aristotle, that intestinal worms are also spontaneously generated. Redi doubted that spontaneous generation ever occurred. (However, he could not rule it out in the case of plant galls: growths formed where insects deposit eggs in plant tissues.) In spite of the wide circulation of Redi's work scientists continued to believe in various forms of spontaneous generation until about a century ago (Farley, 1977). (The success of the canning industry is the final disproof of spontaneous generation of any form of life, with the possible exception of *Clostridium botulinum).* Perhaps the gullibility of scientists in continuing to believe in the myth of spontaneous generation was the motive behind Redi's mischievous creation of another myth, a totally fabricated history of the invention of spectacles which was believed for two centuries.[12]

In the last selection of this chapter Redi describes his observations of the eggs, larvae ("worms"), pupae (also called eggs), and flies produced in various kinds of decaying meat. (One wonders who was kind enough to open his home to Redi's experiments!) Redi observes that the flies are not generated in closed vessels, and describes the control experiments of covering the meat with a veil to allow air, but not flies, access to the meat. One phrase by Redi sums up an entire revolution in thought: "Belief would be vain without the confirmation of experiment."

Francis Bacon, from *Novum Organum,* Second Book, Aphorisms 11–15.

11. The investigation of forms proceeds thus: a nature being given, we must first present to the understanding all the known instances which agree in the same nature, although the subject matter be

considerably diversified. And this collection must be made as a mere history, and without any premature reflection, or too great degree of refinement. For instance: take the investigation of the form of heat.

TABLE I. *Instances agreeing in the Form of Heat*

(1) The rays of the sun, particularly in summer, and at noon.

(2) The same reflected and condensed, as between mountains, or along walls, and particularly in burning mirrors.

(3) Ignited meteors . . .

(28) Other instances.

We are wont to call this *a Table of existence and presence.*

12. We must next present to the understanding instances which do not admit of the given nature, for form (as we have observed) ought no less to be absent where the given nature is absent, than to be present where it is present. If, however, we were to examine every instance, our labor would be infinite.

Negatives, therefore, must be classed under the affirmatives, and the want of the given nature must be inquired into more particularly in objects which have a very close connection with those others in which it is present and manifest. And this we are wont to term a table of deviation or of absence in proximity.

TABLE II. *Proximate Instances wanting the Nature of Heat*

(1) The rays of the moon, stars, and comets, are not found to be warm to the touch, nay, the severest cold has been observed to take place at the full of the moon. Yet the larger fixed stars are supposed to increase and render more intense the heat of the sun, as he approaches them, when the sun is in the sign of the Lion for instance, and in the dog-days.

(2) The rays of the sun in what is called the middle region of the air give no heat, to account for which the commonly assigned reason is satisfactory; namely, that that region is neither sufficiently near to the body of the sun whence the rays emanate, nor to the earth whence they are reflected. And the fact is manifested by snow being perpetual on the tops of mountains, unless extremely lofty. . . .

(32) There are many effects common to cold and heat, however, different in their process; for snowballs appear to burn boys' hands after a little time, and cold no less than fire preserves bodies from putrefaction—besides both heat and cold contract bodies. But it is better to refer these instances and the like to the investigation of cold.

13. In the third place we must exhibit to the understanding the instances in which that nature, which is the object of our inquiries, is

present in a greater or less degree, either by comparing its increase and decrease in the same object, or its degree in different objects; for since the form of a thing is its very essence, and the thing only differs from its form as the apparent from the actual object, or the exterior from the interior, or that which is considered with relation to man from that which is considered with relation to the universe; it necessarily follows that no nature can be considered a real form which does not uniformly diminish and increase with the given nature. We are wont to call this our *Table of degrees or comparative instances.*

TABLE III. *Degrees or Comparative Instances of Heat*

We will first speak of those bodies which exhibit no degree of heat sensible to the touch, but appear rather to possess a potential heat, or disposition and preparation for it. We will then go on to others, which are actually warm to the touch, and observe the strength and degree of it.

(1) There is no known solid or tangible body which is by its own nature originally warm; for neither stone, metal, sulphur, fossils, wood, water, nor dead animal carcasses are found warm. The warm springs in baths appear to be heated accidentally, by flame, subterraneous fire (such as is thrown up by Etna and many other mountains), or by the contact of certain bodies, as heat is exhibited in the dissolution of iron and tin. The degree of heat, therefore, in inanimate objects is not sensible to our touch; but they differ in their degrees of cold, for wood and metal are not equally cold. This, however, belongs to the table of degrees of cold.

(2) But with regard to potential heat and predisposition to flame, we find many inanimate substances wonderfully adapted to it, as sulphur, naptha, and saltpetre. . . .

(41) Heat with regard to the human senses and touch is various and relative, so that lukewarm water appears hot if the hand be cold, and cold if the hand be hot.

14. Anyone may readily see how poor we are in history, since in the above tables, besides occasionally inserting traditions and report instead of approved history and authentic instances (always, however, adding some note if their credit or authority be doubtful), we are often forced to subjoin, "Let the experiment be tried. Let further inquiry be made."

15. We are wont to term the office and use of these three tables the presenting a review of instances to the understanding; and when this has been done, induction itself is to be brought into action. For on an

individual review of all the instances a nature is to be found, such as always to be present and absent with the given nature, to increase and decrease with it, and, as we have said, to form a more common limit of the nature. . . .

René Descartes, *Rules for the Direction of Mind,* Rule III. Translated by E. S. Haldane and G. R. T. Ross. From *The Philosophical Works of Descartes,* vol. 1, Cambridge University Press, New York, 1967. By permission.

RULE III

In the subjects we propose to investigate, our inquiries should be directed, not to what others have thought, nor to what we ourselves conjecture, but to what we can clearly and perspicuously behold and with certainty deduce; for knowledge is not won in any other way.

To study the writings of the ancients is right, because it is a great boon for us to be able to make use of the labours of so many men; and we should do so, both in order to discover what they have correctly made out in previous ages, and also that we may inform ourselves as to what in the various sciences is still left for investigation. But yet there is a great danger lest in a too absorbed study of these works we should become infected with their errors, guard against them as we may. For it is the way of writers, whenever they have allowed themselves rashly and credulously to take up a position in any controverted matter, to try with the subtlest arguments to compel us to go along with them. But when, on the contrary, they have happily come upon something certain and evident, in displaying it they never fail to surround it with ambiguities, fearing, it would seem, lest the simplicity of the explanation should make us respect their discovery less, or because they grudge us an open vision of the truth.

Further, supposing now that all were wholly open and candid, and never thrust upon us doubtful opinions as true, but expounded every matter in good faith, yet since scarce anything has been asserted by any one man the contrary of which has not been alleged by another, we should be eternally uncertain which of the two to believe. It would be of no use to total up the testimonies in favour of each, meaning to follow the opinion which was supported by the greater number of authors: for if it is a question of difficulty that is in dispute, it is more likely that the truth would have been discovered by few than by many. But even though all these men agreed among themselves, what they teach us would not suffice for us. For we shall not, e. g. all turn out to be mathematicians though we know by heart all the proofs that others have elaborated, unless we have an intellectual talent that fits us to resolve difficulties of any kind. Neither, though we have mastered all the arguments of Plato and Aristotle, if yet we have not the capacity for passing a solid judgment on these matters, shall we become Philosophers; we should have acquired the knowledge not of science, but of history.

I lay down the rule also, that we must wholly refrain from ever mixing up conjectures with our pronouncements on the truth of things. This warning is of no little importance. There is no stronger reason for our finding nothing in the current Philosophy which is so evident and certain as not to be capable of being controverted, than the fact that the learned, not content with the recognition of what is clear and certain, in the first instance hazard the assertion of obscure and ill-comprehended theories, at which they have arrived merely by probable conjecture. Then afterwards they gradually attach complete credence to them, and mingling them promiscuously with what is true and evident, they finish by being unable to deduce any conclusion which does not appear to depend upon some proposition of the doubtful sort, and hence is not uncertain.

But lest we in turn should slip into the same error, we shall here take note of all those mental operations by which we are able, wholly without fear of illusion, to arrive at the knowledge of things. Now I admit only two, viz, intuition and induction.[13]

By *intuition* I understand, not the fluctuating testimony of the senses, nor the misleading judgment that proceeds from the blundering construction of imagination, but the conception which an unclouded and attentive mind gives us so readily and distinctly that we are wholly freed from doubt about that which we understand. Or, what comes to the same thing, *intuition* is the undoubting conception of an unclouded and attentive mind, and springs from the light of reason alone; it is more certain than deduction itself, in that it is simpler, though deduction, as we have noted above, cannot by us be erroneously conducted. Thus each individual can mentally have intuition of the fact that he exists, and that he thinks; that the triangle is bounded by three lines only, the sphere by a single superficies, and so on. Facts of such a kind are far more numerous than many think, disdaining as they do to direct their attention upon such simple matters.

But in case anyone may be put out by this new use of the term *intuition* and of other terms which in the following pages I am similarly compelled to dissever from their current meaning, I here make the general announcement that I pay no attention to the way in which particular terms have of late been employed in the schools, because it would have been difficult to employ the same terminology while my theory was wholly different. All that I take note of is the meaning of the Latin of each word, when, in cases where an appropriate term is lacking, I wish to transfer to the vocabulary that expresses my own meaning those that I deem most suitable.

This evidence and certitude, however, which belongs to intuition, is required not only in the enunciation of propositions, but also in discursive reasoning of whatever sort. For example consider this sequence: 2 and 2 amount to the same as 3 and 1. Now we need to see intuitively not only that 2 and 2 make 4, and that likewise 3 and 1 make 4, but further that the third of the above statements is a necessary conclusion from these two.

Hence now we are in a position to raise the question as to why we have, besides intuition, given this supplementary method of knowing, viz. knowing by *deduction,* by which we undserstand all necessary inference from other facts that are known with certainty. This, however, we could not avoid, because many things are known with certainty, though not by themselves evident, but only deduced from true and known principles by the continuous and uninterrupted action of a mind that has a clear vision of each step in the process. It is in a similar way that we know that the last link in a long chain is connected with the first, even though we do not take in by means of one and the same act of vision all the intermediate links on which that connection depends, but only remember that we have taken them successively under review and that each single one is united to its neighbour, from the first even to the last. Hence we distinguish this mental intuition from deduction by the fact that into the conception of the latter there enters a certain movement or succession, into that of the former there does not. Further deduction does not require an immediately presented evidence such as intuition possesses; its certitude is rather conferred upon it in some way by memory. The upshot of the matter is that it is possible to say that those propositions indeed which are immediately deduced from first principles are known now by intuition, now by deduction, i. e. in a way that differs according to our point of view. But the first principles themselves are given by intuition alone, while, on the contrary, the remote conclusions are furnished only by deduction.

These two methods are the most certain routes to knowledge, and the mind should admit no others. All the rest should be rejected as suspect of error and dangerous. But this does not prevent us from believing matters that have been divinely revealed as being more certain than our surest knowledge, since belief in these things, as all faith in obscure matters, is an action not of our intelligence, but of our will. They should be heeded also since, if they have any basis in our understanding, they can and ought to be, more than all things else, discovered by one or other of the ways above mentioned, as we hope perhaps to show at greater length on some future opportunity.

Francesco Redi, from *Experiments on the Generation of Insects.* Translated by M. Bigelow. Open Court, Chicago, 1909, pp. 26–30, 32–34, 36–37.

Although content to be corrected by any one wiser than myself, if I should make erroneous statements, I shall express my belief that the Earth, after having brought forth the first plants and animals at the beginning by order of the Supreme and Omnipotent Creator, has never since produced any kinds of plants or animals, either perfect or imperfect; and everything which we know in past or present times that she has produced, came solely from the true seeds of the plants and animals themselves, which thus, through means of their own, pre-serve their species. And, although it be a matter of daily observation that infinite numbers of worms are produced in dead bodies and decayed plants, I feel, I say, inclined to believe that these worms are all generated by insemination and that the putrefied matter in which they are found has no other office than that of serving as a place, or suitable nest, where animals deposit their eggs at the breeding sea-son, and in which they also find nourishment; otherwise, I assert that nothing is ever generated therein. And, in order, Signor Carlo, to demonstrate to you the truth of what I say, I will describe to you some of those insects, which, being most common, are best known to us.

It being thus, as I have said, the dictum of ancients and moderns, and the popular belief, that the putrescence of a dead body, or the filth of any sort of decayed matter engenders worms; and being desirous of tracing the truth in the case, I made the following experiment:

At the beginning of June I ordered to be killed three snakes, the kind called eels of Aesculapius. As soon as they were dead, I placed them in an open box to decay. Not long afterwards I saw that they were covered with worms of a conical shape and apparently without legs. These worms were intent on devouring the meat, increasing mean-while in size, and from day to day I observed that they likewise increased in number; but, although of the same shape, they differed in size, having been born on different days. But all, little and big, after having consumed the meat, leaving only the bones intact, escaped from a small aperture in the closed box, and I was unable to discover their hiding place. Being curious, therefore, to know their fate, I again prepared three of the same snakes, which in three days were covered with small worms. These increased daily in number and size, remaining alike in form, though not in color. Of these, the largest were white outside, and the smallest ones, pink. When the meat was all consumed, the worms eagerly sought an exit, but I had closed every aperture. On the nineteenth day of the same month some of the worms ceased all movements, as if they were asleep, and appeared to shrink and gradually to assume a shape like an egg. On the twentieth day all the worms had assumed the egg shape, and had taken on a golden white color, turning to red, which in some darkened, becoming almost black. At this point the red, as well as the black ones, changed from soft to hard, resembling somewhat those chrysalides formed by caterpillars, silkworms, and similar insects. My curiosity being thus aroused, I noticed that there was some difference in shape between the red and the black eggs [pupae], though it was clear that all were formed alike of many rings joined together; nevertheless, these rings were more sharply outlined, and more apparent in the black than in the red, which last were almost smooth and without a slight depression at one end, like that in a lemon picked from its stalk, which further distinguished the black egglike balls. I placed these balls separately in glass vessels, well covered with paper, and at the end of eight days, every shell of the red balls was broken, and from each came forth a fly of gray color, torpid and dull, misshapen as if half finished, with closed wings; but after a few minutes they commenced to unfold and to expand in exact proportion to the tiny body, which also in the meantime had acquired symmetry in all its parts. Then the whole creature, as if made anew, having lost its gray color, took on a most brilliant and vivid green; and the whole body had expanded and grown so that it seemed incredible that it could ever have been contained in the small shell. Though the red eggs [pupae] brought forth green flies at the end of eight days, the black ones labored fourteen days to produce certain large black flies striped with white, having a hairy abdomen, of the kind that we see daily buzzing about butchers' stalls. These at birth were misshapen and inactive, with closed wings, like the green ones mentioned above. Not all the black eggs [pupae] hatched after fourteen days; on the contrary, a large part of them delayed until the twenty-first day, at which time there came out some curious flies, quite distinct from the other two broods in size and form, and never before described, to my knowledge, by any historian, for they are much smaller than the ordinary houseflies. They have two silvery wings, not longer than the body, which is entirely black. The lower abdomen is shiny, with an occasional hair, as shown by the microscope, and resembles in shape that of the winged ants. The two long horns, or antennae (a term used by writers of natural history) protrude from the head; the first four legs do not differ from those of the ordinary fly, but the two posterior ones are much larger and longer than would appear to be suitable for such a small body; and they are scaly, like the legs of the locusta marina; they are of the same color, but brighter, so red, in fact, that they would put cinnabar to shame; being all covered with white spots, they resemble fine enamel work. . . .

I continued similar experiments with the raw and cooked flesh of the ox, the deer, the buffalo, the lion, the tiger, the dog, the lamb, the kid, the rabbit; and sometimes with the flesh of ducks, geese, hens, swallows, etc., and finally I experimented with different kinds of fish, such as swordfish, tun, eel, sole, etc. In every case, one or other of the above-mentioned kinds of flies were hatched, and sometimes all were found in a single animal. Besides these, there were to be seen many broods of small black flies, some of which were so minute as to be scarcely visible, and almost always I saw that the decaying flesh and the fissures in the boxes where it lay were covered not alone with worms, but with the eggs from which, as I have said, the worms were hatched. These eggs made me think of those deposits dropped by flies on meats, that eventually become worms, a fact noted by the compilers of the dictionary of our Academy, and also well known to hunters and to butchers, who protect their meats in Summer from filth by covering them with white cloths. Hence great Homer, in the nineteenth book of the Iliad, has good reason to say that Achilles feared lest the flies would breed worms in the wounds of dead Patrocles, whilst he was preparing to take vengeance on Hector.

Having considered these things, I began to believe that all worms found in meat were derived directly from the droppings of flies, and not from the putrefaction of the meat, and I was still more confirmed in this belief by having observed that, before the meat grew wormy, flies had hovered over it, of the same kind as those that later bred in it. Belief would be vain without the confirmation of experiment, hence in the middle of July I put a snake, some fish, some eels of the Arno, and a slice of milk-fed veal in four large, wide-mouthed flasks; having well closed and sealed them, I then filled the same number of flasks in the same way, only leaving these open. It was not long before the meat and the fish, in these second vessels, became wormy and flies were seen entering and leaving at will; but in the closed flasks I did not see a worm, though many days had passed since the dead flesh had been put in them. Outside on the paper cover there was now and then a deposit, or a maggot that eagerly sought some crevice by which to enter and obtain nourishment. Meanwhile the different things placed in the flasks had become putrid and stinking; the fish, their bones excepted, had all been dissolved into a thick, turbid fluid, which on settling became clear, with a drop or so of liquid grease floating on the surface; but the snake kept its form intact, with the same color, as if it had been put in but yesterday; the eels on the contrary, produced little liquid, though they had become very much swollen, and losing all shape, looked like a viscous mass of glue; the veal, after many weeks, became hard and dry. . . .

It is necessary to tell you that although I thought I had proved that the flesh of dead animals could not engender worms unless the semina of live ones were deposited therein, still, to remove all doubt, as the trial had been made with closed vessels into which the air could not penetrate or circulate, I wished to attempt a new experiment by putting meat and fish in a large vase closed only with a fine Naples veil, that allowed the air to enter. For further protection against flies, I placed the vessel in a frame covered with the same net. I never saw any worms in the meat, though many were to be seen moving about on the net-covered frame. These, attracted by the odor of the meat, succeeded at last in penetrating the fine meshes and would have entered the vase had I not speedily removed them. It was interesting, in the meanwhile, to notice the number of flies buzzing about which, every now and then, would light on the outside net and deposit worms there. I noted that some left six or seven at a time there, and others dropped them in the air before reaching the net. . . .

THE USES AND LIMITATIONS OF SCIENTIC METHODS

Several years ago I was lecturing to senior biology students on scientific method when about halfway through the lecture one student, and then all of them, confessed that they hadn't the foggiest idea of what I meant by induction and deduction. I was as stunned as a teacher of Shakespeare would be to discover that his students had not quite got the hang of the English alphabet. Not only was the lecture wasted, but it seemed to me then that all my efforts as a teacher had been wasted. How could we have imagined we were teaching our students science when we had neglected to teach them to think like scientists?

Since that crisis I have learned to be as grateful for many things students don't learn from us as I am for the things they do learn. I am grateful that they have had to learn how to do science by doing science, rather than by studying how it was done in the past. I am even more grateful that they have escaped the danger of learning inadvertently that there is a method of creating scientific theories, when, in fact, there are only methods for testing them.[14]

As Einstein said, "If you want to know the essence of scientific method, don't listen to what a scientist may tell you. Watch what he does" (quoted in Beck, 1961, p. 45). Darwin is a good illustration of how a scientist can be confused about the origins of his own theories. In his autobiography Darwin says that he "distrusted greatly deductive reasoning" and developed his theory "on true Baconian principles, and without any theory collected facts on a wholesale scale." However, Darwin was criticized for deserting "the true method of induction" (Hull, 1973a, pp. 157, 160), and natural selection is now often given a deductive derivation. In fact, Darwin used neither induction nor deduction methodically. Scientists, including Darwin, actually create theories in the same chaotic, capricious, lucky, exhilarating way that everyone else gets good ideas. It is a barely conscious process which is hard to analyze. If we try to describe the process afterwards we are likely instead to defend or explain the theory.[15]

If scientific and nonscientific theories are created in the same way, what is the difference between science and nonscience, or nonsense? The difference has nothing to do with subject matter, since we see science expanding into areas once considered safe from its intrusion. Nor does the difference lie in the fact that science consists of proven truths, and nonscience of conjecture, for there is no way of proving a theory true. The "criterion of demarcation" between science and nonscience, proposed by Popper forty-five years ago and just now becoming widely accepted among scientists, is that scientific theories are capable of being falsified. To be scientific a theory must be stated clearly enough that it can be tested and potentially falsified by any qualified person. Theories are scientific to the degree that they invite falsification, and people are scientific to the degree that they open their own theories to falsification. This criterion serves as a useful signpost for steering scientists away from theories which are not worth the futile effort of trying to test, such as the claims by some advocates of ESP that telepathy works only if there are no skeptics around. It also relieves scientists of anxiety about proposing incorrect theories, since every theory is destined to be falsified eventually. The value of a theory is not in its truth, but in its usefulness in stimulating further research. No scientist should expect a Nobel Prize for a theory which is easily falsified and therefore useless, but neither should a scientist be ashamed of a theory which is eventually falsified by the research which it inspired. The shame belongs to those who state their theories so as to evade falsification.[16]

It is in the attempts to falsify theories—not in the creation of them—that reliable and objective methods for testing theories are most valuable. Fortunately induction, deduction, and experimentation serve better for this purpose than they do for the creation of theories. Only after one has a theory can the application of scientific method begin, by attempting to falsify it using induction, deduction, and experimentation. In scientific method, as with the famous recipe for rabbit stew, we must "First get a rabbit."

Before I proceed to comment on these tools I should admit something which may already be obvious; I am not a professional philosopher of science. It is true that I hold the degree of Doctor of Philosophy, but that in itself does not qualify me to treat ailing philosophies. This is not an apology but a warning that the following revelations on scientific method should not be assumed to reflect a current consensus of philosophers of science (if there were such a consensus). Since my objective is to understand the origins of theories of evolution I am concerned with what scientists have done, not with what some philosophers say they ought to have done.

Induction

It is difficult to define induction because various inductive methods have been proposed, and their advocates were not always consistent.[17] In general, inductive methods have in common the emphasis on experience as the source of knowledge, and the generalization of this knowledge to obtain or test theories. None of the advocates of inductive methods believed that simple enumeration of instances, such as "this crow is black, that crow is black, so is this one, etc." could serve as a source of reliable theories, as many biologists naïvely believed until recently. In biology texts only two decades old one finds simple induction set forth as the one sure method of science, but in practice Bacon's and all other methods of induction are so tedious and complicated that they have little value for scientists. They are as helpful as the advice to a young pianist before his recital debut: "Don't be nervous, kid. Just go out there and hit every goddamn key."

The popular ideal of induction as being the objective gathering of facts without any preconceived theory is refuted by Popper (1972, Ch. 7) in an amusing way. Popper simply asks his audiences to start observing! To expect the scientist to use the inductive method to create theories is to put him into a similar predicament. He naturally will try to narrow the scope of his attention to some subject, which will soon present him with a problem to be solved. Even this problem will usually be too large to be solved by further passive observation, so the scientist creates theories—somehow—to account for the phenomenon which presents the problem. Often induction enters into the formulation of a theory, but not in any methodical way that differs from its use by nonscientists. Induction does provide seemingly innate beliefs or axioms (Descartes's intuitions) which are the basis of theories, but such inductions are not unique to science. An example would be the belief that objects continue to exist even when no one is observing them. This "object concept," so fundamental to normal thought and behavior, has to be learned, starting at about six months of age.[18]

Induction is useful in testing theories in the same commonsense way it is used in creating them. For example, the Copernican theory was tested by the inductive "fact" that the Earth does not move, and the Darwinian theory was tested by the induction that species do not produce new species. As these two examples illustrate, induction is not a perfectly trustworthy means of testing theories. But isn't it possible that *some* method of induction could be reliable, as Bacon and other inductionists hoped? We can never know for certain, as David Hume (1711–1766) demonstrated. The only proof that induction works would be a compilation of examples in which it has worked, and the induction from those examples that it always works. In other words, induction would have to be summoned to testify in its own behalf. Like the sentence "This sentence is true," such a procedure could add nothing to our understanding.[19]

Hume notwithstanding, the brains of animals have evolved as if induction is reliable. Induction—the generalization of experience—is, after all, the basis for all learning. The sun has risen more than 10^{12} times so far, and always precisely at sunrise. Nature selects against those who lie awake at night wondering whether it will rise tomorrow.

Deduction[20]

Deduction, like induction, probably enters into the creation of theories, but not in the methodical way advocated by Descartes. Even rigorously applied deduction cannot produce theories any more reliable than the premises on which the deduction is based. So far, only one indisputable premise has been proposed: the Cartesian postulate "I think." (At least I think the postulate is true for me; I am less certain about you or anyone else.) However, two true premises are required to deduce a new idea that is anything more than a tautology, so deduction will remain incapable of providing any irrefutable theories until someone comes up with a second true premise. Not even Descartes's famous *"Cogito ergo sum"* is a certain deduction, because only one premise, "I think," is stated. There is a hidden premise which Descartes and virtually everyone else takes for granted: "All things that think, are." By leaving this premise unstated Descartes avoided having to prove it. He might have argued that it is known by unerring intuition, but then why not argue that "I am" is also known by intuition? One could also define the verb "to be" so as to include all things that think, but definitions are conventions, not truths. When all the premises are brought out of hiding, Descartes's deduction turns out to be *(sacrebleu!)* a syllogism:

> All things that think, are.
> I think.
> Therefore, I am.

Descartes would have to admit that the conclusion of this syllogism is no more certain than the major premise. Theories produced by other such deductions must be even less certain.

Deduction has always been more reputable among Descartes's countrymen, but until fairly recently English-speaking scientists equated it with "jumping to conclusions." Now most biologists accept deduction as a legitimate part of the testing of theories, in accordance with the hypothetico-deductive method. According to this method, scientists formulate a theory (hypothesis), deduce its consequences, then test the consequences by experiment. If the consequences are falsified, so is the theory. However, this seemingly simple procedure often generates lively controversies. Sometimes theorists deduce incorrect consequences and thus prematurely reject theories. More often theorists dispute the procedures or interpretations of experiments which seem to falsify their theories. Even here, then, the deductive method is no more reliable in the testing of theories than the judgment and objectivity of those testing the theory.

Experimentation

There is little to add about experimentation except to emphasize that it is used to test, rather than to create theories. This is not always clear in research reports, which often make it appear that the theory was discovered as a result of the experiments. It may seem, for example, that Redi discovered that spontaneous generation of insects did not occur in rotting meat only after he had done the experiments. But then we must ask how he knew what experiments to do if he did not already have the theory. Even if he had done experiments at random he would have produced only useless data without a theory. "The experimenter who does not know what he is looking for will never understand what he finds," as Claude Bernard said (quoted in Farley, 1977, p. 3).

The design of experiments narrows our view of nature and makes a mockery of the ideal of the scientist passively observing nature without bias. We can only do experiments involving observable events, so our view of nature is restricted by our sense organs, aided by technology. Secondly, we can only understand those aspects of nature with which we have direct experience; we can comprehend light either as a wave or as a particle, but not as something behaving like both simultaneously. Finally, our view of nature is further restricted because there are only a few ways—often only two ways—in which an experiment can turn out. With all these limitations it is as if we were in the bottom of a well trying to figure out what the world is like based on the things we see passing overhead.

We must conclude that induction, deduction, and experimentation are not capable of creating theories, and that they are not capable of testing them absolutely reliably. You may be wondering why scientists persist in using them. Well, what alternative did you have in mind?

TABLE 6. MAJOR EVENTS AND PEOPLE, 1700-1850

Year	Science / Philosophy	Arts	Politics & War
1700			
	Leibniz (1646-1716) DeMaillet (1656-1738)		
	Berkeley (1685-1753) Linnaeus (1707-1778)	Swift Pope J. S. Bach	Louis XV (r. 1715-1774)
	Montesquieu (1689-1755) Maupertuis (1698-1759) Buffon (1707-1788)	Handel Voltaire	
1750			
	Diderot (1713-1784) Rousseau (1712-1778) Franklin (1706-1790) Hume (1711-1766)		Seven Year's War (French & Indian War, 1755-1763)
	Watt (1736-1819) Lavoisier (1743-1794) Monboddo (1714-1799) Kant (1724-1804) Laplace (1749-1827) Herder (1744-1803) Goethe (1749-1832) Priestley (1733-1804) E. Darwin (1731-1802) Malthus (1766-1834)	Gainsborough Johnson Boswell Gibbon Mozart Schiller	Wesley (1703-1791) Declaration of Independence American Revolution Jefferson (1743-1826) Louis XVI (r. 1774-1792) Bill of Rights French Revolution
1800			
	Lamarck (1744-1829) Cuvier (1769-1832) Wells (1757-1817) Dalton (1766-1844) E. Geoffroy St. Hilaire (1772-1844)	Wordsworth Coleridge Byron Shelley Keats Beethoven	Holy Roman Empire ends (1806) Napoleon (r. 1804-1815) War of 1812 Louis XVIII (r. 1814-1824)

Year	Science / Philosophy	Arts	Politics & War
	Schopenhauer (1788-1860)	Schubert	
	Matthew (1790-1874)		
	Lyell (1797-1875)	Turner	
		Pushkin	
	Faraday (1791-1867)	Balzac	
	C. Darwin (1809-1882)		Queen Victoria (r. 1837-1901)
	Chambers (1802-1871)	Chopin	
			Marx (1818-1883)
1850			

5

The Genesis of Evolutionism: The French Phase

The traditional way of doing the history of evolution theory is by treating each contributor as a precursor of Darwin, judging the contribution by how closely it came to Darwinism, and giving highest honors to the earliest correct contribution. (That some of the honor rubs off on the historian who discovers the earliest precursor may explain why historians have been tempted to see Darwinism in the most unlikely places.) Approaching the history of evolutionism in this way could be compared to Empedocles' explaining the origin of man as the successive accumulation of organs: first we had an arm, and then a liver, and so on, and finally the brain was added to make the complete man. Historians using this approach have contributed much factual information, but they have generated the misconception that evolutionary and other scientific theories grow progressively from a single conception until someone arrives at the final and inevitable truth. By ignoring the historical context in which theories develop, they have also created the impression that theories arise by some sort of spontaneous generation which does not even require rotting meat.

Is not some explanation required for the rejection of an account of the origin of species which had satisfied Jews for at least twenty-seven centuries, and which had been defended by Christendom for half that time? Why did scientists suddenly begin to suspect that species had not always been the same, but had changed to meet the demands for existence? Why did this theory arise not just once, but several times in the single century from 1745 to 1845? Certainly one important factor contributing to the genesis of evolutionism was the maturation of scientific thinking, expressed as the Newtonian and Cartesian view of nature. This mechanistic view is one aspect of the belief that natural phenomena result consistently from causes which can be understood by man, which is a prerequisite for science. (The Greeks also had the belief in the rationalism of nature, but in the eighteenth century scientists adopted the analogies of the fledgling Industrial Revolution. Then as now, technology contributed to science not only tools but modes of thought.) We must also give credit to new discoveries during this period, especially in geology. The increased mining demanded by the Industrial Revolution uncovered fossils and other evidence which suggested that present species had an ancient and varied past. Yet it would be an oversimplification to say that the maturation of science and new discoveries produced the concept of evolution. Evolutionism arose at several times and places under widely differing circumstances, which I find convenient to divide into the French Phase and the British Phase.

Three early French evolutionists, Maupertuis, Diderot, and Lamarck, were products of the Enlightenment. This movement was characterized by the belief that nature was orderly, either obeying a rational god (as the deists thought) or simply obeying natural laws (as atheists believed). The Enlightenment was the philosophical counterpart of the moral outrage over the oppressive rule of Louis XV and the Catholic church. So long as Frenchmen believed that the king ruled by "divine right" granted by an irrational God, they had to accept these abuses. The Enlightened, however, suggested that since God had left the planets to obey natural laws, he certainly was not concerned with who happened to be king on a tiny portion of one of those planets. If there were a god, he cared no more for the alliance of king and Pope than for the conjunction of Mars and Jupiter. Natural law, according to the Enlightened, could govern not only the planet but also its people, if they were not corrupted by aristocracy and theology.[1]

In addition to the Enlightenment, the thinking of Gottfried Wilhelm Leibniz (1646–1716) was important in the development of evolutionism in France. Indeed, Leibniz himself had speculated in a little-known work, *Protogaea* (1691), that

> perhaps, at some time or somewhere in the universe, the species of animals are, or were, or will be, more subject to change than they are at present in ours; and several animals which possess something of the cat, like the lion, tiger, and lynx, could have been of the same race and could be now like new subdivisions of the ancient species of cats. So I always return to what I have said more than once, that our determinations of physical species are provisional and proportional to our knowledge. (Quoted in Glass, 1959a, p. 38)

Leibniz's influence on evolutionism was due largely to his concepts of the "monad" and the Great Chain of Being. The monad was essentially the atom of Democritus, Epicurus, and Lucretius, except that Leibniz granted it an intelligence to account for the apparently rational design found in nature. With this concept each organism could be regarded as a transitory combination of monads. We see in the monad a return to the Greek faith that nature, in spite of its apparent complexity, must have an underlying simplicity.

The Great Chain of Being was another simple idea which Leibniz borrowed from the Greeks. In this instance, however, there was experimental support for the concept. First, the exploration of new lands, especially in America, revealed an increasing variety of new species similar to, yet distinct from, species familiar to the Old World. It began to appear that for any two species one could find another intermediate to them. In a similar way the increasing number of new fossil species filled in the links of the Great Chain of Being. The missing link between plants and animals was thought to have been found in 1744, when Abraham Trembley published a study on the *Hydra*.[2] The discovery that these "polyps" can reproduce by budding also supported the concept of monads fulfilling their life-force. Finally, the anatomical research of Louis-Jean-Marie Daubenton showed that the internal structures of animals were homologous in different species. For example, the hoof of the horse was found to have bones similar to those of the human hand, as would have been expected if the two species were linked on the Great Chain of Being.

The major challenge to the Great Chain of Being was the improved taxonomic system of Carolus Linnaeus (1707–1778), first published in *Systema Natura* in 1735. Although Linnaeus himself doubted the fixity of species on occasion (Glass, 1959c), his binomial system emphasized the distinctiveness of species by giving them names. Eighteenth-century French scientists followed Georges-Leclerc, Comte de Buffon (1707–1788), who overcame this problem simply by dismissing the Linnaean system as artificial. This situation contradicts the common assumption that a rational system of taxonomy was essential to the development of evolutionism.[3]

Pierre-Louis Moreau de Maupertuis (1698–1759)

Maupertuis was one of the most respected scientists of the Enlightenment, but he was virtually forgotten after 1750 when his thin skin got pricked by Voltaire's sharp pen. We have A. O. Lovejoy and Bentley Glass to thank for rehabilitating his memory and pointing out his evolutionist ideas.[4] Maupertuis became a student of philosophy in Paris at age sixteen, but found the curriculum still stifled by Scholasticism under the Jesuits. In 1717 he turned to music and then to mathematics. For his work in mathematics and biology he was elected to the Academy of Sciences at age twenty-five. In 1728 he visited London, became convinced of the superiority of Newton's theory of gravity over that of Descartes, and returned to become the foremost evangelist of Newtonian mechanics in Europe. For a time he was Voltaire's protegé and instructor in the new science. In 1735 he was selected to conduct an expedition to measure the length of a degree of longitude in Lapland. This distance, when compared to the length of a degree in Peru, confirmed

Newton's prediction that the Earth was slightly flattened at the poles. On the return voyage Maupertuis suffered shipwreck, but managed to save himself and the Lapp maiden with whom he had fallen in love. Frederick the Great, following the recommendation of Voltaire, then invited Maupertuis to Berlin. He served Frederick in the War of Austrian Succession, and was captured briefly when his horse bolted into enemy lines—to the great enjoyment of Voltaire. Between 1745 and 1753 Maupertuis was head of the Berlin Academy of Sciences. There he had the misfortune of becoming embroiled in a childish dispute with another scientist, who accused him of stealing an idea from Leibniz. Maupertuis disproved the charge, but in doing so he incurred the animosity of Voltaire, ever the champion of losers. Voltaire's brilliant sarcasm directed at "the great flattener" in *Micromegas* (1752) and other works contributed to the decline in Maupertuis's health. He died in Switzerland while returning to France.

Most of Maupertuis's biological work was done in Berlin, where he turned his home into a menagerie of dogs, birds, and exotic animals for the study of heredity. He also pioneered in human genetics with a thorough study of a family in which extra fingers recurred. In *Vénus physique* (1745) he explained his genetic theories, together with his ideas of embryology and the origins of races and species. In contrast to the present situation, in which geneticists, embryologists, anthropologists, and evolutionists have trouble keeping up a conversation among themselves, Maupertuis saw these as inseparable subjects. All were the consequences of the monads of Leibniz. The most interesting innovation in Maupertuis's genetics—the only one which distinguishes it from the idea of Lucretius (*De Rerum Natura* IV, 11. 1209–1232)—is the notion that the "particles" pair up at conception, and the particle from one parent can be dominant over the homologous particle from the other parent. Maupertuis also revived as "an audacious guess" Hippocrates' theory of pangenesis (*On the Sacred Disease* and *On Airs, Waters, and Places* 14). This concept, which we shall have to return to later, holds that the hereditary particles come from all parts of the body.

In *Vénus physique* (see first selection in this chapter) Maupertuis emphasizes the stability of species, but suggests that occasional races begin as departures from the natural design, as the result of chance events affecting the hereditary particles. If the same events were repeated for several generations, or if the climate were favorable, the race could become fixed as a new species. Hiding behind the pseudonym of Dr. Baumann, he suggested the evolutionary origin of all species in *Système de la Nature* (1751). (Quoted in Glass, 1959b, p. 77. See also Lovejoy, 1904, p. 249 for a similar passage.) Maupertuis suggested that the theory be tested experimentally by surgically removing an organ for many generations. He did not realize that the theory was already falsified by the fact that Jewish males were born with normal prepuces.

In 1750 Maupertuis published the *Essai de Cosmologie,* in which he approaches the idea of natural selection without appreciating it as a mechanism in the continuing formation of new species.

> May we not say that, in the fortuitous combination of the productions of Nature, since only those creatures *could* survive in whose organizations a certain degree of adaptation was present, there is nothing extraordinary in the fact that such adaptation is actually found in all these species which now exist? Chance, one might say, turned out a vast number of individuals; a small proportion of these were organized in such a manner that the animals' organs could satisfy their needs. A much greater number showed neither adaptation nor order; these last have all perished. . . . Thus the species which we see today are but a small part of all those that a blind destiny has produced. (Quoted in Lovejoy, 1904, pp. 242–243)

Maupertuis thus grasped the destructive role of natural selection in eliminating the unfit, but he failed to see that new species could emerge from such a process in the same way that statues emerge as the sculptor chisels away the surrounding stone. Even in this glimpse of natural selection, Maupertuis went beyond most of his enlightened contemporaries, who could not imagine the extinction of a single link in a rationally designed Great Chain of Being. The opinion of Thomas Jefferson was typical: "Such is the economy of nature, that no instance can be produced, of her having permitted any one race of her animals to become extinct; of her having formed any link in her great work so weak as to be broken."[5]

DENIS DIDEROT (1713—1784)

Voltaire and history have been kinder to Diderot than to Maupertuis. From unpromising beginnings as the son of a provincial cutler, student for the priesthood in Paris, lawyer's apprentice, and starving hack writer, Diderot eventually became the chief editor of the *Encyclopédie*—the Bible of the Enlightenment. His rise to fame was by no means steady. One of his first works, *Pensées philosophiques* (*Philosophical Thoughts,* 1746), was condemned by Parlement and burned by the chief executioner because it championed individual reason over authority. *Pensées philosophiques* was published anonymously, else the very title would have branded Diderot as a *philosophe*—i.e., a dangerous radical. In 1748 Diderot brought out anonymously *Les bijoux indiscrets,* which polite English translators call *The Indiscrete Toys.* This was a satire on the sexual proclivities of Louis XV and Madame Pompadour, in which the hero possesses a ring capable of shutting the flattering mouths of women while compelling their private parts to speak only the truth. The church and police, finding no redeeming social value in the work, condemned it while ignoring the well-known deeds which it satirized. The last straw was *Lettre sur les Aveugles* (*Letter on the Blind*, 1749), which propounded a doctrine of moral relativism by demonstrating that, for example, to a blind man minor thievery is a more serious crime than indecent exposure. Diderot was denounced as the author of these three works, and spent three months in prison at Vincennes. (The Bastille, not surprisingly, was already full.)

Diderot, together with Jean le Rond D'Alembert (1717–1738), the famous mathematician, had already been selected to edit the *Encyclopedia, or Descriptive Dictionary of Sciences, Arts and Trades,* and for almost twenty years afterwards he labored on its thirty-five volumes. Behind the innocuous title lurked the manifesto of the Enlightenment—or at least that portion which got past the censors. The *Encyclopedia* turned out to be a preface to the French and the Industrial revolutions. During the period of the *Encyclopedia* Diderot also composed several novels, plays, essays, and commentaries on the arts. After the *Encyclopedia* failed to earn him the acclaim enjoyed by Voltaire and Rousseau, Diderot decided to write only for himself and posterity. Most of his later work was published long after his death. In 1765 the aging and needy Diderot sold his library to Catherine II of Russia, and he spent 1773 and 1774 in her court at St. Petersburg. Apparently he hoped to convert Catherine into the philosopher-monarch which the flickering Enlightenment had settled on as a necessary compromise between despotism and anarchy. After his return to Paris, Diderot continued to write until the end.[6]

Diderot glimpsed the role of natural selection in the origin of species in 1749, several years before he professed evolutionism. (For those who confuse natural selection with evolution this will take some getting used to.) The selectionist passage from *Letter on the Blind* is put into the mouth of Nicholas Saunderson (1682–1739), who had been a brilliant professor of mathematics in spite of his blindness. The words could as easily have come from Empedocles or Lucretius:

> Imagine, then, if you will, that the order which impresses you has always subsisted; but let me believe that it is not at all so; and that if we returned to the birth of things and time, and perceived matter stirring and chaos unravelling itself, we should encounter a multitude of shapeless beings for every well-organized being. If I have nothing to object to you regarding the present state of things, I can at least question you about their past condition. I can ask you, for example, who has told you, Leibniz, Clarke and Newton that in the first instant of the formation of animals, some were not without heads and others without feet? I can imagine that these had no stomach, and those had no intestines; that those in whom a stomach, a palate and teeth seemed to promise survival were doomed by some fault of the heart or lungs; that the monsters were successively annihilated; that all the faulty combinations of matter have disappeared, and that only those remain in which their mechanism does not involve any important conflict, and which can subsist by themselves and perpetuate themselves.[7]

Diderot's transformist ideas were first expressed anonymously in the *Pensées sur l'interpretation de la Nature* (1754).[8] This paean to experimentation was largely inspired by Francis Bacon. The first selection from Diderot, *Pensées* XII, can be read simply as an exposition on the Great Chain of Being, rather than as a theory of evolution, but I include it here because it reveals the influence not only of Leibniz, but of Buffon, Daubenton, Trembley, and Maupertuis (Dr. Baumann). The next selection, Question 2 from *Pensées* LVIII, is explicity transformist. In the closing sentences the atheist Diderot makes use of irony to avoid another jail term.

JEAN BAPTISTE PIERRE ANTOINE DE MONET DE LAMARCK (1744–1829)

Lamarck was the last of eleven children of a somewhat impoverished member of the lesser nobility. His father and brothers were professional soldiers, but Lamarck was offered to the church. At age eleven he went to Paris to study for the priesthood under the Jesuits, but when his father died in 1759 he lost no time in riding off to enlist in the Seven Years War. He immediately distinguished himself by refusing to join a general retreat after all the superior officers in his company were killed. (This was only the first of many instances when Lamarck would refuse to give up an indefensible position.) His military career was cut short at age seventeen when one of his friends made use of his head for the purpose of lifting him. Following surgery to his neck Lamarck worked briefly as a bank clerk in Paris, and then began to study medicine. That profession, too, was terminated prematurely when Lamarck caught the French mania for natural history. He devoted increasing amounts of time to botany, often in the company of Rousseau. In 1778 he published *Flore françoise (sic)*, a popular key to the identification of French flowers. Buffon, pleased by Lamarck's rejection of the Linnaean system, used his influence with Louis XVI to secure a number of prestigious but low-paying positions for Lamarck. In his spare time Lamarck acquired six children and a wife (in that order). Later he had two more children and two or three more wives.

In 1789 Lamarck obtained a position at the *Jardin du Roi*, just in time for the French Revolution. Lamarck suddenly found himself having to defend the King's Garden to the people who would later take the king's head. As an aristocrat, Chevalier de Lamarck seemed poorly cast in the role of defender of what had been an elitist toy. He succeeded, however, for the Garden was reorganized under the Museum d'Histoire Naturelle. (It is noteworthy that science was not cast aside during the revolution; if anything it was enlivened by the enthusiasm for remaking the world. See Guerlac, 1961.) Citizen Lamarck was named "professor of insects and worms" at the Museum. The title "worms"—the Linnaean grab-bag for soft, wet animals—indicates the low esteen for those animals and for Lamarck. He had little knowledge of invertebrates, but threw himself into the work with enthusiasm and intelligence. In fact he brought a fresh perspective to zoology with the term "invertebrate." Before Lamarck taxonomists had followed Aristotle in considering the presence or absence of blood, rather than of vertebrae, as the major difference between "higher" and "lower" animals. Another Lamarckian innovation is the term *"biologie,"* which acknowledged the return to the study of the principles of life, abandoned since the overthrow of Aristotle. As one of the first to use the word "biology," Lamarck was christening a new science.

Almost two centuries after Bacon and Descartes it was still debated whether science should be based upon bare observations or upon axioms. Lamarck was definitely on the Cartesian side of this question. Beginning in the 1790s Lamarck became increasingly tiresome because of his grand schemes to bring all of science under a comprehensive philosophy based on a few laws. Among Lamarck's droll opinions was his continued acceptance of the four classical elements and the rejection of the improved chemistry of Antoine Lavoisier (1743–1794). After one of his books was ignored in 1794, Lamarck imaged (or realized?) that he was being laughed at and conspired against. (Since Lavoisier was beheaded in that year of the Reign of Terror, it was perhaps a good time for scientists to be paranoid.) In spite of his suspicions Lamarck persisted with his speculations on meteorology, geology, chemistry, and physics, while engaged in his principle responsibility of sorting out the "insects and worms." All of these studies came together in 1800 with the realization that species have been transformed in the past as the result of gradual environmental changes. Lamarck's reluctance to believe that any species becomes extinct may have led him to evolution as a way by which species could survive in altered form in spite of environmental changes. (See Burkhardt, 1977, pp. 131–135.) Paradoxically, Lamarck saw evolution as a way of escaping total extinction of a species, while we see extinction as an inevitable part of evolution. Lamarck's evolutionism, described in *Philosophie zoologique* (1809), got no better reception than his other theories. When Lamarck presented the Emperor Napoleon with a copy of the book, he was reduced to tears by Napoleon's insulting reluctance to accept what he thought was a work on meteorology. Lamarck continued to publish dozens of articles until 1820, but the last eleven years of his life were spent in blindness and poverty. He was buried in a trench, his bones dug up five years later to make room for others.

Most people who know of Lamarck at all associate his name with the "inheritance of acquired character"—the so-called Lamarckian Principle. It is true that Lamarck's careless writing sometimes gives the impression that he believed that direct modifications of an organism could be inherited. This simpleminded view goes back at least to the biblical tale of Jacob's producing spotted kids by placing spotted twigs in front of the goats (Gen. 30 : 37–43).[9]

Lamarck, however, meant only the inheritance of the indirect effects of the environment, due to increased use or disuse of an organ. According to Lamarck, changes in conditions create new needs for an organism, and the degree of use of an organ to meet those needs leads to heritable changes in the organ. Lamarck claimed no originality for the idea, which was a commonplace at the time.

The selection by Lamarck is from *Philosphie zoologique,* which he wrote as a text for his students—the one audience which could not ignore him. In grand Lamarckian fashion he intended to encompass the entire field of zoology. (Part II is nothing less than a physical explanation of Life!) Part I is an overview of taxonomy, including the evolution of species. His taxonomic and evolutionary theories were tied up in the Great Chain of Being (or rather, several separate chains for the major phyla). He believed that the natural tendency for organisms to increase their complexity in advancing up the Chain of Being was at least as important in their transformation as the inheritance of acquired characteristics.[10] The supposed tendency of species to progress toward increased complexity would eventually result in there being no more simple organisms. Lamarck overcame this problem by suggesting the continuous spontaneous generation of microorganisms (Part II, Ch. 4). Lamarck was of course aware of the experiments of Redi and others, but he argued that one could not apply studies of insects to the very simple organisms. A more serious problem resulted from Lamarck's adoption of the "nervous fluid" as the mechanism by which heritable effects of use and disuse are impressed upon an organ. Lamarck argued weakly that plants have similar fluids, but it is hard to see how he could escape having to create a second theory to account for the evolution of plants. Moreover, it is hard to see how any new organ could arise at all if only the effects of use and disuse were inherited; how can an animal increase the use of an organ which it does not have?[11]

Lamarck's theory of evolution was more reasonable when the most accepted theory of genetics was pangenesis. Even Darwin was compelled to supplement natural selection with the inheritance of acquired characteristics. As we shall see in the last chapter, Lamarckism is still periodically revived as a serious rival to orthodox neo-Darwinism. Each generation must seemingly decide anew between the crazy ideas of a Lamarck or a Velikovsky and the crazy ideas of a Darwin or an Einstein.[12]

After Lamarck only a few Frenchmen, notably Lamarck's colleague Etienne Geoffroy St. Hilaire (1772–1844) and to a lesser degree his son Isidore Geoffroy St. Hilaire (1805–1861), were willing to advocate the transformation of species. Only the publication of the *Origin of Species* in 1859 succeeded in dragging French biology, kicking and screaming, into an appreciation of the concept which it had pioneered.[13] Even now French biologists are less than enchanted with natural selection. Since the death of a scientific idea can be as revealing as its birth, it may be worthwhile to consider the causes of the demise of French evolutionism after Lamarck. Lamarck himself certainly deserves some of the blame. Knowing that many people were already conditioned to ridicule his ideas, he should have known better than to write about a shorebird acquiring long legs by "[acting] in such a way that its body should not be immersed in the liquid," or of a giraffe getting a long neck by its effort to browse on tree leaves (pp, 119, 120 of Elliot's translation of *Zoological Philosophy*). If the effects of sticking one's neck out were inherited, then Lamarck's descendants would have rivalled even the giraffe.

Even if Lamarck had been more cautious, however, it is doubtful that his theory could have survived the social and scientific conditions of post-revolutionary France. These conditions were distilled in the brain of the eminent comparative anatomist Baron Léopold Chrétien Frédérick Dagobert Cuvier (1769–1832), one of the biggest names in biology. Cuvier belonged to a generation for whom the memory of royal oppression was less vivid than memories of the Terror. His was the generation of Napoleon I and the restoration of monarchy. Evolution belonged to the previous generation of atheism and regicide. One anecdote reveals what a formidable opponent evolutionism had in a fully awakened Cuvier. One of his students, dressed in a red costume with horns and hooves, burst in upon the sleeping Cuvier. "Wake up, thou man of catastrophes. I am the devil. I have come to devour you." Cuvier eyed the intruder sleepily and replied, "I doubt whether you can. You have horns and hooves. You only eat plants" (Millar, 1972, p. 14).

Cuvier's hostility to evolutionism was partly the result of his political conservatism. Although he was too good a paleontologist to believe in the literal Genesis, he did try to make science and Christianity agree as much as possible, for the good of social stability. Consequently, he rejected Lamarck's uniformitarianism and belief in an ancient Earth, in favor of the theory that geological changes were the result of catastrophic events such as a Noachian Deluge. In this way Cuvier accounted for the changes in fossil species, which Lamarck had attributed to evolution. Cuvier was also a conservative in science. He devoted his life to the Baconian measurement of bones and organs and was appalled by Lamarck's bold deductions. Cuvier may also have been reluctant to believe that the species he labored so hard over were merely transients upon the Earth.

Cuvier could also cite serious scientific objections to support his antievolutionism. First, he pointed to the absence of transitional forms in the fossil record. Sudden changes in fossil species from one stratum to another were thought to be inconsistent with evolutionism, but consistent with catastrophism. Secondly, the mummified animals brought from Egypt as part of the loot of the Napoleonic Wars were essentially identical to present species.

Cuvier dismissed Lamarck's argument that the mummies were from a region where a stable climate had not forced evolution, and that two or three thousand years were insignificant in any case (*Zoological Philosophy*, pp. 41–43). Finally, from his studies of comparative anatomy, Cuvier believed that no single organ changes alone, but that the appearance of one organ must be correlated with that of another. (Horns and hooves with a vegetarian digestive tract, for example.) Thus Cuvier could not understand how a single organ, like the giraffe's neck, could have evolved by itself. So extreme was Cuvier's antievolutionism that shortly before his own death he wrote a eulogy of Lamarck which was an obvious attack upon his ideas. He came not to praise Lamarck, but to bury him, together with evolutionism.[14]

From *The Earthly Venus,* Pierre-Louis Moreau de Maupertuis. Translated by S. B. Boas. Johnson Reprint Corp., New York, 1966.

"Attempt at an Explanation of the Preceding Phenomena"

In order to explain all the phenomena above: the accidental production of varieties, the succession of such varieties from one generation to the next, and finally the establishment or the destruction of these breeds, this, I believe, is what faces us. If what I am about to say is revolting to you, just consider it as an effort toward a satisfactory explanation. I do not expect it to be complete, for the phenomena are most complex. At least much shall be accomplished if I have been able to link these phenomena to others on which they are dependent.

We should take for granted facts that experience forces upon us:

(1) That seminal fluid from members of each species of animal contains a multitude of parts suitable to the formation of animals of the same species;

(2) That in the seminal fluid of each individual the parts suitable for the formation of features similar to those of that individual are normally in greater number and have a stronger affinity for one another. There are also many others which may form different features;

(3) As to the matter of the seminal fluid of each animal from which parts resembling it are to be formed, it would be an audacious guess, but might not be unlikely, to suggest that each part furnishes its germs. Experiments might throw light on this point. If it were tried for a long time to mutilate some animals of the same breed, generation after generation, perhaps we might find the amputated parts diminishing little by little. Finally, one might see them disappear.

The guesses above seem necessary and, once we admit them, it may seem possible to explain the many phenomena we have explored.

Parts similar to those of the father and mother, being the most numerous as well as having the greatest affinity, will be the ones to unite most easily and then will form animals like the ones from which they came.

Chance or a shortage of family traits will at times cause other combinations, and then we may see a white child born of black parents, or even a black child from white parents, though this is a much rarer phenomenon than the former.

I am speaking here only of these strange occurrences when a child born of parents of the same race has traits which he does not inherit from them, for we know that when the races are mixed, the child inherits from both.

The unusual unions of parts which are not the parts similar to those of the parents are really freaks to the bold who seek an explanation of Nature's wonders. For the wise man, satisfied with the spectacle, they are beauties.

To begin with, these latter productions are accidental, for the parts whose origin is ancestral are the more abundant in the seeds. Therefore after a few generations, or even in the next generation, the original species will regain its strength and the child, instead of resembling its father or mother, will resemble some distant ancestor. In order to create species from races that become established, it is really necessary to have the same types unite for several generations. The parts suitable to recreate the original trait, since they are less numerous in each generation, are either lost or remain in so small a quantity that a new chance event would be needed to reproduce the original species. However, though I imagine the basic stock of all these varieties is to be found in the seminal fluids themselves, I do not exclude the possible influence of climate and food. It would seem that the heat of the Torrid Zone is more favorable to the particles that compose black skin than to those that make up white skin. And I simply do not know how far this kind of influence of climate and food may go after many centuries.

It would indeed be something to occupy the attention of Philosophers if they would try to discover whether certain unnatural characters induced in animals for many generations were transmitted to their descendants. Whether tails or ears cut off from generation to generation did diminish in size or even finally disappear would be of importance.

One thing is certain, and that is that all variations which may characterize new breeds of animals and plants tend to degenerate. They are the sports of Nature, only preserved through art or discipline, for her original creations always tend to return.

Denis Diderot, *Pensées sur l'interpretation de la Nature.* Translated by C. Leon Harris and Anita Morreale from *Chef d'oeuvres,* Paris: La Renaissance du Livre, pp. 7–8, 138–139.

XII

It seems that nature takes pleasure in varying the same mechanism of one thing in an infinity of different ways. She abandons a style of production only after she has mutiplied the individuals in all possible facets. When one considers the animal kingdom, and notices that among the quadrupeds there is none which does not have functions and parts, especially internal, entirely similar to those of another quadruped, doesn't one willingly believe that there was only one first animal, the prototype of all animals, in whom nature has only lengthened, shortened, transformed, multiplied or obliterated certain organs? Imagine the fingers of the hand joined, and the material of the nails so abundant that, becoming extended and expanded, it envelops and covers the whole; instead of the hand of a man, you have the hoof of a horse. When one sees the successive metamorphoses of the developing prototype [*l'enveloppe du prototype*], whatever it has been, approaching one kingdom from another kingdom by imperceptible degrees, and populating the confines of the two kingdoms (if it is permitted to use the term confines where there is no real division), and populating, I say, the confines of the two kingdoms with uncertain, ambiguous beings, largely devoid of form, of qualities, and of functions in one, and invested with forms, qualities, functions in the other, who would not feel inclined to believe that there was ever one first being, the prototype of all beings? But whether this conjecture is admitted with Dr. Baumann [Maupertuis] as true, or rejected with M. de Buffon as false, one cannot deny that it is necessary to embrace it as a hypothesis essential to the progress of experimental physics, to that of rational philosophy, to the discovery and the explanation of phenomena which depend on organization. For it is evident that nature could not conserve so much resemblance in the parts, and effect so much variety in the forms, without having often made perceptible in one organism that which she took from another. This is a woman who loves to masquerade, and whose different disguises she lets fall piece by piece, giving to those who pursue her assiduously some hope of knowing someday her entire person.

LVIII. Question 2.

Just as in the animal and vegetable kingdoms an individual commences, so to speak, grows, survives, declines and dies, could it not be the same with entire species? If faith did not teach us that animals sprang from the hands of the Creator as we see them; and if it were permitted to have the least uncertainty about their beginning and their end, could not the philosopher abandoned to his conjectures suspect that animals have had throughout eternity these particular elements, scattered and intermingled among the mass of matter; that it happened that these elements united, because it was possible for them to; that the embryo passed through an infinity of organizations and developments; that it had in succession movement, sensation, ideas, thoughts, reflections, conscience, sentiments, passions, signals, gestures, sounds, speech, language, laws, science and arts; that millions of years passed between each of these developments; that perhaps there are other developments to go through, and other growths to come, which are unknown to us; that it has had or will have a stationary state; that it withdraws or will withdraw from this state by an eternal decay, during which its faculties leave it as they made their entry; that it will disappear forever from nature, or rather, that it will continue to exist, but under a form and with faculties altogether different from those by which it was distinguished in this instant of duration? Religion spares us many digressions and much work. If it had not enlightened us on the origins of the world and on the universal system of beings, how many different hypotheses would we not be tempted to accept as the secret of nature? These hypotheses being all equally false, they would all have appeared to us equally probable. The question, *why does something exist,* is the most embarrassing one which philosophy can pose; and only revelation can respond.

Jean Baptiste Pierre Antoine de Monet de Lamarck, from *Philosophie zoologique (Zoological Philosophy),* Part I, Chapter 7. Translated by Hugh Elliot. Macmillan, New York, 1914.

I shall show in Part II., that when the will guides an animal to any action, the organs which have to carry out that action are immediately stimulated to it by the influx of subtle fluids (the nervous fluid), which become the determining factor of the movements required. This fact is verified by many observations, and cannot now be called in question.

Hence it follows that numerous repetitions of these organised activities strengthen, stretch, develop and even create the organs necessary to them. We have only to watch attentively what is happening all around us, to be convinced that this is the true cause of organic development and changes.

Now every change that is wrought in an organ through a habit of frequently using it, is subsequently preserved by reproduction, if it is common to the individuals who unite together in fertilisation for the propagation of their species. Such a change is thus handed on to all succeeding individuals in the same environment, without their having to acquire it in the same way that it was actually created.

Furthermore, in reproductive unions, the crossing of individuals who have different qualities or structures is necessarily opposed to the permanent propagation of these qualities and structures. Hence it is that in man, who is exposed to so great a diversity of environment, the accidental qualities or defects which he acquires are not preserved and propagated by reproduction. If, when certain peculiarities of shape or certain defects have been acquired, two individuals who are both affected were always to unite together, they would hand on the same peculiarities; and if successive generations were limited to such unions, a special and distinct race would then be formed. But perpetual crossings between individuals, who have not the same peculiarities of shape, cause the disappearance of all peculiarities acquired by special action of the environment. Hence, we may be sure that if men were not kept apart by the distances of their habitations, the crossing in reproduction would soon bring about the disappearance of the general characteristics distinguishing different nations.

If I intended here to pass in review all the classes, orders, genera and species of existing animals, I should be able to show that the conformation and structure of individuals, their organs, faculties, etc., etc., are everywhere a pure result of the environment to which each species is exposed by its nature, and by the habits that the individuals composing it have been compelled to acquire; I should be able to show that they are not the result of a shape which existed from the beginning, and has driven animals into the habits they are known to possess.

It is known that the animal called the *ai* or sloth *(Bradypus tridactylus)* is permanently in a state of such extreme weakness that it only executes very slow and limited movements, and walks on the ground with difficulty. So slow are its movements that it is alleged that it can only take fifty steps in a day. It is known, moreover, that the organisation of this animal is entirely in harmony with its state of feebleness and incapacity for walking; and that if it wished to make other movements than those which it actually does make it could not do so.

Hence on the supposition that this animal had received its organisation from nature, it has been asserted that this organisation forced it into the habits and miserable state in which it exists.

This is very far from being my opinion; for I am convinced that the habits which the ai was originally forced to contract must necessarily have brought its organisation to its present condition.

If continual dangers in former times have led the individuals of this species to take refuge in trees, to live there habitually and feed on their leaves, it is clear that they must have given up a great number of movements which animals living on the ground are in a position to perform. All the needs of the ai will then be reduced to clinging to branches and crawling and dragging themselves among them, in order to reach the leaves, and then to remaining on the tree in a state of inactivity in order to avoid falling off. This kind of inactivity, moreover, must have been continually induced by the heat of the climate; for among warm-blooded animals, heat is more conducive to rest than to movement.

Now the individuals of the race of the ai have long maintained this habit of remaining in the trees, and of performing only those slow and little varied movements which suffice for their needs. Hence their organisation will gradually have come into accordance with their new habits; and from this it must follow:

1. That the arms of these animals, which are making continued efforts to grasp the branches of trees, will be lengthened;

2. That the claws of their digits will have acquired a great length and a hooked shape, through the continued efforts of the animal to hold on;

3. That their digits, which are never used in making independent movements, will have entirely lost their mobility, become united and have preserved only the faculty of flexion or extension all together;

4. That their thighs, which are continually clasping either the trunk or large branches of trees, will have contracted a habit of always being separated, so as to lead to an enlargement of the pelvis and a backward direction of the cotyloid cavities;

5. Lastly, that a great many of their bones will be welded together, and that parts of their skeleton will consequently have assumed an arrangement and form adapted to the habits of these animals, and different from those which they would require for other habits.

This is a fact that can never be disputed; since nature shows us in innumerable other instances the power of environment over habit and that of habit over the shape, arrangement and proportions of the parts of animals.

Since there is no necessity to cite any further examples, we may now turn to the main point elaborated in this discussion.

It is a fact that all animals have special habits corresponding to their genus and species, and always possess an organisation that is completely in harmony with those habits.

It seems from the study of this fact that we may adopt one or other of the two following conclusions, and that neither of them can be verified.

Conclusion adopted hitherto: Nature (or her Author) in creating animals, foresaw all the possible kinds of environment in which they would have to live, and endowed each species with a fixed organisation and with a definite and invariable shape, which compel each species to live in the places and climates where we actually find them, and there to maintain the habits which we know in them.

My individual conclusion: Nature has produced all the species of animals in succession, beginning with the most imperfect or simplest, and ending her work with the most perfect, so as to create a gradually increasing complexity in their organisation; these animals have spread at large throughout all the habitable regions of the globe, and every species has derived from its environment the habits that we find in it and the structural modifications which observation shows us.

The former of these two conclusions is that which has been drawn hitherto, at least by nearly everyone: it attributes to every animal a fixed organisation and structure which never have varied and never do vary; it assumes, moreover, that none of the localities inhabited by animals ever vary; for if they were to vary, the same animals could no longer survive, and the possibility of finding other localities and transporting themselves thither would not be open to them.

The second conclusion is my own: it assumes that by the influence of environment on habit, and thereafter by that of habit on the state of the parts and even on organisation, the structure and organisation of any animal may undergo modifications, possibly very great, and capable of accounting for the actual condition in which all animals are found.

In order to show that this second conclusion is baseless, it must first be proved that no point on the surface of the earth ever undergoes variation as to its nature, exposure, high or low situation, climate, etc., etc.; it must then be proved that no part of animals undergoes even after long periods of time any modifications due to a change of environment or to the necessity which forces them into a different kind of life and activity from what has been customary to them.

Now if a single case is sufficient to prove that an animal which has long been in domestication differs from the wild species whence it sprang, and if in any such domesicated species, great differences of conformation are found between the individuals exposed to such a habit and those which are forced into different habits, it will then be certain that the first conclusion is not consistent with the laws of nature, while the second, on the contrary, is entirely in accordance with them.

Everything then combines to prove my statement, namely: that it is not the shape either of the body or its parts which gives rise to the habits of animals and their mode of life; but that it is, on the contrary, the habits, mode of life and all the other influences of the environment which have in course of time built up the shape of the body and of the parts of animals. With new shapes, new faculties have been acquired, and little by little nature has succeeded in fashioning animals such as we actually see them.

Can there be any more important conclusion in the range of natural history, or any to which more attention should be paid than that which I have just set forth?

THE ILLUSION OF METHOD IN SCIENTIC CREATIVITY

Every important theory is fundamentally simple. For that reason brilliant theories often surprise us most by taking so long and requiring so much genius to be created. No longer faced with the confusion of unresolved phenomena which existed before the theory, we fail to appreciate the creativity which brought forth the theory out of the confusion. However, once we have seen the chaotic state of knowledge about fossils, anatomy, and taxonomy before evolutionism, our question changes from "Why did no one think of evolutionism before?" to "How did anyone ever think of evolutionism?"

My favorite daydreams involve the summoning up of the dearly departed to ask them the latter question. When I asked Maupertuis how he got the idea of evolution he told me it came from the Great Chain of Being and his genetic studies. I protested that he was not the only one who accepted the Great Chain of Being, and that, with all due respect to his pioneering efforts in genetics, they were not adequate to demonstrate evolution. Maupertuis simply shrugged. I next summoned up Diderot, who sarcastically answered my question with his own: "If I had been concentrating on how I was getting the idea of evolutionism, I couldn't have gotten it, could I?" Lamarck (who had somehow collected his bones for the occasion) delivered a long lecture describing his brilliant and indisputable deductions. When I objected that he was presenting a justification rather than a chronicle of creation, he accused me of being involved in a plot with Cuvier.

I should not have been surprised at the disappointing answers to my question. Each of us knows how good ideas simply drop in on the mind unexpectedly and unexplainably. Most students of creativity admit that it is an act which is usually kept secret even from oneself. Fortunately they have been able to tell us a great deal about creativity, even if they cannot tell us what it is. The problem is that a theory can only be created once by each person, and it is too fleeting a phenomenon to permit study. Biologists are frequently confronted by this situation in which a phenomenon cannot be studied directly. Creativity, the functioning of an organ, and life itself are likely to be destroyed by the process of studying them. In such cases we resort to a model system: a simpler animal, a controlled laboratory situation, or a mathematical equation manifesting the phenomenon. Somehow I have gotten the idea that visual illusions are such a model of the creative process.[15] Like the creation of theories, visual illusions can be considered as attempts by the brain to interpret phenomena. Consider, for example, the famous Necker cube illusion. Most readers will have no difficulty perceiving this figure as a cube, even though we all know that a three-dimensional object cannot be drawn on a two-dimensional surface. Few of us can see the figure as a two-dimensional drawing even if we try. The brain insists on theorizing that the figure is a cube. We can actually "watch" our brains trying out alternative theories as the "cube" is spontaneously reversed. First the brain theorizes that it is a cube below and to the right of the observer, then that it is above and to the left. By concentrating one can hold the "cube" in one position, just as one can concentrate on creating a theory instead of just letting it happen. With this and other illusions we are permitted to observe at leisure private processes like those by which the brain may create scientific theories.

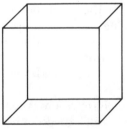

Figure 3. Necker Cube

Just as people of other cultures have trouble comprehending Western scientific theories, they may also have trouble seeing this and other illusions. We have experienced cubes—even lived in them—all our lives. At an early age we had the opportunity to learn that a retinal image like that of the Necker "cube" should be interpreted in three dimensions. Without that experience the Necker "cube" would be just a meaningless flat diagram. The Zulus are seldom exposed to cubes, corners, or straight lines, and they are not subject to illusions such as the Necker cube.[16] In cultures which do not represent objects in two dimensions a photograph of an elephant (or other familiar object) is not interpreted as a picture of an elephant. Only after the trunk, the legs, the tail, and so on are pointed out is the elephant perceived with a sudden insight. What a genius the prehistoric cave artist must have seemed to his audience as he explained his drawings and made animals suddenly appear right before their eyes!

As I mentioned in the last chapter, induction enters into the subconscious creation of at least some theories. There is a model of this in the well-known demonstration of the blind spot. If you shut your left eye and focus with the right on the bold X in the following line, and then move the book back and forth **X** (approximately twenty centimeters away), a distance can be found **O** at which the bold O can no longer be seen. The disappearance of the bold O is no illusion; it is focused on a portion of the retina where there are no receptors—where the optic nerve exits. There is the illusion, however, that nothing is missing. One might expect to "see" a black hole in the page or in any scene viewed with one eye, but we have the illusion that the visual scene is complete. Indeed, if it were not for this demonstration most people would not be aware of the blind spot, even though we look at things with one eye almost daily. What is happening in effect is that by induction the brain makes a guess about what is hidden in the blind spot. An even more remarkable feat of induction occurs when a uniformly colored pencil is placed on the page and its end is slowed advanced toward the bold O. First the tip of the pencil vanishes. Then as it moves past the O it reappears on the other side of the blind spot. At that moment the pencil suddenly appears complete! No portion is missing, even though we know the brain cannot possibly have any information about the portion in the blind spot. One can easily fool the poor brain into thinking that two identical pencils are one by laying them on the page almost end-to-end in a straight line, with the ends separated by the O. The brain believes the most reasonable theory, that instead of two short pencils there is one long one. Whoever said seeing is believing had it backwards.

There is another illusion which represents the unconscious role of deduction in the creation of theories. I call it the Rocking Chair Illusion; there may be another name, but I have never seen this illusion described elsewhere. The illusion is best seen from a rocking chair facing a window about two meters away. The view beyond the window must be at least fifty meters away; nearer objects spoil the illusion. As one rocks back and forth there is the illusion that the distant view grows and shrinks while the window frame remains the same size. One might have expected just the opposite, because the size of the window's image on the retina changes much more than that of the distant scene. I believe the explanation for this illusion is that we have learned early that nearby objects remain the same size even though their retinal images change in size. Perhaps we learned this as babies by feeling no increase in the size of toys as we brought them toward our mouths. In any case it is a useful perceptual rule; imagine the disorientation if walls seemed to grow and shrink as we walked around in a room! This size constancy is more important, and we have had more opportunitites to learn it, for nearby objects than for distant ones. This explains why the window does not seem to change size. But the brain receives the indisputable information that the retinal images of the window and the distant scene do not retain the same relative sizes. How is the brain to make sense of this? Somewhere in the visual apparatus a deduction is being made. If it were verbal and we could tap into it, it might go something like this: The retinal images of the distant scene and of the window change sizes relative to each other. Windows stay the same size. Therefore, the distant scene is shrinking and growing.

We must resist the temptation to imagine a little man in the brain creating these hypotheses and whispering them to our conscious selves. The explanatory value of such little men is limited, for we must then imagine a second little man in his brain, and a third in his, and so on. What is actually taking place is more like the electrical events taking place within a computer. (At least that is what neurophysiologists now believe. Perhaps the next technological revolution will render that analogy as obsolete as Descartes's fluid-mechanical model of the brain.) Visual illusions, though interesting and perhaps useful as models of creativity, are not as emotionally satisfying as the real thing. No scientist who has lost sleep because of the thrill of creating his own theory will underestimate the power of inspiration. We must go to another model to study this emotional component of creativity. One such model of the creative scientist happens to be a chimpanzee named Sultan, who one day discovered that he could connect two sticks and rake a banana into his cage. He got so excited over his creativity that he forgot to eat the banana.[17]

6

The Genesis of Evolutionism: The British Phase

Erasmus Darwin (1731—1802)

Like many rebellious young men in 1811, Percy Bysshe Shelley amused himself "with reading Darwin." Not Charles Darwin, who was then only two years old, but his equally controversial grandfather, the poet-evolutionist Erasmus Darwin.[1]

Erasmus Darwin spent most of his life in the English Midlands, the haunts of Isaac Newton's and Robin Hood's spirits. At age nineteen Darwin entered Cambridge, and four years later went to the University of Edinburgh, the preeminent choice for a medical education. At age twenty-five he began to practice medicine, soon settling for twenty-five years at Lichfield, just north of Birmingham. His first wife and three of their five children died in Lichfield; one of the survivors, Robert, became the father of Charles Darwin. As a widower Dr. Darwin fathered and raised two daughters, then married a woman who insisted that he move to Derby, where they raised a second litter of seven children.

Dr. Darwin was apparently gross, clumsy, and obese, but so witty that he was often mentioned in the same breath with another resident of Lichfield, Samuel Johnson. (Somehow the two managed to avoid each other on most occasions.) Once when asked whether his severe stammering was a handicap, Darwin replied "N-n-no, sir, it g-g-gives me t-t-time for reflection, and s-s-saves m-m-me from asking impertinent q-q-questions." Another of Darwin's famous sayings was that "a fool is a man who never tried an experiment." In his medical practice Darwin studiously avoided being thought a fool, often by trying the curative powers of large doses of electricity on his unfortunate patients. However, his experiments must have been less lethal than the standard remedies, for his reputation was so great that King George III invited Darwin to become his physician. Darwin declined the offer and otherwise neglected opportunities to become wealthy. This was largely because of his refusal to turn away any patient, regardless of his ability to pay. He apparently forgot that even Robin Hood stole from the rich.

In those days doctors concocted their own medicines from plants, so they were virtually the only ones interested in botany. (This was before the passion for natural history had spread from France to the English gentry.) Darwin's botanical knowledge went far beyond his practical needs, as he demonstrated in his first long poem, *The Botanic Garden*. Part II, published in 1789 (two years before Part I!), made him one of the favorite poets of England, and was to earn the praise of Cowper, Coleridge, Wordsworth, Shelley, and Keats. It could not have hurt that the poem was an anthropomorphic description of the sex lives of plants. However, Darwin's objective was not to pander but to propagate his theory that plants have organs and feelings like those of humans. Some modern readers have seen evolutionism foreshadowed in this idea, but none of Darwin's contemporaries would have.

Erasmus Darwin is seldom mentioned in poetry texts and anthologies because his informative but contrived style was supplanted by the Romanticism of Wordsworth and Coleridge. Likewise, his enlightened political and religious views were shunned in the early nineteenth century by an England horrified by the very real threat that revolution would spread to its own shores. So thoroughly was Dr. Darwin expunged from English thought that when Charles Lyell in 1832 sought a name for the transformation of species he had to import the term "Lamarckism." Lyell was apparently unaware that Darwinism (à la Erasmus) had preceded Lamarckism by several years. We can see why Darwin was expunged from the English consciousness by considering the activities of the Lunar Society, which Darwin helped establish in the 1760s. Among the members of the Lunar Society were James Watt (1736–1819), of steam-engine fame, and the Reverend Dr. Joseph Priestley (1733–1804), discoverer of oxygen. Its frequent guests included William Herschel (1738–1822), the foremost astronomer of the time, and Josiah Wedgwood (1730–1795), the potter and other grandfather-to-be of Charles Darwin. The Lunatics, as they called themselves, met monthly to consider ideas from biblical miracles to steam-powered aircraft. Located as they were in the foundry of the Industrial Revolution, many of their less bizarre ideas were put to use. Darwin himself was responsible for dozens of inventions. Englishmen were quite willing to be enriched by such profitable ideas, but not with the political and religious ideas of the Lunar Society. Darwin and other Lunatics incurred the wrath of many by attempting to abolish the slave trade and by supporting the French and American Revolutions. Darwin was a deist or atheist, when he thought about religion at all, and Priestley was notorious for disputing the result of the Council of Nicea's vote on the Trinity.[2] Before 1790 such opinions might be excused as the usual quirks of the scientific mind. England had temporarily depleted its stock of intolerance during the Civil War and with the extraordinary trick of importing George I from Germany to prevent the accession of a Catholic. John Wesley had begun in the 1730s to arouse religious passions, but they did not immediately manifest themselves as bigotry. After the American and French revolutions, however, religious and political attitudes hardened. The citizens of Birmingham were not amused when the Lunar Society decided to celebrate the second anniversary of the Storming of the Bastille. They rioted for five days, yelling "No philosophers—Church and King forever!" They burned Priestley's home containing the results of years of scientific research, and convinced him to seek the healthier climate of Pennsylvania.

Darwin was then in Derby, beyond the reach of the mob. Tempers had cooled somewhat by 1794 when he published his first explicit ideas on evolution, in Part I of *Zoonomia*.[3] *Zoonomia* was primarily an attempt to classify diseases in the same way that Linnaeus had classified species, so evolution entered into it only indirectly. Reviewers found it easy to ignore the evolutionism and thereby avoid rousing the rabble. *Zoonomia* became a huge success. Its accounts of drunkenness, spitting, and various disorders moved one reviewer to predict that it would "do for medicine what Sir Isaac Newton's *Principia* had done for Natural Philosophy." *Zoonomia* did not quite do that, but it did win Darwin an international reputation in medicine. (As Charles Darwin noted in Krause [1879, p. 102], *Zoonomia* was also "honoured by the Pope by being placed in the 'Index Expurgatorius.' ") By the turn of the century, however, with England facing daily the threat of invasion by Napoleon, critics were no longer inclined to overlook Darwin's evolutionism. Even the Under-Secretary for Foreign Affairs attacked his ideas in a parody of *The Botanic Garden*. Darwin took the precaution of dying before publishing further evolutionary views in *The Temple of Nature or The Origin of Society* (1803). The frightened critics condemned that poem too for such heretical lines as the following:

> "*Organic Life* beneath the shoreless waves
> Was born and nursed in Ocean's pearly caves;
> First forms minute, unseen by spheric glass,
> Move on the mud, or pierce the watery mass;
> There, as successive generations bloom,
> New powers acquire, and larger limbs assume;
> Whence countless groups of vegetables spring,
> And breathing realms of fin, and feet, and wing.
>
> Canto I, 11. 295–302[4]

What motivated Darwin to become an evolutionist? His enlightened political and religious views tempt one to link him in the great chain of French evolutionism from Maupertuis to Lamarck. Darwin did share the Enlightenment faith in human progress, and this may have carried over into a progressive view of the development of species. Darwin (like every scientist of his time) was also influenced by Buffon. Yet Darwin differed from the French evolutionists in not basing evolutionism on the Great Chain of Being or on the concept of the monad. Darwin, having translated one of Linnaeus's works in the 1780s, was one of the major proponents of the Linnaean system, and therefore would not have believed in a linear progression of species along a single Chain of Being. And instead of the monad Darwin postulated that every organism developed from a "filament" in the semen which was nourished by the mother (*Zoonomia,* Ch. 39, 3.2–4.1). It is thus only a coincidence that Darwin arrived at a theory similar to that which Lamarck later proposed independently. According to Darwin all hereditary variations are due to differences in the material properties of the filaments from the father or in the nutrient particles of the mother. These differences produce variations in the "irritabilities, sensibilities, voluntarities, and associabilities" of the organism. (We may pass over Darwin's definitions of irritabilities, sensibilities, voluntarities, and associabilities, which are merely his four categories for classifying diseases.) These variations produce variations in the use of organs, which, by some unspecified mechanism, result in heritable changes in the organs. Ultimately new species may result.[5]

The first selection, from the chapter "On Generation" in Part I of *Zoonomia,* is a syntactically garbled compilation of evidence of evolution. This evidence is:

1. The analogy of evolution with metamorphosis and postnatal development.

2. Effects of domestication, which Darwin thought were direct effects rather than the effects of artificial selection. (Darwin's lost opportunity to cite Maupertuis here suggests that he had not read of the latter's genetic studies.)

3. Supposedly inherited effects of embryonic accidents. (Darwin also adduces this as evidence against the theory that organisms simply unfold from a preformed state—that is, against *evolution* in the old sense of the word. Like Aristotle and Maupertuis, Darwin makes no clear distinction between embryology and the origin of species.)

4. Comparative anatomy.

5. The inheritance of acquired characters, especially those developed in satisfying "lust, hunger, and security." (This is the brief anticipation of Lamarck's theory. In the passage on sexual competition Darwin passes over natural selection, without realizing its general applicability as a means of evolution.)

Finally, Darwin concludes that all "warm-blooded animals have arisen from one living filament." In subsequent paragraphs, not quoted here, he postulates four filaments as the origins of "cold-blooded" vertebrates, insects, so-called worms, and plants.

WILLIAM CHARLES WELLS (1757–1817)

The religious climate in England remained hostile to the concept of the transformation of species throughout the early nineteenth century. This was not only because of suppression by church and state, but also because of scientists' reinterpreting their role to be the discovery of proofs of God, rather than the discovery of the laws of nature. "Natural Philosophy" was transformed into "Natural Theology." During this period scientists abandoned the kind of speculation which Coleridge called "Darwinizing," and returned to the safe, plodding Baconian tradition of induction. Scientists such as W. C. Wells, Johann Friedrich Blumenbach (1752–1840), James Cowles Prichard (1786–1848), and William Lawrence (1783–1867) could suggest that the races of man arose by natural biological processes, but they dared not stray so far from Genesis and direct experience as to suggest that species arose by evolution. Like many of today's creationists, they failed to see that to admit evolution within species is to give up Genesis, for there is no barrier preventing a race from continuing to diverge to form a new species, genus, family, etc. In those days (and up until quite recently) transformation or evolution was thought of only in connection with the origin of species, so none of their contemporaries would have labelled—or libelled—Wells and others as evolutionists. For example, Charles Lyell (1797–1875), while criticizing evolutionism in volume 2 of *Principles of Geology* (1832), nevertheless referred approvingly (p. 62) to "the writings of Blumenbach, Prichard, Lawrence and others, for convincing proofs that the varieties of form, colour, and organization of different races of men, are perfectly consistent with the generally received opinion, that all the individuals of the species have originated from a single pair."[6] However, the modern historian of evolution cannot simply ignore Wells and others, because the present definition of evolution includes changes within a species. Thus Wells, Blumenbach, Prichard, and Lawrence must be said to have been evolutionists, but in a very restricted sense. From our perspective their opinions seem a compromise between Genesis and Darwin. It is appropriate, therefore, that we compromise between ignoring them altogether and discussing all of them in detail. I have therefore decided to discuss only one of the four—Wells. I choose him because he is the only one to have proposed natural selection as a mechanism in his restricted theory of evolution.

William Charles Wells could have served as the prototype of post-revolutionary British attitudes. In his autobiographical "Memoir"[7] he described himself as a "constitutional Tory" who was never "able to hear, with the least patience, any serious defence of the conduct of the French." Wells had been raised in Charleston, South Carolina, but his Scotch father forced him to wear a plaid coat and blue bonnet to ward off disloyal influences. We can imagine the persecution he suffered as the American Revolution was heat-ing up, and how that could have nourished his self-confessed stubbornness, violent temper, and propensity to use the vocabulary of the Charleston docks. At age eleven he was sent to study in Scotland, and spent two years at the University of Edinburgh. He returned to Charleston in 1771 to become apprenticed to a physician, but when hostilities broke out in 1775 he went back to Edinburgh to complete his medical study. In 1778 he became a military surgeon in Holland, but soon resigned his commission over a dispute with a superior officer which resulted in a brief stay in prison. Because the British appeared to be succeeding in the Carolinas, Wells returned in 1781 to look after his father's printing business. Yorktown soon proved this to be a miscalculation, and Wells was forced to flee to St. Augustine, where he established a newspaper, became a captain of Loyalist volunteers, and made up for lost time "in female society." Two years later he returned to Charleston and avoided a mob of American patriots only by being jailed for three months over a lawsuit. He then sailed back to Florida (adding shipwreck to his list of achievements), and from there to London. In 1785 Wells began to practice medicine—apparently not very successfully. At the end of his life he could only boast of finally being out of debt and of amassing an estate of £350. (One suspects a dysfunction of the bedside manner as the cause of his not becoming wealthy.) In 1800 Wells suffered an attack of "apoplexy" (a stroke) which left him unable to follow the arguments of others, but left his own reasoning intact. He later suffered from other symptoms which suggest heart failure.

In spite of poor health Wells was a prolific—if uninspired—contributor to science. His "Essay on Single Vision with Two Eyes" (1792) had the distinction of being criticized by Darwin in *Zoonomia*. His "Essay on Dew" (1814), however, was cited by John Herschel (1792–1871) as a model of induction.

The second selection in this chapter is from a description of a lady with one black arm, which Wells first read before the Royal Society in 1813. Wells is lead to speculate that Negroes are found mostly in Africa, and the lighter-skinned races in colder climates, because of some difference in their tolerance to diseases, which is associated with skin color. (Compare this with a similar passage in the selection by Maupertuis.) There is a clear statement of the principle of natural selection in the suggestion that the first inhabitants of Africa were of various skin colors, but that those with darker skins survived better and therefore proliferated.

PATRICK MATTHEW (1790–1874)

Of all the pre-Darwinians discussed in this book, only Patrick Matthew conceived of the evolution of species by means of natural selection. In Charles Darwin's words, he "most expressly and clearly anticipated my views." Yet virtually nothing is known about him.[8] Matthew was born on a farm in Scotland, studied at the University of Edinburgh, travelled in Europe, became a wealthy grain merchant, and devoted much of his time to his estate in Scotland. The most interesting of Matthew's activities were those on behalf of the victims of the Industrial Revolution. Britain had rushed into the modern era dragging with her the baggage of feudal laws and customs designed by and for the rich and aristocratic. These laws, which were perhaps sensible when the rich and titled were essential to society, became unjustified with an economic system which depended more on engineers, craftsmen, and workers in the "dark Satanic mills." Moreover, those laws neglected the growing number of people who found no place in the machinery of the system. This situation had built up in the early nineteenth century to the brink of revolution, and began to ease only gradually after the Tories lost ground in parliamentary elections following the death of George IV in 1830. Parliament's refusal to grant the reforms of the Chartist Movement in 1839 caused riots, and industrial unrest continued throughout the century. Unlike many scientists of conscience who could think of nothing better to do for the poor than to satisfy their craving for gee-whiz science lectures, Matthew became an activist defender of the common man and an opponent of anachronistic laws of inheritance and aristocracy. He was a member of the Chartist Movement, but resigned over its advocacy of violence. Matthew's awareness of the struggle for economic survival may have disposed him to see the struggle for survival in nature.

Another of Matthew's interests was colonialism, which was then being encouraged to create markets for British products and places to export surplus people. It may seem odd that a man who defended the downtrodden Briton would condone the exploitation of other races. However, Matthew and many other nineteenth-century Englishmen whom we would now call racists undoubtedly thought of themselves as charitably fulfilling the "white man's burden" to elevate the "inferior" races. (Matthew devoted one appendix in his book *On Naval Timber and Arboriculture* to the wanderlust of the British as proof of their superiority.) Matthew was much concerned with the possible effects of foreign climates on British settlers, and this may have stimulated his interest in natural selection.

Matthew's theory of evolution by natural selection was published as an appendix to *On Naval Timber and Arboriculture* (1831), which is mostly about shipbuilding and the production of trees for that purpose. Naturally the appendix went unnoticed until Matthew himself pointed it out after the publication of the *Origin of Species*. This raises the question of why Matthew allowed his theory to remain buried for nearly three decades, rather than broadcast the creation of what might have come to be known as "Matthewism." There are four reasonable explanations:

1. As Matthew noted, "the age was not ripe for such ideas."

2. About a year later Lyell published volume 2 of *Principles of Geology*, with its convincing arguments against evolution (or Lamarckism, as it then became known). This may have discouraged Matthew from pursuing his theory.
3. Matthew may not have realized the importance that would be attached to the theory.
4. Matthew lacked the inductive basis needed to convince other scientists.
The last two of these possible reasons are supported by the following statement by Matthew:

> "To me the conception of this law of Nature [selection] came intuitively as a self-evident fact, almost without an effort of concentrated thought. Mr. Darwin here seems to have more merit in the discovery than I have had—to me it did not appear a discovery. He seems to have worked it out by inductive reason, slowly and with due caution to have made his way synthetically from fact to fact onwards; while with me it was by a general glance at the scheme of Nature that I estimated this select production of species of an *a priori* recognisable fact—an axiom, requiring only to be pointed out to be admitted by unprejudiced minds of sufficient grasp.[9]

Matthew's book is now quite rare, so I have reprinted in the third selection the entire appendix dealing with evolution, or "diverging ramification," as he terms it. Matthew begins by rejecting the opinion (held by Wells and most others at the time) that there is an objective difference between varieties and species. He concludes that if man in a few years has been able to produce new varieties, then nature, with millions of ages in which to work, could have produced new species. Matthew argues that the interrupted sequence of fossils in the geological record can be explained either by a series of divine creations or by a natural power of species to change to accommodate sudden environmental changes. Matthew accepts the latter hypothesis, agreeing with the prevailing catastrophism of paleontologists following Cuvier. He may not have been aware that his countryman, Lyell, had just published volume 1 of *Principles of Geology*, which eventually convinced geologists of uniformitarianism—the view that past changes in the Earth were not global catastrophies, but gradual events like those now occurring.[10]
Like Dr. Darwin, Matthew repeats Linnaeus's suggestion that new species could have arisen as hybrids, and he does not exclude what we now call Lamarckism. (Matthew even suggests that memories and learned behavior can be inherited, and proposes the use of insects to study this possibility.) This was a tactical error considering the devastating impact Lyell had on Lamarckism. It is clear, however, that Matthew considered natural selection to be equally important as a mechanism in the origin of species.
After Darwin published the *Origin of Species* in 1859 Matthew claimed priority and began advertising himself as the "Discoverer of the principle of Natural Selection." This so grated on the modest Darwin that he could

hardly hide his delight upon learning that both he and Matthew had been preceded by Wells. "Talking of the 'Origin,' " he wrote in 1865,

> 'a Yankee has called my attention to a paper attached to Dr. Wells's famous 'Essay on Dew,' which was read in 1813 to the Royal Soc., but not printed, in which he applies most distinctly the principle of Natural Selection to the Races of Man. So poor old Patrick Matthew is not the first, and he cannot, or ought not, any longer to put on his title-pages, 'Discoverer of the principle of Natural Selection'! (F. Darwin, 1901, vol. 2, p. 225)

Unfortunately poor old Patrick Matthew was already dead.

OTHER PRE-DARWINIAN EVOLUTIONISTS

At least a dozen scientists had proposed theories of evolution before 1837, when Darwin began his first notebook on the subject; and at least two dozen others kept reinventing the idea before the publication of the *Origin of Species.* This large number of pre-Darwinian evolutionists has given rise to the suspicion that Darwin is underserving of the lavish praise given him in the last century. C. D. Darlington, in particular, has tried to show that "deep down in Darwin's unconscious he must have known that the past contained the origins of his ideas and that his predecessors were not quite so cheap as he made them out to be," and that Darwin's "Historical Sketch" in the *Origin of Species* "reads like the confession of an unhappy man, written under fearful stress" (Darlington, 1959, pp. 61, 64; see also Darlington, 1961). However, Darlington and others with such views neglect to inform us why, if Darwin was so jealous of priority, he waited twenty years to publish his theory, or why the *Origin of Species* was like a sudden revelation. Perhaps the correct perspective on Darwin's so-called precursors is provided by considering the discouraging effects of the evolutionist theories which he knew. Before 1837 only the ideas of Erasmus Darwin and of Lamarck were known to English biologists interested in evolution. Darwin's attitude toward them was typical of the attitude of Victorian biologists. He wrote to Huxley that "the history of error is quite unimportant, but it is curious to observe how exactly and accurately my grandfather . . . gives Lamarck's theory" (F. Darwin and Seward, 1903, vol. 1, p. 125). Charles Darwin could hardly have been interested in plagiarizing their theories.[11]

After publication of the second volume of Lyell's *Principles of Geology* in 1832, and after Robert Chambers's (1802–1871) popular *Vestiges of the Natural History of Creation* appeared in 1844, no literate Englishman could claim the idea of evolution as his own. Nor would many of them have wished to. Lyell's equation of evolutionism with Lamarckism certainly did not have a salutary effect on evolutionism. And the *Vestiges,* to which Chambers did not

TABLE 7. Evolutionists Before *The Origin of Species.*

A list of those who conceived of evolution and/or natural selection as applied to the origin of species prior to 1858. Parentheses in the first column of dates indicate that evolution was thought to be confined to races within species. Parentheses in the second column of dates indicate that natural selection was not regarded as a mechanism of evolution. I trust the reader knows by now that such a list cannot be used as a score-sheet for a supposed race for the first successful theory of evolution, or a chronicle of steady progress toward Darwinism. This list is based on Darwin's Historical Sketch in later editions of the *Origin of Species,* and on Gillispie (1970-1980) and Glass et. al. (1959).

	Evolution	Natural Selection
Empedocles		(5th cent. B.C.)
Lucretius		(1st cent. B.C.)
Maupertuis	1745	(1750)
Diderot	1754	(1749)
E. Darwin	1794	
Lamarck	1800	
Prichard	(1808)	
Wells	(1813)	1813
Lawrence	(1819)	
Grant	1826	
Buzareingnes, E. Geoffroy St. Hilaire	1828	
Matthew	1831	1831
von Buch, Rafinesque, H. C. Watson	1836	
Herbert	1837	
Spencer	1840	
Haldeman	1843	
Chambers	1844	
d'Halloy	1846	
Schleiden	1848	
I. Geoffroy St. Hilaire	(1850)	
Freke	1851	
Naudin, Unger	1852	
Baumgärtner, Keyserling, Schaaffhausen	1853	
Lecoq	1854	
Büchner, Powell, Wallace	1855	
Nägeli	1856	

even dare sign his name, scandalized scientists because of its gross errors as much as it did theologicans because of its unorthodoxy. Darwin's attitude toward the *Vestiges* is revealed in a letter written in 1855: "At times I really feel as much ashamed of myself as the author of *Vestiges* ought to be of himself." The climate in England was such that of the dozen or so scientists with whom Darwin discussed his ideas before 1859, he converted only two. Moreover, especially in Europe, evolution still bore the taint of the Enlightenment and of the Romanticism of German *Naturphilosophie*. In the 1850s, according to August Weismann (1834–1914), German scientists never mentioned evolution, because "the over speculation of *Naturphilosophie* had left in their minds a deep antipathy to all far-reaching deductions. . . .[12] It is true that by the late 1830s evolution was part of the spirit of the times, but although the spirit was willing the evidence needed to convince scientists appeared to be weak until Darwin mobilized it. That Darwin was able to overcome the negative attitude created by his predecessors justifies our continuing to use the term "Darwinism," rather than "Maupertuisism" or "Matthewism."

But we need not be dogmatic. Each reader can judge for himself how much credit is due to those listed in the following table of pre-Darwinians. First you may ask yourself which of those names you would ever have heard of if Darwin had not lived. Secondly, you may imagine yourself in an analogous situation. Suppose you had cleared some land, plowed it, planted seeds, and tended the crop. What would you say to someone who demanded the entire harvest because he had previously thrown some seeds on the land while passing?

Erasmus Darwin from *Zoonomia,* Part I, Chapter 39, Section 4.8. Third edition, London, 1801.

When we revolve in our minds, first, the great changes, which we see naturally produced in animals after their nativity, as in the production of the butterfly with painted wings from the crawling caterpillar; or of the respiring frog from the subnatant tadpole; from the feminine boy to the bearded man, and from the infant girl to the lactescent woman; both which changes may be prevented by certain mutilations of the glands necessary to reproduction.

Secondly, when we think over the great changes introduced into various animals by artificial or accidental cultivation, as in horses, which we have exercised for the different purposes of strength or swiftness, in carrying burthens or in running races; or in dogs, which have been cultivated for strength and courage, as the bull-dog; or for acuteness of his sense of smell, as the hound and spaniel; or for the swiftness of his foot, as the greyhound; or for his swimming in the water, or for drawing snow-sledges, as the rough-haired dogs of the north; or lastly, as a play-dog for children, as the lap-dog; with the changes of the forms of the cattle, which have been domesticated from the greatest antiquity, as camels, and sheep; which have undergone so total a transformation, that we are now ignorant from what species of wild animals they had their origin. Add to these the great changes of shape and colour, which we daily see produced in smaller animals from our domestication of them, as rabbits, or pigeons; or from the difference of climates and even of seasons; thus the sheep of warm climates are covered with hair instead of wool; and the hares and partridges of the latitudes, which are long buried in snow, become white during the winter months; add to these the various changes produced in the forms of mankind, by their early modes of exertion; or by the diseases occasioned by their habits of life; both of which became hereditary, and that through many generations. Those who labour at the anvil, the oar, or the loom, as well as those who carry sedan-chairs, or who have been educated to dance upon the rope, are distinguishable by the shape of their limbs; and the diseases occasioned by intoxication deform the countenance with leprous eruptions, or the body with tumid viscera, or the joints with knots and distortions.

Thirdly, when we enumerate the great changes produced in the species of animals before their nativity; these are such as resemble the form or colour of their parents, which have been altered by the cultivation or accidents above related, and are thus continued to their posterity. Or they are changes produced by the mixture of species as in mules; or changes produced probably by the exuberance of nourishment supplied to the fetus, as in monstrous births with additional limbs; many of these enormities of shape are propagated, and continued as a variety at least, if not as a new species of animal. I have seen a breed of cats with an additional claw on every foot; of poultry also with an additional claw, and with wings to their feet; and of others without rumps. Mr. Buffon mentions a breed of dogs without tails, which are common at Rome and at Naples, which he supposes to have been produced by a custom long established of cutting their tails close off. There are many kinds of pigeons, admired for their peculiarities, which are monsters thus produced and propagated. And to these must be added, the changes produced by the imagination of the male parent, as will be treated of more at large in No. VI. of this Section.

When we consider all these changes of animal form, and innumerable others, which may be collected from the books of natural history;

we cannot but be convinced, that the fetus or embryon is formed by apposition of new parts, and not by the distention of a primordial nest of germes, included one within another, like the cups of a conjurer.

Fourthly, when we revolve in our minds the great similarity of structure which obtains in all the warm blooded animals, as well quadrupeds, birds, and amphibious animals, as in mankind; from the mouse and bat to the elephant and whale; one is led to conclude, that they have alike been produced from a similar living filament. In some this filament in its advance to maturity has acquired hands and fingers, with a fine sense of touch, as in mankind. In others it has acquired claws or talons, as in tygers and eagles. In others, toes with an intervening web, or membrane, as in seals and geese. In others it has acquired cloven hoofs, as in cows and swine; and whole hoofs in others, as in the horse. While in the bird kind this original living filament has put forth wings instead of arms or legs, and feathers instead of hair. In some it has protruded horns on the forehead instead of teeth in the fore part of the upper jaw; in others tushes instead of horns; and in others beaks instead of either. And all this exactly as is daily seen in the transmutations of the tadpole, which acquires legs and lungs, when he wants them; and loses his tail, when it is no longer of service to him.

Fifthly, from their first rudiment, or primordium, to the termination of their lives, all animals undergo perpetual transformations; which are in part produced by their own exertions in consequence of their desires and aversions, of their pleasures and their pains, or of irritations, or of associations; and many of these acquired forms or propensities are transmitted to their posterity. See Sect. XXXI.1.

As air and water are supplied to animals in sufficient profusion, the three great objects of desire, which have changed the forms of many animals by their exertions to gratify them, are those of lust, hunger, and security. A great want of one part of the animal world has consisted in the desire of the exclusive possession of the females; and these have acquired weapons to combat each other for this purpose, as the very thick, shield-like, horny skin on the shoulder of the boar is a defence only against animals of his own species, who strike obliquely upwards, nor are his tushes for other purposes, except to defend himself, as he is not naturally a carnivorous animal. So the horns of the stag are sharp to offend his adversary, but are branched for the purpose of parrying or receiving the thrusts of horns similar to his own, and have therefore been formed for the purpose of combating other stags for the exclusive possession of the females; who are observed, like the ladies in the times of chivalry, to attend the car of the victor.

The birds, which do not carry food to their young, and do not therefore marry, are armed with spurs for the purpose of fighting for the exclusive possession of the females, as cocks and quails. It is certain that these weapons are not provided for their defence against other adversaries, because the females of these species are without this armour. The final cause of this contest amongst the males seems to be, that the strongest and most active animal should propagate the species, which should thence become improved.

Another great want consists in the means of procuring food, which has diversified the forms of all species of animals. Thus the nose of the swine has become hard for the purpose of turning up the soil in search of insects and roots. The trunk of the elephant is an elongation of the nose for the purpose of pulling down the branches of trees for his food, and for taking up water without bending his knees. Beasts of prey have acquired strong jaws or talons. Cattle have acquired a rough tongue and a rough palate to pull off the blades of grass, as cows and sheep. Some birds have acquired harder beaks to crack nuts, as the parrot. Others have acquired beaks adapted to break the harder seeds, as sparrows. Others for the softer seeds of flowers, or the buds of trees, as the finches. Other birds have acquired long beaks to penetrate the moister soils in search of insects or roots, as wood-cocks; and others broad ones to filtrate the water of lakes, and to retain aquatic insects, as ducks. All which seem to have been gradually produced during many generations by the perpetual endeavour of the creatures to supply the want of food, and to have been delivered to their posterity with constant improvement of them for the purposes required.

The third great want amongst animals is that of security, which seems much to have diversified the forms of their bodies and the colour of them; these consist in the means of escaping other animals more powerful than themselves. Hence some animals have acquired wings instead of legs, as the smaller birds, for the purpose of escape. Others great length of fin, or of membrane, as the flying fish, and the bat. Others great swiftness of foot, as the hare. Others have acquired hard or armed shells, as the tortoise and the echinus marinus.

Mr. Osbeck, a pupil of Linnaeus, mentions the American frog-fish, lophius histrio, which inhabits the large floating islands of sea-weed about the Cape of Good Hope, and has fulcra resembling leaves, that the fishes of prey may mistake it for the sea-weed, which it inhabits. Voyage to China, p. 113.

The contrivances for the purposes of security extend even to vegetables, as is seen in the wonderful and various means of their concealing or defending their honey from insects, and their seeds from birds. On the other hand swiftness of wing has been acquired by hawks and swallows to pursue their prey; and a proboscis of admirable structure has been acquired by the bee, the moth, and the humming bird, for the purpose of plundering the nectaries of flowers. All which seem to have been formed by the original living filament, excited into action by the necessities of the creatures, which possess them, and on which their existence depends.

From thus meditating on the great similarity of the structure of the warm-blooded animals, and at the same time of the great changes they undergo both before and after their nativity; and by considering in how minute a portion of time many of the changes of animals above described have been produced; would it be too bold to imagine, that in the great length of time, since the earth began to exist, perhaps millions of ages before the commencement of the history of mankind, would it be too bold to imagine, that all warm-blooded animals have arisen from one living filament, which THE GREAT FIRST CAUSE endued with animality, with the power of acquiring new parts, attended with new propensities, directed by irritations, sensations, volitions, and associations; and thus possessing the faculty of continuing to improve by its own inherent activity, and of delivering down those improvements by generation to its posterity, world without end?

William Charles Wells, from *Two Essays: One Upon Single Vision With Two Eyes; the Other on Dew. A Letter to the Right Hon. Lloyd, Lord Kenyon, and an Account of a Female of the White Race of Mankind, Part of Whose Skin Resembles that of a Negro; with Some Observations on the Causes of the Differences in Colour and Form Between the White and Negro Races of Men.* London, 1818.

On considering the difference of colour between Europeans and Africans, a view has occurred to me of this subject, which has not been given by any author, whose works have fallen into my hands. I shall, therefore, venture to mention it here, though at the hazard of its being thought rather fanciful than just.

There is no circumstance, perhaps, in which these two races differ so much, as in their capacity to bear, with impunity, the action of the causes of many diseases. The fatality to Europeans of the climate of the middle parts of Africa, which are, however, inhabited by negroes without injury to their health, is well known. Let it then be supposed, that any number of Europeans were to be sent to that country, and that they were to subsist themselves by their bodily labour; it seems certain, that the whole colony would soon become extinct. On the other hand, the greater liability of negroes in Europe to be attacked with fatal diseases is equally well established. If, therefore, a colony of the former race were brought to Europe, and forced to labour in the open air for their subsistence, many of them would quickly die, and the remainder, from their inability to make great bodily exertions in cold weather, and their being frequently diseased, would be prevented from working an equal number of days in the year with the whites. The consequence would be, that without taking farther into account the unfriendliness of the climate to them, their gains would be inadequate to the maintenance of themselves and their families. They would thence become feeble, and be rendered still more incapable of supporting life by their labour. In the mean time, their children would die from want, or diseases induced by deficient or improper nourishment, and in this way, a colony of the negro race in a cold country would quickly cease to exist.

This difference in the capacity of the two races to resist the operation of the causes of many diseases, I assume as a fact, though I am utterly unable to explain it. I do not, however, suppose, that their different susceptibility of diseases depends, properly, on their difference of colour. On the contrary, I think it probable, that this is only a sign of some difference in them, which, though strongly manifested by its effects in life, is yet too subtle to be discovered by an anatomist after death; in like manner as a human body, which is incapable of receiving the smallpox, differs in no observable thing from another, which is still liable to be affected with that disease.

Regarding then as certain, that the negro race are better fitted to resist the attacks of the diseases of hot climates than the white, it is reasonable to infer, that those, who only approach the black race, will be likewise better fitted to do so, than others who are entirely white. This is, in fact, found to be true, with regard to the mixture of the two races; since mulattoes are much more healthy in hot climates than whites. But amongst men, as well as among other animals, varieties of a greater or less magnitude are constantly occurring. In a civilized country, which has been long peopled, those varieties, for the most part, quickly disappear, from the intermarriages of different families. Thus, if a very tall man be produced, he very commonly marries a woman much less than himself, and their progeny scarcely differs in size from their countrymen. In districts, however, of very small extent, and having little intercourse with other countries, an accidental difference in the appearance of the inhabitants will often descend to their late posterity. The clan of the Macras, for instance, possess both sides of Loch-Duich in Scotland; but those who inhabit one side of the loch are called the black Macras, and the others the white, from a difference which has always been observed in their complexions. Again, those who attend to the improvement of domestic animals, when they find individuals possessing, in a greater degree than common, the qualities they desire, couple a male and female of these together, then take the best of their offspring as a new stock, and in this way proceed, till they approach as near the point in view, as the nature of things will permit. But, what is here done by art, seems to be done, with equal efficacy, though more slowly, by nature, in the formation of varieties of mankind, fitted for the country which they inhabit. Of the accidental varieties of man, which would occur among the first few and scattered inhabitants of the middle regions of Africa, some one would be better fitted than the others to bear the diseases of the country. This race would constantly multiply, while the others would decrease, not only from their inability to sustain the attacks of disease, but from their incapacity of contending with their more vigorous neighbours. The colour of this vigorous race I take for granted, from what has been already said, would be dark. But the same disposition to form varieties still existing, a darker and a darker race would in the course of time occur, and as the darkest would be the best fitted for the climate, this would at length become the most prevalent, if not the only race, in the particular country in which it had originated.

In like manner, that part of the original stock of the human race, which proceeded to the colder regions of the earth, would in process of time become white, if they were not originally so, from persons of this color being better fitted to resist the diseases of such climates, than others of a dark skin.

Patrick Matthew, from "Accommodation of Organized Life to Circumstance, by Diverging Ramifications," an appendix to *On Naval Timber and Aboriculture; with Critical Notes on Authors who have Recently Treated the Subject of Planting.* London, 1831.

Throughout this volume, we have felt considerable inconvenience, from the adopted dogmatical classification of plant, and have all along been floundering between species and variety, which certainly under culture soften into each other. A particular conformity, each after its own kind, when in a state of nature, termed species, no doubt exists to a considerable degree. This conformity has existed during the last forty centuries. Geologists discover a like particular conformity—fossil species—through the deep deposition of each great epoch, but they also discover an almost complete difference to exist between the species or stamp of life, of one epoch from that of every other. We are therefore led to admit, either of a repeated miraculous creation; or of a power of change, under a change of circumstances, to belong to living organized matter, or rather to the congeries of inferior life, which appears to form superior. The derangements and changes in orga- nized existence, induced by a change of circumstance from the inter- ference of man, affording us proof of the plastic quality of superior life, and the likelihood that circumstances have been very different in the different epochs, though steady in each, tend strongly to heighten the probability of the latter theory.

When we view the immense calcareous and bituminous formations, principally from the waters and atmosphere, and consider the oxida- tions and depositions which have taken place, either gradually, or during some of the great convulsions, it appears at least probable, that the liquid elements containing life have varied considerably at differ- ent times in composition and in weight; that our atmosphere has contained a much greater proportion of carbonic acid or oxygen; and our waters, aided by excess of carbonic acid, and greater heat result- ing from greater density of atmosphere, have contained a greater quantity of lime and other mineral solutions. Is the inference then unphilosophic, that living things which are proved to have a circum- stance-suiting power—a very slight change of circumstance by cul- ture inducing a corresponding change of character—may have gradu- ally accommodated themselves to the variations of the elements containing them, and, without new creation, have presented the di- verging changeable phenomena of past and present organized exist- ence.

The destructive liquid currents, before which the hardest mountains have been swept and comminuted into gravel, sand, and mud, which intervened between and divided these epochs, probably extending over the whole surface of the globe, and destroying nearly all living things, must have reduced existence so much, that an unoccupied field would be formed for new diverging ramifications of life, which, from the connected sexual system of vegetables, and the natural instincts of animals to herd and combine with their own kind, would fall into specific groups, these remnants, in the course of time, moulding and accommodating their being anew to the change of circumstances, and to every possible means of subsistence, and the millions of ages of regularity which appear to have followed between the epochs, probably after this accommodation was completed, affording fossil deposit of regular specific character.

There are only two probable ways of change—the above, and the still wider deviation from present occurrence,—of indestructible or molecular life (which seems to resolve itself into powers of attraction and repulsion under mathematical figure and regulation, bearing a slight systematic similitude to the great aggregations of matter), gradually uniting and developing itself into new circumstance-suited living aggregates, without the presence of any mould or germ of former aggregates, but this scarcely differs from new creation, only it forms a portion of a continued scheme or system.

In endeavouring to trace, in the former way, the principle of these changes of fashion which have taken place in the domiciles of life, the following questions occur: Do they arise from admixture of species nearly allied producing intermediate species? Are they *the diverging ramifications* of the living principle under modification of circumstance? Or have they resulted from the combined agency of both? Is there only one living principle? Does organized existence, and perhaps all material existence, consist of one Proteus principle of life capable of gradual circumstance-suited modifications and aggregations, without bound under the solvent or motion-giving principle, heat or light? There is more beauty and unity of design in this continuing balancing of life to circumstance, and greater conformity to those dispositions of nature which are manifest to us, than in total destruction and new creation. It is improbable that much of this diversification is owing to commixture of species nearly allied, all changes by this appears very limited, and confined within the bounds of what is called Species; the progeny of the same parents, under great difference of circumstance, might, in several generations, even become distinct species, incapable of co-reproduction.

The self-regulating adaptive disposition of organized life may, in part, be traced to the extreme fecundity of Nature, who, as before stated, has, in all the varieties of her offspring, a prolific power much beyond (in many cases a thousandfold) what is necessary to fill up the vacancies caused by senile decay. As the field of existence is limited and pre-occupied, it is only the hardier, more robust, better suited to circumstance individuals, who are able to struggle forward to maturity, these inhabiting only the situations to which they have superior adaptation and greater power of occupancy than any other kind; the weaker, less circumstance-suited, being prematurely destroyed. This principle is in constant action, it regulates the colour, the figure, the capacities, and instincts; those individuals of each species, whose colour and covering are best suited to concealment or protection from enemies, or defence from vicissitude and inclemencies of climate, whose figure is best accommodated to health, strength, defence, and support; whose capacities and instincts can best regulate the physical energies to self-advantage according to circumstances—in such immense waste of primary and youthful life, *those* only come forward to maturity from the strict ordeal by which Nature tests their adaptation to her standard of perfection and fitness to continue their kind by reproduction.

From the unremitting operation of this law acting in concert with the tendency which the progeny have to take the more particular qualities of the parents, together with the connected sexual system in vegetable, and instinctive limitation to its own kind in animals, a considerable uniformity of figure, colour, and character, is induced, constituting species; the breed gradually acquiring the very best possible adaptation of these to its condition which it is susceptible of, and when alteration of circumstance occurs, thus changing in character to suit these as far as its nature is susceptible of change.

This circumstance-adaptive law, operating upon the slight but continued natural disposition to sport in the progeny (seedling variety), does not preclude the supposed influence which volition or sensation may have over the configuration of the body. To examine into the disposition to sport in the progeny, even when there is only one parent, as in many vegetables, and to investigate how much variation is modified by the mind or nervous sensation of the parents, or of the living thing itself during its progress to maturity; how far it depends upon external circumstance, and how far on the will, irritability and muscular exertion, is open to examination and experiment. In the first place, we ought to investigate its dependency upon the preceding links of the particular chain of life, variety being often merely types or approximations of former parentage; thence the variation of the family, as well as of the individual, must be embraced by our experiments.

This continuation of family type, not broken by casual particular aberration, is mental as well as corporeal, and is exemplified in many of the dispositions or instincts of particular races of men. These innate or continuous ideas or habits, seem proportionally greater in the insect tribes, those especially of shorter revolution; and forming an abiding memory, may resolve much of the enigma of instinct, and the foreknowledge which these tribes have of what is necessary to completing their round of life, reducing this to knowledge, or impressions, and habits, acquired by a long experience. This greater continuity of existence, or rather continuity of perceptions and impressions, in insects, is highly probable; it is even difficult in some to ascertain the particular stops when each individual commences, under the different phases of egg, larva, pupa, or if much consciousness of individuality exists. The continuation of reproduction for several generations by the females alone in some of these tribes, tends to the probability of the greater continuity of existence, and the subdivisions of life by cuttings, at any rate must stagger the advocate of individuality.

Among the millions of *specific varieties* of living things which occupy the humid portion of the surface of our planet, as far back as can be traced, there does not appear, with the exception of man, to have been any particular engrossing race, but a pretty fair balance of powers of occupancy,—or rather, most wonderful variation of circumstance parallel to the nature of every species, as if circumstance and species had grown up together. There are indeed several races which have threatened ascendency in some particular regions, but it is man alone from whom any general imminent danger to the existence of his brethren is to be dreaded.

As far back as history reaches, man had already had considerable influence, and had made encroachments upon his fellow denizens, probably occasioning the destruction of many species, and the production and continuation of a number of varieties or even species, which he found more suited to supply his wants, but which, from the infirmity of their condition—not having undergone selection by the law of nature, of which we have spoken, cannot maintain their ground without his culture and protection.

It is, however, only in the present age that man has begun to reap the fruits of his tedious education, and has proven how much "knowledge is power." He has now acquired a dominion over the material world, and a consequent power of increase, so as to render it probable that the whole surface of the earth may soon be overrun by this engrossing anomaly, to the annihilation of every wonderful and beautiful variety of animated existence, which does not administer to his wants principally as laboratories of preparation to befit cruder elemental matter for assimilation by his organs.

Rhyme and Reason

By now readers may have begun to suspect that I believe the social environment of the scientist plays a role in his creativity. The suspicion is justified. I am aware, however, that the relationships of scientists to their cultures are seldom as straightforward as they may appear in this book. For one thing the interaction of science and society is complicated by being a reciprocal relationship: science modifies its own cultural environment, as it did in the Industrial Revolution. Secondly, it is not true, as Swift charged in *Gulliver's Travels*, that "new systems of Nature are but new Fashions, which . . . vary in every Age." Good science, like good art, outlives any human culture. Finally, if scientific theories were strictly determined by culture, biologists, physicists, and chemists would do well to become sociologists, for the natural laws which they seek would be found in the collective thoughts of society.

Scientists, like people, are too complicated to be understood simply as products of public events and ideas. This is a fact which becomes immediately obvious to me whenever I try to understand my contemporaries or myself. However, history permits us to stand back, to view the portraits of past scientists without being distracted by the brush-strokes of their personal lives. What we then often see affecting their creativity is a certain "spirit of the times"—what Goethe called the *Zeitgeist.* I believe the foregoing account of the pre-Darwinians shows such a spirit moving upon the face of biology in the late 1830s, giving scientists with very different interests and circumstances a similar idea. This rise in evolutionism cannot have been due to some new scientific breakthrough, for most of the evidence for evolution had already been summarized years earlier, especially by Erasmus Darwin and by Matthew. The only reasonable candidate for such a breakthrough might by uniformitarianism, but that did not even make Lyell an evolutionist. We must look outside of science for the zeitgeist.

Like most spirits, the spirit of the early nineteenth century is too evanescent to permit close scrutiny, but we can let Wordsworth and Tennyson serve as mediums to summon him up. They should be up to the task, for both poets were interested in science and informed on the evolutionary thought of their times. William Wordsworth, of course, knew of Erasmus Darwin's ideas, and in his early years he dabbled in chemistry with Humphrey Davy (1778–1829). Moreover, Wordsworth had the rare understanding to realize that "the knowledge both of the Poet and the Man of science is pleasure," and to appreciate the creative scientific mind "for ever voyaging through strange seas of thought, alone." Alfred, Lord Tennyson, Wordsworth's successor as Poet Laureate, was himself a pre-Darwinian evolutionist. Apparently he was under the influence of Goethe, the "him" of the first verse of *In Memoriam:*

> I held it truth, with him who sings
> To one clear harp in divers tones,
> That men may rise on stepping-stones
> On their dead selves to higher things.

T. H. Huxley (L. H. Huxley, 1900, vol. 2, p. 359) said of Tennyson that he was "the only poet since the time of Lucretius, who has taken the trouble to understand the work and tendency of men of science."[13]

One clue to the zeitgeist during the rise of evolutionism is Wordsworth's "Ode: Intimations of Immortality from Recollections of Early Childhood," written between 1803 and 1806. Wordsworth was at that time discouraged over the outcome of the French Revolution, the mental decay of Coleridge caused by opium, and his own declining sensitivity to nature. (He no longer was so moved by nature that he had to lean against a wall!) Yet we can now see the Ode as not only a private complaint, but a warning that the confident youth of the British nation was coming to an end. Nature would lose its charm like a solved puzzle, and her exploiters would become her slaves. Hearts would grieve "to think what man has made of man." Wordsworth put on a brave show of optimism, but with the Victorian period his dismal prophecy became undeniable. Tennyson's *In Memoriam,* written between 1833 and 1850, was an expression of grief over the death of a friend, but more than that it was a lament over Britain's lost innocence. The fair works of nature were no longer linked to the human soul. Even those who had never heard of Malthus realized that life was a struggle for survival. Without hope for earthly salvation, Tennyson turned to evolution in the hope that his generation could at least serve as stepping-stones to higher things.[14]

But let the poets speak.

From "Ode: Intimations of Immortality from Recollections of Early Childhood," by William Wordsworth

1

There was a time when meadow, grove, and stream,
The earth, and every common sight,
    To me did seem
    Apparelled in celestial light,
The glory and the freshness of a dream.
It is not now as it hath been of yore;—
    Turn wheresoe'er I may,
      By night or day,
The things which I have seen I now can see no more.

2

    The Rainbow comes and goes,
    And lovely is the Rose,
    The Moon doth with delight
Look round her when the heavens are bare;
    Waters on a starry night
    Are beautiful and fair;
    The sunshine is a glorious birth;
    But yet I know, where'er I go,
That there hath past away a glory from the earth.

10
Then sing, ye Birds, sing, sing a joyous song!
    And let the young Lambs bound
    As to the tabor's sound!
We in thought will join your throng,
    Ye that pipe and ye that play,
    Ye that through your hearts to-day
    Feel the gladness of the May!
What though the radiance which was once so bright
Be now for ever taken from my sight,
    Though nothing can bring back the hour
Of splendour in the grass, of glory in the flower;
    We will grieve not, rather find
    Strength in what remains behind;
    In the primal sympathy
    Which having been must ever be;
    In the soothing thoughts that spring
    Out of human suffering;
    In the faith that looks through death,
In years that bring the philosophic mind.

From *In Memoriam,* by Alfred, Lord Tennyson

54
Oh yet we trust that somehow good
    Will be the final goal of ill,
    To pangs of nature, sins of will,
Defects of doubt, and taints of blood;

That nothing walks with aimless feet;
    That not one life shall be destroyed,
    Or cast as rubbish to the void,
When God hath made the pile complete;

That not a worm is cloven in vain;
    That not a moth with vain desire
    Is shrivelled in a fruitless fire,
Or but subserves another's gain.

Behold, we know not anything;
    I can but trust that good shall fall
    At last—far off—at last, to all,
And every winter change to spring.

So runs my dream: but what am I?
　An infant crying in the night:
　An infant crying for the light:
And with no language but a cry.

55

The wish, that of the living whole
　No life may fail beyond the grave,
　Derives it not from what we have
The likest God within the soul?

Are God and Nature then at strife,
　That Nature lends such evil dreams?
　So careful of the type she seems,
So careless of the single life;

That I, considering everywhere
　Her secret meaning in her deeds,
　And finding that of fifty seeds
She often brings but one to bear,

I falter where I firmly trod,
　And falling with my weight of cares
　Upon the great world's altar-stairs
That slope through darkness up to God,

I stretch lame hands of faith, and grope,
　And gather dust and chaff, and call
　To what I feel is Lord of all,
And faintly trust the larger hope.

56

"So careful of the type?" but no.
　From scarped cliff and quarried stone
　She cries, "A thousand types are gone:
I care for nothing, all shall go.

"Thou makest thine appeal to me:
　I bring to life, I bring to death:
　The spirit does but mean the breath:
I know no more." And he, shall he,

Man, her last work, who seemed so fair,
   Such splendid purpose in his eyes,
   Who rolled the psalm to wintry skies,
Who built him fanes of fruitless prayer,

Who trusted God was love indeed
   And love Creation's final law—
   Though Nature, red in tooth and claw
With ravine, shrieked against his creed—

Who loved, who suffered countless ills,
   Who battled for the True, the Just,
   Be blown about the desert dust,
Or sealed within the iron hills?

No more? A monster then, a dream,
   A discord. Dragons of the prime,
   That tear each other in their slime,
Were mellow music matched with him.

O life as futile, then, as frail!
   O for thy voice to soothe and bless!
   What hope of answer, or redress?
Behind the veil, behind the veil.

TABLE 8. MAJOR EVENTS AND PEOPLE OF THE NINETEENTH CENTURY

Year	Darwin/Wallace	Science	Arts/Politics
1800			
		Cuvier (1769-1832)	President Jefferson
		Zoonomia	Emperor Napoleon
		Malthus (1766-1834)	
	Darwin born	Davy (1778-1829)	Beethoven
	9 Feb. 1809	Dalton (1766-1844)	Goethe
		Philosophie Zoologique	Hegel
		"Account of a Female . . ."	
		Oersted (1777-1851)	War of 1812
		Ampère (1775-1836)	Wordsworth, Coleridge
		Ohm (1789-1854)	Byron, Shelley, Keats
	Wallace born	Faraday (1791-1867)	Turner, Constable
	8 Jan. 1823	Audubon (1785-1851)	Schubert, Mendelssohn
1825			
		Naval Timber . . .	Bolívar
	Beagle voyage	Lyell (1797-1875)	
	27 Dec. 1831-	von Baer (1792-1876)	Balzac, Hugo
	2 Oct. 1836		
	Darwin Opens Note-book		
	Darwin's "Sketch"		Chopin
	Darwin's "Essay"		The Alamo
		Vestiges	First Opium War
	Wallace in the	Helmholtz (1821-	Queen Victoria
	Amazon 1848-52	1894)	
		Gray (1810-1888)	Dickens, Brontë
			Communist Manifesto
1850			
	Wallace "On the	Neanderthal Man	Wagner, Verdi
	Law . . ."	(1856)	
		Hooker (1817-1911)	Tennyson, Whitman
	Linnean Soc. Papers	Bates (1825-1892)	Emerson, Hawthorne
	Origin of Spieces	Spencer (1820-1903)	Longfellow, Melville
	Wallace in Malay	Mendel (1822-1884)	Poe, Thoreau
	Archipelago	Huxley (1825-1895)	John Brown, Garibaldi
	1854-62	Pasteur (1822-1895)	President Lincoln
		Nobel (1833-1896)	U.S. Civil War
		Galton (1822-1911)	Degas, Manet, Monet
		Mendeleev (1834-1907)	Tolstoy, Turgenev
	Darwin's *Descent*	Maxwell (1831-1879)	Dostoevsky
	of Man		Twain, Carroll

Year	Darwin/Wallace	Science	Arts/Politics
1875			
			Tchaikovsky, Strauss
	Darwin died		Gilbert & Sullivan
	19 April 1882	Weismann (1834-1914)	Rodin, Cezanne
		Haeckel (1834-1919)	Renoir
		Hertz (1857-1894)	Fabian Society
		Mach (1838-1916)	Shaw, Kipling
		Java Man (1891)	Ibsen, Strindberg
		Röntgen (1845-1923)	Toulouse-Lautrec
	Wallace's *Darwin-*	Becquerel (1852-1908)	Gaugin, van Gogh
	ism	P. Curie (1859-1906)	Debussey, Mahler
		M. Curie (1867-1934)	
			Dreyfus Affair
1900			

7

Darwin and Wallace: Evolutionary Convergence

On one of the islands of the Malay archipelago in February 1858, a thirty-five-year-old Englishman shivered in a blanket despite the 88° heat. Impatiently he waited for this attack of malaria to abate, so that he could write down a theory which had suddenly occurred to him. The fevered brain of Alfred Russel Wallace was about to converge with that of Charles Darwin, who was himself writing a book on the same theory in moments of good health.

Meanwhile, a thousand kilometers south of Wallace, a lesser gliding possum slept soundly within the curl of its bushy tail. It was slightly tired after a night of gliding through the Australian forest, riding the air that filled the folds of skin stretched between its legs. Just as Wallace did not dream that Darwin had found the same solution to the problem of species, the lesser gliding possum did not dream that the flying squirrel had found the same solution to the problem of locomotion through the trees. Nor did the lesser gliding possum dream that in 121 years a writer, desperate for a novel introduction to Darwinism, would compare him and the squirrel with Wallace and Darwin![1]

Yet the comparison is not so farfetched. It is almost commonplace that scientists with different origins converge upon the same theory independently, just as animals as different as a marsupial and a rodent converged upon similar adaptations in similar environments. Scientists are always driving at theories under the influence of their environments, so it should not be surprising that similar scientific and cultural influences shape similar theories. In the last chapter we saw how many scientists converged upon evolutionism at about the time the Romantic gaze upon the splendors of nature was being replaced by a steely Victorian stare. Suddenly the quaint nonsense of Erasmus Darwin and Lamarck seemed appealing to many as an alternative to the static view of species as perfectly designed. Most scientists, however, could not accept evolutionism without a plausible mechanism for its occurrence. This mechanism was the theory that Darwin and Wallace converged upon.

The simultaneous development of a scientific theory allows for a kind of experiment in history in which hypothetical foundations of the theory can be tested. For example, the hypothesis that scientist X created a particular theory because he had been improperly potty-trained and a Marxist is false or at least incomplete if scientist Y, a properly potty-trained capitalist, conceived of the same theory. Wallace may thus be used as a control to test some of the many conjectures which have been proposed to account for Darwin's theory. Fortunately, Darwin and Wallace have left fairly complete records of the circumstances surrounding their creation of the theory of evolution by natural selection. (It is perhaps too much to hope that further information will come to light regarding Patrick Matthew.) The following parallel biography of Darwin and Wallace prior to the publication of their theory is therefore in the nature of an experiment to determine the shared influences on Darwin's and Wallace's creativity.

CHILDHOOD

The experimental historian could ask for no better subjects than Charles Robert Darwin (1809–1882) and Alfred Russel Wallace (1823–1913). Their origins differed as greatly as those of the possum and the flying squirrel. Charles Darwin was born into a wealthy, genteel, and modestly intellectual family on the same day as Abraham Lincoln. His mother, who was the daughter of Josiah Wedgwood, died when Charles was only eight. His father, Dr. Robert Darwin, was the son of Erasmus Darwin, who was already passing from notoriety to obscurity. Robert Darwin loomed even larger than life to his son—an impressive feat for a man who stood six feet, two inches, and weighed 336 pounds. By current American standards Robert Darwin would be considered an overbearing father, but Charles had as much affection for him as respect. Much has been made of Robert's scolding which stuck in Charles Darwin's mind for sixty years: "You care for nothing but shooting, dogs, and rat-catching, and you will be a disgrace to yourself and all your family." When Darwin recalled these words in his *Autobiography* he was generally acknowledged as the Newton of biology, and may have decided that the scolding was neither an infallible prophecy nor an inescapable curse. He added: "[my] father, who was the kindest man I ever knew, and whose memory I love with all my heart, must have been angry and somewhat unjust when he used such words."[2]

The reason for dwelling on Darwin's father is that several psychohistorians of the Freudian persuasion have tried to find the roots of Darwinism in a supposed Oedipal struggle of Darwin against his father. If such a conjecture is valid we should find a similar relationship between Alfred Russel Wallace and his father. In Wallace's autobiography, however, his father is mentioned only as a necessary explanation for Alfred's having been born. The elder

Wallace had studied law but preferred to live on an inheritance until it was too late to find employment as a lawyer. He then started an unsuccessful magazine of art and literature, and later took occasional jobs as a teacher and librarian. Wallace made no judgment of his father, but one can imagine the thoughts of a young man driven to poverty because of his father's folly. An Oedipal desire to castrate the father would have been superfluous.[3]

EDUCATION

Darwin's genius revealed itself early in his refusal to accept the formal education thought proper for a young gentleman of his time. His seven years at the Shrewsbury School run by Samuel Butler's father was recalled as "simply a blank." Toward the end of this period, when Darwin was about sixteen, his interests in chemistry were rewarded with ridicule by Butler, who considered the smoke and fumes more appropriate for those destined to labor in factories. Darwin said of himself that he was "a very ordinary boy, rather below the common standard in intellect." However, this ordinary boy often had an extraordinary collection of pebbles, shells, eggs, and so on in his pockets. He attributed his zeal for collecting to some "innate" tendency, because none of his family shared it.[4]

At age sixteen Darwin was sent to Edinburgh University in hopes that it might be able to transmute him into a physician. However, at about the same time Darwin realized that his father would leave him enough property to live well without working, and that was "sufficient to check any strenuous effort to learn medicine." Moreover, Darwin was bored by all of the courses except chemistry. It was particularly "fearful to remember" the lectures in Materia Medica given at eight in the morning by a Dr. Duncan, who was "so very learned that his wisdom [had] left no room for his sense." Duncan's lectures consisted of reading aloud his grandfather's notes, including a reminiscence which began, "When I was in Leyden in 1719. . ." Students always had a supply of peas with which to pelt the professor on such occasions. Darwin was also haunted by two operations on children he witnessed in the days before anesthetics. However, Darwin's interest in natural history swelled to fill the vacuum left by medicine. He contributed several papers to the local scientific society, and became acquainted with Robert Edmund Grant (1793–1874), whose enthusiasm for Lamarckism failed to excite any resonance in the seventeen-year-old. Charles, of course, knew and approved of similar ideas in his grandfather's *Zoonomia*, but was apparently not then interested in the origin of species.[5]

After his second year at Edinburgh, Robert Darwin had reason to suspect that his son would not carry on the Darwin tradition in medicine. He therefore sent Charles to Cambridge University to see if he had the makings of a clergyman. Dr. Darwin had acquired Erasmus's attitude toward religion, and perhaps thought that giving his son to the church would serve them both right. Or perhaps, as Charles believed, his father thought having a country clergyman for a son would be preferable to having an idle sporting man. In any case there was nothing in the proposition incompatible with Charles's ambition to live comfortably and to indulge his interests in natural history. The decision was not made lightly, however, for Charles had to decide whether he could declare a belief in all the dogmas of the Church of England.

> As I did not then in the least doubt the strict and literal truth of every word in the Bible, I soon persuaded myself that our Creed must be fully accepted. It never struck me how illogical it was to say that I believed in what I could not understand and what is in fact unintelligible. I might have said with entire truth that I had no wish to dispute any dogma; but I never was such a fool as to feel and say 'credo quia incredible!' (Barlow, 1958, p. 57)

After brushing up on Greek, Darwin entered Cambridge where three years were "sadly wasted . . . and worse than wasted." He got into a "sporting set, including some dissipated low-minded young men [and] sometimes drank too much, with jolly singing and playing at cards afterwards." Based on my observations of students, I doubt that Darwin's greatness can be attributed to these facets of his education.

Somewhat more promising were Darwin's interests in painting, music, Shakespeare, Milton, Wordsworth, Coleridge, Shelley, Byron, and beetles (Barlow, 1958, pp. 61, 138). Letters to his friends were filled with entomological gossip and requests for caterpillars and dung beetles. Through these interests Darwin impressed Professor J. S. Henslow (1796–1861) as someone "a little superior to the common run of youths," and soon he became known as "the man who walks with Henslow." It was at Reverend Henslow's in 1831 that Darwin met Lyell, whose first volume of *Principles of Geology* was just coming out. Perhaps this meeting helped awaken in Darwin an interest in geology. At Edinburgh he had found the lectures on geology so boring that at Cambridge he did not bother to attend the "eloquent and interesting" lectures of Adam Sedgwick (1785–1873). He made up for this neglect with a three-week outing in Wales with Sedgwick in August 1831. At Cambridge Darwin also came under the influence of Alexander von Humboldt (1769–1859) through his *Personal Narrative of Travels to the Equinoctial Regions of the New Continent, During the Years 1799–1804*. Reading this book moved Darwin to plan an expedition to the Canary islands. A second influential book was *Introduction to the Study of Natural Philosophy* by John Herschel (1792–1871), son of Erasmus Darwin's colleague. Herschel's book inspired "a burning zeal to add even the most humble contribution to the noble structure of Natural Science."[6]

However doubtful the value of Darwin's formal education, it was infinitely superior to the opportunities available to Wallace. He and his brothers and sisters were directly engaged in the struggle for survival. Alfred left school at age thirteen to help an older brother in the surveying and architecture business. Quitting school after only six years meant primarily that his sleep would no longer be troubled by nightmares brought on by having to assist in the teaching of reading, writing, diction, and arithmetic. Wallace made up for his limited education by reading widely, thanks to his father's sometime job as librarian, and membership in a book club. It was surveying rather than books that stimulated Wallace's interest in mathematics, geology, and especially botany. Wallace later gave thanks to poverty for forcing him to work outdoors (Wallace, 1905, vol. 1, pp. 195–196).

In 1843 Wallace's father died, and each member of the family was forced to look out for himself. Wallace went to London for no particular reason. He was then twenty-one, shy, without prospects, and by his own assessment, devoid of any talent other than an appreciation of beauty and a sense of justice. Eventually he was so desperate that he went to Leicester to return to teaching. His enthusiasm for teaching English, writing, arithmetic, Latin, surveying, and mapping was still lacking, but so was his enthusiasm for hunger. And Leicester had the advantage of a good library where he could lose himself in natural history. It was at the Leicester Library that Wallace met H. W. Bates (1825–1892), who convinced him to add entomology to his interests. It was also there that Wallace read two books which were to affect him profoundly: Humboldt's *Personal Narratives* and Malthus's *Essay on Population*. It was also there that Wallace acquired a lifelong interest in hypnotism, psychic research, and spiritualism, which seems so out of place in a man who only briefly as a child felt "something like religious fervour."[7]

During the second year at Leicester Wallace's brother died, leaving him a surveying business which was thriving because of railroads. Back in Wales, Wallace prospered for a while, continued his study of natural history, gave popular-science lectures to workmen, and read Darwin's account of the voyage of the *Beagle*. Soon, however, there was a financial panic, and as relief from the onerous task of collecting debts, Wallace began to dream of repeating the journeys of Humboldt and Darwin.

VOYAGES

When Darwin returned from his ramble with Sedgwick in August 1831, there was a letter from Henslow inviting Darwin to sail around the world as naturalist aboard the *Beagle:*

I [Henslow] have been asked . . . to recommend . . . a Naturalist as companion to Captain Fitz-Roy, employed by Government to survey the southern extremity of

America. I have stated that I consider you to be the best qualified person I know of who is likely to undertake such a situation. I state this not on the supposition of your being a *finished* naturalist, but as amply qualified for collecting, observing, and noting, anything worthy to be noted in Natural History. . . .Captain Fitz-Roy wants a man (I understand) more as a companion than a mere collector, and would not take any one, however good a naturalist, who was not recommended to him likewise as a gentleman.

Although Darwin's function would be primarily to prevent the captain's going bonkers from loneliness, Henslow considered it such a fine opportunity that he nearly accepted it himself. Hence the careful wording of the second sentence.

Darwin was still a dependent on his father, and reluctantly turned down the offer when Robert expressed several objections. (In those days it was not unusual for young men to heed the advice of their parents.) Robert Darwin did allow the loophole that if Charles could find "any man of common sense" who would recommend it, he would give his consent. Fortunately for science, Charles's uncle, Josiah Wedgwood, had such good sense. In thus extracting permission from his father, Charles tried to console him by pointing out that he would have to be "deuced clever to spend more than [his] allowance whilst on board the *Beagle.*" Robert had probably heard that one before, for he replied, "But they all tell me you are very clever."[8]

Actually, any father should have been concerned about a son undertaking a voyage of several years on the *Beagle.* Sailors referred to boats of her class as "coffins" because of their habit of becoming swamped in heavy seas. She was so rotten that the departure had to be delayed to rebuild the decks. Nor was Captain Fitz-Roy altogether seaworthy. At twenty-six, only four years older than Darwin, he had already shown signs of the instability common among sea captains. Class-consciousness and discipline prevented captains from fraternizing with other officers and the crew; hence, Fitz-Roy's need for a companion of his social class who was not am employee. Before departure Darwin was completely charmed by this *"beau ideal* of a Captain," but at sea he discovered that "some part of the organization of his brain wants mending" (Himmelfarb, 1962, p. 61). Darwin, the liberal Whig, and Fitz-Roy the Tory, clashed mainly over the latter's defense of slavery, but they managed to end the five-year journey in close quarters cordially.[9]

Darwin left on the *Beagle* in the last days of 1831 and returned on 2 October 1836. Enough has been written about the voyage—including Darwin's still-popular *Voyage of the Beagle*—to make a detailed treatment unnecessary here.[10] However, we must note the observations which Darwin, himself, considered important in leading him from orthodoxy to revolution:

> During the voyage of the *Beagle* I had been deeply impressed by discovering in the Pampean formation great fossil animals covered with armour like that on

the existing armadillos; secondly, by the manner in which closely allied animals replace one another in proceeding southwards over the Continent; and thirdly, by the South American character of most of the productions of the Galápagos archipelago, and more especially by the manner in which they differ slightly on each island of the group; none of these islands appearing to be very ancient in a geological sense. It was evident that such facts as these, as well as many others, could be explained on the supposition that species gradually become modified; and the subject haunted me. (Barlow, 1958, pp. 118–119)

These words, written four decades after the voyage, present a misleading picture of Darwin immediately grasping the inescapable evidence of evolution. However, his field notes and *Diary* written on the spot contain scarcely a hint that Darwin was considering evolution. Even after four years of the voyage Darwin accepted the conventional explanation for the origin and distribution of species: that God created different species at different "centers of creation" from which they dispersed. After "industriously collecting all the animals, plants, insects & reptiles" of Charles Island in the Galápagos on 26 and 27 September 1835, Darwin noted in his *Diary* that "it will be very interesting to find from future comparisons to what district or 'centre of creation' the organized beings of this archipelago must be attached" (Barlow, 1934, p. 337). As late as 18 January 1836 Darwin was inspired by the marsupials of Australia to think again about centers of creation:

I had been lying on a sunny bank & was reflecting on the strange character of the animals of this country as compared to the rest of the World. An unbeliever in every thing beyond his own reason might exclaim, "Surely two distinct Creators must have been at work; their object, however, has been the same & certainly the end in each case is complete." [But] it cannot be thought so. The one hand has surely worked throughout the universe. A Geologist perhaps would suggest that the periods of Creation have been distinct & remote the one from the other; that the Creator rested in his labor. (Barlow, 1934, p. 383)[11]

Why did it take Darwin so long to see what now seems so obvious? Was he reluctant, as an "unfinished" naturalist, to propose such a revolutionary idea? I think not, for as a raw recruit in geology he had not hesitated to theorize. He confessed his tendencies to the cautious Henslow before the voyage: "As yet I have only indulged in hypotheses, but they are such powerful ones that I suppose, if they were put into action for but one day, the world would come to an end." On the voyage he conceived a new (and still accepted) theory of the formation of coral reefs before he had even seen a coral reef![12]

There are perhaps two important reasons why Darwin did not immediately convert to evolutionism on the *Beagle*. First, one's world view resists being transformed by an undigested mass of observations. Darwin was raised and educated in a culture permeated by creationism and natural theology, which were just as indelibly embossed within the grooves of his brain as evolutionism and natural selection are within ours. (It is true that Darwin embraced uniformitarianism almost immediately, but his education in catastrophist geology had been only brief.) The candid evolutionist of today must admit that if he were shown the undisputed remains of the Garden of Eden and Noah's Ark, he would still require some time to adjust his thinking to conform to Genesis.

Secondly, Darwin's chief interest aboard the *Beagle* was geology. Henslow had given Darwin the first volume of Lyell's *Principles of Geology* as a going-away present, warning him not to believe a word of it. Darwin ignored the warning and became the first to see the New World with Lyellian eyes. Darwin devoted most of his energies to collecting as many geological facts as possible and fitting them into the new conceptual scheme. Moreover, he saw the opportunity to make a name for himself in geology by creating new theories—building "geological castles in the air," as he put it. Biological specimens could be packed away for later study in England; not even Darwin would have hoped that they would prove as revolutionary as his geological insights.[13]

When Darwin returned in 1836, Wallace was still a lad of thirteen, just beginning to learn surveying. Twelve years of poverty, relieved by beetles and botanizing, lay between him and his own voyage to South America. By 1847 Wallace's favorite subject had become the "variations, arrangements, distribution, etc., of species." Robert Chambers's sensational *Vestiges of the Natural History of Creation* (1844) had suggested to him that evolution might explain these phenomena.

> Although I saw that it really offered no explanation of the process of change of species, yet the view that change was effected, not through any unimaginable process, but through the known laws of reproduction commended itself to me as perfectly satisfactory and as affording the first steps towards a more complete and explanatory theory.

In a letter to Bates late in 1845 Wallace (revealing an intuitive grasp of the hypothetico-deductive approach) wrote that the evolutionism of the *Vestiges* "furnishes both an incitement to the collection of facts & an object to which to apply them when collected." In 1847 Wallace and Bates began seriously to plan for a voyage to South America to gather facts "towards solving the problem of the origin of species." To finance the trip they intended to sell duplicates of their collections in London to other victims of beetle mania. They met in London the following spring to study the British Museum collections and to buy books and equipment, and departed aboard the *Mischief* on 20 April 1848.[14]

For more than four years Wallace explored the Amazon and Rio Negro, penetrating deep into areas previously unknown to Europeans. Wallace seldom mentions it in his books, but he could easily have vanished without a trace on numerous occasions. In contrast to Darwin's frequent complaints of illness, Wallace's letters and books usually ignore his suffering from tropical diseases. (His brother died of yellow fever shortly after joining Alfred in 1851.) As if he had not suffered enough during the four years in South America, Wallace's ship burned on the return voyage in 1852. Most of his hard-won collection was lost, but Wallace was rescued after ten days adrift in a small boat. Back in England later that year Wallace found that he had earned just enough from his expedition to support himself while preparing for the next one. He spent the next two years writing the *Narrative of Travels on the Amazon and Rio Negro,* a small book on palm trees, and several brief reports. He also continued to study in the British Museum, where he first met Darwin briefly in early 1854.

By this time South America was relatively crawling with collectors, so Wallace chose for his next venture the Malay archipelago. Between 1854 and 1862 he travelled more than 20,000 kilometers among the Moluccas, Borneo, Sumatra, Java, New Guinea, Celebes and many smaller islands. Wallace's numerous scientific contributions made his reputation and led to correspondence with the leading biologists of England, including Darwin. Both Darwin and Wallace were impressed by the differences in species on opposite sides of geological barriers like seas, rivers, and mountain ranges. For both, such evidence would provide the first solid clues in solving the problem of the origin of species.[15]

THE CONCEPTION OF EVOLUTION BY NATURAL SELECTION

Darwin's five-year voyage around the world had changed him so markedly that his father greeted him with the observation that "the shape of his head is quite altered." But that was nothing compared to the changes taking place *within* his head. Further alterations occurred in the next few years while Darwin was creating the theory that altered all our heads. As a seasoned naturalist of twenty-eight, Darwin had discovered a life that was more fun than that of an idle sporting man, or even that of a clergyman. He forgot his plans to become a minister, while spending much of his last month on the *Beagle* thinking about religion. Somewhere on the Atlantic Darwin jettisoned his belief in the literal Genesis, clearing his mind of obstacles which made Sedgwick and other pious scientists blind to evolution[16]

Soon after returning to England Darwin found himself being transformed from a robust sailor to a semi-invalid. Nearly every day for the next thirty years would be interrupted by vomiting and weakness which prevented travel and socializing, and reduced his working time to only a few hours a day. When Freud was in fashion some psychohistorians diagnosed Darwin's illness as the result of stress caused by the symbolic slaying of God with the sword of evolution, which was a substitute for the Oedipal conflict with his father. One can only admire such a confident analysis of a man who never submitted to the couch. After studying Darwin's case as well as one can after more than a century, Colp (1977, p. 141) was able to conclude only that Darwin's "feelings about his evolutionary theory were a major cause of his illness."[17]

In 1839 Darwin underwent a more felicitous change—marriage to his cousin, Emma Wedgwood. Darwin talked himself into matrimony by a sort of double-entry bookkeeping. In one column he listed the liabilities and assets of not marrying: "freedom to go where one liked—choice of Society *and little of it.* . . .Not forced to visit relatives. . . ." In the opposite column he listed the consequences of marrying: "Children—(if it please God)—constant companion, (friend in old age) who will feel interested in one, object to be beloved and played with—better than a dog anyhow." (But remember Darwin's great love of dogs.) In the summation Darwin reviewed the disadvantages of marriage—"poor slave, you will be worse than a negro." But finally the romantic in him won out. "Never mind, trust to chance—keep a sharp look out.—There is many a happy slave—." Darwin was more tactful in letters to Emma. Shortly before the wedding he wrote to her, "I think you will humanize me, and soon teach me there is greater happiness than building theories and accumulating facts in silence and solitude." She was, in fact, a "wise adviser and cheerful comforter throughout life."[18]

Before we come to the greatest event in Darwin's life it is worth a few more lines of preparation to remind ourselves that the gulf separating the Darwinian view from that prevailing in the late 1830s was as wide as that which now prevents evolutionists and creationists from engaging in meaningful dialogue. Many historians have attempted to minimize the extent of the Darwinian revolution by pointing to his precursors as evidence that evolutionism was already "in the air." Lest we make the same mistake, we should review the prevailing ideas of the origin of species prior to the publication of Darwin's and Wallace's theory.

As we saw in the last chapter, Darwin was indeed not the first to suggest evolution or natural selection. However, it is one thing for prior evolutionists to have proposed the idea, but quite another thing to have convinced scientists. At the exalted height occupied by established science, what filled the air was not evolutionism, but special creation, design, and fixity of species. Fossils, geographical distribution of species, comparative anatomy, and all that Darwin taught us to see as the result of evolution were then seen as the proofs of God's handiwork. Darwin succeeded in erecting a new framework for these ideas by showing the superiority of evolution as an explanation. This raises the question of why other scientists, especially geologists, were so slow to accept the reasonable suggestions of Lamarck, Erasmus Darwin, Matthew, and others. It was not because they regarded creationism and catastrophism as entirely satisfactory; even fundamentalists must have been embarrassed by the need for a whole series of Edens to replenish the Earth after each catastrophe. Part of the explanation for their reluctance was a conservative social climate which was hostile to ideas associated with the Enlightenment. Another reason was that most theories of evolution were not satisfactory as explanations of how evolution could have occurred. Of course Genesis is not a satisfactory explanation either, but at least it had the dignity of age.[19]

Darwin's and Wallace's studies of geographical distribution lose all significance unless one appreciates how they conflicted with prevailing views. Why would God have found it necessary to create a distinct variety or species of finch on each of the Galápagos islands, which are so similar to each other? And if God did go to the trouble of making special finches for the Galápagos, why would he have made them more similar to birds on the mainland of South America than to birds on other Pacific islands? The presence of continental birds on islands contradicted the notion that God created each species for its habitat. Certainly it is within the power of the Almighty to establish as many centers of creation as needed, but as an increasing multitude of centers had to be hypothesized there was a conflict with the underlying faith in the simplicity of nature. The solution of Darwin and Wallace met the demand for simplicity: a few South American finches arrived by chance on the Galápagos, then evolved in accordance with the new selection pressures imposed on the islands. Slight differences in the individuals on each island led to the different species now present, by the process of evolutionary divergence. Lyell lived at a happy time for this argument, for he provided the vast lengths of time required for such evolution.[20]

However, it is still doubtful whether Darwin and Wallace could have prevailed without an alternative to the argument of design. For much of the early nineteenth century scientists, under the banner of natural theology, had awed the public with the striking and beautiful adaptations supposed to be the proof that God had designed each species individually. Darwin and Wallace had to explain how species came to be adapted without a supernatural designer. This is the significance of natural selection. In a way, Darwin and Wallace should have been grateful to the natural theologians for emphasizing adaptation; they had only to replace design as a final cause with natural selection as an efficient cause.[21]

There is one last question: Why was natural selection overlooked so long, but eventually accepted so readily? It is not more intuitively obvious than design or inheritance of acquired character, and we shall see that there are logical problems with it as a scientific theory. The way for natural selection was undoubtedly prepared by the *Essay on the Principle of Population* by Thomas Malthus (1766–1834). This essay, first published in 1798 and enlarged in 1803, proposed that a limited supply of food would always dictate a "struggle for existence," even if war and disease were eradicated. This is because population tends to grow geometrically, while the means of subsistence increases only arithmetically. That is, an uncontrolled population might double in twenty-five years, but the amount of food and other resources could seldom double in that time. Darwin and Wallace both credited Malthus with providing the key to natural selection by suggesting the inevitability of a struggle in which only the fittest survive.[22]

Malthus presents us with another enigma in the chain of circumstances leading to the Darwinian revolution. That is the mystery of why it took forty years for someone to see the evolutionary implications of the Malthusian Principle—a principle that was common knowledge, widely used as an excuse for laissez-faire economic policies. Some historians maintain that there is no enigma—that this is just another case of Darwin capitalizing on an idea that was already in the air. Marxist historians, inclined to see scientific developments on a grander scale than mere individual creativity, have been especially prone to speak of Darwinism as merely "an extension to the animal and vegetable world of *laisser-faire* economics" (to use Bertrand Russell's phrase). It is undeniable that Malthus played a major role in shaping the zeitgeist in which evolutionism arose in Britain, but it is as erroneous to say that the Malthusian view was the only source of Darwinism as it would be to say that it played no role at all.

The comparative historical approach shows what an oversimplification it is to portray Darwinism as a footnote to economics. Such an explanation would be hard enough to defend in light of the independent creation of the same theory by such diverse characters as Matthew the Chartist, Darwin the upper-class "liberal or radical," and Wallace the socialist. It becomes impossible in view of the conception of natural selection by Empedocles, Maupertuis, and Diderot. A Marxist might have predicted the conception of natural selection by the Tory Wells, but not by the other British evolutionists, and certainly not by an ancient Sicilian or Enlightened Frenchmen.

Historians who make such simpleminded assertions ignore the fact that the Malthusian Principle was intended and interpreted as an argument *against* change. Malthus first wrote his essay to rebut the Enlightenment delusion that human progress can grow out of social reform, and later revised it to justify the social and economic measures for dealing with the population explosion which resulted from the Industrial Revolution. Malthus reasoned that progress is impossible unless there is an unlimited food supply, so policies to improve the plight of the poor were misguided so long as total food supply remained the same. Advocates of laissez-faire could thus ignore starving children in good conscience. Many scientists, notably Lyell, perceived the biological implications of the Malthusian Principle as an argument *against* evolution. Since species were already well adapted for survival, any tendency to change would result in extermination. As R. M. Young (1969, p. 116) has said, "far from being a mechanism for change, [the Malthusian Principle] was a defense of the *status quo* both in nature and in society." Only by individual creative insight were Darwin and Wallace able to see in it an explanation for adaptation and evolution.[23]

By this time we should be able to appreciate the development of Darwin's and Wallace's theory of evolution by natural selection. For Darwin, at least, the record of this development has been abundant since the rediscovery and publication of his notebooks on "Transmutation of Species," written between July 1837 and July 1839. These notebooks are especially valuable because, unlike the autobiographical accounts of the theory, Darwin did not intend them to be read by anyone else. (Indeed he would have been amazed that anyone could decipher his handwriting.) On the other hand, since they were not intended as a chronicle of his daily thoughts, it is likely that he omitted many important ideas which were too obvious to note. Thus the notebooks require interpretation, and laborers in the "Darwin industry" will be mining them for decades to come. A consensus on the detailed route to Darwin's final theory has not yet emerged, but (to the chagrin of some revisionists) there is general agreement with the version Darwin presented to the public decades later. At the very least the notebooks reveal an intellect groping with a confusing array of facts, rather than a scoundrel stealing the theories of others. Instead of attempting a synthesis or analysis of recent studies, it therefore seems justified and more economical of space simply to elaborate on Darwin's own account, as presented in his *Autobiography*.[24]

When Darwin stepped off the *Beagle* he was immediately immersed in a sea of work. Examining the collections he had shipped to Henslow required a few months at Cambridge. Then Darwin had to move to "dirty, odious London" to arrange for their further study by specialists. He also set to work on his *Journal of Researches* (1839), which is now the popular *Voyage of the Beagle*. In addition, he supervised the production of the five-volume *Zoology of the Voyage of H. M. S. Beagle* (1839–1843), wrote an important but unfortunate paper "On the Parallel Roads of Glen Roy" (1839), presented two lesser papers at the Geological Society, and was prevailed upon to become Secretary of that society. As if this were not enough to kill even a well man, Darwin also began a book on volcanoes and coral reefs which eventually made three volumes, published between 1842 and 1846, and found time to read Wordsworth and Coleridge. And, oh yes, he courted and married Emma.

Darwin already had fears of a short life, and was seemingly driven to accomplish all he could while he could.[25]

Darwin states that his reviewing of the *Beagle* collections convinced him of the transmutation of species. The origin of species was not entirely a separate problem from geology, but we may still wonder that Darwin allowed himself to be diverted from volcanoes, coral reefs, and glacial action, on which he was gaining reknown. I believe G. J. Grinnell (1974) has hit upon the major stimulus for Darwin's interest in transmutation—the jarring realization that each of the Galápagos finches (now called Darwin's finches) was a distinct species. This was so jarring because it meant that each island would have been a separate "center of creation." Darwin had been so reluctant to imagine God hopping from island to island creating a separate species for each one that he insisted they were merely varieties, not even worth collecting. It was Captain Fitz-Roy who thought the finches were good species and who had them collected, because their diverse beaks illustrated the "admirable provision of Infinite Widsom by which each created thing is adapted to the place of which it is intended." "Fitz-Roy's finches" might be a more just name for them, for without Fitz-Roy, Darwin and the ornithologist John Gould (1804–1881) would not even have had specimens for study. Only after Gould sided with Fitz-Roy did Darwin grudgingly admit that the finches were distinct species. He quickly saw that admitting Gould's remarks implied that the finches had greatly changed after they arrived at their respective islands. "If there is the slightest foundation for these remarks the zoology of Archipelagoes will be well worth examining; for such facts would undermine the stability of species.[26]

Charles Darwin began to wonder why it was so difficult to answer the question whether the finches were species or varieties if species were separately created. Of course his grandfather and others had used that mystery as a basis for evolutionism, but Darwin was not content simply to accept their ideas. He began collecting facts on varieties and species in a notebook labelled B and entitled "Zoonomia." "In July [1837] opened first notebook on 'Transmutation of Species'—Had been greatly struck from about month of previous March on character of S. American fossils—& species on Galapagos Archipelago. These facts origin (especially latter) of all my views."[27]

Darwin described his manner of working in the *Autobiography:*

> After my return to England it appeared to me that by following the example of Lyell in Geology, and by collecting all facts which bore in any way on the variation of animals and plants under domestication and nature, some light might perhaps be thrown on the whole subject. My first notebook was opened in July 1837. I worked on true Baconian principles, and without any theory collected facts on a wholesale scale, more especially with respect to domesticated

productions, by printed enquiries, by conversation with skillful breeders and gardeners, and by extensive reading.

By the time Darwin wrote the above he had evidently forgotten that his notes were not entirely restricted to facts. Very early he speculated on the spontaneous generation of "monads" (Notebook B, pp. 18, 19), as if the development of his own theory were recapitulating previous stages in the development of evolutionism.[28]

Darwin was not about to jeopardize his blossoming career in geology by vainly announcing his views prematurely. He anticipated the probable reaction such a step would have provoked by alluding to the "persecution of early Astronomers," in Notebook C (p. 123). On 28 March 1837, when Darwin was presumably in the throes of conceiving his monumental insight, he opened a letter to his trusted mentor Henslow as follows: "I have been waiting to see if anything particular should occur to write about. But such has not been the case." In his *Journal of Researches* he allowed himself only veiled hints at transmutation of species. In order to obtain information without arousing suspicion he pretended even to his closest friends, Charles Lyell and William Darwin Fox, that he was merely writing a book with the innocent title "Varieties and Species."[29]

Darwin meant by "following the example of Lyell" that he tried to infer the causes of past changes in species by looking at the causes of present changes—namely artificial selection.

I soon perceived that selection was the keystone of man's success in making useful races of animals and plants. But how selection could be applied to organisms living in a state of nature remained for sometime a mystery to me.[30]

In October 1838 [actually 28 September 1838], that is, fifteen months after I had begun my systematic enquiry, I happened to read for amusement Malthus on *Population,* and being well prepared to appreciate the struggle for existence which everywhere goes on from long-continued observation of the habits of animals and plants, it at once struck me that under these circumstances favourable variations would tend to be preserved, and unfavourable ones to be destroyed. The result of this would be the formation of new species.[31]

Here, then, I had at last got a theory by which to work; but I was so anxious to avoid prejudice, that I determined not for some time to write even the briefest sketch of it. In June 1842 I first allowed myself the satisfaction of writing a very brief abstract of my theory in pencil in 35 pages; and this was enlarged during the summer of 1844 into one of 230 pages, which I had fairly copied out and still possess.[32]

But at that time I overlooked one problem of great importance; and it is astonishing to me, except on the principle of Columbus and his egg, how I could have overlooked it and its solution. This problem is the tendency in organic beings descended from the same stock to diverge in character as they become modified. That they have diverged greatly is obvious from the manner in which species of all kinds can be classed under genera, genera under families, families under suborders, and so forth; and I can remember the very spot in the road, whilst in my carriage, when to my joy the solution occurred to me; and this was long after I had come to Down [in September 1842]. The solution, as I believe, is that the modified offspring of all dominant and increasing forms tend to become adapted to many and highly diversified places in the economy of nature.[33]

This last paragraph should puzzle many readers, since we now see divergence as a foregone conclusion once natural selection is admitted. The passage became especially puzzling after the discovery of Notebook B, in which Darwin sketched in early 1837 a "Tree of Nature" with radiating branches representing species. Gruber and Barrett (1974, pp. 117–118, 141–144) suggest that Darwin simply forgot this earlier idea of divergence and later rediscovered it. However, the "Tree of Nature" occurred during Darwin's monad phase, in which he must have thought of each limb as a randomly developing monad with its branches becoming species. At that time Darwin had no idea why the branches grew as they did, so that species became adapted to their environments. The distinctly remembered insight was probably Darwin's first realization of how natural selection shaped the Tree of Life by pruning the unfit twigs.

There is also an early reference to "wedging" in Notebook D135, where Darwin first mentions Malthus (Gruber and Barrett, 1974, p. 456). However, this "wedging" does not refer to a splitting of one species into two, but to "a force like a hundred thousand wedges trying [to] force every kind of adapted structure into the gaps in the economy of nature, or rather forming gaps by thrusting out weaker ones." The violence of the metaphor—so out of harmony with natural theology, Romanticism and, in a sense, uniformitarianism—suggests another way in which Malthus had influenced Darwin.

Sometime after 1844, then, Darwin had the answer to the "mystery of mysteries." He had a purely scientific explanation for the origin of species, adaptation, and divergence. And, unlike Patrick Matthew, Darwin knew he had something important, for he left instructions with Emma for publishing the 1844 Essay in case he died. Nowadays a scientist in Darwin's position, pressured to obtain grants, would dash off a quick note to *Science* or *Nature* and stay by the phone for a call from Stockholm. This is essentially what Wallace later did, except, of course, neither of those journals, nor the phone, nor the Nobel Prize had yet been invented. Darwin, however, showed his Essay only to Joseph Hooker (1817–1911), with whom he had begun to collaborate soon after the voyage. Hooker was unimpressed. Darwin then proceeded to sacrifice eight years from 1846 to 1854 to the anatomy and classification of thousand of barnacles. This work established Darwin as a sound inductive biologist, but even he wondered whether it was worth so much time.[34]

Darwin's long delay from 1844 to 1859 has been attributed to several causes: fear of being branded a materialist, fear of offending his wife's religious sensitivities, failure to convince Hooker and others of his theory, and so on. All of these may have contributed, but it is also significant that *Vestiges of the Natural History of Creation* came out in the same year Darwin wrote his Essay. That, alone, would have convinced a prudent scientist not to venture upon the stormy sea of transmutation without some weighty facts for ballast. No one can read the *Origin of Species* and not be painfully aware of the extensive compiling of facts and the experimentation Darwin evidently felt compelled to do during his long "wait." It is all the more impressive considering that he had only a few good working hours per day, and that the *Origin* is only an "abstract" of a work which would have been four times as long.[35]

What finally moved Darwin to begin this big book in May 1856 was the urging of Lyell, who was first let in on Darwin's secret in April of that year. Lyell's concern was due to his having read Wallace's recent paper from Sarawak "On the Law which Has Regulated the Introduction of New Species." This law, that "every species has come into existence coincident in both space and time with a pre-existing closely allied species," was a clear warning that there was now a second evolutionist with the experience and ability to arrive at the same theory as Darwin. Darwin reluctantly considered writing a brief paper to establish priority, but the words multiplied to become his "big book."[36]

As we saw earlier, Wallace had been leaning toward evolutionism since 1845, when he read *Vestiges*. His inclinations were reinforced by the distributions of species in South America (including Darwin's description of the Galápagos) and on the Malay archipelago. The latter case was especially striking, there being a sharp line (now known as Wallace's Line) separating the Australian species of the eastern islands from the Oriental or Indian types to the west. The strange character of the Australian animals had been noticed by others (including Darwin in the passage already quoted from his diary of 1836), but Wallace was not burdened by religious biases toward seeing this as evidence for a center of creation. Soon after the 1855 Sarawak paper, Wallace began collecting notes for his own book, which would apparently have been a refutation of Lyell's antievolutionism. One of the major arguments Wallace intended to use was the difficulty of distinguishing between species and varieties. Beddall (1968) presents the best analysis of Wallace's thinking which led to his conception of natural selection in February 1858. For our purposes, however, we may let Wallace speak for himself.[37]

> At the time in question I was suffering from a sharp attack of intermittent fever, and every day during the cold and succeeding hot fits had to lie down for

several hours, during which time I had nothing to do but to think over any subjects then particularly interesting to me. One day something brought to my recollection Malthus's "Principles of Population," which I had read about twelve years before. I thought of his clear exposition of "the positive checks to increase"—disease, accidents, war, and famine—which keep down the population of savage races to so much lower an average than that of more civilized peoples. It then occurred to me that these causes or their equivalents are continually acting in the case of animals also; and as animals usually breed much more rapidly than does mankind, the destruction every year from these causes must be enormous in order to keep down the numbers of each species, since they evidently do not increase regularly from year to year, as otherwise the world would long ago have been densely crowded with those that breed most quickly. Vaguely thinking over the enormous and constant destruction which this implied, it occurred to me to ask the question, Why do some die and some live? And the answer was clearly, that on the whole the best fitted live. From the effects of disease the most healthy escaped; from enemies, the strongest, the swiftest, or the most cunning; from famine, the best hunters or those with the best digestion; and so on. Then it suddenly flashed upon me that this self-acting process would necessarily *improve the race,* because in every generation the inferior would inevitably be killed off and the superior would remain—that is, *the fittest would survive.* Then at once I seemed to see the whole effect of this, that when changes of land and sea, or of climate, or of food-supply, or of enemies occurred—and we know that such changes have always been taking place—and considering the amount of individual variation that my experience as a collector had shown me to exist, then it followed that all the changes necessary for the adaptation of the species to the changing conditions would be brought about; and as great changes in the environment are always slow, there would be ample time for the change to be effected in the survival of the best fitted in every generation. In this way every part of an animal's organization could be modified exactly as required, and in the very process of this modification the unmodified would die out, and thus the *definite* characters and the clear *isolation* of each new species would be explained. The more I thought over it the more I became convinced that I had at length found the long-sought-for law of nature that solved the problem of the origin of species. For the next hour I thought over the deficiencies in the theories of Lamarck and the author of the "Vestiges," and I saw that my new theory supplemented these views and obviated every important difficulty. I waited anxiously for the termination of my fit so that I might at once make notes for a paper on the subject. The same evening I did this pretty fully, and on the two succeeding evenings wrote it out carefully in order to send it to Darwin by the next post, which would leave in a day or two.

Darwin received Wallace's paper in late spring of 1858 (McKinney, 1972, p. 139). His distress is apparent in a letter to Lyell:

Your words have come true with a vengeance—that I should be forestalled. . . .Please return me the MS., which he does not say he wishes me to publish, but I shall of course, at once write and offer to send to any journal. So all my originality, whatever it may amount to, will be smashed, though my book, if it will ever have any value, will not be deteriorated; as all the labour consists in the application of the theory.

After struggling with his conscience for a week Darwin suggested to Lyell and Hooker that they might publish parts of his Essay and a letter to Asa Gray, along with Wallace's paper. Darwin, however, left the matter entirely in the hands of these two upstanding gentlemen. The death from smallpox of his retarded son a few days later left him in no condition to control events in any case. On the first of July, 1858, Lyell and Hooker presented to the Linnean Society both Darwin's and Wallace's contributions, which comprise this chapter's selection.[38]

It was not clear even to Darwin whether he was intending to steal a portion of the credit due to Wallace. As it turned out, it would have been only petit larceny. The Linnean Society papers were almost completely ignored, with even the president of the society summarizing 1858 as a year unmarked "by any of those striking discoveries which at once revolutionize" science (Beddall, 1968, pp. 304–305). It was the *Origin of Species,* published as an abstract, of the "big book" in November 1859, that gave the name "Darwinism" to the theory discovered independently by Matthew, Wallace, and Darwin. Wallace certainly did not feel that he had been cheated. He consistently referred to the theory as Darwin's, in spite of Darwin's objections; he dedicated a book to Darwin; and he entitled a collection of his American lectures *Darwinism.* Darwin was equally generous to Wallace, as he could well afford to be. Seldom have such great scientists been such great men. Those who have come to think of J. D. Watson's *Double Helix* as the standard of scientific ethics will have the cockles of their hearts warmed by reading the letters between Darwin and Wallace.[39]

In the space available I cannot do justice to the breadth and depth of reasoning in the *Origin of Species.* I can only hope that some will be moved to read this classic, although I must warn that most readers of the *Origin* will agree with Darwin that it "is a very good book, but oh! my gracious, it is tough reading." It would also take too much space even to summarize Darwin's subsequent works, which include books on fertilization of orchids, the expression of emotions, behavior of plants, the action of earthworms, and the descent of man. Wallace, too, made subsequent contributions too numerous to mention. It is especially regrettable that I cannot enliven this chapter with Wallace's cranky campaigns against vaccination, the fundamentalist Flat-Earth Society, belief in extraterrestrial life, and in favor of land nationalization, séances, and freedom of and from religion.[40]

The task of this chapter is essentially completed, and we should be ready to see whether we have learned anything about the creation of the theory of evolution by natural selection, and about scientific creativity in general. If what I have previously said is valid—that no supposed basis for Darwin's creativity should be admitted unless it was also present in Wallace's case— then there are only three possibly essential roots to the theory:

1. Darwin's and Wallace's appreciation of variation within species and the difficulty of distinguishing among varieties and species.

2. Their understanding of geographical distribution of species, witnessed directly and with a Lyellian perspective. (Matthew, too, was a student of the distribution of trees and people, but he was not a Lyellian.)

3. Their appreciation, thanks to Malthus, of the struggle for survival among members of the same species.[41]

This example is consistent with what I have previously suggested about creativity; namely:

1. Theories are realized "in a sudden flash of insight . . . we hardly know *how* or *whence* (Wallace's words, quoted in George, 1964, p. 280). This is not to say that the underlying process, about which we know little, may not require a long gestation.

2. There is no conscious method for the creation of theories, but induction, deduction, and experimentation are used to test them.

3. Theories are influenced by the zeitgeist, both positively and negatively. In the case of Darwinism, the social theories of Malthus had a positive effect on the conception of natural selection, but prevailing ideas of creationism had a negative effect on evolutionism.

On the Tendency of Species to Form Varieties; and on the Perpetuation of Varieties and Species by Natural Means of Selection. By Charles Darwin, Esq., F. R. S., F. L. S., & F. G. S., and Alfred Wallace, Esq. Communicated by Sir Charles Lyell, F. R. S., F. L. S., and J. D. Hooker, Esq., M. D., V. P. R. S., F. L. S., &c. *Journal of the Linnean Society of London* (Zoology) 3 (1859) 45–62.[42]

My Dear Sir,—The accompanying papers, which we have the honour of communicating to the Linnean Society, and which all relate to the same subject, viz. the Laws which affect the Production of Varieties, Races, and Species, contain the results of the investigations of two indefatigable naturalists, Mr. Charles Darwin and Mr. Alfred Wallace.

These gentlemen having, independently and unknown to one another, conceived the same very ingenious theory to account for the appearance and perpetuation of varieties and of specific forms on our planet, may both fairly claim the merit of being original thinkers in this important line of inquiry; but neither of them having published his views, though Mr. Darwin has for many years past been repeatedly urged by us to do so, and both authors having now unreservedly placed their papers in our hands, we think it would best promote the interests of science that a selection from them should be laid before the Linnean Society.

Taken in the order of their dates, they consist of:—

1. Extracts from a MS. work on Species, by Mr. Darwin, which was sketched in 1839, and copied in 1844, when the copy was read by Dr. Hooker, and its contents afterwards communicated to Sir Charles Lyell. The first Part is devoted to "The Variation of Organic Beings under Domestication and in their Natural State;" and the second chapter of that Part, from which we propose to read to the Society the extracts referred to, is headed, "On the Variation of Organic Beings in a state of Nature; on the Natural Means of Selection; on the Comparison of Domestic Races and true Species."

2. An abstract of a private letter addressed to Professor Asa Gray, of Boston, U.S., in October 1857, by Mr. Darwin, in which he repeats his views, and which shows that these remained unaltered from 1839 to 1857.

3. An Essay by Mr. Wallace, entitled "On the Tendency of Varieties to depart indefinitely from the Original Type." This was written at Ternate in February 1858, for the perusal of his friend and correspondent Mr. Darwin, and sent to him with the expressed wish that it should be forwarded to Sir Charles Lyell, if Mr. Darwin thought it sufficiently novel and interesting. So highly did Mr. Darwin appreciate the value of the views therein set forth, that he proposed, in a letter to Sir Charles Lyell, to obtain Mr. Wallace's consent to allow the Essay to be published as soon as possible. Of this step we highly approved, provided Mr. Darwin did not withhold from the public, as he was strongly inclined to do (in favor of Mr. Wallace), the memoir which he had himself written on the same subject, and which, as before stated, one of us had perused in 1844, and the contents of which we had both of us been privy to for many years. On representing this to Mr. Darwin, he gave us permission to make what use we thought proper of his memoir, &c.; and in adopting our present course, of presenting it to the Linnean Society, we have explained to him that we are not solely considering the relative claims to priority of himself and his friend, but the interests of science generally; for we feel it to be desirable that views founded on a wide deduction from facts, and matured by years of reflection, should constitute at once a goal from which others may start, and that, while the scientific world is waiting for the appearance

of Mr. Darwin's complete work, some of the leading results of his labours, as well as those of his able correspondent, should together be laid before the public.

We have the honor to be yours very obediently,

Charles Lyell
Jos. D. Hooker

J. J. Bennett, Esq.,
Secretary of the Linnean Society

I. Extract from an Unpublished Work on Species, by C. Darwin, Esq., Consisting of a Portion of a Chapter Entitled, "On the Variation of Organic Beings in a State of Nature; on the Natural Means of Selection; on the Comparison of Domestic Races and True Species"

De Candolle, in an eloquent passage, has declared that all nature is at war, one organism with another, or with external nature. Seeing the contented face of nature, this may at first well be doubted; but reflection will inevitably prove it to be true. The war, however, is not constant, but recurrent in a slight degree at short periods, and more severely at occasional more distant periods; and hence its effects are easily overlooked. It is the doctrine of Malthus applied in most cases with tenfold force. As in every climate there are seasons, for each of its inhabitants, of greater and less abundance, so all annually breed; and the moral restraint which in some small degree checks the increase of mankind is entirely lost. Even slow-breeding mankind has doubled in twenty-five years; and if he could increase his food with greater ease, he would double in less time. But for animals without artificial means, the amount of food for each species must, *on an average,* be constant, whereas the increase of all organisms tends to be geometrical, and in a vast majority of cases at an enormous ratio. Suppose in a certain spot there are eight pairs of birds, and that *only* four pairs of them annually (including double hatches) rear only four young, and that these go on rearing their young at the same rate, then at the end of seven years (a short life, excluding violent deaths, for any bird) there will be 2048 birds, instead of the original sixteen. As this increase is quite impossible, we must conclude either that birds do not rear nearly half their young, or that the average life of a bird is, from accident, not nearly seven years. Both checks probably concur. The same kind of calculation applied to all plants and animals affords results more or less striking, but in very few instances more striking than in man.

Many practical illustrations of this rapid tendency to increase are on record, among which, during peculiar seasons, are the extraordinary numbers of certain animals; for instance, during the years 1826 to 1828, in La Plata, when from drought some millions of cattle perished, the whole country actually *swarmed* with mice. Now I think it cannot be doubted that during the breeding-season all the mice (with the exception of a few males or females in excess) ordinarily pair, and therefore that this astounding increase during three years must be attributed to a greater number than usual surviving the first year, and then breeding, and so on till the third year, when their numbers were brought down to their usual limits on the return of wet weather. Where man has introduced plants and animals into a new and favourable country, there are many accounts in how surprisingly few years the whole country has become stocked with them. This increase would necessarily stop as soon as the country was fully stocked; and yet we have every reason to believe, from what is known of wild animals, that *all* would pair in the spring. In the majority of cases it is most difficult to imagine where the checks fall—though generally, no doubt, on the seeds, eggs, and young; but when we remember how impossible, even in mankind (so much better known than any other animal), it is to infer from repeated casual observations what the average duration of life is, or to discover the different percentage of deaths to births in different countries, we ought to feel no surprise at our being unable to discover where the check falls in any animal or plant. It should always be remembered, that in most cases the checks are recurrent yearly in a small, regular degree, and in an extreme degree during unusually cold, hot, dry, or wet years, according to the constitution of the being in question. Lighten any check in the least degree, and the geometrical powers of increase in every organism will almost instantly increase the average number of the favoured species. Nature may be compared to a surface on which rest ten thousand sharp wedges touching each other and driven inwards by incessant blows. Fully to realize these views much reflection is requisite. Malthus on man should be studied; and all such cases as those of the mice in La Plata, of the cattle and horses when first turned out in South America, of the birds by our calculation, &c., should be well considered. Reflect on the enormous multiplying power *inherent and annually in action* in all animals; reflect on the countless seeds scattered by a hundred ingenious contrivances, year after year, over the whole face of the land; and yet we have every reason to suppose that the average percentage of each of the inhabitants of a country usually remains constant. Finally, let it be borne in mind that this average number of individuals (the external conditions remaining the same) in each country is kept up by recurrent struggles against other species or against external nature (as on the borders of the Arctic regions, where the cold checks life), and that ordinarily each individual of every species holds its place, either by its own struggle and capacity of acquiring nourishment in some period of Its lIfe, from the egg upwards; or by the struggle of its parents (in short-lived organisms, when the main check occurs at longer intervals) with other individuals of the *same* or *different* species.

But let the external conditions of a country alter. If in a small degree, the relative proportions of the inhabitants will in most cases simply be slightly changed; but let the number of inhabitants be small, as on an island, and free access to it from other countries be circumscribed, and let the change of conditions continue progressing (forming new stations), in such a case the original inhabitants must cease to be as perfectly adapted to the changed conditions as they were originally. It has been shown in a former part of this work, that such changes of external conditions would, from their acting on the reproductive system, probably cause the organization of those beings which were most affected to become, as under domestication, plastic. Now, can it be doubted, from the struggle each individual has to obtain subsistence, that any minute variation in structure, habits, or instincts, adapting that individual better to the new conditions, would tell upon its vigour and health? In the struggle it would have a better *chance* of surviving; and those of its offspring which inherited the variation, be it ever so slight, would also have a better *chance.* Yearly more are bred than can survive; the smallest grain in the balance, in the long run, must tell on which death shall fall, and which shall survive. Let this work of selection on the one hand, and death on the other, go on for a thousand generations, who will pretend to affirm that it would produce no effect, when we remember what, in a few years, Bakewell effected in cattle, and Western in sheep, by this identical principle of selection?

To give an imaginary example from changes in progress on an island:—let the organization of a canine animal which preyed chiefly on rabbits, but sometimes on hares, become slightly plastic; let these same changes cause the number of rabbits very slowly to decrease, and the number of hares to increase; the effect of this would be that the fox or dog would be driven to try to catch more hares: his organization, however, being slightly plastic, those individuals with the lightest forms, longest limbs, and best eyesight, let the difference be ever so small, would be slightly favoured, and would tend to live longer, and to survive during that time of the year when food was scarcest; they would also rear more young, which would tend to inherit these slight peculiarities. The less fleet ones would be rigidly destroyed. I can see no more reason to doubt that these causes in a thousand generations would produce a marked effect, and adapt the form of the fox or dog to the catching of hares instead of rabbits, than that greyhounds can be improved by selection and careful breeding. So would it be with plants under similar circumstances. If the number of individuals of a species with plumed seeds could be increased by greater powers of dissemination within its own area (that is, if the check to increase fell chiefly on the seeds), those seeds which were provided with ever so little more down, would in the long run be most disseminated; hence a greater number of seeds thus formed would germinate, and would tend to produce plants inheriting the slightly better-adapted down.

Besides this natural means of selection, by which those individuals are preserved, whether in their egg, or larval, or mature state, which are best adapted to the place they fill in nature, there is a second agency at work in most unisexual animals, tending to produce the same effect, namely, the struggle of the males for the females. These struggles are generally decided by the law of battle, but in the case of birds, apparently, by the charms of their song, by their beauty or their power of courtship, as in the dancing rock-thrush of Guiana. The most vigorous and healthy males, implying perfect adaptation, must generally gain the victory in their contests. This kind of selection, however, is less rigorous than the other; it does not require the death of the less successful, but gives to them fewer descendants. The struggle falls, moreover, at a time of year when food is generally abundant, and perhaps the effect chiefly produced would be the modification of the secondary sexual characters, which are not related to the power of obtaining food, or to defence from enemies, but to fighting with or rivalling other males. The result of this struggle amongst the males may be compared in some respects to that produced by those agriculturists who pay less attention to the careful selection of all their young animals, and more to the occasional use of a choice mate.

II. Abstract of a Letter from C. Darwin, Esq., to Prof. Asa Gray, Boston, U.S., dated Down, September 5th, 1857

1. It is wonderful what the principle of selection by man, that is the picking out of individuals with any desired quality, and breeding from them, and again picking out, can do. Even breeders have been astounded at their own results. They can act on differences inappreciable to an uneducated eye. Selection has been *methodically* followed in *Europe* for only the last half century; but it was occasionally, and even in some degree methodically, followed in most ancient times. There must have been also a kind of unconscious selection from a

remote period, namely in the preservation of the individual animals (without any thought of their offspring) most useful to each race of man in his particular circumstances. The "roguing," as nurserymen call the destroying of varieties which depart from their type, is a kind of selection. I am convinced that intentional and occasional selection has been the main agent in the production of our domestic races; but however this may be, its great power of modification has been indisputably shown in later times. Selection acts only by the accumulation of slight or greater variations, caused by external conditions, or by the mere fact that in generation the child is not absolutely similar to its parent. Man, by this power of accumulating variations, adapts living beings to his wants—may be said to make the wool of one sheep good for carpets, of another for cloth, &c.

2. Now suppose there were a being who did not judge by mere external appearances, but who could study the whole internal organization, who was never capricious, and should go on selecting for one object during millions of generations; who will say what he might not effect? In nature we have some *slight* variation occasionally in all parts; and I think it can be shown that changed conditions of existence is the main cause of the child not exactly resembling its parents; and in nature geology shows us what changes have taken place, and are taking place. We have almost unlimited time; no one but a practical geologist can fully appreciate this. Think of the Glacial period, during the whole of which the same species at least of shells have existed; there must have been during this period millions on millions of generations.

3. I think it can be shown that there is such an unerring power at work in *Natural Selection* (the title of my book), which selects exclusively for the good of each organic being. The elder De Candolle, W. Herbert, and Lyell have written excellently on the struggle for life; but even they have not written strongly enough. Reflect that every being (even the elephant) breeds at such a rate, that in a few years, or at most a few centuries, the surface of the earth would not hold the progeny of one pair. I have found it hard constantly to bear in mind that the increase of every single species is checked during some part of its life, or during some shortly recurrent generation. Only a few of those annually born can live to propagate their kind. What a trifling difference must often determine which shall survive, and which perish!

4. Now take the case of a country undergoing some change. This will tend to cause some of its inhabitants to vary slightly—not but that I believe most beings vary at all times enough for selection to act on them. Some of its inhabitants will be exterminated; and the remainder will be exposed to the mutual action of a different set of inhabitants,

which I believe to be far more important to the life of each being than mere climate. Considering the infinitely various methods which living beings follow to obtain food by struggling with other organisms, to escape danger at various times of life, to have their eggs or seeds disseminated, &c. &c., I cannot doubt that during millions of generations individuals of a species will be occasionally born with some slight variation, profitable to some part of their economy. Such individuals will have a better chance of surviving, and of propagating their new and slightly different structure; and the modification may be slowly increased by the accumulative action of natural selection to any profitable extent. The variety thus formed will either coexist with, or, more commonly, will exterminate its parent form. An organic being, like the woodpecker or misseltoe, may thus come to be adapted to a score of contingencies—natural selection accumulating those slight variations in all parts of its structure, which are in any way useful to it during any part of its life.

5. Multiform difficulties will occur to every one, with respect to this theory. Many can, I think, be satisfactorily answered. *Natura non facit saltum* answers some of the most obvious. The slowness of the change, and only a very few individuals undergoing change at any one time, answers others. The extreme imperfection of our geological records answers others.

6. Another principle, which may be called the principle of divergence, plays, I believe, an important part in the origin of species. The same spot will support more life if occupied by very diverse forms. We see this in the many generic forms in a square yard of turf, and in the plants or insects on any little uniform islet, belonging almost invariably to as many genera and families as species. We can understand the meaning of this fact amongst the higher animals, whose habits we understand. We know that it has been experimentally shown that a plot of land will yield a greater weight if sown with several species and genera of grasses, than if sown with only two or three species. Now, every organic being, by propagating so rapidly, may be said to be striving its utmost to increase in numbers. So it will be with the offspring of any species after it has become diversified into varieties, or sub-species, or true species. And it follows, I think, from the foregoing facts, that the varying offspring of each species will try (only few will succeed) to seize on as many and as diverse places in the economy of nature as possible. Each new variety or species, when formed, will generally take the place of, and thus exterminate its less well-fitted parent. This I believe to be the origin of the classification and affinities of organic beings at all times; for organic beings always *seem* to branch and sub-branch like the limbs of a tree from a common trunk,

the flourishing and diverging twigs destroying the less vigorous—the dead and lost branches rudely representing extinct genera and families.

This sketch is *most* imperfect; but in so short a space I cannot make it better. Your imagination must fill up very wide blanks.

III. On the Tendency of Varieties to depart indefinitely from the Original Type. By Alfred Russel Wallace

One of the strongest arguments which have been adduced to prove the original and permanent distinctness of species is, that *varieties* produced in a state of domesticity are more or less unstable, and often have a tendency, if left to themselves, to return to the normal form of the parent species; and this instability is considered to be a distinctive peculiarity of all varieties, even of those occurring among wild animals in a state of nature, and to constitute a provision for preserving unchanged the originally created distinct species.

In the absence or scarcity of facts and observations as to *varieties* occurring among wild animals, this argument has had great weight with naturalists, and has led to a very general and somewhat prejudiced belief in the stability of species. Equally general, however, is the belief in what are called "permanent or true varieties,"—races of animals which continually propagate their like, but which differ so slightly (although constantly) from some other race, that the one is considered to be a *variety* of the other. Which is the *variety* and which the original *species,* there is generally no means of determining, except in those rare cases in which the one race has been known to produce an offspring unlike itself and resembling the other. This, however, would seem quite incompatible with the "permanent invariability of species," but the difficulty is overcome by assuming that such varieties have strict limits, and can never again vary further from the original type, although they may return to it, which, from the analogy of the domesticated animals, is considered to be highly probable, if not certainly proved.

It will be observed that this argument rests entirely on the assumption, that *varieties* occurring in a state of nature are in all respects analogous to or even identical with those of domestic animals, and are governed by the same laws as regards their permanence or further variation. But it is the object of the present paper to show that this assumption is altogether false, that there is a general principle in nature which will cause many *varieties* to survive the parent species, and to give rise to successive variations departing further and further from the original type, and which also produces, in domesticated animals, the tendency of varieties to return to the parent form.

The life of wild animals is a struggle for existence. The full exertion of all their faculties and all their energies is required to preserve their own existence and provide for that of their infant offspring. The possibility of procuring food during the least favourable seasons, and of escaping the attacks of their most dangerous enemies, are the primary conditions which determine the existence both of individuals and of entire species. These conditions will also determine the population of a species; and by a careful consideration of all the circumstances we may be enabled to comprehend, and in some degree to explain, what at first sight appears so inexplicable—the excessive abundance of some species, while others closely allied to them are very rare.

The general proportion that must obtain between certain groups of animals is readily seen. Large animals cannot be so abundant as small ones; the carnivora must be less numerous than the herbivora; eagles and lions can never be so plentiful as pigeons and antelopes; the wild asses of the Tartarian deserts cannot equal in numbers the horses of the more luxuriant prairies and pampas of America. The greater or less fecundity of an animal is often considered to be one of the chief causes of its abundance or scarcity; but a consideration of the facts will show us that it really has little or nothing to do with the matter. Even the least prolific of animals would increase rapidly if unchecked, whereas it is evident that the animal population of the globe must be stationary, or perhaps, through the influence of man, decreasing. Fluctuations there may be; but permanent increase, except in restricted localities, is almost impossible. For example, our own observation must convince us that birds do not go on increasing every year in a geometrical ratio, as they would do, were there not some powerful check to their natural increase. Very few birds produce less than two young ones each year, while many have six, eight, or ten; four will certainly be below the average; and if we suppose that each pair produce young only four times in their life, that will also be below the average, supposing them not to die either by violence or want of food. Yet at this rate how tremendous would be the increase in a few years from a single pair! A simple calculation will show that in fifteen years each pair of birds would have increased to nearly ten millions! whereas we have no reason to believe that the number of birds of any country increases at all in fifteen or in one hundred and fifty years. With such powers of increase the population must have reached its limits, and have become stationary, in a very few years after the origin of each species. It is evident, therefore, that each year an immense number of birds must perish—as many in fact as are born; and as on the lowest calculation the progeny are each year twice as numerous as their parents, it follows that, whatever be the average number of individuals existing in any given country, *twice that number must perish annually,*—a striking result, but one which seems at least highly probable, and is perhaps under rather than over the truth. It would therefore appear that, as far as the continuance of the species and the keeping up the average number of individuals are concerned, large broods are superfluous. On the average all above *one* become food for hawks and kites, wild cats and weasels, or perish of cold and hunger as winter comes on. This is strikingly proved by the case of particular species; for we find that their abundance in individuals bears no relation whatever to their fertility in producing offspring. Perhaps the most remarkable instance of an immense bird population is that of the passenger pigeon of the United States, which lays only one, or at most two eggs, and is said to rear generally but one young one. Why is this bird so extraordinarily abundant, while others producing two or three times as many young are much less plentiful? The explanation is not difficult. The food most congenial to this species, and on which it thrives best, is abundantly distributed over a very extensive region, offering such differences of soil and climate, that in one part or another of the area the supply never fails. The bird is capable of a very rapid and long-continued flight, so that it can pass without fatigue over the whole of the district it inhabits, and as soon as the supply of food begins to fail in one place is able to discover a fresh feeding-ground. This example strikingly shows us that the procuring a constant supply of wholesome food is almost the sole condition requisite for ensuring the rapid increase of a given species, since neither the limited fecundity, nor the unrestrained attacks of birds of prey and of man are here sufficient to check it. In no other birds are these peculiar circumstances so strikingly combined. Either their food is more liable to failure, or they have not sufficient power of wing to search for it over an extensive area, or during some season of the year it becomes very scarce, and less wholesome substitutes have to be found; and thus, though more fertile in offspring, they can never increase beyond the supply of food in the least favourable seasons. Many birds can only exist by migrating, when their food becomes scarce, to regions possessing a milder, or at least a different climate, though, as these migrating birds are seldom excessively abundant, it is evident that the countries they visit are still deficient in a constant and abundant supply of wholesome food. Those whose organization does not permit them to migrate when their food becomes periodically scarce, can never attain a large population. This is probably the reason why woodpeckers are scarce with us, while in the tropics they are among the most abundant of solitary birds. Thus the house sparrow is more abundant than the redbreast, because its food is more constant and plentiful—seeds of grasses being preserved during the winter, and our farm-yards and stubble-fields furnishing an almost inexhaustible supply. Why, as a general rule, are aquatic, and especially sea birds, very numerous in individuals? Not because they are more prolific than others, generally the contrary; but because their food never fails, the sea-shores and river-banks daily swarming with a fresh supply of small mollusca and crustacea. Exactly the same laws will apply to mammals. Wild cats are prolific and have few enemies; why then are they never as abundant as rabbits? The only intelligible answer is, that their supply of food is more precarious. It appears evident, therefore, that so long as a country remains physically unchanged, the numbers of its animal population cannot materially increase. If one species does so, some others requiring the same kind of food must diminish in proportion. The numbers that die annually must be immense; and as the individual existence of each animal depends upon itself, those that die must be the weakest—the very young, the aged, and the diseased,—while those that prolong their existence can only be the most perfect in health and vigour—those who are best able to obtain food regularly, and avoid their numerous enemies. It is, as we commenced by remarking, "a struggle for existence," in which the weakest and least perfectly organized must always succumb.

Now it is clear that what takes place among the individuals of a species must also occur among the several allied species of a group,—viz. that those which are the best adapted to obtain a regular supply of food, and to defend themselves against the attacks of their enemies and the vicissitudes of the seasons, must necessarily obtain and preserve a superiority in population; while those species which from some defect of power or organization are the least capable of counteracting the vicissitudes of food, supply, &c., must diminish in numbers, and, in extreme cases, become altogether extinct. Between these extremes the species will present various degrees of capacity for ensuring the means of preserving life; and it is thus we account for the abundance or rarity of species. Our ignorance will generally prevent us from accurately tracing the effects to their causes; but could we become perfectly acquainted with the organization and habits of the various species of animals, and could we measure the capacity of each for performing the different acts necessary to its safety and existence under all the varying circumstances by which it is surrounded, we might be able even to calculate the proportionate abundance of individuals which is the necessary result.

If now we have succeeded in establishing these two points—1st, *that the animal population of a country is generally stationary, being kept down by a periodical deficiency of food, and other checks;* and, 2nd, *that the comparative abundance or scarcity of the individuals of the several species is entirely due to their organization and resulting habits, which, rendering it more difficult to procure a regular supply of food and to provide for their personal safety in some cases than in others, can only be balanced by a difference in the population which have to exist in a given area*—we shall be in a condition to proceed to the consideration of *varieties,* to which the preceding remarks have a direct and very important application.

Most or perhaps all the variations from the typical form of a species must have some definite effect, however slight, on the habits or capacities of the individuals. Even a change of colour might, by rendering them more or less distinguishable, affect their safety; a greater or less development of hair might modify their habits. More important changes, such as an increase in the power or dimensions of the limbs or any of the external organs, would more or less affect their mode of procuring food or the range of country which they inhabit. It is also evident that most changes would affect, either favourably or adversely, the powers of prolonging existence. An antelope with shorter or weaker legs must necessarily suffer more from the attacks of the feline carnivora; the passenger pigeon with less powerful wings would sooner or later be affected in its powers of procuring a regular supply of food; and in both cases the result must necessarily be a diminution of the population of the modified species. If, on the other hand, any species should produce a variety having slightly increased powers of preserving existence, that variety must inevitably in time acquire a superiority in numbers. These results must follow as surely as old age, intemperance, or scarcity of food produce an increased mortality. In both cases there may be many individual exceptions; but on the average the rule will invariably be found to hold good. All varieties will therefore fall into two classes—those which under the same conditions would never reach the population of the parent species, and those which would in time obtain and keep a numerical superiority. Now, let some alteration of physical conditions occur in the district—a long period of drought, a destruction of vegetation by locusts, the irruption of some new carnivorous animal seeking "pastures new"—any change in fact tending to render existence more difficult to the species in question, and tasking its utmost powers to avoid complete extermination; it is evident that, of all the individuals composing the species, those forming the least numerous and most feebly organized variety would suffer first, and, were the pressure severe, must soon become extinct. The same causes continuing in action, the parent species would next suffer, would gradually diminish in numbers, and with a recurrence of similar unfavourable conditions might also become extinct. The superior variety would then alone remain, and on a return to favourable circumstances would rapidly increase in numbers and occupy the place of the extinct species and variety.

The *variety* would now have replaced the *species,* of which it would be a more perfectly developed and more highly organized form. It would be in all respects better adapted to secure its safety, and to prolong its individual existence and that of the race. Such a variety *could not* return to the original form; for that form is an inferior one, and could never compete with it for existence. Granted, therefore, a "tendency" to reproduce the original type of the species, still the variety must ever remain preponderant in numbers, and under adverse physical conditions *again alone survive.* But this new, improved, and populous race might itself, in course of time, give rise to new varieties, exhibiting several diverging modifications of form, any of which, tending to increase the facilities for preserving existence, must, by the same general law, in their turn become predominant. Here, then, we have *progression and continued divergence* deduced from the general laws which regulate the existence of animals in a state of nature, and from the undisputed fact that varieties do frequently occur. It is not, however, contended that this result would be invariable; a change of physical conditions in the district might at times materially modify it, rendering the race which had been the most capable of supporting existence under the former conditions now the least so, and even causing the extinction of the newer and, for a time, superior race, while the old or parent species and its first inferior varieties continued to flourish. Variations in unimportant parts might also occur, having no perceptible effect on the life-preserving powers; and the varieties so furnished might run a course parallel with the parent species, either giving rise to further variations or returning to the former type. All we argue for is, that certain varieties have a tendency to maintain their existence longer than the original species, and this tendency must make itself felt; for though the doctrine of chances or averages can never be trusted to on a limited scale, yet, if applied to high numbers, the results come nearer to what theory demands, and, as we approach to an infinity of examples, become strictly accurate. Now the scale on which nature works is so vast—the numbers of individuals and periods of time with which she deals approach so near to infinity, that any cause, however slight, and however liable to be veiled and counteracted by accidental circumstances, must in the end produce its full legitimate results.

Let us now turn to domesticated animals, and inquire how varieties produced among them are affected by the principles here enunciated. The essential difference in the condition of wild and domestic animals is this,—that among the former, their well-being and very existence depend upon the full exercise and healthy condition of all their senses and physical powers, whereas, among the latter, these are only partially exercised, and in some cases are absolutely unused. A wild animal has to search, and often to labour, for every mouthful of food—to exercise sight, hearing, and smell in seeking it, and in avoiding dangers, in procuring shelter from the inclemency of the seasons, and in providing for the subsistence and safety of its offspring. There is no muscle of its body that is not called into daily and hourly activity; there is no sense or faculty that is not strengthened by continual exercise. The domestic animal, on the other hand, has food provided for it, is sheltered, and often confined, to guard it against the vicissitudes of the seasons, is carefully secured from the attacks of its natural enemies, and seldom even rears its young without human assistance. Half of its senses and faculties are quite useless; and the other half are but occasionally called into feeble exercise, while even its muscular system is only irregularly called into action.

Now when a variety of such an animal occurs, having increased power or capacity in any organ or sense, such increase is totally useless, is never called into action, and may even exist without the animal ever becoming aware of it. In the wild animal, on the contrary, all its faculties and powers being brought into full action for the necessities of existence, any increase becomes immediately available, is strengthened by exercise, and must even slightly modify the food, the habits, and the whole economy of the race. It creates as it were a new animal, one of superior powers, and which will necessarily increase in numbers and outlive those inferior to it.

Again, in the domesticated animal all variations have an equal chance of continuance; and those which would decidedly render a wild animal unable to compete with its fellows and continue its existence are no disadvantage whatever in a state of domesticity. Our quickly fattening pigs, short-legged sheep, pouter pigeons, and poodle dogs could never have come into existence in a state of nature, because the very first step towards such inferior forms would have led to the rapid extinction of the race; still less could they now exist in competition with their wild allies. The great speed but slight endurance of the race horse, the unwieldy strength of the ploughman's team, would both be useless in a state of nature. If turned wild on the pampas, such animals would probably soon become extinct, or under favourable circumstances might each lose those extreme qualities which would never be called into action, and in a few generations would revert to a common type, which must be that in which the various powers and faculties are so proportioned to each other as to be best adapted to procure food and secure safety,—that in which by the full exercise of every part of his organization the animal can alone continue to live. Domestic varieties, when turned wild, *must* return to something near the type of the original wild stock, *or become altogether extinct.*

We see, then, that no inferences as to varieties in a state of nature can be deduced from the observation of those occuring among domestic animals. The two are so much opposed to each other in every circumstance of their existence, that what applies to the one is almost sure not to apply to the other. Domestic animals are abnormal, irregular, artificial; they are subject to varieties which never occur and never can occur in a state of nature: their very existence depends altogether on human care; so far are many of them removed from that just proportion of faculties, that true balance of organization, by means of which alone an animal left to its own resources can preserve its existence and continue its race.

The hypothesis of Lamarck—that progressive changes in species have been produced by the attempts of animals to increase the development of their own organs, and thus modify their structure and habits—has been repeatedly and easily refuted by all writers on the subject of varieties and species, and it seems to have been considered that when this was done the whole question has been finally settled; but the view here developed renders such an hypothesis quite unnecessary, by showing that similar results must be produced by the action of principles constantly at work in nature. The powerful retractile talons of the falcon- and the cat-tribes have not been produced or increased by the volition of those animals; but among the different varieties which occurred in the earlier and less highly organized forms of these groups, *those always survived longest which had the greatest facilities for seizing their prey.* Neither did the giraffe acquire its long neck by desiring to reach the foliage of the more lofty shrubs, and constantly stretching its neck for the purpose, but because any varieties which occurred among its antitypes with a longer neck than usual *at once secured a fresh range of pasture over the same ground as their shorter-necked companions, and on the first scarcity of food were thereby enabled to outlive them.* Even the peculiar colours of many animals, especially insects, so closely resembling the soil or the leaves or the trunks on which they habitually reside, are explained on the same principle; for though in the course of ages varieties of many tints may have occurred, *yet those races having colours best adapted to concealment from their enemies would inevitably survive the longest*. We have also here an acting cause to account for that balance so often observed in nature,—a deficiency in one set of organs always being compensated by an increased development of some others— powerful wings accompanying weak feet, or great velocity making up for the absence of defensive weapons; for it has been shown that all varieties in which an unbalanced deficiency occurred could not long continue their existence. The action of this principle is exactly like that of the centrifugal governor of the steam engine, which checks and corrects any irregularities almost before they become evident; and in like manner no unbalanced deficiency in the animal kingdom can ever reach any conspicuous magnitude, because it would make itself felt at the very first step, by rendering existence difficult and extinction almost sure soon to follow. An origin such as is here advocated will also agree with the peculiar character of the modifications of form and structure which obtain in organized beings—the many lines of divergence from a central type, the increasing efficiency and power of a particular organ through a succession of allied species, and the remarkable persistence of unimportant parts such as colour, texture of plumage and hair, form of horns or crests, through a series of species differing considerably in more essential characters. It also furnishes us with a reason for that "more specialized structure" which Professor Owen states to be a characteristic of recent compared with extinct forms, and which would evidently be the result of the progressive modification of any organ applied to a special purpose in the animal economy.

We believe we have now shown that there is a tendency in nature to the continued progression of certain classes of *varieties* further and further from the original type—a progression to which there appears no reason to assign any definite limits—and that the same principle which produces this result in a state of nature will also explain why domestic varieties have a tendency to revert to the original type. This progression, by minute steps, in various directions, but always checked and balanced by the necessary conditions, subject to which alone existence can be preserved, may, it is believed, be followed out so as to agree with all the phenomena presented by organized beings, their extinction and succession in past ages, and all the extraordinary modifications of form, instinct, and habits which they exhibit.

Ternate, February, 1858

SURVIVAL OF THE FITTEST: AN AXIOM TO GRIND

We have just witnessed with Darwin and Wallace an event in the history of science analogous to evolutionary convergence. There are also parallels to evolutionary divergence: scientists becoming specialized and isolated from one another and eventually forming two different sciences. I first became aware of this in the late 1960s as a graduate student in biophysics. Working on the boundary between physics and biology allowed me to spy into both camps. I was struck by the differences in thinking which had arisen since natural history diverged from natural philosophy. Most noticeable was the faith of most biologists that new theories represented progress toward truth, in contrast to the physicists' unconcern with the truth of their theories so long as they were useful and interesting. At the time it seemed odd that the less precise science inspired more confidence among its practitioners, but I now see this as merely one example of a general truth, which I call Harris's First Law of Knowledge. *Belief in the truth of a theory is inversely proportional to the precision of the science.* In fact, this law applies to assertions made in fields outside science, as may be seen by considering the following areas, listed in order of decreasing precision and increasing dogmatism: mathematics, physics, biology, sociology, economics, politics, philosophy, psychology, theology. Harris's First Law of Knowledge is an illustration of itself. If the law belonged in the fuzzy realm of religion instead of the merely vague field of psychology I could state it with the moral conviction of a commandment instead of a mere law of human nature.

Anyway, I soon realized that physicists' lack of concern about absolute truth resulted partly from the revolution in physics in the early part of this century, when Einstein's Theories of Relativity, the Heisenberg Uncertainty Principle, and other theories of physics revealed inescapable limits to our ability to judge length, time, mass, energy, etc. Indeed, instead of increasing confidence in our ability to understand truth, progress in physics raised doubts about the reality of truth, itself, and our ability to know truth by induction and the objective study of reality (D'Espagnat, 1979). Biologists have not yet had a comparable shock which would shake their faith that we are getting closer to the truth about life.

Another reason why physicists are less concerned with the truth of their theories is their awareness, arising from a closer acquaintance with mathematics and the example set by Newton, that all theories are deduced from untestable assumptions, called axioms (what Descartes called intuitions). For example, all of classical Euclidean geometry is based on five axioms (plus several definitions and common notions). Few people are upset about this, for most would intuitively accept the truth of axioms such as Euclid's first, that one can "draw a straight line from any point to any point," and the fifth axiom that "if a straight line falling on two straight lines makes the interior angles on the same side less than two right angles, the two straight lines, if projected indefinitely, will meet on that side on which are the angles less than the two right angles." Newton also used the axiomatic method in deducing his theory of universal gravitation from three "Axioms, or Laws of Motion." Again, there seemed no reason to doubt the truth of such laws as Newton's first, which states that "every body continues in its state of rest, or of uniform motion in a right line, unless it is compelled to change that state by forces impressed upon it." Newton's successful explanation of the motion of planets justified the use of axioms even though inductive philosophers doubted its validity. Any lingering doubts about axioms were eventually soothed by Kant's idea, in *Critique of Pure Reason,* that there are such a priori truths as Euclid's and Newton's axioms.

The first hint that axioms might not be innate truths came in the late nineteenth century, when several mathematicians created an entirely new geometry by negating Euclid's fifth axiom so that even parallel lines would eventually intersect. Non-Euclidean geometry turned out to be interesting, incapable of disproof, and more useful than classical geometry for dealing with theories of curved space. A more serious blow to axioms came in 1905 when Einstein overthrew intuitive ideas of space and time with two postulates: that the laws of electromagnetism will remain the same even in a moving frame of reference, and that the speed of light will be the same regardless of the motion of the observer with respect to the body emitting light (Einstein et al. 1923, pp. 37, 38). Taken separately the two postulates seemed innocuous; together they revolutionized physics with the Special Theory of Relativity.

Biology has had neither a Newton to show how axioms can be used creatively, nor an Einstein to show the irrelevance of the truth of those axioms. Or rather, biology's Newton—Darwin—reinforced the opposite tendency of searching for true laws of nature by induction. It has always seemed to me unlikely that this difference in scientific approach is anything but a historic artifact. Surely nature did not use one philosophy of science for life and another for the nonliving.[43]

As a student I wondered whether biologists might profitably borrow the axiomatic approach of the physicists. Could Darwin have deduced his theory by the logic of Newton? Suddenly it occurred to me that this is precisely what Darwin had done, unknowingly. The central idea of Darwin's theory is that a fitter organism has a greater chance of surviving and reproducing in a particular environment because of adaptations which it possesses. What is an adaptation? Anything which increases the chances for survival and repro-duction. Fitness is thus essentially the greater ability to survive and repro-duce. Thus "survival of the fittest," Darwin's shorthand for this idea, postu-lates that the organisms which tend to survive and reproduce are those which have a greater ability to survive and reproduce. This is a circular argument—a tautology. "Survival of the fittest" may thus be taken as an untestable truism—an axiom.[44]

Calling "survival of the fittest" an axiom is justified because of its close analogy with another important axiom. Newton's First Law postulated that an object remains at rest or in a state of uniform motion unless affected by a force, but Newton had already defined force as "an action exerted upon a body, in order to change its state, either of rest, or of uniform motion in a right line." A clearer but less flattering comparison may be made with Calvin Coolidge's great insight into the causes of unemployment: "When many people are out of work, unemployment results."

The circularity of "survival of the fittest" may be so obvious that many readers might wonder why I am going on about it. The reason is that the majority of evolutionists reject the notion. In many cases they have rightly rejected the claim that natural selection—not merely "survival of the fittest"—is circular. For example, in a 1975 paper I erroneously stated that natural selection is a tautology, not realizing that "survival of the fittest" is only part of natural selection. Natural selection can also refer to any natural means of selecting those that will survive, by whatever criterion. There is no difficulty in imagining the opposite situation: complete randomness in the survival of organisms. Thus there is nothing circular about this aspect of natural selection, in contrast to "survival of the fittest." Defenders of natural selection are therefore partially correct in stating that natural selection is not a tautology. Unfortunately for them, however, it is of more interest to know which organisms will survive than to know that survival is not merely a matter of luck. At least Darwin thought so, for he continued to search for a theory of evolution long after he realized that some kind of natural selection occurs. Modern evolutionists must also think "survival of the fittest" is the more interesting part of natural selection, judging from the effort spent to measure fitness.[45]

Because of the importance of "survival of the fittest," most evolutionists feel a compulsion to defend it against the charge of circularity, as if the charge somehow reflected adversely on evolution theory or the concept of evolution. There is no doubt that the charge has often been intended as such an attack, especially by creationists. It is peculiar that no one makes similar attacks on Newton's theory or on gravity itself. A more serious reason for rejecting the idea that "survival of the fittest" is circular is Popper's criterion of demarcation. If "survival of the fittest" is a tautology it cannot be falsified. (We know that the fittest survive on Jupiter without having to bother to go there.) Unfalsifiability, far from being a virtue in a theory, means that "survival of the fittest" is not a scientific theory. If it is a theory at all, it does not belong in the realm of science, but perhaps in that region occupied by the theory of demonic possession. However, there is no reason not to retain "survival of the fittest" in science as an axiom. As we have already seen in the case of Empedocles, it is not sufficient in itself for evolution, but must be used in conjunction with other axioms and definitions to produce a theory of evolution.[46]

I doubt that Darwin would readily accept any of this. To him fitness was observable in the adaptations possessed by species. What Darwin meant by "survival of the fittest" was really "survival of those with traits conferring a greater chance of surviving." The circumference is increased, but the circle is unbroken.[47] So certain was Darwin that adaptations promote survival of the species possessing them that he staked his entire theory on it. "If it could be proved that any part of the structure of any one species had been formed for the exclusive good of another species, it would annihilate my theory, for such could not have been produced through natural selection." The catch here is in the words "if it could be proved." How does one prove that a structure was formed for the exclusive good of any species, or for any reason whatever? At best one can only show that a structure benefits a species—not that it was produced for that purpose. There are, in fact, features of organisms which are detrimental to the survival and reproduction of the species possessing them and correspondingly beneficial to their competitors. Most striking is the release of chemicals by certain species of plants which are toxic to those species. Does self-toxicity render "survival of the fittest" and Darwin's theory not only falsifiable but falsified? Some might say that it ought to, but in practice scientists seldom reject a theory which is satisfactory in most cases, simply because it fails in a few cases. Instead they introduce ad-hoc assumptions to save the theory. The following remark by Whittaker and Feeny (1971, p. 758) is typical in its logic, though unusual in its candor. "Self-toxicity is an evolutionary paradox. One supposes that some selective advantage from productions of toxic compounds outweighs the disadvantages of self-inhibition." Saving a theory in this way may seem intellectually dishonest, but it is necessary to scientific progress. Newton knew that the orbit of Mercury was slightly inconsistent with his theory of gravitation, but he retained his theory anyway. Who dares suggest that Newton ought to have scrapped his theory for the good of science?[48]

There is a tacit admission that "survival of the fittest" is not testable in the fact that no one has ever tried to test it. The surprising fact is that no evolutionist has ever thought it worth his time to test the most important idea in evolution and in all of biology. If fitness really means anything besides the ability to survive it ought to be easy enough to set up a situation in which fitness is measured independently of survival. Evolutionists could then agree in advance that if the fittest do not survive they will no longer consider themselves Darwinians. As Bacon would say, "Let the experiment be tried!" Of course what would really happen in the event that those defined as the fittest did not survive is that the definition of fitness would be scrapped, not "survival of the fittest." Again, that is as it should be. Good theories are harder to come by than good definitions, so they are not lightly dismissed. But the inability to falsify "survival of the fittest" as a practical matter ought to serve as a clue that it is not a testable theory, but an axiom.

There is much to be gained by taking "survival of the fittest" as an axiom, judging from the lesson Einstein taught physicists. Like him, we might begin to look for alternative axioms. I can't imagine what such alternatives will be, any more than nineteenth-century physicists could imagine alternatives to Newtonian mechanics. But perhaps the Einstein of biology is reading this now. Even if nothing better than Darwin's theory is created, the search for alternatives is in itself preferable to the blind assumption that the final truth has already been found. In the words of Popper (1972, p. 266), "Whenever a theory appears to you as the only possible one, take this as a sign that you have neither understood the theory nor the problem which it was intended to solve." Or to quote Harris's Second Law of Knowledge: *The creativity of a scientist is directly proportional to how much he knows, and inversely proportional to how much he believes.*[49]

8

Darwinism is Dead: Long Live Neo-Darwinism

You may be wondering why I am about to abuse your patience with another chapter in the history of evolutionism. If Darwin's theory is still accepted as the cause of evolution, what more is there to add? Quite a lot, as it turned out. For roughly half a century advances in cellular biology and genetics cast serious doubt upon the efficiency of natural selection. It was only in the 1930s that these advances were reconciled with natural selection to form the prevailing synthetic or neo-Darwinian theory of evolution. There is neither space nor necessity for a complete review of cell biology and genetics, but I would like to review the major developments which affected evolution theory.[1]

CHARLES DARWIN'S PROVISIONAL HYPOTHESIS OF PANGENESIS

In order to appreciate the evolutionary implications of modern genetics we should first consider the ideas of heredity in Darwin's time. I could as well have said "in Hippocrates' time," for little progress had been made in the intervening centuries. Around 1840 Darwin in fact conceived what he thought was the original theory of pangenesis, only to learn later that the basic idea had appeared in the Hippocratic writings, *On the Sacred Disease* and *On Airs, Waters and Places* 14. Darwin gave away too much in saying that Hippocrates' ideas "seem almost identical with mine," but the two theories did share the assumption that all parts of an organism contributed to the formation of its offspring. Darwin's new twist was that instead of particles from all parts of the body simply collecting to form corresponding parts in the embryo, there were "gemmules" which reproduced themselves to varying degrees before affecting development of the offspring.[2]

Darwin's hypothesis has been criticized as "almost his only venture in the field of pure speculation" (Dobzhansky et al., 1977, p. 15). Actually it was no more speculative than natural selection. Darwin arrived at pangenesis by the same route he had successfully travelled to get to natural selection: by creating a theory which appeared to explain a confusing array of phenomena. It was simply Darwin's misfortune that most of the phenomena were either erroneous or irrelevant in the case of pangenesis. In the erroneous category were:

1. "How the effect of increased or decreased use of a limb can be transmitted to the child." (Darwin had never completely rejected this Lamarckian notion, and relied on it increasingly to answer criticisms of natural selection.)[3]

2. "How the male sexual element can act not solely on the ovules, but occasionally on the mother-form." (That is, how the offspring of a male and female can be affected by previous matings of its mother with another male.)

3. "How a hybrid can be produced by the union of the cellular tissue of two plants independently of the organs of generation," by grafting.

The remaining facts are still accepted, but only the last turned out to be relevant to heredity.

4. "How a limb can be reproduced on the exact line of amputation, with neither too much nor too little added."

5. "How of two allied forms, one passes in the course of its development through the most complex metamorphoses, and the other does not do so, though when mature both are alike in every detail of struture."

6. "How the same organism may be produced by such widely different processes as budding and true seminal generation."

7. "How it is possible for a character possessed by some remote ancestor suddenly to reappear in the offspring."[4]

Darwin first published his theory of pangenesis in *The Variation of Animals and Plants under Domestication* (1868), from which the first selection of this chapter is taken. Darwin considered this theory to be as important as natural selection, but only Wallace and Lyell shared his enthusiasm (F. Darwin, 1901, vol. 1, pp. 300–301). Few English biologists at that time were prepared to think in terms of cells and gemmules, so most of Darwin's colleagues maintained an embarrassed silence. One exception was Francis Galton (1822–1911), whose life was so interesting and whose work was so far-reaching that I need not apologize for a brief biographical digression.

Galton shared with Darwin the distinction of having inherited his clever gemmules from the same grandfather, Erasmus Darwin. Also like Charles Darwin, Galton's hereditary wealth decided him against a career in medicine. He too was afflicted with the urge to travel, and his explorations in southwest Africa got him elected to the Geographical and Royal societies. Galton never held an academic position, so he was able to range over such fields as meteorology and musical instruments. He was the first to suggest that fingerprints were a means of positive identification. Galton's few courses in mathematics had convinced him that anything could be measured, so he attempted to determine the power of prayer, and he developed a scale to measure feminine beauty. More important, he developed the foundation of statistics and applied them to human heredity. An offshoot of this work was his advocacy of eugenics.

Galton attempted to find evidence for pangenesis by transfusing blood from rabbits of various colors into silver-grey rabbits, to see whether the offspring of the silver-greys would acquire colors from the blood donors. They did not. Galton concluded that the evidence weighed against pangenesis, but Darwin simply pointed out that he had never said gemmules circulated in the blood. In 1876 Galton countered with his own theory of heredity. Instead of all parts of the body contributing to the offspring, only one part, a hypothetical "stirp," contributed. Material from the stirp of both parents combined to form the stirp of the embryo, and only a small part of the offspring's stirp influenced its development. Consequently only a small portion of the hereditary substance could be influenced by the rest of the body. Thus the inheritance of acquired characters occurred only rarely. Few biologists noticed Galton's proposal that the reproductive material was isolated until it was suggested independently by Weismann.[5]

AUGUST FRIEDRICH LEOPOLD WEISMANN (1834–1914)

Darwin's and Galton's ideas of heredity attracted more interest on the continent, especially among German-speaking scientists who were discovering a new world within the cell. Improved microscopes, especially those by the firm of Carl Zeiss, together with methods for preserving, staining, and slicing tissue had already established the basics of cellular behavior by the time Darwin published his theory of pangenesis. Schleiden and Schwann had found evidence that all living tissues are composed of cells; Virchow had proposed that all cells come from preexisting cells; and Nägeli had discovered that when cells divide their nuclei divide with them.[6]

Weismann was a major contributor to cell biology in this period, and provided the convincing arguments against pangenesis and the inheritance of acquired characters. He is therefore often regarded as the first neo-Darwinian, because he first attempted a synthesis of natural selection and cellular biology. August Weismann's father had been a professor of classics, and his mother a painter and musician. Weismann, himself, became an accomplished pianist. In fact, it may have been his music teacher who ignited his interest in science, by introducing him to butterfly collecting. Weismann hoped to become a chemist, but studied medicine instead on the advice of his father and a friend, who happened to be famous chemist Friedrich Wöhler (1800–1882). In 1856 Weismann became a physician's assistant, and two years later he set up his own practice. Later he served as personal physician to Archduke Stephen of Austria and in his spare time studied the structure of heart cells and the development of flies. He also visited many other European scientists. In 1863 Weismann stopped pretending that medicine was his main interest and accepted a position teaching comparative anatomy and zoology at the University of Freiburg. Soon he was forced to stop his research and even his reading because of a rare eye disease. During the following decade of virtual blindness he became a leading advocate of Darwinism in Germany, and like Wallace "out-Darwined Darwin" by insisting that natural selection was the the only cause of evolution.

Between 1874 and 1884 Weismann's vision improved enough to allow the study of life histories of the tiny aquatic animals *Daphnia* and *Hydromedusae*. These studies reinforced Weismann's rejection of the inheritance of acquired characters by showing that in those animals the cells which eventually carry out reproduction appear in the very early stages of development. Thus there is little opportunity for the environment to influence them. It also seemed unlikely that gemmules collected from the mature animal could effect reproduction by pangenesis. This research was the germ of Weismann's theory of the "continuity of the germ plasm," which he announced in 1883 in his inaugural lecture as Pro-Rector of Freiburg University. The second selection of this chapter is from that lecture. At this stage Weismann's theory resembled Galton's stirp theory. In the following year Weismann once more became nearly blind. He devoted much of his remaining years to refining his theory by incorporating the research of others. In particular he moved the germ plasm inside the cell nucleus after the discovery of Oskar Hertwig (1849–1922) and Herman Fol (1845–1892) that the nuclei of sperm and egg cells unite during fertilization. Later he assumed that the hereditary material was found in the "loops," now called chromosomes. A polished version of his theory was published in 1885 in the influential essay "The Continuity of the Germ-Plasm as the Foundation of a Theory of Heredity."[7]

Weismann's continued efforts to integrate the latest discoveries regarding cells with Darwin's views of evolution must have seemed old-fashioned to many of his contemporaries who were looking for the causes of evolution within the molecules of the cell. Nägeli, for example, published in 1884 an influential book which argued that evolution was the result of self-directing physical forces operating within the "idioplasm." The idioplasm was analogous to the germ plasm in other respects. Although Nägeli allowed that selection played some role in eliminating the unfit, he was more inclined to explain adaptation by Lamarckian influences on the idioplasm. Nägeli can thus be regarded as one of the first in a continuing line of neo-Lamarckians.

JOHANN GREGOR MENDEL (1822–1884)

No one could have predicted the source of the next great mutation in evolution theory. Johann Mendel was born into a peasant family in Silesia, in what is now northern Czechoslovakia. Ordinarily peasant boys were needed on the farm, but Johann's father sacrificed to permit his son to get an education. In 1841 Johann's father was partially crushed by a tree trunk and was forced to sell his holdings. Johann's sister gave her share of the proceeds to Johann, who had decided to study for the priesthood. For two years at the Olmütz Philosophical Institute Johann studied physics and mathematics, but not biology. He was always an excellent student, and was recommended by his physics professor to the Altbrünn Monastery in Brünn (now Brno, Czechoslovakia). Thus at age twenty-one Mendel became an Augustinian novice and took the name Gregor. Gregor began a four-year course of study at Brünn Theological College in 1845, and was ordained a priest in 1847. The following year was marked by revolution throughout Europe, but Gregor's greatest departure from his vow of obedience seems to have been a failure to wear the college cap to lectures.

Gregor was spared from the usual duties of priests by being unable to stomach the sight of sick people. He was instead assigned as a deputy teacher of high school mathematics in 1849. In the following year he revealed a profound ignorance of biology by failing the teachers' qualifying examination. He was then sent to the University of Vienna for two years to study practical and mathematical physics, chemistry, zoology, paleontology, systematic botany, and plant physiology, which included the new cellular theories. In 1853 Gregor reluctantly left the charms of Vienna to resume teaching at Brünn. Three years later he again applied to take the teachers' exam, but had to withdraw because of sickness. At age thirty-four Mendel seemed an ordinary fat, jolly priest.

In 1856 Mendel began the classic studies in peas which will be described shortly. His interest in botany is not as surprising as one might suppose. His father had raised fruit trees, he lived in an agricultural region, and his monastery encouraged botanizing. Mendel stated in his famous paper of 1865 that he had begun simply to produce new color variants in ornamental flowers. However, he must have had more than a practical interest to have read *Zoonomia, Origin of Species,* and other theoretical works (Iltis, 1932, p. 103). Perhaps because of his mathematical training he noticed the striking regularity of the simple ratios of plant types obtained from second-generation hybrids. For the next seven years he kept the small monastery garden filled with artificially fertilized pea plants—his "children." The pea weevil forced him to switch to other species such as hawkweeds and thistles. These studies were more difficult, and they too withered when Mendel became too fat to collect specimens in the field, after his eyes were damaged by the strong light needed for hawkweed studies, and after his election as abbot in 1868 took too much of his time. He did, however, continue to do interesting studies on meteorology and honeybees.

Mendel's last years were increasingly occupied with his duties as prelate and as chairman of a bank. The latter office resulted from his support for the German Liberal Constitutional Party. In 1872 that party earned his enmity by passing a stiff tax on church property to help finance government support of religion. Mendel alone refused to pay the assessment on monastery property, so the government took over one of its estates and confiscated the rents from the monastery's sugar factory and two dairy farms. The resulting stress may have contributed to the fatal effects on his heart and kidneys of obesity and twenty cigars per day.[8]

Now we come to the intricate task of analyzing the evolutionary implications of Mendel's research on hybridization. This requires not merely an understanding of what Mendel said, but what later scientists thought he said. As Fisher (1936), Brannigan (1979) and Olby (1979) have noted, twentiety-century interpreters of Mendel's work have usually conflated it with their own ideas of heredity. Consequently we need to examine Mendel's role in three stages:

1. From the presentation of the research in 1865 until its "rediscovery" in 1900. In this period Mendel's work had virtually no influence on evolutionism.

2. The first two decades of this century, when Mendelism was interpreted as an argument against natural selection as a major factor in evolution.

3. The past half-century, when Mendelism and natural selection have been considered the two foundations of neo-Darwinism. This last phase will be analyzed in the following section on Haldane.

First let us see what Mendel actually said. We must forget all we know about genes and assume only what Mendel knew: that during fertilization parental cells combine, then multiply to form a new organism. Joseph Gottlieb Kölreuter (1733–1806), Carl Friedrich Gärtner (1772–1850), Charles Darwin, and many other students of heredity had already used hybridization to study the mechanisms of inheritance, but their work was complicated because they produced hybrids from two varieties which differed in many traits. They could say only whether a hybrid resembled one parental variety more than the other. Since hybrids usually inherit something from both parents the pre-Mendelians assumed that hybrids were simply a blend of parental traits. The trouble for Darwin was that natural selection would have to try to rescue a favorable adaptation from being swamped by all the ordinary traits in the population in which it bred. However, Gärtner and Kölreuter had found that instead of hybrids remaining intermediate between their parents they tended to become like one or the other parental variety after several generations. This too was a problem, for it suggested that species resisted evolutionary change.[9]

Mendel's approach to the study of hybridization was more like that of a physicist than of a biologist. Just as a physicist studying a rolling object would isolate the separate effects of weight, friction, air resistance, etc., Mendel decided to study the inheritance of one trait at a time. After preliminary studies he chose seven traits in the pea, genus *Pisum*. One such trait was the shape of the seeds normally produced when the flowers are self-fertilized. With artificial fertilization Mendel was able to cross a plant which normally produces only round seeds with a plant which normally produces only wrinkled seeds. He found that the resulting hybrids produced only round seeds. Thus the trait for round seeds, designated *A,* was *dominating* over the *recessive* trait for wrinkled seeds, *a*. None of the hybrid seeds was intermediate, as would have been expected from a blending theory of inheritance. Yet the recessive trait somehow survived in the reproductive cells of the hybrids, for one-fourth of their self-fertilized offspring produced only wrinkled seeds. A ratio of three dominating to one recessive also obtained for the other six traits in the offspring of hybrids.[10]

Three-to-one ratios were not entirely new; Darwin had reported one in *Variation of Animals and Plants under Domestication* (vol. 2, p. 92). Mendel, however, went a generation further in order to get at the underlying cause. He found that one-third of the plants raised from the round seeds of the hybrid offspring produced only round seeds, while two-thirds of them produced round and wrinkled seeds in the ratio of 3 : 1. In other words, one-half of the offspring of hybrids were themselves hybrids, one-fourth were like the dominating parental variety, and one-fourth were like the recessive parent. Mendel explained these results by assuming that in the hybrid *(Aa)* the dominating and recessive traits *segregate* to produce equal numbers of reproductive cells (pollen and "germinal" cells) of each type. Thus the offspring of the self-fertilizing hybrid would have an equal probability of receiving an *A* or an *a* from the pollen and an equal probability of receiving an *A* or an *a* from the egg cell. One-fourth of the resulting offspring (50% x 50%) would receive only *A,* one-half would receive one *A* and one *a* to become *Aa,* and one-fourth would receive only *a*. Hence the 1 : 2 : 1 ratio. Since *Aa* plants appear like *A,* there is a ratio of 3 : 1 dominating to recessive. The 3 : 1 ratio for one trait was not at all affected by the presence of any of the other six traits. Thus, as Mendel noted in italics, each trait assorted independently of the other traits.[11]

What are the evolutionary implications of Mendel's research? There was in fact less here than meets the modern eye. Any direct contribution by Mendel to evolution came from clarifying the previous research on hybrids, as Mendel implies in the second paragraph of his paper, and as Brannigan (1979) and Olby (1979) have recently reminded us. These major points of clarification are 1) that traits are never lost or weakened by associating with other traits, and 2) that each trait is transmitted independently of others. If Mendel thought of himself as creating a new theory of evolution he was certainly modest about it. Thus I believe Brannigan and Olby go too far in suggesting that Mendel was proposing a new theory of evolution, based on the idea that new species originate from hybrids, as Linnaeus and E. Darwin had suggested. Actually Mendel makes just the opposite point in the section dealing with "Subsequent Generations from Hybrids" (see selection in this chapter). He describes how, in self-fertilizing species, the hybrid form not only fails to develop into a new species, but splits into two separate varieties and all but disappears. As previously shown, four seeds produced by a hybrid will most likely be in the ratio of $1A : 2Aa : 1a$. If the plant from each of these four seeds produces four more seeds, then in the next generation there will be $6A : 4Aa : 6a$. (The two Aa plants will each produce $1A$, $1a$, and $2Aa$ seeds.) In subsesquent generations the proportion of the hybrid form Aa will get smaller, while the numbers of the two new varieties, A and a, get larger. Thus in self-fertilizing species Mendel shows how varieties (and species) become distinct as the hybrid parent disappears. Moreover, even in the absence of natural selection a single individual Aa in a population of A could give rise to a new variety, a. I do not believe Mendel was proposing this as a new theory of evolution, but only as an explanation for the finding of Gärtner and Kölreuter that hybrids revert to parental forms.[12]

The brilliance of Mendel's discoveries is seen in the ability of any college freshman with a grasp of Mendel's principles to answer the "questions about the breeding of animals" which Darwin brooded over so many years. Yet no one in Mendel's and Darwin's time appreciated Mendel's contributions. There are probably many reasons, but one of them must have been that few biologists and practical breeders could understand Mendel's arguments. Biology has always been a refuge for those who love science and hate mathematics, so many biologists were (and are) leery of mathematical theories. Mendel sent his paper to the foremost biologist of the time, Nägeli, who either did not understand it or would not believe it. For whatever reason, Nägeli neglected to mention it in his important book of 1884, in which he presented his own theory that evolution resulted from forces within the idioplasm. Probably Darwin never heard of Mendel's work and would not have understood it. He regretted that he "did not proceed far enough at least to understand something of the great leading principles of mathematics; for men thus endowed seem to have an extra sense" (Barlow, 1958, p. 58). Even if he had understood Mendel's work he might have regarded it as a threat to Darwinism, as Wallace did.[13]

Lately several historians have argued that Mendel's work was not forgotten and therefore could not have been rediscovered. Whether or not that is so, there is no doubt that Mendelism had a greater and different importance after 1900. In that year Hugo De Vries (1848–1935), Carl Erich Correns (1864–1933), and Erich von Tschermak-Seysenegg (1871–1962) independently reported that their own studies had been anticipated by Mendel. Shortly afterwards Lucien Cuénot (1866–1951) and William Bateson (1861–1926) made similar announcements and extended Mendelism to animals. Mendel's "discoverers" inevitably interpreted his work in light of the cellular theories of Weismann and others, which Mendel could not have known. Thus the impression was created that Mendel himself believed that each character was determined by a pair of independent particles, now called genes, each one of which was inherited from each parent. In fact this was merely the most likely explanation consistent with later theories of cell function. Hence Mendel is still widely credited as the father of a new science, which after a prolonged gestation Bateson christened "genetics." Doubts about paternity are difficult to settle in science, but we can at least say that the midwives had as much to do with shaping the infant science as Mendel did.[14]

After Mendel's work was reintroduced at the turn of the century it entered the second phase of its career in which it seemed to argue against natural selection as a cause of evolution. How this came about can be glimpsed by a brief look at the ideas of de Vries and Bateson. Hugo De Vries was a plant physiologist who became interested in evolution after reading *Origin of Species.* In 1889 he published *Intracellular Pangenesis,* in which he modified Darwin's theory of pangenesis by incorporating Weismann's idea of a separate germ plasm. Instead of gemmules, De Vries hypothesized "pangens," which were confined within cells where they exerted their inherited effects on the organism. De Vries began to study hybridization in order to determine whether evolution was caused by a gradual change in the number of pangens affecting a particular trait, or by the sudden appearance or disappearance of pangens. He was swayed to the latter view by discovering a number of spontaneously occurring true-breeding "mutants" of the evening primrose, *Oenothera lamarckiana.* In 1901–1903 he published his mutation theory of evolution, which stressed that most evolution occurs rapidly during periods when a species is mutating rapidly.[15]

De Vries did not consider his theory to be in conflict with natural selection, but Bateson commandeered it for his own battle against adherents to Darwin's belief that *"natura non facit saltum."* This brings us back to Francis Galton. In 1889 Galton proposed a mathematical "law of ancestral heredity," according to which each trait of an organism was intermediate between the trait in each of its parents, barring environmental disturbances. Galton's work was continued by Frank Raphael Walter Weldon (1860–1906) and by

Karl Pearson (1857–1936), whom Galton recommended as first Galton Professor of Eugenics at University College, London. Pearson and cohorts comprised the "ancestrian" or "biometrician" faction, which did battle with Bateson's "mendelian" faction. By some process of mental transference the impression arose that Darwin's theory of evolution was incompatible with Mendel's research. Both factions relied heavily upon polemics, but the biometricians also depended on statistical techniques which they were in the process of developing. Bateson could not understand the mathematics, but then neither could most other biologists. More damaging to the biometrician's cause were new studies confirming the basic accuracy of Mendel's findings. Thomas Hunt Morgan (1866–1945) and his colleagues in the United States were demonstrating with the fruitfly *Drosophila* that heredity was indeed affected by genes attached to pairs of chromosomes, that each parent contributed one chromosome per pair, and that genes were usually stable but could suddenly mutate. Thus for reasons which were compelling at the time many biologists became convinced by 1920 that the Mendelians must be right and the biometricians wrong. Darwin too was found to have been wrong, on the principle of guilt by assocation.[16]

JOHN BURDON SANDERSON HALDANE (1892–1964)

Darwin staked his theory of evolution by natural selection on the evidence that evolution had occurred slowly. "[Species] have changed in the manner required by the theory, for they have changed slowly and in a graduated manner" (Ch. 7 of later editions of *The Origin of Species*). Thus the victory of the Mendelians seemed to be defeat for natural selection. A few men, however, saw the fallacy of portraying Mendel and Darwin as antagonists. The suddenness with which a new trait occurred in an individual did not necessarily imply anything about the speed with which a new variety becomes self-sustaining within a species. Evolution could result either from a mutation occurring simultaneously in a large number of individuals, or from a few mutated individuals gradually leaving more offspring inheriting the mutation. The question is, Which is more important—mutation rate or natural selection? The only practical way to answer that question was by mathematics.

The answer was worked out in the 1920s and 1930s by three men: Ronald Aylmer Fisher (1890–1962), J. B. S. Haldane (1892–1964), and Sewall Wright (1889–   ). Using different approaches they all converged on essentially the same conclusion: the rate of occurrence of spontaneous mutations has little effect on evolution, compared to natural selection. That is, mutations are important only because they provide the heritable variations from which nature selects. I have selected J. B. S. Haldane to illustrate this era of evolutionism. There is no special reason for favoring him except that he was such a fantastic character, and that he establishes continuity with a topic of the next chapter.[17]

Haldane's entry into science is no mystery, since it was a dominant trait in his father, the Oxford physiologist John Scott Haldane (1860–1936). "JBS" grew up surrounded by scientific books, apparatus, and associates of his father. By age five he could read German and could write English with enough facility to leave about the mansion little notes with the endearing message "I hate you." At Eton his brilliance and arrogance made him an ideal subject for ingenious tortures devised by his peers. JBS was happier after his 200-pound anatomy left no doubt that he would pulverize anyone who crossed him. He naturally went to Oxford where he associated with the likes of Aldous and Julian Huxley, grandsons of "Darwin's bulldog." Although JBS excelled at science and mathematics, his only degree was in classics.

By the time he graduated from Oxford JBS had already contributed to original research in his father's study of respiration, especially the effects of gasses in mines, diving suits, and other unlikely places. In the process JBS got to demonstrate his loyalty to the family motto "Suffer." For one experiment J. S. had his son recite Shakespeare while breathing methane gas that had collected in a mine. JBS hardly got past "Friends, Romans, countrymen" before collapsing. To J. S. and JBS self-experimentation was a logical approach to human physiology, because they were the only subjects who could describe what was happening, and because they were more nearly human than rats or guinea pigs. It was also easier on the animals, not that JBS had any sympathy with the extreme antivivisectionists.

In 1908 JBS and his twelve-year-old sister, Naomi, began a line of research which eventually led to the topic of this chapter. In the course of a breeding program involving 300 guinea pigs they noted that certain traits tended to be inherited together, even though they were determined by different genes. This was the first discovery of linkage in animals, but Morgan and others reported it in *Drosophila* before JBS and Naomi could publish in 1915.[18] This paper was written in a trench in France, for JBS had volunteered for the Black Watch Regiment on the outbreak of the World War. His assignment was to try out experimental bombs and mortars, often by sneaking up to enemy lines at night and tossing them. The obvious delight with which he sent German anatomy airborne earned him the nickname "Bombo," among others. After the Germans started using chlorine gas the Lord Chancellor, who just happened to be JBS's uncle, asked the Haldanes to study the problem. Afterwards JBS was sent back to France to advise on defense against gas, but instead he rejoined his regiment. Still somewhat disabled from having tested chlorine on himself, he was wounded. Fortunately a volume by Anatole France came between him and a lethal fragment. After recovering JBS conducted bombing classes, and further embroidered his reputation by demonstrating the handling of explosive in crowded busses and before other unwilling audiences. Eventually he ended up in Mesopotamia fighting Turks, and was wounded by a bomb. (A British bomb, but not his own.) For the next year he enjoyed a leisurely recuperation in India.

In 1919 JBS accepted a fellowship at Oxford to work with his father and to teach physiology in spite of lacking a science degree. (In the first year he managed to stay just ahead of the students.) His research often involved calculating the lethal dose of a chemical, then swallowing just less than that amount to test the calculation. The objective was not merely to make himself miserably ill, but to determine the effects of upsetting the acidity of the blood. Between 1923 and 1932 he was at Cambridge, primarily to supervise research on enzymes. There he conducted the research on the mathematics of evolution, which he summarized in *The Causes of Evolution* (1932). There he also originated, independently of A. I. Oparin (1894–   ), the theory that life originated in a "hot, dilute soup" of organic molecules produced by the action of ultraviolet light on CO_2, methane, ammonia, etc. Haldane also began his prodigious output in the despised art of interpreting science for the public.[19]

JBS also fell in love at Cambridge. Unfortunately the lady was already married, and the only way to correct that situation was to provoke the husband to sue for divorce on the grounds of adultery. Haldane's wartime experiences with chaplains and bureaucrats had reinforced his native skepticism about authority, and had confirmed his belief that the wisest course was always to do the opposite of what society demanded. He and his beloved therefore announced their intention to commit adultery, and carefully saw to it that the injured husband's private detective was able to follow them to the hotel. They were married in 1925. This scandalized the guardians of Cambridge morality, the Sex Viri (pronounced "sex weary"), but Haldane rejected their demand that he resign. The rather sad epilogue to this and Haldane's second marriage was that he was never able to father the son he desperately wanted.

In 1933 Haldane moved to University College, London and became Weldon Professor of Biometry in 1936. His job was to direct genetics research after the retirement of Karl Pearson, while R. A. Fisher took over the statistical work as second Galton Professor of Eugenics. During this period Haldane showed increasing sympathy for Russian Communism. Not only was this the ultimate means of thumbing his nose at society, but it seemed to be the only alternative to the kind of government that had produced a worldwide depression and was standing by while Hitler enslaved his neighbors. Moreover, while lecturing in Russia as the guest of Nikolai Ivanovich Vavilov (1887–1943), JBS had been impressed with Lenin's support of science. Indeed Marxism itself claimed to be a science, so in 1937 it seemed only natural for JBS to become a Marxist.[20]

During World War II Haldane maintained a delicate balance of devotion to science and Marxism on one hand and to loyalty and duty to country on the other. When Franco invited Hitler to test aerial bombardment on Spaniards, Haldane was there to make his own study of how the British could defend themselves against bombing. Haldane was entrusted with secret research even while criticizing the government's conduct of the war and echoing the Party line that it was only a "phony war." (The line changed, of course, after Hitler broke his promise and invaded Russia.) More than once Haldane risked his life studying escape from submarines by submerging himself in ice water at high pressure while breathing poor air. In one such study gas bubbles formed in his spinal cord, resulting in pain for the rest of his life.

If Haldane's devotion to science explains his attraction to Communism, it also explains his gradual disaffection. The crisis occurred when Trofim Lysenko convinced Stalin that his own theory of heredity could increase farm production. Initially Haldane defended Lysenko's theories, and even excused his having Vavilov imprisoned by comparing it with a politically motivated criticism of his father's work. In 1948, however, Lysenko completely suppressed the "Morgano-Weismannites" in Russia, and Haldane had to admit that his earlier fear had come true: "It may possibly be that as a result of [the association of science with the state] in Russia science will undergo somewhat the same fate as overtook Christianity after its association with the State in the time of Constantine" (Haldane, 1933, p. 137). He resigned from the party but remained a Marxist. He could never bring himself to give aid and comfort to the McCarthyites by openly criticizing Stalin or Russia.

In 1957 JBS and Helen Spurway (1915–   ), a colleague he had married in 1945, left for India. He gave as the reason the British and French attack on Egypt during the Suez Crisis; but probably more important were the economic advantages, his imminent retirement, and the opportunity to contribute to a culture he loved. Haldane and his Indian students migrated through a series of institutes—some of them consisting of his own apartment—where they studied genetics and animal behavior. Each new move was another lesson that he had not left bureaucratic stupidity on the shores of Britain. In 1963 he was stricken with cancer of the rectum while in Florida for a conference on the origin of life. He spent his last months in Haldanian fashion, filming his own obituary for the BBC, writing the poem "Cancer's a Funny Thing," and continuing his research in India.

The conclusion of Haldane, Fisher, and Wright that natural selection rather than mutation was the major cause of evolution began to be applied to field studies in the 1940s. This reconciliation of Mendel and Darwin is now the orthodox neo-Darwinian or synthetic theory of evolution. "Orthodox" is the correct term, for most biologists are as incapable of imagining evolution by any other means as fundamentalists are of imagining the origin of life without God. It is important, however, to keep in mind that there are several limitations and qualifications to the orthodox view.[21]

First, natural selection does occur, as Haldane points out in the last reading in this chapter. However, that nature selects the fittest is still a logical and mathematical tautology, as Haldane (1935) realized.

Second, Fisher, Haldane, and Wright necessarily assumed a "bean-bag" model in which each gene behaved independently of others. This is certainly an oversimplification, but considering exchange of genes between chromosomes (crossing over), linkage, and other interactions would have made the mathematics impossibly messy. Only since around 1970 have techniques for analyzing protein structures taken population genetics out of the realm of pure theory. It is thus too early to say whether those mathematical simplifications were inconsequential, or whether the mathematical support for neo-Darwinism will be rendered invalid.

Third, neo-Darwinism is based on the assumption that mutations occur spontaneously or by chance. This does not mean that they occur without cause, but that specific mutations are not selectively induced by the environment or by the organism, as neo-Lamarckism requires. The situation is not quite as bad as when Darwin wrote the following in Chapter 5 of the *Origin*: "I have hitherto sometimes spoken as if the variations . . . were due to chance. This, of course, is a wholly incorrect expression, but it serves to acknowledge plainly our ignorance of the causes of each particular variation." We now know many causes of mutations, and there is evidence that most mutations do indeed occur by chance. One such line of evidence is that the genetic variance in a population increases with the size of the population. The majority of these mutations are harmful, which implies that organisms generally have no control over mutations. On the other hand, in a real situation it would take only one lucky mutant to start a better-adapted variety, and no one could prove afterwards that the mutant did not induce the beneficial mutation by its own physiological processes during the struggle for survival. No study of DNA has so far revealed a violation of the Central Dogma that information flows *from* DNA, not *to* it from some other kind of molecule. But negative evidence is always tentative, and no one claims that DNA holds no more surprises. The best course would seem to be to accept spontaneity of mutations as an axiom, rather than as a proven fact.[22]

A final limitation of neo-Darwinism is that it requires the assumption that selection has a rather direct effect on the frequency of occurrence of genes in a population, depending on the contribution to fitness by each gene. However, recent findings suggest that there is a large gap between the genetic level (genotype) and the anatomical and physiological level (phenotype) where selection occurs. It is an oversimplification to speak of a particular gene for a single adaptation, because the same adaptation can result from numerous different combinations of genes. A recent challenger to neo-Darwinism, the neutral theory of evolution, makes use of this fact to argue that most evolutionary change results from random "drift" of genes which are neutral with respect to fitness and selection. Not only can the same phenotype result from different genotypes, but the converse can also happen. Different phenotypes can result from almost identical genotypes. The genes of humans and chimpanzees are ninety-nine percent identical. That may or may not be surprising, depending on one's esteem for chimps or men, but it means that only one percent of man's four feet of DNA makes the difference between man and *Pan*. These few genes may have a regulatory power over many others. Not all beans in the bag are equal to or independent of the others. It has long been observed, by the way, that adult humans are more like infant chimps than adult chimps, especially in their capacity for play, exploration, learning, and so on. Perhaps this one percent are the genes which make us human by keeping us from growing up.[23]

Every orthodoxy must expect to be challenged, but not every challenger is worthy to become the next orthodoxy. It is too soon to say whether the neutral theory and other challengers will be neo-Darwinism's Martin Luther, or whether they will go the way of Huss and Wycliffe.

Charles Darwin, from *The Variation of Animals and Plants under Domestication,* Chapter 27, "Provisional Hypothesis of Pangenesis." Appleton, New York, 1905.

Conclusion

The hypothesis of Pangenesis, as applied to the several great classes of facts just discussed, no doubt is extremely complex, but so are the facts. The chief assumption is that all the units of the body, besides having the universally admitted power of growing by self-division, throw off minute gemmules which are dispersed through the system. Nor can this assumption be considered as too bold, for we know from the cases of graft-hybridisation that formative matter of some kind is present in the tissues of plants, which is capable of combining with that included in another individual, and of reproducing every unit of the whole organism. But we have further to assume that the gemmules grow, multiply, and aggregate themselves into buds and the sexual elements; their development depending on their union with other nascent cells or units. They are also believed to be capable of transmission in a dormant state, like seeds in the ground, to successive generations.

In a highly-organised animal, the gemmules thrown off from each different unit throughout the body must be inconceivably numerous and minute. Each unit of each part, as it changes during development, and we know that some insects undergo at least twenty metamorphoses, must throw off its gemmules. But the same cells may long continue to increase by self-division, and even become modified by absorbing peculiar nutriment, without necessarily throwing off modified gemmules. All organic beings, moreover, include many dormant gemmules derived from their grandparents and more remote progenitors, but not from all their progenitors. These almost infinitely numerous and minute gemmules are contained within each bud, ovule, spermatozoon, and pollen-grain. Such an admission will be declared impossible; but number and size are only relative difficulties. Independent organisms exist which are barely visible under the highest powers of the microscope, and their germs must be excessively minute. Particles of infectious matter, so small as to be wafted by the wind or to adhere to smooth paper, will multiply so rapidly as to infect within a short time the whole body of a large animal. We should also reflect on the admitted number and minuteness of the molecules composing a particle of ordinary matter. The difficulty, therefore, which at first appears insurmountable, of believing in the existence of gemmules so numerous and small as they must be according to our hypothesis, has no great weight.

The units of the body are generally admitted by physiologists to be autonomous. I go one step further and assume that they throw off reproductive gemmules. Thus an organism does not generate its kind as a whole, but each separate unit generates its kind. It has often been said by naturalists that each cell of a plant has the potential capacity of reproducing the whole plant; but it has this power only in virtue of containing gemmules derived from every part. When a cell or unit is from some cause modified, the gemmules derived from it will be in like manner modified. If our hypothesis be provisionally accepted, we must look at all the forms of asexual reproduction, whether occurring at maturity or during youth, as fundamentally the same, and dependent on the mutual aggregation and multiplication of the gemmules. The re-growth of an amputated limb and the healing of a wound is the same process partially carried out. Buds apparently include nascent cells, belonging to that stage of development at which the budding occurs, and these cells are ready to unite with the gemmules derived from the next succeeding cells. The sexual elements, on the other hand, do not include such nascent cells; and the male and female elements taken separately do not contain a sufficient number of gemmules for independent development, except in the cases of parthenogenesis. The development of each being, including all the forms of metamorphosis and metagenesis, depends on the presence of gemmules thrown off at each period of life, and on their development, at a corresponding period, in union with preceding cells. Such cells may be said to be fertilised by the gemmules which come next in due order of development. Thus the act of ordinary impregnation and the development of each part in each being are closely analogous processes. The child, strictly speaking, does not grow into the man, but includes germs which slowly and successively become developed and form the man. In the child, as well as in the adult, each part generates the same part. Inheritance must be looked at as merely a form of growth, like the self-division of a lowly-organised unicellular organism. Reversion depends on the transmission from the forefather to his descendants of dormant gemmules, which occasionally become developed under certain known or unknown conditions. Each animal and plant may be compared with a bed of soil full of seeds, some of which soon germinate, some lie dormant for a period, whilst others perish. When we hear it said that a man carries in his constitution the seeds of an inherited disease, there is much truth in the expression. No other attempt, as far as I am aware, has been made, imperfect as this confessedly is, to connect under one point of view these several grand classes of facts. An organic being is a microcosm—a little universe, formed of a host of self-propagating organisms, inconceivably minute and numerous as the stars in heaven.

August Weismann. From *Essays upon Heredity and Kindred Biological Problems,* E. B. Poulton, S. Schönland and A. E. Shipley (eds.). Clarendon Press, Oxford, 1889. "On Heredity," translated by A. E. Shipley.

It is well known that Darwin has attempted to explain the phenomena of heredity by means of a hypothesis which corresponds to a considerable extent with that just described. If we substitute gemmules for molecules we have the fundamental idea of Darwin's provisional hypothesis of pangenesis. Particles of an excessively minute size are continually given off from all the cells of the body; these particles collect in the reproductive cells, and hence any change arising in the organism, at any time during its life, is represented in the reproductive cell. Darwin believed that he had by this means rendered the transmission of acquired characters intelligible, a conception which he held to be necessary in order to explain the development of species. He himself pointed out that the hypothesis was merely provisional, and that it was only an expression of immediate, and by no means satisfactory knowledge of these phenomena.

It is always dangerous to invoke some entirely new force in order to understand phenomena which cannot be readily explained by the forces which are already known.

I believe that an explanation can in this case be reached by an appeal to known forces, if we suppose that characters acquired (in the true sense of the term) by the parent cannot appear in the course of the development of the offspring, but that all the characters exhibited by the latter are due to primary changes in the germ.

This supposition can obviously be made with regard to the above-mentioned colony with its constituent elements differentiated into somatic and reproductive cells. It is conceivable that the differentiation of the somatic cells was not primarily caused by a change in their own structure, but that it was prepared for by changes in the molecular structure of the reproductive cell from which the colony arose.

The generally received idea assumes that changes in the external conditions can, in connection with natural selection, call forth persistent changes in an organism; and if this view can be accepted it must be as true of all Metazoa [multicellular animals] as it is of unicellular or of homogeneous multicellular organisms. Supposing that the hypothetical colonies, which were at first entirely made up of similar cells, were to gain some advantages, if in the course of development, the molecules of the reproductive cells, from which each colony arose became distributed irregularly in the resulting organism, there would be a tendency towards the perpetuation of such a change, wherever it appeared as the result of individual variability. As a result of this change the colony would no longer remain homogeneous, and its cells would become dissimilar from the first, because of the altered arrangement of the molecules in the reproductive cells. Nothing prevents us from assuming that, at the same time, the nature of a part of the molecule may undergo still further change, for the molecules are by nature complex, and may split up or combine together.

If then the reproductive cells have undergone such changes that they can produce a heterogeneous colony as the result of continual division, it follows that succeeding generations must behave in exactly the same manner, for each of them is developed from a portion of the reproductive cell from which the previous generation arose, and consists of the same reproductive substance as the latter.

From this point of view the exact manner in which we imagine the subsequent differentiation of the colony to be potentially present in the reproductive cell, becomes a matter of comparatively small importance. It may consist in a different molecular arrangement, or in some change of chemical constitution, or it may be due to both these causes combined. The essential point is that the differentiation was originally due to some change in the reproductive cells, just as this change itself produces all the differentiations which appear in the ontogeny of all species at the present day. No one doubts that the reason why this or that form of segmentation takes place, or why this or that species finally appears, is to be found in the ultimate structure of the reproductive cells. And, as a matter of fact, molecular differentiation and grouping, whether present from the beginning or first appearing in the course of development, plays a role which can be almost directly observed in certain species. The first segmentation furrow divides the egg of such species into an opaque and a clear half, or, as is often the case among Medusae, into a granular outer layer and a clear central part, corresponding respectively with the ectoderm and endoderm which are formed at a later period. Such early differentiations are only the visible proofs of certain highly complex molecular rearrangements in the cells, and the fact appears to indicate that we cannot be far wrong in maintaining that differentiations which appear in the course of ontogeny depend upon the chemical and physical constitution of the molecules in the reproductive cell.

At the first appearance of the earliest Metazoa alluded to above, only two kinds of cells, somatic and reproductive, arose from the segmentation of the reproductive cell. The reproductive cells thus formed must have possessed exactly the same molecular structure as the mother reproductive cell, and would therefore pass through precisely the same developmental changes. We can easily imagine that all the succeeding stages in the development of the Metazoa have been due to the same causes which were efficient at the earliest period. Variations in the molecular structure of the reproductive cells would continue to appear, and these would be increased and rendered permanent by means of natural selection, when their results, in the alteration of certain cells in the body, were advantageous to the species. The only condition necessary for the transmission of such changes is that a part of the reproductive substance (the germ-plasm) should always remain unchanged during segmentation and the subsequent building up of the body, or in other words, that such unchanged substance should pass into the organism, and after the lapse of a variable period, should reappear as the reproductive cells. Only in this way can we render to some extent intelligible the transmission of those changes which have arisen in the phylogeny of the species; only thus can we imagine the manner in which the first somatic cells gradually developed in numbers and in complexity.

It is only by supposing that these changes arose from molecular alterations in the reproductive cell that we can understand how the reproductive cells of the next generation can originate the same changes in the cells which are developed from them; and it is impossible to imagine any way in which the transmission of changes, produced by the direct action of external forces upon the somatic cells, can be brought about.

The difficulty or the impossibility of rendering the transmission of acquired characters intelligible by an appeal to any known force has been often felt, but no one has hitherto attempted to cast doubts upon the very existence of such a form of heredity.

There are two reasons for this: first, observations have been recorded which appear to prove the existence of such transmission; and secondly, it has seemed impossible to do without the supposition of the transmission of acquired characters, because it has always played such an important part in the explanation of the transformation of species.

It is perfectly right to defer an explanation, and to hesitate before we declare a supposed phenomenon to be impossible, because we are unable to refer it to any of the known forces. No one can believe that we are acquainted with all the forces of nature. But, on the other hand, we must use the greatest caution in dealing with unknown forces; and clear and indubitable facts must be brought forward to prove that the supposed phenomena have a real existence, and that their acceptance is unavoidable.

It has never been proved that acquired characters are transmitted, and it has never been demonstrated that, without the aid of such transmission, the evolution of the organic world becomes unintelligible.

Gregor Mendel, from "Experiments on Plant Hybrids." Translated by William Bateson. Reprinted from *Journal of the Royal Horticultural Society,* 1901.

Introductory Remarks

Experience of artificial fertilisation, such as is effected with ornamental plants in order to obtain new variations in colour, has led to the experiments which will here be discussed. The striking regularity with which the same hybrid forms always reappeared whenever fertilisation took place between the same species induced further experiments to be undertaken, the object of which was to follow up the developments of the hybrids in their progeny.

To this object numerous careful observers, such as Kölreuter, Gärtner, Herbert, Lecoq, Wichura and others, have devoted a part of their lives with inexhaustible perseverance. Gärtner especially, in his work "Die Bastarderzeugung im Pflanzenreiche" (The Production of Hybrids in the Vegetable Kingdom), has recorded very valuable observations; and quite recently Wichura published the results of some profound investigations into the hybrids of the Willow. That, so far, no generally applicable law governing the formation and development of hybrids has been successfully formulated can hardly be wondered at by anyone who is acquainted with the extent of the task, and can appreciate the difficulties with which experiments of this class have to contend. A final decision can only be arrived at when we shall have before us the results of detailed experiments made on plants belonging to the most diverse orders.

Those who survey the work in this department will arrive at the conviction that among all the numerous experiments made, not one has been carried out to such an extent and in such a way as to make it possible to determine the number of different forms under which the offspring of hybrids appear, or to arrange these forms with certainty according to their separate generations, or definitely to ascertain their statistical relations.

It requires indeed some courage to undertake a labour of such far-reaching extent; this appears, however, to be the only right way by which we can finally reach the solution of a question the importance of which cannot be overestimated in connection with the history of the evolution of organic forms.

The paper now presented records the results of such a detailed experiment. This experiment was practically confined to a small plant group, and is now, after eight years' pursuit, concluded in all essentials. Whether the plan upon which the separate experiments were conducted and carried out was the best suited to attain the desired end is left to the friendly decision of the reader.

SELECTION OF THE EXPERIMENTAL PLANTS

The value and utility of any experiment are determined by the fitness of the material to the purpose for which it is used, and thus in the case before us it cannot be immaterial what plants are subjected to experiment and in what manner such experiments are conducted.

The selection of the plant group which shall serve for experiments of this kind must be made with all possible care if it be desired to avoid from the outset every risk of questionable results.

The experimental plants must necessarily—

1. Possess constant differentiating characters.

2. The hybrids of such plants must, during the flowering period, be protected from the influence of all foreign pollen, or be easily capable of such protection.

The hybrids and their offspring should suffer no marked disturbance in their fertility in the successive generations.

Accidental impregnation by foreign pollen, if it occurred during the experiments and were not recognized, would lead to entirely erroneous conclusions. Reduced fertility or entire sterility of certain forms, such as occurs in the offspring of many hybrids, would render the experiments very difficult or entirely frustrate them. In order to discover the relations in which the hybrid forms stand towards each other and also towards their progenitors it appears to be necessary that all members of the series developed in each successive generation should be, *without exception,* subjected to observation.

At the very outset special attention was devoted to the *Leguminosae* on account of their peculiar floral structure. Experiments which were made with several members of this family led to the result that the genus *Pisum* was found to possess the necessary qualifications.

Some thoroughly distinct forms of this genus possess characters which are constant, and easily and certainly recognizable, and when their hybrids are mutually crossed they yield perfectly fertile progeny. Furthermore, a disturbance through foreign pollen cannot easily occur, since the fertilising organs are closely packed inside the keel and the anther bursts within the bud, so that the stigma becomes covered with pollen even before the flower opens. This circumstance is of especial importance. As additional advantages worth mentioning, there may be cited the easy culture of these plants in the open ground and in pots, and also their relatively short periods of growth. Artificial fertilisation is certainly a somewhat elaborate process, but nearly always succeeds. For this purpose the bud is opened before it is perfectly developed, the keel is removed, and each stamen carefully extracted by means of forceps, after which the stigma can at once be dusted over with the foreign pollen.

In all, thirty-four more or less distinct varieties of Peas were obtained from several seedsmen and subjected to a two years' trial. In the case of one variety there were noticed, among a larger number of plants all alike, a few forms which were markedly different. These, however, did not vary in the following year, and agreed entirely with another variety obtained from the same seedsman; the seeds were therefore doubtless merely accidentally mixed. All the other varieties yielded perfectly constant and similar offspring; at any rate, no essential difference was observed during two trial years. For fertilisation twenty-two of these were selected and cultivated during the whole period of the experiments. They remained constant without any exception.

Their systematic classification is difficult and uncertain. If we adopt the strictest definition of a species, according to which only those individuals belong to a species which under precisely the same circumstances display precisely similar characters, no two of these varieties could be referred to one species. According to the opinion of experts, however, the majority belong to the species *Pisum sativum;* while the rest are regarded and classed, some as sub-species of *P. sativum,* and some as independent species, such as *P. quadratum, P. saccharatum,* and *P. umbellatum.* The positions, however, which may be assigned to them in a classificatory system are quite immaterial for the purposes of the experiments in question. It has so far been found to be just as impossible to draw a sharp line between the hybrids of species and varieties as between species and varieties themselves.

DIVISION AND ARRANGEMENT OF THE EXPERIMENTS

If two plants which differ constantly in one or several characters be crossed, numerous experiments have demonstrated that the common characters are transmitted unchanged to the hybrids and their progeny; but each pair of differentiating characters, on the other hand, unite in the hybrid to form a new character, which in the progeny of the hybrid is usually variable. The object of the experiment was to observe these variations in the case of each pair of differentiating characters, and to deduce the law according to which they appear in the successive generations. The experiment resolves itself therefore into just as many separate experiments as there are constantly differentiating characters presented in the experimental plants.

The various forms of Peas selected for crossing showed differences in the length and colour of the stem; in the size and form of the leaves; in the position, colour, and size of the flowers; in the length of the flower stalk; in the colour, form, and size of the pods; in the form and size of the seeds; and in the colour of the seed-coats and of the albumen. Some of the characters noted do not permit of a sharp and certain separation, since the difference is of a "more or less" nature, which is often difficult to define. Such characters could not be utilised for the separate experiments; these could only be applied to characters which stand out clearly and definitely in the plants. Lastly, the result must show whether they, in their entirety, observe a regular behaviour in their hybrid unions, and whether from these facts any conclusion can be come to regarding those characters which possess a subordinate significance in the type.

The characters which were selected for experiment relate:

1. To the *difference in the form of the ripe seeds*. These are either round or roundish, the depressions, if any, occur on the surface, being always only shallow; or they are irregularly angular and deeply wrinkled *(P. quadratum)*.

2. To the *difference in the colour of the seed albumen* (endosperm). The albumen of the ripe seeds is either pale yellow, bright yellow and orange coloured, or it possesses a more or less intense green tint. This difference of colour is easily seen in the seeds as their coats are transparent.

3. To the *difference in the colour of the seed-coat*. This is either white, with which character white flowers are constantly correlated; or it is grey, grey-brown, leather-brown, with or without violet spotting, in which case the colour of the standards is violet, that of the wings purple, and the stem in the axils of the leaves is of a reddish tint. The grey seed-coats become dark brown in boiling water.

4. To the *difference in the form of the ripe pods*. These are either simply inflated, not contracted in places; or they are deeply constricted between the seeds and more or less wrinkled *(P. saccharatum)*.

5. To the *difference in the colour of the unripe pods*. They are either light to dark green, or vividly yellow, in which colouring the stalks, leaf-veins, and calyx participate.

6. To the *difference in the position of the flowers*. They are either axial, that is, distributed along the main stem; or they are terminal, that is, bunched at the top of the stem and arranged almost in a false umbel; in this case the upper part of the stem is more or less widened in section *(P. umbellatum)*.

7. To the *difference in the length of the stem*. The length of the stem is very various in some forms; it is, however, a constant character for each, in so far that healthy plants, grown in the same soil, are only subject to unimportant variations in this character.

In experiments with this character, in order to be able to discriminate with certainty, the long axis of 6 to 7 ft. was always crossed with the short one of ¾ ft. to 1½ ft.

Each two of the differentiating characters enumerated above were united by cross-fertilisation. There were made for the

1st	trial	60	fertilisations	on	15	plants
2nd	"	58	"	"	10	"
3rd	"	35	"	"	10	"
4th	"	40	"	"	10	"
5th	"	23	"	"	5	"
6th	"	34	"	"	10	"
7th	"	37	"	"	10	"

From a larger number of plants of the same variety only the most vigorous were chosen for fertilisation. Weakly plants always afford uncertain results, because even in the first generation of hybrids, and still more so in the subsequent ones, many of the offspring either entirely fail to flower or only form a few and inferior seeds.

Furthermore, in all the experiments reciprocal crossings were effected in such a way that each of the two varieties which in one set of fertilisation served as seed-bearer in the other set was used as the pollen plant.

The plants were grown in garden beds, a few also in pots, and were maintained in their naturally upright position by means of sticks, branches of trees, and strings stretched between. For each experiment a number of pot plants were placed during the blooming period in a greenhouse, to serve as control plants for the main experiment in the open as regards possible disturbance by insects. Among the insects which visit Peas the beetle *Bruchus pisi* might be detrimental to the experiments should it appear in numbers. The female of this species is known to lay the eggs in the flower, and in so doing opens the keel; upon the tarsi of one specimen, which was caught in a flower, some pollen grains could clearly be seen under a lens. Mention must also be made of a circumstance which possibly might lead to the introduction of foreign pollen. It occurs, for instance, in some rare cases that certain parts of an otherwise quite normally developed flower wither, resulting in a partial exposure of the fertilising organs. A defective development of the keel has also been observed, owing to which the stigma and anthers remained partially uncovered. It also sometimes happens that the pollen does not reach full perfection. In this event there occurs a gradual lengthening of the pistil during the blooming period, until the stigmatic tip protrudes at the point of the keel. This remarkable appearance has also been observed in hybrids of *Phaseolus* and *Lathyrus.*

The risk of false impregnation by foreign pollen is, however, a very slight one with *Pisum,* and is quite incapable of disturbing the general result. Among more than 10,000 plants which were carefully examined there were only a very few cases where an indubitable false impregnation had occurred. Since in the greenhouse such a case was never remarked, it may well be supposed that *Bruchus pisi,* and possibly also the described abnormalities in the floral structure, were to blame.

THE FORMS OF THE HYBRIDS

Experiments which in previous years were made with ornamental plants have already afforded evidence that the hybrids, as a rule, are not exactly intermediate between the parental species. With some of the more striking characters, those, for instance, which relate to the form and size of the leaves, the pubescence of the several parts, &c., the intermediate, indeed, is nearly always to be seen; in other cases, however, one of the two parental characters is so preponderant that it is difficult, or quite impossible, to detect the other in the hybrid.

This is precisely the case with the Pea hybrids. In the case of each of the seven crosses the hybrid-character resembles that of one of the parental forms so closely that the other either escapes observation completely or cannot be detected with certainty. This circumstance is of great importance in the determination and classification of the forms under which the offspring of the hybrids appear. Henceforth in this paper those characters which are transmitted entire, or almost unchanged in the hybridisation, and therefore in themselves consti-tute the characters of the hybrid, are termed the *dominant,* and those which become latent in the process *recessive.* The expression "re-cessive" has been chosen because the characters thereby desig-nated withdraw or entirely disappear in the hybrids, but nevertheless reappear unchanged in their progeny, as will be demonstrated later on.

It was furthermore shown by the whole of the experiments that it is perfectly immaterial whether the dominant character belongs to the seed-bearer or to the pollen-parent; the form of the hybrid remains identical in both cases. This interesting fact was also emphasised by Gärtner, with the remark that even the most practised expert is not in a position to determine in a hybrid which of the two parental species was the seed or the pollen plant.

Of the differentiating characters which were used in the experi-ments the following are dominant:

1. The round or roundish form of the seed with or without shallow depressions.

2. The yellow colouring of the seed albumen.

3. The grey, grey-brown, or leather-brown colour of the seed-coat, in association with violet-red blossoms and reddish spots in the leaf axils.

4. The simply inflated form of the pod.

5. The green colouring of the unripe pod in association with the same colour in the stems, the leaf-veins and the calyx.

6. The distribution of the flowers along the stem.

7. The greater length of stem.

With regard to this last character it must be stated that the longer of the two parental stems is usually exceeded by the hybrid, a fact which is possibly only attributable to the greater luxuriance which appears in all parts of plants when stems of very different length are crossed. Thus, for instance, in repeated experiments, stems of 1 ft. and 6 ft. in length yielded without exception hybrids which varied in length between 6 ft. and 7½ ft.

The hybrid seeds in the experiments with seed-coat are often more spotted, and the spots sometimes coalesce into small bluish-violet patches. The spotting also frequently appears even when it is absent as a parental character.

The hybrid forms of the seed-shape and of the albumen are developed immediately after the artificial fertilisation by the mere influence of the foreign pollen. They can, therefore, be observed even in the first year of experiment, whilst all the other characters naturally only appear in the following year in such plants as have been raised from the crossed seed.

THE GENERATION FROM THE HYBRIDS

In this generation there reappear, together with the dominant characters, also the recessive ones with their peculiarities fully developed, and this occurs in the definitely expressed average proportion of three to one, so that among each four plants of this generation three display the dominant character and one the recessive. This relates without exception to all the characters which were investigated in the experiments. The angular wrinkled form of the seed, the green colour of the albumen, the white colour of the seed-coats and the flowers, the constrictions of the pods, the yellow colour of the unripe pod, of the stalk, of the calyx, and of the leaf venation, the umbel-like form of the inflorescence, and the dwarfed stem, all reappear in the numerical proportion given, without any essential alteration. *Transitional forms were not observed in any experiment.*

Since the hybrids resulting from reciprocal crosses are formed alike and present no appreciable difference in their subsequent development, consequently the results can be reckoned together in each experiment. The relative numbers which were obtained for each pair of differentiating characters are as follows:

Expt. 1. Form of seed.—From 253 hybrids 7,324 seeds were obtained in the second trial year. Among them were 5,474 round or roundish ones and 1,850 angular wrinkled ones. Therefore the ratio 2.96 to 1 is deduced.

Expt. 2. Colour of albumen.—258 plants yielded 8,023 seeds, 6,022 yellow, and 2,001 green; their ratio, therefore, is 3.01 to 1.

In these two experiments each pod yielded usually both kinds of seeds. In well-developed pods which contained on the average six to nine seeds, it often happened that all the seeds were round (Expt. 1) or all yellow (Expt. 2); on the other hand there were never observed more than five wrinkled or five green ones in one pod. It appears to make no difference whether the pods are developed early or later in the hybrid or whether they spring from the main axis or from a lateral one. In some few plants only a few seeds developed in the first formed pods, and these possessed exclusively one of the two characters, but in the subsequently developed pods the normal proportions were maintained nevertheless.

As in separate pods, so did the distribution of the characteres vary in separate plants. By way of illustration the first ten individuals from both series of experiments may serve.

Plants	Experiment 1 Form of Seed.		Experiment 2 Color of Albumen.	
	Round	Angular	Yellow	Green
1	45	12	25	11
2	27	8	32	7
3	24	7	14	5
4	19	16	70	27
5	32	11	24	13
6	26	6	20	6
7	88	24	32	13
8	22	10	44	9
9	28	6	50	14
10	25	7	44	18

As extremes in the distribution of the two seed characters in one plant, there were observed in Expt. 1 an instance of 43 round and only 2 angular, and another of 14 round and 15 angular seeds. In Expt. 2 there was a case of 32 yellow and only 1 green seed, but also one of 20 yellow and 19 green.

These two experiments are important for the determination of the average ratios, because with a smaller number of experimental plants they show that very considerable fluctuations may occur. In counting the seeds, also, especially in Expt. 2, some care is requisite, since in some of the seeds of many plants the green colour of the albumen is less developed, and at first may be easily overlooked. The cause of this partial disappearance of the green colouring has no connection with the hybrid-character of the plants, as it likewise occurs in the parental variety. This peculiarity is also confined to the individual and is not inherited by the offspring. In luxuriant plants this appearance was frequently noted. Seeds which are damaged by insects during their development often vary in colour and form, but, with a little practice in sorting, errors are easily avoided. It is almost superfluous to mention that the pods must remain on the plants until they are thoroughly ripened and have become dried, since it is only then that the shape and colour of the seed are fully developed.

Expt. 3. Colour of the seed-coats.—Among 929 plants 705 bore violet-red flowers and grey-brown seed-coats; 224 had white flowers and white seed-coats, giving the proportion of 3.15 to 1.

Expt. 4. Form of pods.—Of 1,181 plants 882 had them simply inflated, and in 299 they were constricted. Resulting ratio, 2.95 to 1.

Expt. 5. Colour of the unripe pods.—The number of trial plants was 580, of which 428 had green pods and 152 yellow ones. Consequently these stand in the ratio 2.82 to 1.

Expt. 6. Position of flowers.—Among 858 cases 651 had inflorescences axial and 207 terminal. Ratio, 3.14 to 1.

Expt. 7. Length of stem.—Out of 1,064 plants, in 787 cases the stem was long, and in 277 short. Hence a mutual ratio of 2.84 to 1. In this experiment the dwarfed plants were carefully lifted and transferred to a special bed. This precaution was necessary, as otherwise they would have perished through being overgrown by their tall relatives. Even in their quite young state they can be easily picked out by their compact growth and thick dark-green foliage.

If now the results of the whole of the experiments be brought together, there is found, as between the number of forms with the dominant and recessive characters, an average ratio of 2.98 to 1, or 3 to 1.

The dominant character can have here a *double signification*—viz. that of a parental character, or a hybrid-character. In which of the two significations it appears in each separate case can only be determined by the following generation. As a parental character it must pass over unchanged to the whole of the offspring; as a hybrid-character, on the other hand, it must maintain the same behaviour as in the first generation.

THE SECOND GENERATION FROM THE HYBRIDS

Those forms which in the first generation exhibit the recessive character do not further vary in the second generation as regards this character; they remain constant in their offspring.

It is otherwise with those which possess the dominant character in the first generation. Of these *two*-thirds yield offspring which display the dominant and recessive characters in the proportion of 3 to 1, and thereby show exactly the same ratio as the hybrid forms, while only *one*-third remains with the dominant character constant.

The separate experiments yielded the following results:

Expt. 1. Among 565 plants which were raised from round seeds of the first generation, 193 yielded round seeds only, and remained therefore constant in this character; 372, however, gave both round and wrinkled seeds, in the proportion of 3 to 1. The number of the hybrids, therefore, as compared with the constants is 1.93 to 1.

Expt. 2. Of 519 plants which were raised from seeds whose albumen was of yellow colour in the first generation, 166 yielded exclusively yellow, while 353 yielded yellow and green seeds in the proportion of 3 to 1. There resulted, therefore, a division into hybrid and constant forms in the proportion of 2.13 to 1.

For each separate trial in the following experiments 100 plants were selected which displayed the dominant character in the first generation, and in order to ascertain the significance of this, ten seeds of each were cultivated.

Expt. 3. The offspring of 36 plants yielded exclusively grey-brown seed-coats, while of the offspring of 64 plants some had grey-brown and some had white.

Expt. 4. The offspring of 29 plants had only simply inflated pods; of the offspring of 71, on the other hand, some had inflated and some constricted.

Expt. 5. The offspring of 40 plants had only green pods; of the offspring of 60 plants some had green, some yellow ones.

Expt. 6. The offspring of 33 plants had only axial flowers; of the offspring of 67, on the other hand, some had axial and some terminal flowers.

Expt. 7. The offspring of 28 plants inherited the long axis, and those of 72 plants some the long and some the short axis.

In each of these experiments a certain number of the plants came constant with the dominant character. For the determination of the proportion in which the separation of the forms with the constantly persistent character results, the two first experiments are of especial importance, since in these a larger number of plants can be compared. The ratios 1.93 to 1 and 2.13 to 1 gave together almost exactly the average ratio of 2 to 1. The sixth experiment gave a quite concordant result; in the others the ratio varies more or less, as was only to be expected in view of the smaller number of 100 trial plants. Experiment 5, which shows the greatest departure, was repeated, and then, in lieu of the ratio of 60 and 40, that of 65 and 35 resulted. *The average ratio of 2 to 1 appears, therefore, as fixed with certainty.* It is therefore demonstrated that, of those forms which possess the dominant character in the first generation, two-thirds have the hybrid-character, while one-third remains constant with the dominant character.

The ratio of 3 to 1, in accordance with which the distribution of the dominant and recessive characters results in the first generation, resolves itself therefore in all experiments into the ratio of 2 : 1 : 1 if the dominant character be differentiated according to its significance as a hybrid-character or as a parental one. Since the members of the first generation spring directly from the seed of the hybrids, *it is now clear that the hybrids form seeds having one or other of the two differentiating characters, and of these one-half develop again the hybrid form, while the other half yield plants which remain constant and receive the dominant or the recessive characters in equal numbers.*

THE SUBSEQUENT GENERATIONS FROM THE HYBRIDS

The proportions in which the descendants of the hybrids develop and split up in the first and second generations presumably hold good for all subsequent progeny. Experiments 1 and 2 have already been carried through six generations, 3 and 7 through five, and 4, 5, and 6 through four, these experiments being continued from the third generation with a small number of plants, and no departure from the rule has been perceptible. The offspring of the hybrids separated in each generation in the ratio of 2 : 1 : 1 into hybrids and constant forms.

If *A* be taken as denoting one of the two constant characters, for instance the dominant, *a,* the recessive, and *Aa* the hybrid form in which both are conjoined, the expression $A + 2Aa + a$ shows the terms in the series for the progeny of the hybrids of two differentiating characters.

The observation made by Gärtner, Kölreuter, and others, that hybrids are inclined to revert to the parental forms, is also confirmed by the experiments described. It is seen that the number of the hybrids which arise from one fertilisation, as compared with the number of forms which become constant, and their progeny from generation to generation, is continually diminishing, but that nevertheless they could not entirely disappear. If an average equality of fertility in all plants in all generations be assumed, and if, furthermore, each hybrid forms seed of which one-half yields hybrids again, while the other half is constant to both characters in equal proportions, the ratio of numbers for the offspring in each generation is seen by the following summary, in which *A* and *a* denote again the two parental characters, and *Aa* the hybrid forms. For brevity's sake it may be assumed that each plant in each generation furnishes only 4 seeds.

				Ratios		
Generation	A	Aa	a	A :	Aa :	a
1	1	2	1	1 :	2 :	1
2	6	4	6	3 :	2 :	3
3	28	8	28	7 :	2 :	7
4	120	16	120	15 :	2 :	15
5	496	32	496	31 :	2 :	31
n				2^n-1 :	2 :	2^n-1

In the tenth generation, for instance, $2^n-1 = 1023$. There result, therefore, in each 2,048 plants which arise in this generation, 1,023 with the constant dominant character, 1,023 with the recessive character, and only two hybrids.

J. B. S. Haldane, from *The Causes of Evolution,* Chapter Four, "Natural Selection." Cornell University Press, Ithaca, New York, 1966. By permission.

The best example known to me where the effects of selection have been watched over many generations is described by Todd (1930), in the case of the organism of which different races cause scarlet fever, puerperal fever, and erysipelas, *Streptococcus haemolyticus.* It rapidly loses its virulence for animals when bred in artificial media. This phenomenon was at first taken for a Lamarckian inheritance of the effects of disuse, and its analysis by Todd is typical of the results obtained when such phenomena are carefully studied. He found that his *Streptococcus* when grown on agar produced hydrogen peroxide. But occasionally a variant appears which gives rather different colonies, is less virulent, and produces much less peroxide. We do not know how these variants arise because the details of the process of reproduction in bacteria are not known. There is no reason to think that bacterial mutation is a phenomenon essentially different from mutation in higher organisms, and it is not even clear that it is commoner.

Now the normal type of bacteria, when grown on agar, make enough peroxide to kill themselves, or at any rate to slow down their growth very greatly. When parasitic they are protected by the catalase of their hosts. This is a widely distributed enzyme which destroys hydrogen peroxide. Hence the glossy and non-virulent type is the only survivor after a few weeks of culture. But if a little catalase is added to the medium the virulent type grow as well as the non-virulent, and can be preserved in culture indefinitely. These bacteria divide about once every half-hour, so Todd's experiments, which lasted thirty-nine days at a minimum, covered some 2000 bacterial generations, corresponding to about 50,000 years in human evolution, and a century even with so rapidly breeding a creature as *Drosophila.* It took Calmette and Guerin (1924) fourteen years, or about 25,000 generations, to convert the bovine tubercle bacillus into a harmless and indeed beneficial organism by growing it on artificial media. There is thus no reason to put down such modifications of bacteria to anything but natural selection, acting on the results of mutation.

The following example, from the work of Harrison (1920), shows natural selection at work among the moths of the species *Oporabia autumnata.* About 1800 a mixed wood of pine, birch, and alder on Eston Moor in Yorkshire was divided into two parts separated by half a mile of heather. In 1885, after a storm, the pines were replaced by birch in the southern portion, while in the northern birches and alders are now rare. Presumably in 1800 the two populations were similar. By 1907 they were quite different. In the pine-wood 96 per cent. belong to a dark variety, 4 per cent. to a light. In the birch-wood about 15 per cent. are dark and 85 per cent. light. The reason for this is fairly clear. In the pine-wood owls, nightjars, and bats feed on the moths, leaving their wings when the bodies are eaten. Although only 4 per cent. of the moths in the pine-wood are light, the majority of the wings lying on its grass belong to the light variety, which is thus some thirty times as likely to be caught as the dark. We do not know for certain what advantage the light-coloured insect enjoys in the birch-wood, where birds and bats are relatively rare. But as the light race lays its eggs later than the dark they are less likely to hatch in the same year instead of (as normally) in the spring, an event which entails the death of the larvae during the winter. It may be added that an attempt to make the pine-wood insects lighter in colour by feeding them for three generations on birch met with no success.

It is perfectly true, as critics of Darwinism never tire of pointing out, that in these observations no new character appears in the species as the result of selection. Novelty is only brought about by selection as the result of the combination of previously rare characters. Supposing that in a population fifteen characters, not correlated, are each present in 1 per cent. of the individuals. The combination of all fifteen would only be present in one in 10^{30}, *i.e.* 1 per (English, not American) quintillion. This is a large number even on the evolutionary scale. The earth's land surface is only 10^{18} square centimetres. There have not been 10^{30} higher plants in the whole of geological history (10^9 years), including all members of all many-celled plant species. The combination of all fifteen characters would not occur in practice even once in the whole history of plants larger than unicellular.

Now suppose that natural selection acts on all these fifteen characters, so that they are found in 99 per cent. not in 1 per cent. of the species. The combination of all fifteen would now be found in 86 per cent. of the population. It would, in fact, be the normal character. No one has ever observed this happening in nature, because, owing to the slowness of natural selection, it would probably require ten thousand years of observation in a favourable case. But, as Darwin realised, it has happened as the result of artificial selection. A middle-white pig differs from a wild boar in some thirty to forty distinct respects. Some may be due to the action of the same gene on several organs. Others require several genes. Some of these genes were doubtless present as rarities in the wild species. Others may have turned up after domestication, but if so they had probably often occurred in the wild species.

It is important to realise that the combination of several genes may give a result quite unlike the mere summation of their effects one at a time. This is obviously to be expected if genes act chemically. Thus in *Primula sinensis* a dark stem (recessive) is associated with no great change in colour of acid-sapped (red and purple) flowers. But blue (recessive) flowers, which have a neutral sap, when growing on a dark stem, are mottled. The same recessive dark stem genes, along with genes for a green stem, give plants which will not set seed, though they give good pollen. So selection acting on several characters leads, not merely to novelty, but to novelty of a kind unpredictable with our present scientific knowledge, though probably susceptible of a fairly straightforward biochemical explanation.

We have seen that there is no question that natural selection does occur. We must next consider what would be the effect of selection of a given intensity. The mathematical theory of natural selection where inheritance is Mendelian has been mainly developed by R. A. Fisher, S. Wright, and myself. One of the more important results are summarised in the Appendix, but I shall deal with a few of them here. The first question which arises is how we are to measure that intensity. I shall confine myself to organisms, such as annual plants and insects, where generations do not overlap. The more general case, exemplified by man, can only be treated by means of integral equations. Suppose we have two competing types A and B, say dark and light moths or virulent and non-virulent bacteria. Then if in one generation the ratio of A to B changes from r to $r(1 + k)$ we shall call k the coefficient of selection. Of course k will not be steady. In one year an early spring will give an advantage to early maturing seeds. In the next year a late frost will reverse the process. Nor will it be constant from one locality to another, as is clear in the case of the moths just cited. We must take average values over considerable periods and areas. The value of k will increase with the proportion of individuals killed off by selection, but after selection has become intense enough to kill off about 80 per cent. of the population it increases rather slowly, roughly as the logarithm of the number killed off per survivor—sometimes even as the square root of the logarithm. In what follows I shall suppose k to be small.

The effect of selection of a given intensity depends entirely on the type of inheritance of the character selected and the system of mating. I will confine myself for the moment to characters inherited in an alternative manner, in a population either mating at random or self-fertilised. If two races do not cross, or if the inheritance is cytoplasmic, and if u_n is the ratio of A to B after n generations, then $u_n = e^{kn} u_o$, or $kn = \log_e \frac{u_n}{u_o}$. If the character is due to a single dominant gene, and u_n is the ratio of dominant to recessive genes, then

$$k_n = u_n - u_o + \log_e \frac{u_n}{u_o}.$$

This means that selection is rapid when populations contain a reasonable proportion of recessives, but excessively slow, in either direction, when recessives are very rare. Thus if $k = {}^1$, i.e. 1001 of one type survive to breed for every 1000 of the other, it would take 11,739 generations to increase the number of dominants from one in a million to one in two, but 321,444 generations to increase the number of recessives in the same way. It is not surprising that the only new types which have been known to spread through a wild population under constant observation are dominants. For example, the black form of the peppered moth, *Amphidasys betularia,* which replaced the original form in the industrial districts of England and Germany during the nineteenth century, is a dominant. When the character is due to several rare genes the effect of selection is also very slow even if the genes are dominant. But however small may be the selective advantage the new character will spread, provided it is present in enough individuals of a population to prevent its disappearance by mere random extinction. Fisher has shown that it is only when k is less than the reciprocal of the number of the whole population that natural selection ceases to be effective. An average advantage of one in a million will be quite effective in most species. . . .

One more application of mathematics, and I have done. Under what conditions can mutation overcome selection? This is quite a simple problem. Let p be the probability that a gene will mutate in a generation. We saw that p is probably usually less than a millionth, and so far always less than a thousandth. Let k be the coefficient of selection measuring the selective disadvantage of the new type, k being considerably larger than p. Then equilibrium is reached when the proportion of unfavourable to favourable phenotypes is $\frac{p}{k}$ if the mutant is recessive, $\frac{p}{k}$ if it is dominant. The above calculations refer to a random mating population. The ratio is always $\frac{2p}{k}$ in a self-fertilised population.

Hence, unless k is so small as to be of the same order as p, the new type will not spread to any significant extent. Even under the extreme conditions of Muller's X-ray experiments, when mutation was a hundred and fifty times more frequent than in the normal, a disadvantage of one in two thousand would have kept any of the new recessive types quite rare. Thus until it has been shown that anywhere in nature conditions produce a mutation rate considerably higher than this, we cannot regard mutation as a cause likely by itself to cause larger changes in a species. But I am not suggesting for a moment that selection alone can have any effect at all. The material on which selection acts must be supplied by mutation.

Neither of these processes alone can furnish a basis for prolonged evolution. Selection alone may produce considerable changes in a highly mixed population. A selector of sufficient knowledge and power might perhaps obtain from the genes at present available in the human species a race combining an average intellect equal to that of Shakespeare with the stature of Carnera. But he could not produce a race of angels. For the moral character or for the wings he would have to await or produce suitable mutations.

The Art of Science

I have tried to show throughout this book that scientific theories are the creations of individual scientists who have been influenced by their cultures, that theories are based on axioms which are merely assumptions, and that theories can never be proved true. Undoubtedly many readers will have been given the impression that scientific theories are purely arbitrary: that one theory is about as good as another. Indeed I have encouraged that view as an antidote to the too-common notion that theories are derived only from facts, requiring nothing more of a scientist than the dogged application of *the* scientific method. I have undoubtedly overshot the target, and would now like to readjust our sights in the opposite direction.

There are, in fact, criteria by which axioms and theories are judged. However, one must not expect that these criteria were derived scientifically, for the theoretical basis of such criteria would then have to be judged by the criteria which the theory is supposed to establish. There may be a school of philosophy competent to deal with criteria for choosing one theory over another, but if there is no one has bothered to tell scientists. The perhaps surprising fact is that nowhere in science education are future scientists told how to judge whether an axiom or theory is good. Instead these criteria are part of the unspoken legacy handed down from one generation of scientists to the next. Presumably science students learn to identify good theories by example, for teachers rarely waste time on bad ones. When teachers do discuss a bad theory they are likely to label it as such, if only by an air of boredom. The criteria I shall propose are therefore merely those I have absorbed in this haphazard fashion, and I shall not attempt to justify them. However, in their defense I will mention that others have suggested similar criteria, and that scientists who hear of them respond with either a shock of recognition or a bored acknowledgment of things they knew without thinking.

The first criterion will come as no surprise. *A good axiom or theory must be canonical.* That is, it must not directly contradict accepted facts. For example, it is now generally accepted as fact that an organism cannot selectively effect mutations within itself. Thus neo-Lamarckians are not likely to gain a following until they can disprove that fact. The disproof of facts is not unheard of. Once upon a time it was a fact that species were unalterable.

The second criterion is also unexceptionable. *A good axiom or theory must be productive.* A good axiom must contribute toward the production of a good theory, and a good theory must produce explanations, predictions, or at least experiments capable of potentially falsifying the theory. "There is a god" is a perfectly good axiom except that it has never been necessary for the creation of any scientific theory. Adding it makes no difference except to clutter up the theory. The axiom of spontaneous mutations, however, is an essential part of the neo-Darwinian theory. One reason why special creation is not a good theory is that it fails this criterion of productivity. If we answer "God made it so" to every question, scientists might as well just go home. In contrast the neo-Darwinian theory has proved very beneficial for the employment situation of biologists with mathematical inclinations.

The theories which scientists create and use on a day-to-day basis are usually adequate if they are canonical and productive. Occasionally, however, a theory is created which is not only adequate but evokes an emotional response comparable to that felt when experiencing great art. Such theories, like great art, have a beauty more profound than the sensual pleasure of the eye or ear. They evoke the feeling of having glimpsed truth like a crystal— clear, hard, pure. Understanding such a theory is like learning the truth about war from Picasso's *Guernica,* or experiencing the majesty of Heaven by listening to Bach. Such theories rise as far above the adequate as the works of Picasso and Bach rise above pretty pictures and pleasant tunes.

Like great art, great scientific theories are characterized by an almost universal scope and an economy of expression. *Guernica* would not move us if Picasso had merely tried to represent the bombing of one Spanish town in 1937, or if he had cluttered the huge canvas with details. Attempts to popularize Bach with the latest musical clichés only muddle and trivialize. Likewise great theories must also reach beyond the experience of the theoretician to encompass the experiences and experiments of others. And they must do so with simplicity. Mendel's ratios would not be important if they applied only to peas, which may explain why Mendel lost enthusiasm after working with other species. The ratio 2.9838 : 1 is actually more consistent with Mendel's data than 3 : 1. However, the latter is more compelling because it is more likely to represent an underlying simplicity in nature.

I have tried to find a word which connotes both universality and economy. The best I can do is suggest the trivial word that many scientists of my generation utter on first hearing of a great theory. On formal occasions they call great theories beautiful or elegant, but for my third criterion I shall use the colloquial. *A great theory must be neat.*[24]

Physicists are the least abashed about admitting the role of neatness in creating and accepting theories. P. A. M. Dirac (1902–   ) credits Einstein with introducing "the view that something that is beautiful mathematically, is bound to be correct physically. . . . The proof [of a complex theory] comes not really from experiments. The real foundations come from the beauty of the theory. . . . It is the essential beauty of the theory which, I feel, makes us believe in it." Keats said it more neatly:

> "Beauty is truth, truth beauty,"—that is all
> Ye know on earth, and all ye need to know.[25]

Biologists are apt to distrust an aesthetic criterion as being a departure from scientific method. Yet even some biologists of the previous century were not immune to the neatness of their own theories. Patrick Matthew wrote that "there is more beauty and unity of design in [his theory of] continual balancing of life to circumstance." At the end of the *Origin of Species* Darwin confessed to seeing "grandeur" in the evolutionary view of life. Very early he had rejected the idea of special creation as implying a "miserable, limited [and] cramped" view of God (Notebooks B216, D36–37). With characteristic candor and wit J. D. Watson (1928–   ) admitted the role of aesthetics not only in appreciating the completed theory but in creating it. In *The Double Helix* (1968, p. 63) he stated that a tentative model of DNA structure was disappointing because it allowed too many possible variations, none of which was "prettier" than the others. Parts of another model just "smelled bad" (p. 69). Eventually he and F. H. C. Crick (1916–   ) conceived of the double helical model of DNA partly because it was "aesthetically elegant," and "a structure this pretty just had to exist" (p. 131). What Watson thought was pretty was not the spiral-staircase contraption he built to represent DNA, but the simple concept which unified so many phenomena.

Scientists are so partial to neat theories that they sometimes retain them in spite of ugly facts which make them no longer canonical. Scientists can better afford to indulge their aesthetic sensitivities than nature can. Living things often have to depend on messy facts that work, rather than neat theories that don't. I learned this as a novice graduate student when looking at cockroach eyes to see whether they had taken advantage of my neat theory of how they could perceive color. To my surprise they had not. Eventually I accepted the possibility that during their several hundred million years of evolution cockroaches might have learned something I hadn't.

We can summarize the preceding by saying that scientists are constrained in their creativity by the requirements that axioms and theories be canonical and productive, but those constraints are relaxed by an appreciation for neatness. This is really not very different from the situation of the artist. Poets, even modern ones, are constrained by rhyme, meter, or some other dictate of their muse. Yet those constraints are forgiving enough to have permitted Tennyson to rhyme "stone" and "gone" for the sake of beauty. Scientists also have something like poetic license. It is that which allows the connoisseur of biology to perceive the individual styles of Patrick Matthew, Charles Darwin, and Alfred Russel Wallace as clearly as the connoisseur of poetry distinguishes the styles of Byron, Shelley, and Keats.[26]

9

Modern Times: Marxism, Lysenkoism, and Sociobiology

A great theory inevitably arouses controversies, because its scope reaches into other subject areas. It is easy to forget this in the case of evolutionism. It has survived so many challenges over the last two centuries that it seems to many people that only a few die-hard creationists can see any controversy in neo-Darwinism. Such complacency presents two threats to evolutionism. First, we might underestimate the seriousness of attempts to suppress evolutionism, just as biologists are largely ignoring creationists' attempts to dilute the teaching of evolution in public schools. The second threat is that biologists will brush aside even valid criticisms of neo-Darwinism. Both dangers are well illustrated by the two controversies of this section—Lysenkoism and sociobiology.

These two controversies also illustrate how evolutionary theories invade nonscientific areas: Lysenkoism had severe political consequences in Russia; sociobiology has the potential for changing man's perception of himself, with unforeseeable results. They also provide an opportunity to complete our study of the major historical and social factors which have influenced the course of science. Marxism has replaced Christianity as the single most important influence in human thought, and it is becoming increasingly important in scientific thought even in non-Marxist countries.

MARXISM

Certain aspects of this chapter may seem more suited to a text on abnormal psychology or the legacy of the Dark Ages unless we first consider the philosophical basis of Marxism. Of course we cannot do this thoroughly: Marxist theory has baroque intricacies that would have impressed even Thomas Aquinas, and Marxism has evolved into as many denominations as Protestantism. Strictly speaking, "Marxism" refers only to the economic theories of Karl Marx (1818–1883) which he set forth in *Capital* and, with Friedrich Engels (1820–1895), in *The Communist Manifesto*. This economic system has been adapted to practical requirements by Lenin, Mao Zedong, and others, and Marxist interpretations have been extended to almost every aspect of intellectual interest, including science. Engels, with Marx's approval, applied the Marxist perspective to physics and evolution. In spite of the complexity and diversity of Marxist views—some of which are violently debated among those who call themselves Marxists—there is a core of thought shared by all real Marxists. It is called *dialectical materialism*. In this chapter I shall restrict myself to the applications of dialectical materialism to science.[1]

It is convenient to divide dialectical materialism into its material and then its dialectical aspects. Strictly speaking Marxist materialism is the same as the materialism of Democritus, Epicurus, Diderot, Darwin, and others. It assumes that natural phenomena, including human behavior, are determined by the properties of matter, and not by abstract ideas. Marx's contribution was to infer that the most important motive of man is therefore the securing of the material requirements for life. Thus each person's behavior is ultimately determined by the mode of production in his society—whether that mode is feudalism, capitalism, socialism, or communism. The laws, sermons, and theories of politicians, preachers, and scientists do interact with the mode of production, but they are all merely parts of the "superstructure" of the mode of production, which is devoted to justifying and perpetuating that mode of production. Thus Marxists tend to view scientific theories as merely the products and the tools of the mode of production. This is just the opposite of the common view that a theory is a purely objective induction or deduction from fact, without any influence by culture. Regarding the origin of Darwinism, Marx, Engels, and many of their followers ignored all of Darwin's biological research and emphasized the derivation of natural selection from Malthus's laissez-faire ideas, and the use of natural selection by "social Darwinians" to justify the worst aspects of capitalism.[2]

However, there are aspects of Darwinism with which Marx was favorably impressed, namely its materialism and its view of continuous, progressive change through struggle. "Darwin's book is very important and serves me as a natural-scientific basis for the class struggle in history."[3] Marx saw the class struggle as arising from the materialist requirement for humans to compete for the necessities of life. This view, called *historical materialism*, holds that history evolves because of the inevitable conflicts among social classes in their economic struggle for survival. There is a major difference between Darwin and Marx, however: to Darwin change resulted from conflicts between an organism and any other internal or external, organic or inorganic entity; to Marx change resulted from what he called "contradictions" within a single entity. "Contradiction" does not refer to a logical inconsistency, but to two

opposite and interdependent aspects of a single whole. Contradictions are
the basis for change; external forces are the conditions of change. *Bourgeoisie*
and *proletariat* are contradictions in Marxist terms; they are opposite yet
interdependent, because each is defined only in relation to the other.
Conflicts developing between such contradictions inevitably result in progressive change, according to a set of laws called *dialectics*.

The term "dialectics" refers to the Socratic method of philosophizing by
means of dialogue. Just as two opponents in an argument may arrive at
agreement by a give-and-take discussion, so do history and nature, according to Marx, develop by the dialectical resolution of contradictions. There
are three major laws of dialectics, which Marx adapted from G. W. F. Hegel
(1770–1831):

1. *The transformation of quantity into quality.* Changing the quantity of something eventually causes a revolutionary change in its quality. For example,
the accumulation of many small variations can suddenly result in a new
species.

2. *The mutual interpenetration of opposites.* This is essentially the basis of Marx's
idea of contradiction, as explained above. Engels (1940, p. 224) gave as
examples of interpenetrating opposites identity/difference, necessity/
chance, and cause/effect.

3. *Negation of the negation.* In the resolution of a contradiction an opposite
does not extinguish the other and then survive; both opposites vanish but
form a new synthesis, just as a seed vanishes in forming a new plant.

Some Marxists consciously apply the dialectical laws, but even those who
do not often have an altered perspective. Marxists tend more than others to
view nature and history as a continuous struggle punctuated by revolutions.
This may seem strange to most of us, but it is just as valid as the conventional
view of gradual change, which may have originated with Aristotle. One
advantage Marxists have is that they are not deluded into thinking that their
perspective is natural and objective. Rather, they remind all scientists that
our views depend on our social contexts. Stephen Jay Gould gives an interesting example of this: Russian paleontologists may have been more willing
to accept his and Eldredge's theory that most evolution occurs relatively
rapidly in brief periods which interrupt long, uneventful stretches, because
of their study of the law of transformation of quantity into quality.[4]

In accordance with the dialectical laws, Marxists suppose that societies go
through a sequence of inevitable economic stages, with each new stage
emerging from the mutual negation of contradictions within the previous
stage. Marx predicted that all capitalist societies would give way to socialism
as the means of production becomes concentrated in the hands of a shrinking bourgeoisie, which will then be easily overthrown by a growing and
increasingly miserable proletariat. Because of the lawfulness of this process

(in the dialectical sense, at least), Marxism is also referred to as *scientific socialism.* The socialist stage comes about, by definition, when the means of production falls into the hands of the workers. For a short time after the overthrow of the bourgeoisie the form of government would be "dictatorship by the proletariat," but this would soon give way to a classless society. Without classes there would be no contradictions within society, and therefore no conflicts for police and other government functionaries to resolve. The state would therefore wither away, and the socialist society would quietly evolve into the highest stage, communism.

Marx saw more clearly into the defects of laissez-faire capitalism than do most capitalists, but he did not foresee the ability of modern capitalist societies to forestall indefinitely the coming of socialism by such measures as the minimum wage, unemployment insurance, collective bargaining, and antitrust laws.[5] (Paradoxically these measures, which delay the advent of socialism, have been widely denounced as socialist.) Marx would have argued that by such measures the bourgeoisie and their legislative servants are merely delaying the inevitable. (Hence the hatred of liberals by many Marxists.) Marx was not content to let history unfold at the leisurely pace which suited capitalists. He urged that Marxists must accelerate the coming of socialism by combining theory and practice. "The philosophers have only *interpreted* the world, in various ways; the point, however, is to *change* it" (Engels, 1969, p. 61). Thus there are no armchair Marxists. Every real Marxist is committed to socialism. This is the trait of Marxist biologists which most often brings them into conflict with non-Marxists. Inclined to see scientific theories as subjective products and tools of ideology, and regarding Marxism itself as a science, they may see nothing strange in using extraordinary means to promote scientific theories which promote socialism and to suppress those which they view as retarding the progress toward socialism. In effect, the Marxist scientist has a criterion for judging theories which may override even the requirements that they be canonical and productive. To argue that this criterion of socialism is irrational would be fruitless, for the criterion of neatness is just as irrational. Many Marxists have even a second additional criterion, which results from Marx's urging that theory be combined with practice. According to this criterion a good theory must result in successful application. This helps explain why many Marxists are impatient with "bourgeois" science, that is, science not directed toward serving the masses. We shall soon see what a powerful criterion this was when used against the fruit-fly geneticists.

One final point before reading the following. Difficult as it may be in these revolutionary times, one must struggle against the stereotype of all Marxists as violent fanatics. It is true that Lysenko used Marxism as an excuse for violence, but it is also true that his victims—martyrs for reason, justice, and decency—were often better Marxists than Lysenko. We must not add insult to their injuries by confusing Marxism itself with Lysenko's perversion of it. No reasonable person would condemn all Christians because the Holy Inquisition forced Galileo to recant a scientific theory, or because some creationists attempt to use the power of the government to impose their views on students. By the same token we should judge Marxists by their individual deeds.

TROFIM DENISOVICH LYSENKO (1898–1976)

One consequence of the Marxist notion that thoughts are determined by economics is that there is little interest in Russia in the kind of biographical insight I have tried to encourage in this book. Thus we shall probably never know what lay behind Lysenko's "dejected mien . . [the] sullen look creeping along the earth as if, at very least, he were ready to do someone in."[6] T. D. Lysenko was born into a peasant family in Karlovka, in the Ukraine. He studied agronomy at the Horticultural Institute of Poltava, and graduated from Kiev Agricultural Institute in 1925. Lysenko's ambition was soon nourished when, as head of the legumes-breeding division at Gandzha Breeding Station in the late 1920s, he was the subject of a *Pravda* article. What really launched his career was a noisy campaign for "vernalization," following a random success by his father. Denis N. Lysenko had obtained increased yield on one crop of winter wheat after wetting and freezing the seeds, then sowing them in the spring instead of the autumn. Actually there was little new in this procedure, which Lysenko called "vernalization." It could accelerate harvesting by a few days and perhaps avoid frost damage, but the investment in labor in the spring was tremendous. Perhaps the major advantage of vernalization was that during the usually idle spring months it kept farmers too busy to brood over Stalin's having just collectivized their lands. Lysenko, having been promoted to a new post in Odessa, began in 1930 to create a whole new science to explain vernalization. His revolutionary theory was that plants pass through qualitatively different stages in their development from seed to maturity, and that each stage requires different conditions. Vernalization supposedly worked by accelerating a particular stage. This is really about all there was to the theory.

In the early thirties Soviet ideologists began for the first time to apply Marxist philosophy to science, with the Central Committee of the Communist Party as the ultimate judge of the correctness of theories. Suddenly Lysenko, or more likely his politically astute colleague I. I. Prezent, saw in historical materialism the perfect analogy to the theory of developmental phases. In 1935 Lysenko published a paper in which he sought support for his theory from dialectical materialism. In the same year in a speech to all the members of government Lysenko explained his vernalization scheme and accused those who opposed him of being "kulak-wreckers," that is, agricultural saboteurs. Stalin cheered. "Bravo, comrade Lysenko, bravo!"[7]

A word of explanation may be in order for those to whom the attention of a head of state on behalf of an individual scientist seems a novelty. In the 1930s collectivization of agriculture was proving to be a disaster, Russia was feeling threatened by more industralized countries such as Germany, and Stalin must have been wondering how long it would be before he joined his victims in Siberia. Continued food shortages twenty years after the revolution could only mean, to a Marxist, that there was something wrong with the Soviet economic system. Lysenko promised salvation for Russia and for Stalin. Instead of the three or four years granted to the bourgeois practitioners of foreign genetics to develop improved cereals, Lysenko would do it with his home-grown method of vernalization in only two and one-half years.

With the unkind assistance of Stalin's terror, Lysenko was able to repress many of his adversaries. One by one his rivals for the powerful post of President of the Lenin All-Union Academy of Agricultural Sciences (LAAAS) were arrested, leaving Lysenko in 1938 to take this position as virtual dictator of agriculture and biology. Others were arrested for opposing Lysenko or for trying to remain neutral. Although they comprised a minuscule proportion of the millions of Stalin's victims, the number of repressed anti-Lysenkoites was large enough to attract the notice of Solzhenitsyn in *The Gulag Archipelago* (1973). (Compare, however, Joravsky, 1970, pp. 112–130.) Here I shall mention only the most noted case: Nikolai Ivanovich Vavilov (1887–1943), whom I have already noted as Haldane's host in Russia. Vavilov was head of the All-Union Institute of Plant Breeding, and was therefore subordinate to Lysenko. His crime was to continue to seek desirable varieties of grain from foreign countries, rather than to convert Russian grain to desirable types by vernalization. Even worse, Vavilov had studied Mendelian genetics in England with William Bateson, and he opposed Lysenko's own theory of heredity, to be described later. Vavilov's spirit is apparent in his prophetic words spoken in 1939 after years of compromise with Lysenko: "We shall go to the pyre, we shall burn, but we shall not retreat from our convictions" (Medvedev, 1969, p. 58). Vavilov was arrested by secret police in August 1940. On the strength of testimony from informers and frightened colleagues he was sentenced to death for "belonging to a rightist conspiracy, spying for England, . . . sabotage in agriculture," etc., etc. (Medvedev, 1969, p. 72). His execution was delayed, however, and because of the German invasion in October 1941 he was evacuated to a windowless basement death cell. The following summer his sentence was commuted to ten years imprisonment, but weakened by malnutrition he died in January 1943. In 1955 he was accorded Russia's substitute for resurrection: posthumous rehabilitation.

Although Lysenko's methods make our own Joe McCarthy seem like a bleeding-heart liberal in comparison, they were not quite adequate to silence all of Lysenko's opponents. Only after Lysenko's speech to the LAAAS in 1948, from which the first selection of this chapter is taken, could he have his own way with Soviet Agriculture and biology. That speech, which Lysenko pointedly announced had been approved by the Central Committee, and which had in fact been read in advance by Stalin, made "Mendelism-Weismannism-Morganism" an outlaw science. Genetics texts were removed from libraries or rewritten to agree with Lysenko. Biology teachers had to ignore cell muclei and chromosomes. Those who persisted in studying the principles of heredity in such animals as fruit flies, rather than directly attacking the problems of agriculture, were reviled as "fly-lovers and man-haters" and reassigned to meaningless tasks. Cultures of *Drosophila* were sought out and liquidated. Not even relevance to human needs was an absolute guard against Lysenkoism, for medical genetics, the study of genetically caused diseases, was curtailed. On the other hand, scientists who toadied to Lysenko rose in stature regardless of their ability. Some Lysenkoites, such as A. I. Oparin, had undeniable talent; others were so incompetent that they really believed in Lysenko's theories. Lysenko himself became the object of a personality cult. His portrait was nearly as common as Stalin's, and his praises were sung by schoolchildren.

When Stalin died in 1953 there were attempts to depose Lysenko, but these were quickly thwarted by Khrushchev. Thus while Watson's and Crick's announcement of the double-helical model of DNA was sparking the revolution in molecular biology in the rest of the world, most Soviet biologists remained ignorant of the significance of DNA. Incredibly, Zhores Medvedev and a few others managed to publish some theoretical studies of molecular genetics by disguising them as cybernetics research.

And what were the achievements of Lysenko that justified three decades of repression? None. Russian agricultural productivity fell increasingly behind that of countries which used hybrids and other techniques based on bourgeois genetics. In fact, it is tempting to suspect that Lysenko was the greatest kulak-wrecker of all. However, this is probably crediting him with too much subtlety. A more mundane explanation is a simple lust for power, which every reader will easily recognize from examples in his own society. For thirty years Lysenko escaped detection by refusing to perform controlled experiments, appealing to the practical-mindedness of Stalin, Khrushchev, and the farmers, and by showing off the successes of his model farms which had the benefits of the best equipment. Finally, however, after two years of poor harvests, both Khrushchev and Lysenko were deposed in

1964. Unlike so many of their victims, both were permitted to die of natural causes. Lysenko still directed a large institute until he died.[8]

Let us now consider the theory of heredity which Lysenko and Prezent announced in 1935. This is not easy because of Lysenko's fuzzy and inconsistent use of language, but we can detect at least two major elements:

1. That the environment can directly affect the heredity of an organism. For example, vernalization worked by "shattering" the heredity of wheat and allowing it to develop a new heredity more rapidly.

2. The inheritance of acquired characters.

The second premise is often identified with Lamarckism, so Lysenkoism is often referred to as Lamarckian or neo-Lamarckian. This, however, is too hard on poor Lamarck, for it was not the most important part of Lamarck's theory, and it was held by many others, including Darwin. Moreover, Lamarck at least tried to incorporate some of the science of his time; Lysenko reached back into prescientific thought. For example, one product of his theory was the idea of "cluster planting" trees. It is well-known that trees planted closely together should be thinned to prevent their having to compete for light and nutrients. Lysenko, however, rejected the idea of competition within species as contrary to the ideal of class solidarity. Instead he believed that the weak trees in a cluster would "sacrifice themselves for the good of the species."[9] There was in fact more interest in scientific Lamarckism in Russia (and elsewhere) before Lysenko's rise than afterwards. In 1925 Russia offered Paul Kammerer (1880–1926) his own institute to continue studies of the inheritance of acquired characters in amphibians, in spite of the discovery that some of his specimens had been faked by someone. Kammerer was preparing to leave for Moscow when he committed suicide. Outside Russia neo-Lamarckism was found guilty by association with Kammerer and later with Lysenko, and has remained anathema to most biologists every since.[10]

Lamarckism was never rejected by Lysenko, but in Russia it was simply eclipsed by Lysenkoism—or Michurinism, as Lysenko and most Russians prefer to call it. Indeed Lysenkoism did owe less to Lamarck than to Ivan Vladimirovich Michurin (1855–1935), the "Russian Luther Burbank." Michurin claimed to have phenomenal success with tree grafting, and attributed this to the scion teaching the stock desirable traits. Michurin believed he could change any tree simply by grafting onto it a branch with desirable traits to act as an instructor. All things are possible for the man who will not listen to reason.[11]

We are not likely to profit from further study of Lysenko's ideas, but it is interesting to consider the basis for his condemnation of "Mendelism-Weismannism-Morganism" in the selection from the speech of 1948. First Lysenko cleverly plays to the postwar suspicions of all things foreign, and to the idea that bourgeois genetics has no practical applications. His main point, however, is that gene theory is "idealistic," in contrast to his own "materialistic" theory. No, this is not a faulty translation or misprint. Lysenko really believed that the idea of material hereditary factors was idealistic, while the idea of plants sacrificing themselves for the species and teaching other plants how to serve man was materialistic. The use of the terms "materialistic" and "idealistic" is exactly opposite to the custom of most people, and it is a reversal of what Marx and Engels meant by those words.

> Those who asserted the primacy of spirit to nature . . . comprised the camp of idealism. The others, who regarded nature as primary, belong to the various schools of materialism. These two expressions, idealism and materialism, originally signify nothing else but this; and here too they are not used in any other sense. What confusion arises when some other meaning is put into them. . . . (Engels, 1969, p. 20)

Over the years, however, this meaning of materialism became conflated with dialectical and historical materialism, according to which all things are in flux. Lenin was largely responsible for this revisionism. In a discussion of modern physics he wrote: "The recognition of immutable elements, 'of the immutable substance of things', and so forth, is not materialism, but *metaphysical*, i.e., anti-dialectical materialism."[12] (Lenin, 1970, p. 249) Now we can see how Mendel's assertion of unchanged hereditary factors and Weismann's theory of isolated germ plasm could be interpreted as anti-materialist, therefore idealistic. It made no difference that Morgan and his students had shown that genes do mutate; mutation was too slow and was caused by external forces, not internal contradicitions. On the other hand, Lysenko's theory that organisms struggle within themselves to bring about hereditary changes is materialistic in the sense that Lenin used the term. This also explains how Mendel and Weismann, both supporters of Darwin, could be charged with anti-Darwinism. Darwin was a materialist, as Marx noted; Mendel and Weismann were idealists, as just proved; therefore Mendel and Weismann were anti-Darwinians. Q.E.D.[13]

It is evident that through the misuse of the term "materialism," Lysenkoism was actually a perversion of materialism. There is an even more profound sense in which this is true. According to Marx and the classical materialists, laws of nature do not precede or determine the behavior of matter. Rather, those laws are created by the human brain from observing how matter behaves. Thus to ignore natural phenomena such as the experiments of Mendel and Morgan, and to give priority instead to abstract dialectical laws is to be not materialistic but idealistic. Lysenkoism was a complete distortion of Marxism, unless by Marxism we mean Groucho Marx's genius for pursuing a ridiculous premise to its logical conclusion.

EDWARD OSBORNE WILSON 1929

E. O. Wilson shares with the opponents of Lysenkoism the unenviable distinction of having been attacked by Marxists for his ideas of evolution. Of course being picketed, charged with Nazism and genocide, and doused with water are not to be compared with the fates of Vavilov and others in Russia. Still, the Marxist reaction to sociobiology is dramatic enough to suggest that the differences between Marx and Wilson will be worth looking into.[14]

E. O. Wilson has been collecting and observing animals, especially insects, since his high school years in Alabama. By age seventeen he had decided to become an entomologist specializing in ants. His mother, a descendant of farmers, and his father, a government accountant, did nothing to discourage this odd ambition. Wilson studied biology at the University of Alabama—the choice of that college having been dictated by its low tuition. After earning the B. S. degree he remained at Alabama for his M. S., following a brief stint as a state entomologist. During that period he conducted one of the first thorough studies of the imported fire ant. Later Wilson made further contributions to entomology as a graduate student at Harvard. After earning his Ph.D. in 1955 he remained at Harvard, where he is now Baird Professor of Science and curator of entomology at the Museum of Comparative Zoology. Wilson has participated in expeditions to such places as the West Indies, New Caledonia, Australia, and New Guinea. These journeys led to coauthorship of a book on *The Theory of Island Biogeography* (1967)—the subject which proved so inspiring to Darwin and Wallace.

In 1971 Wilson published *The Insect Societies*, the final chapter of which stated the goal of sociobiology: to be able to predict features of social organization in all natural species from a knowledge of "population parameters combined with information on the behavioral constraints imposed by the genetic constitution of the species." Essentially sociobiology seeks to apply neo-Darwinian theory to animal behavior. In *Sociobiology: The New Synthesis* (1975a), Wilson presented the theoretical basis for achieving this goal, described numerous applications to various species, and in the last twenty-nine pages of the 575-page text suggested applications to human social behavior. He was subsequently startled by the controversy over those concluding pages. Undaunted, however, he pursued the topic in the Pulitzer-Prize-winning book *On Human Nature*, which Wilson (1978a, p. xii) describes as "not a work of science, [but] a work about science."[15]

To most people who have read only criticism of Wilson, sociobiology probably means the theory that human behavior is caused by genes. Wilson (1978a, p. 230), however, defines sociobiology as "the scientific study of the biological basis of all forms of social behavior in all kinds of organisms, including man." Obviously sociobiology is too vast a subject to review in the space remaining here, so I will simply outline how sociobiology fits into evolutionary theory. In the process we may be able to see the source of the conflict between Marxists' and sociobiologists' attempts to explain the evolution of human society.

First it will be helpful to consider the scientific precursors of sociobiology (Barlow, 1980). The term "sociobiology" was used as early as 1946 and 1948 (Wilson, 1978b, p. 3), but as a science it goes back at least to Charles Darwin. From the very beginning of his search for a theory of evolution he kept notebooks on "Man, Mind and Materialism." (See the transcripts of the M and N notebooks in Gruber and Barrett, 1974.) In the *Origin of Species* he included a chapter on instinct, and even dared to hint that "much light will be thrown on the origins of man and his history." In *The Descent of Man* (1871) he freely discussed the evolution of "intellectual and moral faculties." Around the turn of the century, however, behavior became the monopoly of psychologists, who showed little interest in nonhuman species, except for the white rat and a few other models of man. The perspective was broadened by anthropologists and sociologists, but the emphasis was still on what made people different from each other, rather than on what they had in common because of a shared evolutionary heritage.

Only in the last few decades have biologists reclaimed animal behavior as a scientific discipline in its own right. Geneticists quickly noted behavioral differences among various strains of fruit flies and other species, indicating that some behavior is genetically programmed. Behavior genetics is now a thriving discipline, and there are numerous examples of genetically determined behaviors in a wide range of species. On the principle of continuity between man and other animals it is reasonable to suppose that some social behavior in humans may also be genetically based. However, hard evidence for that inference is lacking. For obvious reasons the breeding programs favored by behavior geneticists have not been attempted with humans. Studies of human pedigrees have shown that certain human behaviors are genetically determined, but these behaviors are either inconsequential (inability to smell isobutyrate, for example) or grossly abnormal (various types of mental retardation). Even if social behavior in humans were shown to be associated with a particular genotype it would be difficult to show that the behavior was the primary product of the genes and not a side effect of a physiological disturbance. This is an important point for sociobiologists, for they are interested in how the environment has selected for social behavior, not for other aspects of physiology.

The influence of social behavior on fitness is well-known in many cases, thanks to ethologists, who study animal behavior under natural conditions. They have described numerous types of stereotyped courtship and territorial behavior, notably in fish, birds, and insects. In many cases these have long been shown to be genetically programmed and subject to strong selection. The closest humans come to such stereotyped social behavior seems to be facial expressions, which are also shared with monkeys and apes. Not only would an Eskimo or Bushman understand and resent it if you glared at him, but so would a chimpanzee. (Naturally, Darwin wrote a book on the subject.) However, such stereotypy is rare among primates. Even apes of the same species have "cultural" variations in social behavior, depending on the environment, learning, and so on.[16]

With behavior genetics and ethology already well developed, why does Wilson feel the need for the new discipline of sociobiology? One reason is that too many ethologists have used what Wilson (1975a, pp. 28–30) calls the "advocacy approach to human evolution." Based on studies of a few species of birds, or perhaps one group of primates, many ethologists and popularizers have attempted to push their own diagnosis and cures for whatever social disorder happens to be in fashion. During the Viet Nam War and the outbreak of racial unrest in the United States, books which blamed aggression and racism on our evolutionary precursors crowded the shelves. Now the best sellers are books which explain the differences between the sexes. Wilson hopes to replace advocacy with a truly scientific approach capable of producing falsifiable predictions.

Wilson's hope for a scientific sociobiology rests largely on the fact, noted by Haldane in 1955, that the fitness of an organism depends not only on its own reproductive ability (Darwinian fitness), but also on the reproductive ability of its kin. As far as evolution is concerned it matters not at all whether a gene gets passed on to a son or to a niece. Thus in social animals an organism can increase the chances of getting its genes into the next generation by aiding its kin, who are likely to be carrying many of its genes. For an extreme example, consider the worker honeybee. Even though she never reproduces she can help get her genes into the population by insuring the survival of the queen, her mother. She would therefore have been selected for ability to help maintain the hive, and even to sacrifice her own life in stinging a predator. At first glance such self-sacrifice contradicts "survival of the fittest," but Darwin himself recognized that "fittest" in this case referred not to the individual but to the social group. As Marcus Aurelius noted, "What is not good for the hive, neither is it good for the bee." By aiding the queen in this way the worker in a sense can reproduce, if only by proxy.[17]

The contribution of kin to an individual's fitness was developed mathematically by W. D. Hamilton (1964). He defined the *inclusive fitness* of an organism as its own Darwinian fitness, plus the sum for all genetic kin of their Darwinian fitnesses multiplied by their genetic relatedness (r). For example, the worker honeybee has an individual Darwinian fitness of zero, but an inclusive fitness equal to the Darwinian fitness of the queen multiplied by $\frac{1}{2}$, plus the total Darwinian fitness for the drones multiplied by $\frac{1}{4}$. (The relatedness of the worker to the queen is $\frac{1}{2}$ because she gets one-half of her chromosomes from the queen and one-half from the drone who fertilized the egg from which the worker arose. The relatedness of the worker to a drone is ¼ because the drone receives only one-half the queen's chromosomes, through unfertilized eggs.) If natural selection worked only on Darwinian fitness it could not select directly for the traits of workers. Presumably, however, nature selects for inclusive fitness.

The sacrifice by workers of their own ability to reproduce is an example of altruism, defined by Wilson (1975a, p. 578) as "self-destructive behavior performed for the benefit of others." According to Wilson (1975a, p. 3) the central theoretical problem of sociobiology is to understand "how altruism, which by definition reduces personal fitness, could evolve by natural selection." Hamilton's formulation of inclusive fitness allows for such an understanding in at least some cases. The honeybee is one case, although an unusual one because of the unequal kinships among males and females. In most other sexually reproducing species each offspring, whether male or female, gets one chromosome of every pair from the mother, and the other chromosome of each pair from the father. Thus all offspring have a relatedness of ½ to each parent. To put it another way, each offspring has a fifty-fifty chance of carrying a particular gene from one parent. If a parent and each offspring had exactly the same Darwinian or personal fitness, then the parent would "break even" if it sacrificed its life for that of two offspring. The number of saved offspring needs to be higher if they are less fit, or lower if the parent is less fit. By this calculus similar optimal altruistic strategies can be worked out. This is referred to as the theory of kin selection. The theory predicts that on average (all Darwinian fitnesses equal) an animal would die for two sisters or brothers ($r = $ ½), or for eight cousins ($r = $ ⅛). On average an animal will give up to a sibling anything that will benefit the sibling twice as much as it is worth to the altruist. An organism is expected to contribute four times as much to a sibling as a cousin. One definition of "calculating" fits this kind of altruism, but of course few humans and no animals consciously make such calculations. That is the point. If social animals have been selected to maximize inclusive fitness they ought to behave automatically in this way. Thus the theory of kin selection provides some of the key falsifiable predictions which Wilson needs for a science of sociobiology.

As an example of such a test of sociobiology we can consider the relative contributions by worker and drone honeybees to the maintenance of the hive. As mentioned before each worker shares with each drone only twenty-five percent of her genes. Each worker, however, has a relatedness with other workers in a hive of up to ¾, assuming a single drone fertilized the eggs from which all the workers developed. Workers may therefore be more closely related to their sisters than they would be to their daughters, which may explain why they have been selected to help each other rather than to have daughters. Moreover, workers are up to three times more closely related to other workers than their brother drones are, which may explain why drones are famous for their laziness. Rather than help their sisters they save themselves for the once-in-a-lifetime opportunity to reproduce.

Now these are not true examples of falsifiable predictions, because honeybee behavior was known long before Hamilton proposed this explanation of their division of labor. However, the explanation is rendered more probable by two naturally occurring controls. First, the fact that the workers and drones occupy the same environment rules out any conceivable external cause of the difference in their behavior. Second, social termites, in which both males and females develop from fertilized eggs, share equally in maintaining the colony.[18]

There is another type of altruism besides that toward kin which is also consistent with the idea of inclusive fitness: it is reciprocal altruism. We expect that social animals of the same species will have evolved so as to mutually aid one another, whether or not they are closely related, so long as the inclusive fitness of all is increased. Wilson (1978a, Ch. 7) calls this "soft-core altruism." An analog in humans would be contributing to a charity from which one might some day benefit. Wilson recognizes that in humans there is also (rarely) "hard-core altruism," as when a soldier throws himself on a grenade to save unrelated comrades, or when someone adopts an unrelated child. Lysenko believed in hard-core altruism even among plants, but as far as I know neither Marx nor Engels ever attempted to deal with it in any species. I suspect they would have seen through most soft-core altruism in humans as not really qualifying as self-sacrifice. Almost certainly they would have considered hard-core altruism to be confined within social classes, because of class consciousness. They would have attributed any exceptions to the altruists' overestimating the return on their investments.

Critics of sociobiology frequently charge that it is not falsifiable. I doubt that the criterion of falsifiability can be applied to an entire discipline, but what the critics presumably mean is that none of the theories of sociobiology is falsifiable. There may be something to the charge, for if sociobiological theories can account for suicide, warfare, homosexuality, and other behaviors which are detrimental to Darwinian fitness, what is there that they cannot explain? The problem is that the phenomena are so complex and sociobiology is so rich in theories that alternative explanations and ad-hoc excuses for exceptional cases are always available. However, the same criticism applies to all neo-Darwinian theories. If the success of neo-Darwinism in explaining the giraffe's long neck counts in favor of neo-Darwinism, then the short necks of sheep and antelope ought to count against it. The reason they do not is that there are ad-hoc explanations for short necks. That is why such explanations ought to be discouraged. So much of evolution theory is like this that Popper considers it metaphysical rather than scientific. Personally, I don't believe the situation is that bad, because the central theory of neo-Darwinism—the differential reproductive success of different geno-types—is falsifiable. Moreover, explanations such as those of honeybee be-havior do come very close to being falsifiable.[19]

Unfortunately many sociobiologists do not heed Wilson's (1975a, pp. 27–31) urgings that predictions be stated in a falsifiable form, and that if one must resort to ex post facto explanations (as evolutionists often must), then several competing explanations should also be proposed. The reason for the latter prescription is to avoid the fallacy of "affirming the consequent": that is, concluding that because a phenomenon is consistent with an explanation, therefore the explanation is the only correct one. I shall discuss one example of a study which falls short of Wilson's ideal: Barash's (1977a) study of the "Sociobiology of Rape in Mallards *(Anas platyrhynchos)*: Responses of the Mated Male," which appeared in the prestigious journal *Science*. Barash observed that male mallards frequently responded to the rape of their mates by raping their mates themselves, especially when the female did not force-fully resist the first rapist. His explanation is as follows:

> Given the usual excess of males over females in surface-feeding ducks mates of rape victims do not have the option of an aggressive response [toward the victim], as reported for mates of seemingly adulterous mountain bluebirds, since replacement females are presumably unavailable. Under this circum-stance, optimum male strategy is probably to stick with his mate, but also to introduce his sperm as quickly as possible—hence the forcing of a copulation.

Forced copulations thus "probably represent efforts by the mates of just-raped females to make the best of a bad situation." According to Barash this behavior is "in accord with evolutionary prediction."

First, let us note that, unlike some of Barash's (1980) other studies, this is not an actual test of an "evolutionary prediction," for no one predicted the behavior before it was observed. Rather, it is an ex post facto explanation. This in itself would not be a criticism if Barash had proposed several alternative explanations and attempted to eliminate some of them. One obvious alternative is that the mated male saw in the successful rape of his mate an opportunity to copulate without the usual courtship preliminaries. The seizing of this opportunity might well be genetically programmed, in which case this explanation might not be experimentally distinguishable from Barash's. Alternatively the male might have learned to take advantage of the situation, in which case it should be possible to determine the role of previous experience on the behavior.

Another way to eliminate alternative explanations is to make use of natu-ral controls, such as were available with the honeybees. Such controls might also exist for Barash's study, but he did not report any attempt to find them. His explanation would be strengthened if the rape by mated males did not occur in flocks in which there were plenty of females. Also, since rape and a scarcity of females are not unusual among surface-feeding ducks, it should be possible to show that the same behavior occurs in other species, if his explanation is valid.

There is another defect in Barash's report which is even more pervasive; that is the careless use of language. We may pass over Barash's statement that the behavior of the mated male represents "efforts . . . to make the best of a bad situation." Presumably readers of *Science* would know to read that as "behavior which increases his inclusive fitness." Obviously drakes have little conception of the link between copulation and baby ducklings. More serious, however, is Barash's use of the word "rape." Barash defines rape in the *Science* report simply as "forced copulation." In a popular description of the work, however, Barash (1977b, pp. 67–68) omits a definition, leaving the general reader to supply his own definition from whatever experience he may have had with rape in humans. One can hardly blame the reader for assuming that rape in ducks is like rape in humans, and that Barash's explanation also applies to man. The reader would be in error, however, for human rape is usually motivated by hostility toward the victim or toward all women rather than a scarcity of females or a longing for children. Rape among humans is so severely punished in most societies that it is at least questionable whether it increases the rapist's fitness at all.

The transfer of terms from humans to animals probably results from a desire of the sociobiologist to make theories of animal behavior understandable and appealing to laymen. The attempt is misguided, however, if it leads to the unjustified transfer of concepts and theories between man and animals. Engels's criticism of such transfer is perhaps as just here as when he directed it at Darwin:

> After this trick [of transferring theories from man to animals] has been performed . . . the same theories are transferred back from organic nature to history and the claim is then made that it has been proved that they have the force of eternal laws of human society. The childishness of this procedure is obvious, and it is not worth while wasting any words on it.[20]

Now that we have been drawn into Marxist criticisms we might as well take the bull by the tail and face the situation of the debate between Marxists and sociobiologists. Unlike most commentators I would like to treat the controversy as a real philosophical difference in perception, rather than as an ordinary scientific debate or as political theater. By examining the underlying causes of the controversy we can better understand how all our ideologies affect our scientific perceptions. Most of the Marxist opposition to sociobiology has come from members of the Sociobiology Study Group, collectively and as individuals. This group is made up of members of the

Boston Science for the People, one of about three-dozen affiliates dedicated to socialism and opposed to the use of science for warfare, racism, and other forms of injustice. Most members of Science for the People are white, male college professors, doctors, and students. Two members of the Sociobiology Study Group, Stephen Jay Gould and Richard Lewontin, are colleagues of Wilson at Harvard's Museum of Comparative Zoology. Not all those who subscribe to the views of the Sociobiology Study Group are Marxists, however. Gould, Lewontin and Richard Levins use Marxist philosophy in their scientific thinking, but many who share their criticisms of sociobiology call themselves anarchists, socialists, leftists, or, like Darwin, radicals or liberals. I shall assume that when a Marxist endorses a criticism it is compatible with Marxism, even if non-Marxists also endorse it.[21]

The curious thing about the hostility between Marxists and Wilson is that both camps start from the same premise—scientific materialism. Marx would undoubtedly accept Wilson's definition of scientific materialism as "the view that all phenomena in the universe, including the human mind, have a material basis, are subject to the same physical laws, and can be most deeply understood by scientific analysis." Beyond this there is almost total disagreement. Marx lived in a time when one could still speak of objective laws of nature, discoverable by induction. To Marx scientific materialism was such a law. Wilson, however, recognizes that scientific materialism is not an objectively verifiable law, or even a falsifiable theory. He refers to it as a myth—a serious rival to the two other great mythologies of modern times, traditional religion and Marxism. Wilson (1978b, p. 3) explains the Marxist outcry as the expected reaction to kicking the Marxist sacred cow. In this assumption I believe Wilson and many others underestimate the depth of the Marxist reaction. Many of the Marxist critics cannot be so easily dismissed as worshippers of Marx opposed to scientific materialism, for to be a devotee of Marx is to be an even more dedicated devotee of scientific materialism.

I believe the main reason for disagreement between Marx and Wilson lies in their different applications of scientific materialism. Marx used it as a basis for his theory that all human behavior is ultimately determined by the need to obtain the material requirements for life. Most Marxists take this to mean that human behavior is almost totally flexible in response to the economic forces of society. Wilson rejects that interpretation as untested and wrong. To him scientific materialism means that there are material causes for the social behavior of animals within the patterns of neural connections within their brains, in the responses of their hormonal organs, and so forth. These material causes of social behavior are influenced to varying degrees by the environment, but they are also at least partially controlled by genes.[22]

In spite of this fundamental difference between the Marxist and sociobiological applications of materialism it is doubtful that a controversy would have arisen if Wilson had not suggested that *Homo sapiens* is one of the species whose social behavior is under some genetic control. Wilson guesses that the degree of genetic control is only ten percent (Wade, 1976), but Marxists deny that there are any genes for human social behavior, or if there are, that they are important in light of man's proven capacity to adapt to various situations. The debate between Marxists and sociobiologists at this point looks discouragingly like the debate over "nature versus nurture" which has been going on since Galton coined the phrase. But why should Marxists wish to join in this empty academic debate? The answer is that they view sociobiological and other theories of "biological determinism" as justifying war, racism, sexism, and social inequality while diverting attention from the real cause of those evils, modern market society. They reject the sociobiological inference that war and genocide result partly from an inherited biological tendency to increase one's own inclusive fitness by wiping out those who are not closely related. To make its point that these evils result from modern economic conditions, the Sociobiology Study Group (1976; 1977) has gone so far as to state that " 'primitive' warfare is rarely lethal to more than one, or at most a few, individuals in an episode of warfare," and that "genocide was practically unknown until state-organized societies appeared in history. . . ."[23]

A different but related source of conflict between Marxists and sociobiologists is the Marxist view that scientific theories are inevitably influenced by and are used to support the ruling class of society. "All people doing science are reflecting their general view of the world, politically and socially," says Lewontin. (In Henig, 1979. See also Lewontin, 1969 and Sahlins, 1976, Part II.) With that assumption the standard of science now becomes a political and social one: Does the science further the cause of socialism or hinder it? In the Marxist view sociobiology fails that test by being both a product and a tool of capitalism. In the opening attack againt Wilson, Allen et al. (1975) charged that sociobiology was "the latest attempt to reinvigorate" theories of genetic causes of criminality and racial inferiority which have been used to justify eugenics, forced sterilization, restrictive immigration laws, and the gas chambers of Nazi Germany. Lately they have refrained from accusing Wilson, who describes himself as a liberal (Wade, 1976), of deliberately attempting to revive such practices. For example, Gould, who signed the document just referred to, attributes no motive to Wilson in a later article on sociobiology. (Gould, 1977, Ch. 32, reprinted in Caplan, 1978b, pp. 343–351. See also Gould, 1980b.) The Marxist critics now merely state that Wilson can't help having a bourgeois view of nature because of his status as a white, male Harvard professor.

If the root of the Marxist-sociobiologist conflict is their different world views, then there may be something to this last charge. We have seen throughout this book how the social milieu of the scientist influences his creativity. The individual perspective can never render an objective view of a total situation; it can provide unique insights, but it can also distort. The remedy for this, as Popper (1966, vol. 2, Ch. 23) points out, lies in criticism by other scientists with different points of view. Each critic's perspective may also be distorted, but the distortion will eventually be corrected by the total view. In the case of sociobiology and its Marxist critics I shall leave it to the reader to sort out the insights from the distortions by comparing the following sample of criticisms with what Wilson says in the selection on "Role Playing and Polyethism":

> To construct such a view of human nature, Wilson either must divorce himself from any historical or ethnographic perspective or engage in bad ethnographic and bad historical reporting. His discussion of the economy of scarcity is an excellent example. An economy of scarcity and unequal distribution of rewards is described as an aspect of human nature, as follows: "The members of human societies sometimes cooperate closely in *insectan* fashion, but more frequently they compete for the limited resources allocated to their role sector. The best and most entrepreneurial of the role-actors usually gain a disproportionate share of the rewards, while the least successful are displaced to other, less desirable positions" (p. 554). [Our emphasis.] Note that this description of modern market-economy society is universalized over time and space, consigning the unstated cooperative "exceptions" to an "insectan" form of behavior. It is rather reminiscent of the predetente rhetoric about "insectlike" Chinese millions, identically blue clad and mindlessly regimented into cooperative (and "unnatural") brigades. In fact, there exists a great deal of ethnographic description that completely contradicts this conception of social organization. There are scores of known "egalitarian" societies that do not have more or less desirable positions or inequalities of shares. (See, for example, the literature on Eskimos. . . .)—Sociobiology Study Group, 1977, pp. 137–138.

> The newest wave of human nature determinism has culminated in the publication by E. O. Wilson of *Sociobiology: The New Synthesis.* . . , which announces the creation of a new field, sociobiology, and which asserts that such human cultural manifestations as religion, ethics, tribalism, warfare, genocide, cooperation, competition, entrepreneurship, conformity, indoctrinability, and spite (the list is incomplete) are tendencies that have been established by natural selection and by implication are encoded in the human genome. No evidence at all is presented for a genetic basis of these characteristics, and the arguments for their establishment by natural selection cannot be tested, since such arguments postulate hypothetical situations in human prehistory that are uncheckable. For example, homosexuality is hypothesized to be genetically conditioned (no evidence), and it is then assumed that homosexuals leave fewer offspring than heterosexuals (no evidence and a confusion between homosexual *acts* and total homosexuality), but then it is postulated that the "genes" for homosexuality may have been preserved in human prehistory because homosexuals served as helpers to their close relatives (uncheckable story with no ethnographic evidence from present hunters and gatherers to suggest such a phenomenon).—Lewontin, 1977b, pp. 15–16.

The second main tack is to postulate genes right and left. The technique is a simple one. Start by saying "if there were a gene for spite" and then go on with a long discussion of the consequences, dropping the "if" along the way. There are hypothetical altruist genes, conformer genes, spite genes, learning genes, homosexual genes, and so on. An instance of the technique is on pp. 554–555. "Dahlberg (1947) showed that *if* a single gene appears that is responsible for success and upward-shift in status. . . . Furthermore, there are *many* Dahlberg genes. . . ." [Our emphasis.] Or, again (p. 555), "The homosexual state itself results in inferior genetic fitness. . . .It remains to be said that if such genes really exist they are almost certainly incomplete in penetrance and expressivity." The notion of confirming the existence of behavior genes that only have effect in some unspecified proportion of individuals carrying them *(incomplete penetrance)* and with some unspecified range of manifestation when they do have effect *(variable expressivity)* is interesting. (A standing joke among human geneticists is that, when some trait has defied attempts to unravel its inheritance [if any], it is said to be "a dominant gene with incomplete penetrance and variable expressivity.")—Sociobiology Study Group, 1977, p. 143.

Trofim Denisovich Lysenko from *The Science of Biology Today.* International Publishers, New York, 1948, pp. 9–19. By permission.

1. Biology, the Basis of Agronomy

Agronomy deals with living bodies—plants, animals, micro-organisms. A theoretical grounding in agronomy therefore must include knowledge of biological laws. And the more profoundly the science of biology reveals the laws of the life and development of living bodies, the more effective is the science of agronomy.

In essence, the science of agronomy is inseparable from biology. When we speak of the theory of agronomy we mean the discovered and comprehended laws of the life and development of plants, animals, and micro-organisms.

The methodological level of biological knowledge, the state of the science treating of the laws of the life and development of vegetable and animal forms, *i.e.,* primarily of the science known as genetics for half a century now, is of essential importance for our agricultural science.

2. The History of Biology: A History of Ideological Controversy

The appearance of Darwin's teaching, expounded in his book, *The Origin of Species,* marked the beginning of scientific biology. The primary idea in Darwin's theory is the teaching on natural and artificial selection. Selection of variations favorable to the organism has produced the purposefulness which we observe in living nature: in the structure of organisms and their adaptation to their conditions of life.

Darwin's theory of selection provided a rational explanation of the purposefulness observable in living nature. His idea of selection is scientific and true. In substance, the teaching on selection is a summation of the age-old practical experience of plant and animal breeders who, long before Darwin, produced strains of plants and breeds of animals by the empirical method.

Darwin investigated the numerous facts obtained by naturalists in living nature and analyzed them through the prism of practical experience. Agricultural practice served Darwin as the material basis for the elaboration of his theory of evolution, which explained the natural causation of the utility we see in the structure of the organic world. That was a great advance in the knowledge of living nature.

In Engels' opinion, three great discoveries enabled man's knowledge of the interconnection of natural processes to advance by leaps and bounds: first, the discovery of the cell; second, the discovery of transformation of energy; third, the proof which Darwin first developed in connected form that the stock of organic products of nature surrounding us today, including mankind, is the result of a long process of evolution from a few original unicellular germs, and that these again have arisen from protoplasm or albumen which came into existence by chemical means.

The classics of Marxism, while fully appreciating the significance of the Darwinian theory, pointed out the errors of which Darwin was guilty. Darwin's theory, though unquestionably materialist in its main features, is not free from some serious errors. A major fault, for example, is the fact that, along with the materialist principle, Darwin introduced into his theory of evolution reactionary Malthusian ideas. In our days this major error is being aggravated by reactionary biologists.

Darwin himself recorded the fact that he accepted the Malthusian idea. In his autobiography we read:

"In October 1838, that is, fifteen months after I had begun my systematic enquiry, I happened to read for amusement Malthus on population, and, being well prepared to appreciate the struggle for existence which everywhere goes on from long-continued observation of the habits of animals and plants, it at once struck me that under these circumstances favorable variations would tend to be preserved, and unfavorable ones to be destroyed. The result of this would be the formation of new species. Here then *I had at last got a theory by which to work.*" (My emphasis—T. L.)

Many are still apt to slur over Darwin's error in transferring into his teaching Malthus' preposterous reactionary ideas on population. The true scientist cannot and must not overlook the erroneous aspects of Darwin's teaching.

Biologists should always ponder these words of Engels: "The entire Darwinian teaching on the struggle for existence merely transfers from society to the realm of living nature Hobbes' teaching on war of all against all and the bourgeois economic teaching on competition, along with Malthus' population theory. After this trick has been performed (the absolute justification for which I question, particularly in regard to Malthus' theory), the same theories are transferred back from organic nature to history and the claim is then made that it has been proved that they have the force of eternal laws of human society. The childishness of this procedure is obvious, and it is not worth while wasting any words on it. But if I were to dwell on this at greater length, I should have started out by showing that they are poor *economists* first, and only then that they are poor naturalists and philosophers."

For the propaganda of his reactionary ideas Malthus invented an allegedly natural law. "The cause to which I allude," he wrote, "is the constant tendency in all animated life to increase beyond the nourishment prepared for it."

It must be clear to any progressively thinking Darwinist that, even though Darwin accepted Malthus' reactionary theory, it basically contradicts the materialist principle of his own teaching. Darwin himself, as may be easily noted, being as he was a great naturalist, the founder of scientific biology, whose activity marks an epoch in science, could not be satisfied with the Malthusian theory, since it is, in fact and fundamentally, in contradiction to the phenomena of living nature.

Under the weight of the vast amount of biological facts accumulated by him, Darwin felt constrained in a number of cases radically to alter the concept "struggle for existence," to stretch it to the point of declaring that it was just a figure of speech.

Darwin himself, in his day, was unable to fight free of the theoretical errors of which he was guilty. It was the classics of Marxism that revealed those errors and pointed them out. Today there is absolutely no justification for accepting the erroneous aspects of the Darwinian theory, those based on Malthus' theory of overpopulation with the inference about a struggle presumably going on within species. And it is all the more inadmissible to represent these erroneous aspects as the cornerstone of Darwinism (as I. I. Schmalhausen, B. M. Zavadovsky, and P. M. Zhukovsky do). Such an approach to Darwin's theory prejudices the creative development of its scientific core.

Even when Darwin's teaching first made its appearance, it became clear at once that its scientific, materialist core, the teaching on the evolution of living nature, was antagonistic to the idealism that reigned in biology.

Progressively thinking biologists, both in our country and abroad, saw in Darwinism the only right road to the further development of scientific biology. They took it upon themselves to defend Darwinism against the attacks of the reactionaries, with the Church at their head, and of obscurantists in science, such as Bateson.

Eminent biologists like V. O. Kovalevsky, I. I. Mechnikov, I. M. Sechenov and, particularly, K. A. Timiryazev defended and developed Darwinism with all the passion of true scientists. K. A. Timiryazev, that great investigator, saw distinctly that only on the basis of Darwinism could the science of the life of plants and animals develop successfully, that only by further developing Darwinism and raising it to new heights is biological science capable of helping the tiller of the soil to obtain two ears of corn where only one grows today.

Darwinism, as presented by Darwin, contradicted the idealistic philosophy, and this contradiction grew deeper with the development of the materialist teaching. Reactionary biologists have therefore done everything in their power to empty Darwinism of its materialist elements. The individual voices of progressive biologists like K. A. Timiryazev were drowned out by the chorus of the anti-Darwinists, the reactionary biologists the world over.

In the post-Darwinisn period the overwhelming majority of biologists—far from further developing Darwin's teaching—did all they could to vulgarize Darwinism, to smother its scientific foundation. The most glaring manifestation of such vulgarization of Darwinism is to be found in the teaching of August Weismann, Gregor Mendel, and Thomas Hunt Morgan, the founder of modern reactionary genetics.

3. Two Worlds—Two Ideologies in Biology

Weismannism, followed by Mendelism-Morganism, which made its appearance at the beginning of this century, was primarily directed against the materialist foundations of Darwin's theory of evolution.

Weismann named his conception Neo-Darwinism, but, in fact, it was a complete denial of the materialist aspects of Darwinism. It insinuated idealism and metaphysics into biology.

The materialist theory of evolution of animated nature involves recognition of the necessity of hereditary transmission of individual characteristics acquired by the organism under the conditions of its life; it is unthinkable without recognition of the inheritance of acquired characters. Weismann, however, set out to refute this materialist proposition. In his lectures on evolutionary theory, he asserts that "not only is there no proof of such a form of heredity, but it is inconceivable theoretically." Referring to earlier statements of his in a similar vein, he declares that "thus war was declared against the Lamarckian principle of the direct effect of use and disuse, and there arose a strife which has continued to this day, the strife between the Neo-Lamarckians and the Neo-Darwinians, as the two disputing parties have been called."

Weismann, as we see, speaks of having declared war against Lamarck's principle; but it is easy enough to see that he declared war against that without which there is no materialist theory of evolution, that under the guise of "Neo-Darwinism" he declared war against the materialist foundations of Darwinism.

Weismann denied the inheritability of acquired characters and elaborated the idea of a special hereditary substance to be sought for in the nucleus. "The sought for bearer of the inheritance," he stated, "is contained in the substance of the chromosome." The chromosomes, he said, contain units, each of which "determines a definite part of the organism in its appearance and final form."

Weismann asserts that there are "two great categories of living substance—the hereditary substance or idioplasm, and 'nutritive substance' or trophoplasm." And he goes on to declare that the bearers of the hereditary substance, "the chromosomes, represent a separate world, as it were," a world independent of the organism and its condition of life.

In Weismann's opinion, the living body is but a nutritive soil for the hereditary substance, which is immortal and never generated again.

So, he asserts, "the germ plasm of a species is thus never formed de novo, but it grows and increases ceaselessly; it is handed down from one generation to another . . . . If these conditions be considered from the point of view of reproduction, the germ cells appear the most important part of the individual, for they alone maintain the species, and the body sinks down almost to the level of a mere cradle for the germ cells, a place in which they are formed, and under favorable conditions are nourished, multiply, and attain to maturity." The living body and its cells, according to Weismann, are but the *container and nutritive medium* of the hereditary substance; they themselves can never produce the latter, they "can never bring forth germ cells."

Weismann thus endows the mythical hereditary substance with the property of continued existence; it is a substance which does not develop itself and at the same time determines the development of the mortal body.

Further: ". . . the hereditary substance of the germ cell, *prior* to the reduction division, potentially contains all the elements of the body." And although Weismann does state that "the germ plasm no more contains the determinants of a 'crooked nose' than it does those of a butterfly's tailed wing," he goes on to emphasize that, nevertheless, the germ plasm . . . "contains a number of determinants which so control the whole cell-group in all its successive stages, leading on to the development of the nose, that ultimately the crooked nose must result, just as the butterfly's wing with all its veins, membranes, tracheae, glandular cells, scales, pigment deposits and pointed tail arises through the successive interposition of numerous determinants in the course of cell multiplication."

Hence, according to Weismann, the hereditary substance produces no new forms, does *not* develop with the development of the individual, and is *not* subject to any dependent changes.

An immortal hereditary substance, independent of the qualitative features attending the development of the living body, directing the mortal body, but not produced by the latter—that is Weismann's frankly idealistic, essentially mystical conception, which he disguised as "Neo-Darwinism."

Weismann's conception has been fully accepted and, we might say, carried further by the Mendelian-Morganists.

Morgan, Johannsen and other pillars of Mendelism-Morganism declared from the outset that they intended to investigate the phenomena of heredity independently of the Darwinian theory of evolution. Johannsen, for example, wrote in his principal work: ". . . one of the major aims of our research was to put an end to the harmful dependence of the hereditary theories on speculations in the field of evolution." The purpose of the Morganists in making such declarations was to wind up their investigations by assertions which in the final analysis denied evolution in living nature, or recognized it as a process of purely quantitative changes.

As noted above, the controversy between the materialist and the idealist outlook in biological science has been going on throughout its history. In the present epoch of struggle between two worlds the two opposing and antagonistic trends penetrating the foundations of nearly all branches of biology are particularly sharply defined.

Socialist agriculture, the collective and state farming system, has given rise to a Soviet biological science, founded by I. V. Michurin—a science new in principle, developing in close union with agronomic practice as agronomic biology.

The foundations of the Soviet agro-biological science were laid by Michurin and V. R. Williams, who generalized and developed the best of what science and practice had accumulated in the past. Their work has enriched our knowledge of the nature of plants and soils, our knowledge of agriculture, with much that is new in principle.

Close contact between science and the practice of collective farms and state farms creates inexhaustible opportunities for the development of theoretical knowledge, enabling us to learn ever more and more about the nature of living bodies and the soil.

It is no exaggeration to state that Morgan's feeble metaphysical "science" concerning the nature of living bodies can stand no comparison with our effective Michurinian agro-biological science.

The new vigorous trend in biology, or, more truly, the new Soviet biology, agro-biology, has met with strong opposition on the part of representatives of reactionary biology abroad, as well as of some scientists in our country.

The representatives of reactionary biological science—Neo-Darwinians, Weismannists, or, which is the same, Mendelian-Morganists—uphold the so-called chromosome theory of heredity.

Following Weismann, the Mendelian-Morganists contend that the chromosomes contain a special "hereditary substance" which resides in the body of the organism as if in a case and is transmitted to coming generations irrespective of the qualitative features of the body and its conditions of life. The conclusion drawn from this conception is that new tendencies and characteristics acquired by the organism under the influence of the conditions of its life and development are not inherited and can have no evolutionary significance.

According to this theory, characters acquired by plant and animal organisms cannot be handed down, *are not inherited.*

The Mendel-Morgan theory does not include in the scientific concept "living body" the conditions of the body's life. To the Morganists, environment is only the background—indispensable, they admit—for the manifestation and operation of the various characteristics of the living body, in accordance with its heredity. They therefore hold that qualitative variations in the heredity (nature) of living bodies are entirely independent of the environment, of the conditions of life.

The representatives of Neo-Darwinism, the Mendelian-Morganists, hold that the efforts of investigators to regulate the heredity of organisms by changes in the conditions of life of these organisms are utterly unscientific. They therefore call the Michurinian trend in agrobiology Neo-Lamarckian, which, in their opinion, is absolutely faulty and unscientific.

Actually, it is the other way round.

Firstly, the well-known Lamarckian propositions, which recognize the active role of external conditions in the formation of the living body and the heredity of acquired characters, unlike the metaphysics of Neo-Darwinism (or Weismannism), are by no means faulty. On the contrary, they are quite true and scientific.

Secondly, the Michurinian trend cannot be called either Neo-Lamarckian or Neo-Darwinian. It is creative Soviet Darwinism, rejecting the errors of each, and free from the defects of the Darwinian theory in so far as it included Malthus' erroneous ideas.

Furthermore, it cannot be denied that in the controversy that flared up between the Weismannists and Lamarckians in the beginning of the twentieth century, the Lamarckians were closer to the truth; for they defended the interests of science, whereas the Weismannists were at loggerheads with science and prone to indulge in mysticism.

The true ideological content of Morgan's genetics has been well revealed (to the discomfiture of our geneticists) by the physicist Erwin Schroedinger. In his book, *What Is Life? The Physical Aspects of the Living Cell,* he draws some philosophical conclusions from Weismann's chromosome theory, of which he speaks very approvingly. Here is his main conclusion: ". . . the personal self equals omnipresent, all-comprehending eternal self." Schroedinger regards this conclusion as "the closest the biologist can get to proving God and immortality at one stroke."

We, the representatives of the Soviet Michurinian trend, contend that inheritance of characters acquired by plants and animals in the process of their development is possible and necessary. Ivan Vladimirovich Michurin mastered these possibilities in his experiments and practical activities. The most important point is that Michurin's teaching, expounded in his works, shows every biologist the way to regulating the nature of plant and animal organisms, the way of altering it in a direction required for practical purposes by regulating the conditions of life, *i.e.,* by physiological means.

A sharp controversy, which has divided biologists into two irreconcilable camps, has thus flared up over the old question: Is it possible for features and characteristics acquired by plant and animal organisms in the course of their life to be inherited? In other words, whether qualitative variations of the nature of plant and animal organisms depend on the conditions of life which act upon the living body, upon the organism.

The Michurinian teaching, which is materialist and dialectical in its essence, proves by facts that such dependence does exist.

The Mendel-Morgan teaching, which is metaphysical and idealist in its essence, denies the existence of such dependence, though it can cite no evidence to prove its point.

Edward Osborne Wilson, from *Sociobiology: The New Synthesis.* The Belknap Press of Harvard University Press, Cambridge, 1975, pp. 554–555. By permission.

Role Playing and Polyethism

The superman, like the super-ant or super-wolf, can never be an individual; it is the society, whose members diversify and cooperate to create a composite well beyond the capacity of any conceivable organism. Human societies have effloresced to levels of extreme complexity because their members have the intelligence and flexibility to play roles of virtually any degree of specification, and to switch them as the occasion demands. Modern man is an actor of many parts who may well be stretched to his limit by the constantly shifting demands of his environment. As Goffman (1961) observed, "Perhaps there are times when an individual does march up and down like a wooden soldier, tightly rolled up in a particular role. It is true that here and there we can pounce on a moment when an individual sits fully astride a single role, head erect, eyes front, but the next moment the picture is shattered into many pieces and the individual divides into different persons holding the ties of different spheres of life by his hands, by his teeth, and by his grimaces. When seen up close, the individual, bringing together in various ways all the connections he has in life, becomes a blur." Little wonder that the most acute inner problem of modern man is identity.

Roles in human societies are fundamentally different from the castes of social insects. The members of human societies sometimes cooperate closely in insectan fashion, but more frequently they compete for the limited resources allocated to their role-sector. The best and most entrepreneurial of the role-actors usually gain a disproportionate share of the rewards, while the least successful are displaced to other, less desirable positions. In addition, individuals attempt to move to higher socioeconomic positions by changing roles. Competition between classes also occurs, and in great moments of history it has proved to be a determinant of societal change.

A key question of human biology is whether there exists a genetic predisposition to enter certain classes and to play certain roles. Circumstances can be easily conceived in which such genetic differentiation might occur. The heritability of at least some parameters of intelligence and emotive traits is sufficient to respond to a moderate amount of disruptive selection. Dahlberg (1947) showed that if a single gene appears that is responsible for success and an upward shift in status, it can be rapidly concentrated in the uppermost socioeconomic classes. Suppose, for example, there are two classes, each beginning with only a 1 percent frequency of the homozygotes of the upward-mobile gene.[25] Suppose further that 50 percent of the homozygotes in the lower class are transferred upward in each generation. Then in only ten generations, depending on the relative sizes of the groups, the upper class will be comprised of as many as 20 percent homozygotes or more and the lower class of as few as 0.5 percent or less. Using a similar argument, Herrnstein (1971b) proposed that as environmental opportunities become more nearly equal within societies, socioeconomic groups will be defined increasingly by genetically based differences in intelligence.

A strong initial bias toward such stratification is created when one human population conquers and subjugates another, a common enough event in human history. Genetic differences in mental traits, however slight, tend to be preserved by the raising of class barriers, racial and cultural discrimination, and physical ghettos. The geneticist C. D. Darlington (1969), among others, postulated this process to be a prime source of genetic diversity within human societies.

Yet despite the plausibility of the general argument, there is little evidence of any hereditary solidification of status. The castes of India have been in existence for 2000 years, more than enough time for evolutionary divergence, but they differ only slightly in blood type and other measurable anatomical and physiological traits. Powerful forces can be identified that work against the genetic fixation of caste difference. First, cultural evolution is too fluid. Over a period of decades or at most centuries ghettos are replaced, races and subject people are liberated, the conquerors are conquered. Even within relatively stable societies the pathways of upward mobility are numerous. The daughters of lower classes tend to marry upward. Success in commerce or political life can launch a family from virtually any socioeconomic group into the ruling class in a single generation. Furthermore, there are many Dahlberg genes, not just the one postulated for argument in the simplest model. The hereditary factors of human success are strongly polygenic and form a long list, only a few of which have been measured. IQ constitutes only one subset of the components of intelligence. Less tangible but equally important qualities are creativity, entrepreneurship, drive, and mental stamina. Let us assume that the genes contributing to these qualities are scattered over many chromosomes. Assume further that some of the traits are uncorrelated or even negatively correlated. Under these circumstances only the most intense forms of disruptive selection could result in the formation of stable ensembles of genes. A much more likely circumstance is the one that apparently prevails: the maintenance of a large amount of genetic diversity within societies and the loose correlation of some of the genetically determined traits with success. This scrambling process is accelerated by the continuous shift in the fortunes of individual families from one generation to the next.

Even so, the influence of genetic factors toward the assumption of certain *broad* roles cannot be discounted. Consider male homosexuality. The surveys of Kinsey and his coworkers showed that in the 1940's approximately 10 percent of the sexually mature males in the

United States were mainly or exclusively homosexual for at least three years prior to being interviewed. Homosexuality is also exhibited by comparably high fractions of the male populations in many if not most other cultures. Kallmann's twin data indicate the probable existence of a genetic predisposition toward the condition. Accordingly, Hutchinson (1959) suggested that the homosexual genes may possess superior fitness in heterozygous conditions. His reasoning followed lines now standard in the thinking of population genetics. The homosexual state itself results in inferior genetic fitness, because of course homosexual men marry much less frequently and have far fewer children than their unambiguously heterosexual counterparts. The simplest way genes producing such a condition can be maintained in evolution is if they are superior in the heterozygous state, that is, if heterozygotes survive into maturity better, produce more offspring, or both. An interesting alternatiave hypothesis has been suggested to me by Herman T. Spieth (personal communication) and independently developed by Robert L. Trivers (1974). The homosexual members of primitive societies may have functioned as helpers, either while hunting in company with other men or in more domestic occupations at the dwelling sites. Freed from the special obligations of parental duties, they could have operated with special efficiency in assisting close relatives. Genes favoring homosexuality could then be sustained at a high equilibrium level by kin selection alone. It remains to be said that if such genes really exist they are almost certainly incomplete in penetrance and variable in expressivity, meaning that which bearers of the genes develop the behavioral trait and to what degree depend on the presence or absence of modifier genes and the influence of the environment.

Other basic types might exist, and perhaps the clues lie in full sight. In his study of British nursery children Blurton Jones (1969) distinguished two apparently basic behavioral types. "Verbalists," a small minority, often remained alone, seldom moved about, and almost never joined in rough-and-tumble play. They talked a great deal and spent much of their time looking at books. The other children were "doers." They joined groups, moved around a great deal, and spent much of their time painting and making objects instead of talking. Blurton Jones speculated that the dichotomy results from an early divergence in behavioral development persisting into maturity. Should it prove general it might contribute fundamentally to diversity within cultures. There is no way of knowing whether the divergence is ultimately genetic in origin or triggered entirely by experiential events at an early age.

GETTING BAD MARX IN SCIENCE

When I began this book I had no other objective than an exposition of the development of theories of the origin of species, emphasizing the creativity of the individual scientist under the influence of his culture. However, an unintended theme has repeatedly asserted itself. That theme is the tension between elements of society and the creators of theories of man's origins. Indeed that tension seems proof in itself that scientists do not simply reflect the dominant views of their society, as Marxists claim, but often depart radically from them if their interpretation of evidence leads in that direction. In the case of theories of man's origins such tension is not at all surprising, for it is impossible to say anything about where man came from without saying something about who he is, and thereby coming into conflict with established religion, philosophy, and ideology. If there is any one lesson to be learned from this book it is that whatever the setbacks science may suffer at the hands of dogmatists, they are only temporary. Eventually reason triumphs and dogma stands condemned in the eyes of history. Attempts of the church to impose Aristotle upon Renaissance science provoked the counter-Scholastic rebellion of Bacon, Descartes, and others, and the realization that in matters of science the church is no more infallible than the rest of us. Creationists continue to score minor victories against evolutionism, but the eventual outcome seems foreshadowed by the negative reaction to presidential-candidate Reagan's advocacy of teaching the biblical story of creation in public schools. Those who dreamed of building a glorious Soviet Science of Lysenkoism on the ashes of bourgeois genetics merely destroyed what science they had and brought shame upon themselves and their country.

Time and again we hear the established dogmatists predict the collapse of civilization or some other dire consequence if some new idea of man's origins is not suppressed. Just as often we see the new idea absorbed with no permanent ill effects upon mankind except for a reduced capacity to believe in dogmatic authority. Any temporary harm has usually resulted from the efforts to suppress the idea, rather than from the idea itself. I do not wish to be dogmatic myself, but I will make the following assertion with a confidence backed by induction from all of recorded history: No idea is as dangerous as the idea that some ideas are too dangerous to be expressed.

Tolerance for the views of others may seem a trite sermon to most of us, but it is by no means a lesson that all grown-ups have learned. I wish to consider especially Marxists who are intolerant of others, because Marxism is such a potent force in modern times. One finds scarcely a word in the classics of Marxism respecting the personal freedoms of individuals as opposed to the collective economic freedom of the masses. Marxists have traditionally considered the individual scientist to be just one of the parts of a collective, to be silenced if his creativity threatens the whole. This view may now be more popular than ever because of writers like myself who have emphasized the mutual relationships between scientists and society, and have said perhaps too little about the individual, rational processes of science. Whatever the reason for the conclusion that science is just another part of the superstructure which supports the mode of production, it is a totally illogical conclusion. It reminds me of Engels's lamentations about the "most amazing rubbish" which his and Marx's emphasis on economic determinism had inspired (quoted in Young, 1973, p. 345). Not only is it unreasonable to think that scientists and politicians are really in the same business, it is also dangerous. From such a conclusion it follows almost immediately that one may suppress scientific ideas in whatever way one suppresses political opponents or revolutionaries. It seems to me that Marxist scientists stand to lose the most if ever they convince others that the political motivations of a scientist are relevant to the acceptance or rejection of his theories. One can cite a great many Marxists who knew this. Haldane (1933, p. 208) wrote that "there is a worse evil than intellectual starvation, and that is the deliberate suppression of free thought and free speech." Even Joseph Stalin was capable of saying, if not of believing, that "no science can develop and prosper without the clash of opinions."[26]

The tactics employed by some Marxist opponents of sociobiology are in marked contrast to these ideals. Not content merely to criticize Wilson, Richard Lewontin for example has admitted his intention to "trash" Wilson's book. The stress on Wilson's family has caused him to cancel some lectures. Lewontin says he did not intend that result, but since he expects Wilson to be accountable for the consequences of sociobiology, he must also accept responsibility for the consequences of his own actions.[27]

The threat to sociobiology is not idle. Jonathan Beckwith of Harvard and Jonathan King of MIT used similar tactics and arguments to halt a study of possible behavioral disturbances in children born with an extra sex chromosome. These self-anointed opponents of "biological determinism" were able to nullify the judgment of a granting agency, a Harvard review panel, and a 200-to-30 vote of the Harvard Medical School faculty by intimidating the researcher (Culliton, 1975). One recalls with sadness and alarm the suppression of medical genetics under Lysenko.

As we have seen in the cases of Lysenko and others the suppression of science eventually backfires. I predict the same outcome for Marxist opponents of sociobiology. It may be that Marxists will succeed in alerting the book-trashers to the threat of "biological determinism," but will they be able to stop them from burning the works of Marx, wherein they will find the following?

Within a family, and after further development within a tribe, there springs up
naturally a division of labor, caused by differences of sex and age, a division that
is consequently based on a purely physiological foundation. . . .

Capital, Ch. 14.4.

In its historical and political application, the book is much more important and
copious than Darwin. For certain questions, such as nationality, etc., a natural
basis is found only in this work. For example, the author corrects the Pole
Duchinski, whose findings in regard to the geological differences between
Russia and the West Slavs he generally confirms, that contrary to the Pole's
belief, the Russians are not only no Slavs but, rather, Tartars, etc., but also that
on the existing soil formation of Russia the Slavs became Tartarized and Mon-
golized, just as he (he has been in Africa for a long time) proves the common
Negro type is only a degeneration of a much higher one. . . .

Letter from Marx to Engels, 7 August 1866
Marx (1979, p. 215)

It is now completely clear to me that he, as is proved by his cranial formation and
[curly] hair—descends from the Negroes who had joined Moses' exodus from
Egypt (assuming his mother or grandmother on the paternal side had not
interbred with a *nigger* [in English]. Now this union of Judaism and Gemanism
with a basic Negro substance must produce a peculiar product. The obtrusive-
ness of the fellow is also *Nigger*-like [in English].

Letter from Marx to Engels, 30 July 1862
Marx (1979, p. 468)

I have no doubt that Marxist opponents of biological determinism are
possessed of good intentions. They believe that war, racism, sexism, and
injustice are caused only by social and economic conditions, and that searching for biological causes merely delays correcting the real causes. They also
fear that many people will commit the *naturalistic fallacy* of believing that
what is biologically natural in wild animals is inevitable or desirable in
civilized humans. My own feeling is that "natural" may be an effective word
for selling breakfast cereal and laxatives, but few decent and intelligent
people are going to be transformed into racist, sexist warmongers by sociobiology. Very few people take wild animals or prehistoric men as models for
their social behavior. Even if there were such a danger it would seem to be
more efficient to educate people about the naturalistic fallacy than to attempt to suppress sociobiology.[28]

Avoiding the naturalistic fallacy does not mean that we cannot learn
anything from the examples found in nature. The lesson I have been trying
to present in this section could be learned from natural history as easily as
from human history, by studying the way species evolve so as to survive
changing conditions. Like species evolution, social evolution also requires a
continuous supply of "mutant" ideas. Most of them will be neutral or even

harmful, but a few will provide the basis for better adaptation and survival in the future.[29] However, nature and society can only select among the mutations which are expressed. To suppress new mutations before they are expressed is to invite extinction.

Notes

1. PRESCIENTIC CONCEPTS OF THE ORIGIN OF SPECIES: GENESIS

1. Liberated readers may prefer another version of the Adam and Eve story in which the first woman was Lilith. Lilith was created out of clay, like Adam, and she therefore felt herself to be his equal. She left Adam when he insisted that she take a subordinate position during intercourse. (Graves and Patai, 1964, p. 65.)

2. A common example of a statement which is both true and false is the rule that "There is an exception to every rule." Paul was victim of a similar paradox when he accepted the word of a Cretan that Cretans are always liars (Titus 1:12). See Tarski (1969) for a relatively simple introduction to the logic of truth.

See Horton (1973), Northrup (1950, esp. Ch. 12), Odhiambo (1967), Siu (1957, esp. Ch. 9), and Yukawa (1973) for attempts to reconcile science and prescientific thought. Bohannon's (1973) attempt to relate Shakespeare's *Hamlet* to the Tiv of West Africa provides amusing insight into the problem of transferring concepts between cultures.

3. The universe of the Bible is typical in its smallness. The myth of the Tower of Babel is pointless unless the Hebrews thought men could reach Heaven with Bronze-Age technology.

See entries under "creation" in the index of vol. 13 of MacCulloch (1931), the first chapter of Frazer (1967), Freund (1965), and Brandon (1963) for pertinent discussions of prescientific concepts. Taton (1963) presents an excellent introduction to the growth of scientific knowledge in ancient times.

4. "The Growth of the Hexateuch," and "Introduction and Exegesis to Genesis" by Simpson in vol. 1 of Buttrick (1952).

5. "The History of Israel" by Robinson in vol. 1 of Buttrick (1952).

6. Parts of the story of the Garden of Eden and of the Flood are traced by Biblical scholars to the *Epic of Gilgamesh*. This Sumerian and Babylonian myth may have originated as early as 2000 B. C. For discussions of the influence of this and other myths on Genesis, see Brandon (1963), Frazer (1918), Graves and Patai (1964), and Heidel (1949).

7. These economic conditions are described in timeless fashion by Amos (2:6–8; 5:7–15; 8:4–6). Following this oppression the Prophets transformed the image of JHVH from that of a warrior who could order the slaughter of women and children during the conquest (Deut. 20:16) to that of a defender of the downtrodden.

8. Heidel (1951).

9. The term "Fundamentalist" was first applied to a movement early in this century which held, among other tenets, that the Bible is literally true. Uncapital-

ized, the term now denotes anyone who clings to that belief. Cole (1931) and Furniss (1963) provide useful histories of the Fundamentalists and their opposition to evolution. Although most fundamentalists are Protestants, the term may have to be broadened to include the Hare Krishna movement. See Dasa (1978).

10. For the early history of religious attacks on evolutionists see Ellegard (1958, Ch. 5), Gillespie (1979), and Chapter 1 of A. D. White's immortal *History of the Warfare of Science with Theology in Christendom,* first published in 1896. For three versions of the Huxley-Wilberforce debate see White (1896, pp. 70, 71), Bibby (1959, pp. 69–70), and F. Darwin (1901, vol. 2, pp. 114–116). The Scopes trial and its aftermath are described by L. H. Allen (1967), Cole (1959), de Camp (1968, 1969), Ginger (1958), Grabiner and Miller (1974), Grebstein (1960), Kennedy (1957), Lippman (1928), and Scopes and Presley (1967). The play and film *Inherit the Wind* are vaguely based on this trial. Metzger (1955), Nelkin (1976a, b, 1977a), and Newell (1974) bring the history of antievolution up-to-date. J. R. Moore (1975) provides a bibliography of more than 200 titles which, he states, must be read before deciding between Genesis and evolution! Vanderpool (1973) provides an interesting selection of readings on this question.

11. For a sample of evolutionists' reactions to the California situation see Bartlett et al. (1977), J. A. Moore (1974, 1975), Nelkin (1977a, b), Strickberger (1973), and Wade (1972). Legal aspects of the dispute are discussed by Le Clercq (1974), Lightner (1975), and Mayer (1973). Several articles as well as legal opinions are reprinted in Lightner (1977).

12. The year of Adam's creation was 3,148 years before the building of Solomon's Temple in 968 B. C.—that is, Creation was in 4116 B. C. (Some scholars believe that the Temple was begun in 959 B. C., which would make this and subsequent dates nine years more recent. See Finegan, 1964, p. 197.) The date is deduced from 1 Kings 6:1, Exod. 12:40, and Gen. 47:28, 25:26, 21:5, 11:10–26, 9:28–29, and 5:3–28. According to this chronology the year of the Flood would be 2460 B. C., and that of the Exodus 1448 B. C. Contrary to Gen. 7:23, several Middle Eastern cultures were not interrupted by a Flood around 2460 B. C., and contrary to Gen. 11:1 they already had several languages. (See, for example, La Fay, 1978 and Bermant and Weitzman, 1979.)

13. I am aware of claims that beings from another planet visited Earth in ancient times and genetically enriched mankind, but I cannot bring myself to envision extraterrestrials who just happen to have genetic and reproductive systems complementary to those of women—not to mention a queer sexual preference for creatures from another planet. The improbability of this is discussed in a later chapter. Augustine struggled with this problem, and the problem of Cain, in Book XV of the *City of God.*

14. "Creation cannot be proved. . . .If one should ask, What is the evidence for man's creation? the answer is, None—except Revelation!" (Anon., 1970, pp. 77, 103). "Creation is, of course, unproven and unprovable by the methods of experimental science" (Gish, 1973, p. 134). Gish's assertion is based on a ludicrous interpretation of the criterion of falsifiability. This criterion means only that to qualify as scientific, a theory must have consequences which are potentially falsifiable. It does not mean, as Gish claims, that evolution or creation would have to be witnessed directly. If eye-witness is required for a theory, what then is needed to establish a fact?

15. Kerkut (1960) sets a good example of informed skepticism by challenging as an evolutionist the evidence for evolution. Today, however, he would have a harder time playing devil's advocate.

16. Examples of the confusion of natural selection with evolution can be found in Gish's writings (1973, 1978, Ch. 1). I assume Gish's ally J. N. Moore intended no irony when, in an article which accompanied Gish's in 1973, he admonished readers not to make this mistake.

The selection from Harris (1975) which Gish misinterprets should read: "I have suggested that the neo-Darwinian theory of evolution rests on the axioms that all heritable variations in fitness result from chance mutations and that there is natural selection for fitness. There are several consequences for evolution and for biology in general.

First, the axiomatic nature of the neo-Darwinian theory places the debate between evolutionists and creationists in a new perspective. Evolutionists have often challenged creationists to provide experimental proof that species have been fashioned de novo. Creationists have often demanded that evolutionists show how chance mutations can lead to adaptability, or to explain why natural selection has favored some species but not others with special adaptations, or to explain why natural selection allows apparently detrimental organs to persist. We may now recognize that neither challenge is fair. If the neo-Darwinian theory is axiomatic, it is not valid for creationists to demand proof of the axioms, and it is not valid for evolutionists to dismiss special creation as unproved so long as it is stated as an axiom. [Paleontology and comparisons of protein structures presently support evolution as a fact, but some creationists argue that species were divinely created by processes indistinguishable from evolution. This axiom of special creation by pseudo-natural processes is inferior to the neo-Darwinian axioms because it is apparently not productive of any theories except those which have already been established.]"

Gish's omission of the bracketed portion changes the meaning entirely. But not even Darwin is immune from the bearing of false witness. The anonymous author of a Jehovah's Witness publication (Anon., 1967, Ch. 1) deleted the bracketed portion of the opening sentences from Chapter 6 of *Origin of Species:*

> Long before the reader has arrived at this part of my work, a crowd of difficulties will have occurred to him. Some of them are so serious that to this day I can hardly reflect on them without being to some degree staggered; [but, to the best of my judgment, the greater number are only apparent, and those that are real are not, I think, fatal to the theory.]

17. Readers who suspect me of trifling with their credulity will find these assertions in Anon. (1970, pp. 93, 101), Kofahl (1976), J. N. Moore (1977), Morris (1972, cited in Cloud, 1977), Nelkin (1976b, p. 33, 1977a, pp. 29, 50, 130), and the *New York Times* 1 October 1972, p. 131; 10 March 1974, p. 49. "Streaking" was a short-lived fad in which young people ran naked through public places.

It is not clear how teaching evolution is supposed to cause environmental problems, but remarks such as the following by Senator Scott of Virginia in support of his amendments to weaken the Endangered Species Act are directly traceable to Gen. 1:26: "people should have dominion over fish, wildlife, and plants. Only where the lower species are of benefit to mankind are they important." (*Congressional Record,* 18 July 1978, pp. S11040, and S11043. See also Gen. 9:1–3.)

Regarding Marxism, see Acts 2:44–45, which describes how the earliest Christians "shared all things in common" and divided "everything on the basis of each one's need." Capitalism should be added to the list with Nazism and Marxism, since militant capitalists like Carnegie (1900) and Roosevelt (1913) took their inspiration (or their excuses) from the idea of "survival of the fittest." Something good must be said for an idea which can unite such contrary politico-economic systems.

18. For the moral shortcomings of fundamentalists in the 1920s see de Camp (1968, pp. 478–479, 1969, p. 21). Thomas Paine compared the moral implications of the Bible unfavorably to those of natural philosophy in *The Age of Reason* (1794). For a nonhysterical discussion of the moral implications of evolution see Munson (1971).

19. The analogy of the Watchmaker was popularized by Paley (1802). Other early uses of design may be found in Gray (1963, articles 2 and 13) and in the Bridgewater Treatises of Bell (1833) and others. Uses of design by contemporary fundamentalists are represented by Parker (1978). Further criticism of the design argument may be found in Aulie (1972) and Stebbins (1973).

20. For Hume's argument against design see N. K. Smith (1935, cited in Russett, 1976, p. 35).

21. Actually the creation of new plant species has been almost commonplace since Karpechenko created *Raphanobrassica* by combining radish and cabbage. (See Dobzhansky et al., 1977.) Not everyone accepts the evidence for warm-blooded dinosaurs. See Thomas and Olson (1978) and Marx (1978).

22. In fact Morris (1974, Ch. 6, 1977b, pp. 55–59) and other creationists cite numerous data allegedly proving the inaccuracy of scientific methods of dating, and most of these data give the age of the Earth as much greater than 6,000 years.

Morris attempts to explain the fossil record with the assertion that it was deposited as sediment from the Flood. If so, these sediments—including the Grand Canyon— would have been deposited within a single year (Gen. 7:11, 8:14) around 2460 B. C. Yet even creationists' calculations show that the ages of Cambrian and recent fossils differ by more than one year.

23. Gish (1975) in fact mentioned the discovery of a man's sandal print encrusted with trilobites. However, he was apparently all wet because trilobites lived on the ocean floor. According to Lubenow (1978), Gish now admits that "attempts to reconcile Genesis with geology lead to numerous contradictions, even if one rejects evolution." For further discussion of geological arguments see Aulie (1972), Cloud (1977), and van de Fliert (1969).

24. From historical records we know that the three major ethnic types, Negroid, Caucasoid, and Mongoloid, were present at least by 1000 B. C. Thus the eight passengers on the Ark would have produced these three ethnic types in less than 1,500 years. At that constant rate at least five more ethnic types, as distinct as the previous three, should have arisen since 1000 B. C. If the rate of formation of new races were proportional to population, then with the world population now 500 million times larger than it was during the Flood, there ought to be 500,000,000 x 3 ÷ 1500 = 1 million new ethnic types forming each year. In the United States alone affirmative action programs would have to cope with 60,000 new minorities per year,

and in less than five years each American citizen would be the sole member of his very own race!

25. For a relatively simple statement of this problem and an approach to its solution see Prigogine (1973).

2. THE ORIGIN OF SCIENCE: ANCIENT GREECE

1. We should remember that even the staunchest supporters of democracy in Greece owned slaves.

2. This may be the place to point out that there is a difference between agriculture, medicine, and technology on one hand, and science on the other hand. The cultivation of domestic animals and crops, the medicinal use of drugs, and the construction of tools were once based on trial and error, rather than science. Successful procedures were then formalized into religious or other traditions. Remnants of these prescientific practices survive in planting according to the phase of the moon, folk medicine, and other traditions.

Science seems to have been invented independently in China by the followers of Mo Ti (or Mo Tzu), who lived in the fifth century B. C., during the Warring States period. Many Mohist writings were deliberately destroyed because they were critical of Confucius, but surviving fragments include sophisticated theories and a modern appreciation of cause and effect. Implicit in these writings is the idea that cause must precede effect, which does not occur in many other cultures. Even Aristotle allowed that final causes occurred after their effects. See Needham (1969, p. 225) for Mohist science.

3. As we shall see, Empedocles and Aristotle have also been championed as the first evolutionists. There have always been those who delight in proving that the degenerated brains of modern man have been incapable of an original idea since the Greeks. Among those who consider Anaximander an evolutionist are Clagett (1955, p. 53), Sarton (1927, p. 72, 1952, p. 176), and Nordenskiold (1929, p. 12). Guthrie (1962, pp. 101–104) argues against this conclusion on different grounds from those I use. For sources of the quotations about Anaximander see Guthrie or Burnet (1957, pp. 70–71). See Diogenes Laertius (1950, vol. 1, pp. 130–133) and Gillispie (1970, vol. 1) for the life and thoughts of Anaximander.

4. This is the same Cyrus who freed the Jews from Babylon eight years later. Herodotus (I. 75) says that Thales served as a military engineer in an attack against Cyrus. Thus the dispersal of Ionian science might be considered poetic justice.

5. For the life of Empedocles see Burnet (1957, pp. 197–204), Diogenes Laertius (1950, vol. 2, pp. 366–391), Gillispie (1971, vol. 4), and Lambridis (1976).

6. Among those who regard Empedocles as an evolutionist are Burnet (1957, pp. 242–243), Durant (1966, p. 356), Fothergill (1952, p. 15), and Sarton (1927, p. 87). Burnet interprets the fragments to mean that each of the first animals had both sexes, and that males and females separated later and only then began to reproduce. Burnet must therefore have in mind a definition of evolution which does not require reproduction.

According to Burnet (1957, p. 232), Love and Hate were material rather than abstract. These same physical forces produced the corresponding emotions in humans. Greeks at this time made no distinction between matter and mental states. Greeks also rejected the idea of action at a distance, such as gravity acting through space, so Love and Hate were not like our forces of attraction and repulsion.

7. The most famous Eleatic paradox is Zeno's proof that Achilles can never catch up to a tortoise because by the time Achilles arrives where the tortoise was, the tortoise will have moved farther. For a solution to the paradox see Grünbaum (1955). For contemporaneous views of the Eleatics and the Sophists see Plato's *Parmenides, Protagoras,* and *Sophist,* and Aristotle's *Sophistical Refutations.*

8. *Parts of Animals* I. 1. A. M. Peck, translator.

9. I am assuming that Diogenes Laertius (1950, vol. 1, pp. 148–177) was a more accurate historian than Aristophanes, who portrays Socrates in *The Clouds* as scheming to profit from philosophy and devoting his mind to such concerns as whether a gnat hums out of its mouth or out of its rear end.

10. The quotation is from Plato's *Phaedo,* beginning around section 99. The essence of Socrates is found in this dialogue, especially sections 72–75 and 96–99. The assertion that phenomena of life can be understood from atomic and molecular behavior—reductionism—is still hotly debated by biologists. See for example Ayala and Dobzhansky (1974), Hull (1974, Ch. 5), Koestler (1967), and Koestler and Smythies (1969).

11. For Plato's life see Diogenes Laertius (1950, vol. 1, pp. 276–373), Gillispie (1975, vol. 11), and the supposedly autobiographical *Seventh Letter.*

12. It is doubtful that these views on women were Plato's. He admitted women to the Academy and advocated an equal share for them in government (*Republic* V).

13. See C. U. M. Smith (1976, Ch. 7) for an introduction to the *Timaeus.*

14. For Aristotle's life see Chroust (1973), Diogenes Laertius (1950, vol. 2, pp. 444–483), Gillispie (1970, vol. 1), Grayeff (1974), and Lloyd (1968).

15. For introductions to Aristotle's scientific thought see Grene (1963, 1976), Lloyd (1968), and Randall (1960).

16. This *Scala naturae* became in the Middle Ages the basis for the idea of the Great Chain of Being: that there is a continuous chain linking the Prime Mover, the celestial bodies, man, other animals, plants, and the inanimate. For a discussion of whether Aristotle was an evolutionist, see Torrey and Felin (1937).

17. For the history of science in the last three centuries b. c. see Lloyd (1973), Sarton (1959), and Taton (1963, pp. 262–371).

18. Aristotle rejected the atoms of Democritus not only because of their chaotic motion, but because they would have to have a void between them. Aristotle's logic could not cope with the existence of nothingness. Physicists until early in the present century had the same problem. They found it necessary to postulate an imperceptible ether as the medium in which matter existed and waves were propagated.

19. For the life and thought of Epicurus see Diogenes Laertius (1950, vol. 2, Ch. 10) and Gillispie (1971, vol. 4). Farrington (1966, 1967) has a very different interpretation of Epicurus. Most historians see Epicurus as using scientific explanations of thunder, magnetism, and life primarily to liberate minds from superstitious fears, as one explains the shadows which may frighten children. Farrington argues persuasively that Epicurus was prescribing scientific reasoning as an antidote to the type of state-imposed religion advocated by Plato.

The last sentence of this paragraph is inspired by the passage in *L'Etranger* by Albert Camus, in which Muersault, awaiting his execution, gazes past the bars into the starry night and finds peace in *"la tendre indifference du monde."*

20. For Lucretius see Gillispie (1973, vol. 8), Sarton (1959, pp. 263–279), and Farrington's (1966) unique interpretation.

In addition to the insights of Lucretius and/or Epicurus already discussed, they also recognized the importance of molecular structure to life (*De Rerum Natura* I, ll. 817–823), the likelihood of life on other planets (II, ll. 1067–1076; Diogenes Laertius, 1950, vol. 2, p. 605), and the constant acceleration of falling bodies regardless of their weights (II, ll. 225–242; Diogenes Laertius, 1950, vol. 2, p. 591). The last discovery is generally credited to Galileo, even though *De Rerum Natura* had been known in Italy since 1418. The reason why Lucretius and Epicurus are underrated as scientists may be such boners as their claim that the sun is no larger than it appears to the eye (V, ll. 564–565; Diogenes Laertius, 1950, vol. 2, p. 619).

3. THE INFANTICIDE OF SCIENCE: ROME AND THE MIDDLE AGES

1. None of these emperor-gods seems particularly divine, but the Stoic Marcus Aurelius (121–180) at least deserves respect for the wisdom and comfort we still find in his *Meditations*. Unfortunately he could not follow his own advice: "No longer talk at all about the kind of man that a good man ought to be, but be such" (*Meditations* X. 16). On Roman science see Stahl (1962).

2. See Gibbon's *Decline and Fall of the Roman Empire,* Chapter 16 for this quotation. This chapter in Gibbon is a history of the early church from Gibbon's usual anti-Christian point of view. Most histories of the early church are at the other extreme, relying too heavily on accounts by early Christians, full of miracles such as flames which refuse to burn martyrs. Also religious historians have often had to pay an intellectual price in order to obtain the Nihil Obstat and Imprimatur attesting to a work's freedom from doctrinal error.

3. At this point most students of Roman history have an irresistible urge to speculate on the causes of Roman decline. Preachers blame moral decadence and persecution of Christians; Gibbon blamed the Christians; countless cranks and moralizers blame whatever the current fashion in evil happens to be. It would be foolish of me to join their ranks. Still, I would just like to note that the decline began shortly after the last great ancient scientists, Ptolemy and Galen, died.

4. Early church historians have been grateful enough to Constantine to portray him as a model of Christian virtue. Yet within a year after the Council of Nicaea, he killed his wife, son, and nephew for reasons which those same historians saw fit not to record.

5. The year 476 is usually taken as the start of the Middle Ages, although the transition into that period was of course gradual and occurred at different times in different places. The capture of Constantinople in 1453 is regarded by historians as a convenient date to mark the end of the Middle Ages. The Dark Ages are considered to have covered the first five centuries of the Middle Ages.

6. For the life of Augustine see his *Confessions* and Brown (1967).

7. After he became a Christian Augustine did not insist on this interpretation, but

allowed that Genesis would have to be accepted on faith even if reason could not explain it (*Confessions* XII). Sarton (1927, vol. 1, p. 383) has actually inferred that Augustine was an evolutionist because of his idea of potential creation. See Portatié (1960, pp. 139–143) for a discussion of this point.

8. Other selections from the *City of God* which may interest the student of evolution are XII. 10, 12 in which Augustine argues that the Earth is only a few thousand years old, and XVI. 7, 8, 9 in which he argues that animals on remote islands arose by spontaneous generation after the Flood, that legendary monsters are also creatures of God, and that there could not possibly be men on the opposite side of the Earth.

9. Possibly a few men attempted to revive science in this period. Boethius (475–524) translated Aristotle's *Logic* and wrote on mathematics and astronomy; Isidore, Bishop of Seville (560?–636?), wrote an encyclopedia of Greek science; and the Venerable Bede (673–735) studied tides. Several Jewish scholars wrote treatises on biology and medicine after the Jews were scattered throughout Europe by the Diaspora in 70 A. D. See Taton (1963) for a review of science in this period in Europe and the rest of the world. In the Eastern Roman Empire and among Nestorian Christians in Syria there were attempts to preserve the Greek scientific tradition. In India, China, and America there was some work, mostly related to medicine and the astronomical aspects of religion. With the exception of America (presumably), these cultures had already begun to influence each other.

10. Frederick's book on falconry is available in an English translation (Frederick II, 1943), excerpted in Grant (1974, pp. 657–681). Among the early European scientists should also be mentioned Adelard of Bath (circa 1130?), who wrote that "only when [human knowledge] fails utterly should there be recourse to God"; William of Conches (1080?–1154), who was a follower of Plato and Lucretius until forced to recant; and Thierry of Chartres (died 1155?), who was led to Plato through Augustine. For the next four centuries after the thirteenth many of the greatest minds unfortunately acquired the Arabic obsession with alchemy, and for the next seven centuries many great and lesser minds were devoted to astrology. However, alchemy and astrology did provide the first practical experience in manipulating chemical apparatus and measuring planetary motions. For an introduction to alchemy see Chaucer's "The Canon's Yeoman's Tale." For histories of science in the Middle Ages see Crombie (1959, vol. 1), Grant (1974), Lindberg (1979), Sarton (1927, vol. 1, 1931, vol. 2), Stiefel (1977), Taton (1963), and Thorndike (1923, vols. 1, 2). Regarding the student life in the Middle Ages see Durant (1950, pp. 926–930) and Rashdall (1936, vol. 3, pp. 339–464).

11. Unfortunately, to give Albertus Magnus (1193–1280) the attention he deserves would lead us too far astray. Like Aristotle he considered no detail beneath his notice, but unlike Aristotle he insisted on experience as the final arbiter of truth. Among his extensive biological research is the neat (and still interesting to invertebrate neurophysiologists) demonstration that cicadas sing following decapitation (Thorndike, 1923, vol. 2, p. 541). He cleared the way for a rational study of animals by discrediting medieval bestiaries—compilations of fabulous animal lore usually intended as moral lessons. White (1896, vol. 1, p. 35) gives the following example from a bestiary: "The lioness giveth birth to cubs which remain three days without life. Then cometh the lion, breatheth upon them, and bringeth them to life. . . . Thus it is that Jesus Christ during three days was deprived of life, but God the Father

raised him gloriously." For other selections from bestiaries and from the works of Albertus Magnus see Grant (1974, pp. 644–657, 681–700).

12. Other interesting questions answered by Thomas are LXIX ("Of the Works of the Third Day"), XCI ("The Production of the First Man's Body"), and XCII ("The Production of the Woman").

13. Direct quotations in this selection are from the following biblical sources: a. Jer. 23:24; b. Wisd. 8:1; c. I Cor. 3:7; d. I Cor. 15:38; e. Jer. 1:5.

14. Quoted from Augustine, *Gen. ad lit.*, III, 13. See also *Confessions* XIII. 33.

15. This does not mean that thoughts and fears per se are inherited, although neurophysiology does not entirely rule out the possibility that the physiological basis of specific fears is inherited. See Sagan (1977) for speculation of this sort. All that is implied here is that particular brain structures are responsible for the drives which give rise to the behavior which a more civilized part of the brain normally looks upon with horror. In fact, stimulation of certain parts of the brain can produce fear, rage, hunger, sexual arousal, and so forth. The resulting behavior is not stereotyped like simple reflexes, but is directed to the most appropriate target. Thus social conditions might excite a particular area of the brain, triggering behavior which depends on the social context. See Delgado (1969).

16. Other parallels between the medieval and the more recent "witch-hunt" are brought out by McWilliams (1950). For the Feinberg Law, including the quoted justification, see McKinney's Consolidated Laws of New York, Section 3022 of the Education Law. The Feinberg Law was never repealed, but was finally ruled unconstitutional in 1967 (87 S. Ct. 675). For a history of this period see Caute (1978).

17. This quotation is from White (1896, vol. 1, p. 351). For a fascinating history of witchcraft, demonic possession, and satanic influences see vol. 1, Ch. 11 and vol. 2, Ch. 14–16 of White's book.

18. Compare Sagan's (1972, pp. 272–274) views on the psychological and religious needs satisfied by extraterrestrial guests. My thesis is of course a venture into untestable conjecture, but I think it is supported by a comparison of the anxiety caused by sightings of UFOs in the 1950s with present deliberate attempts to send messages to intelligent extraterrestrials (Sagan et al., 1978), regardless of the risk of attracting invaders. This thesis is also supported by a comparison of films on this theme in the 1950s (see Willis, 1972) with the immensely popular *Close Encounters of the Third Kind* (1977) and *Superman* (1978). (Of course, Superman goes back several decades, but only recently has he been considered worthy of attention by adults.) *Invasion of the Body Snatchers* (1978) may seem an exception, but this film is actually a remake of the 1956 version. I also call attention to the popular books by Erik von Däniken, who argues that humans had extraterrestrial assistance in building the pyramids and other monumental works. The implication is that interplanetary visitors could think of nothing better to do than create tourist attractions in remote parts of the world. I can't imagine why this idea would sell so many books unless their readers are hoping that the visitors will soon return to address more serious problems. See Goran (1978) and Strong (1976) for a critical appraisal of the idea of such visitations. For a scientific evaluation of UFOs see Condon (1969), Menzel and Taves (1977), and Sagan and Page (1972).

19. By "life as we know it" I mean life composed of cells made largely of carbon-

based molecules in an aqueous medium. The planet giving rise to such forms of life would have to lie within a certain range of distances from its sun so that temperatures would not be so high that water evaporates, nor so low that molecular reactions are drastically slowed down. In our own solar system this range lies roughly between the orbits of Venus and Mars (10^8 to 2.3 x 10^8 km), which occupies about two percent of the radius of the solar system (6 x 10^9 km). Thus one out of fifty planets might fall into this suitable range of distances. Therefore, if the average sun has ten planets, only one out of five solar systems could give rise to life as we know it. This number is further reduced by perhaps one out of forty by the requirements of water, minerals, gasses, and pH. (Pollard's [1979] more precise estimate is one out of 10^5 to 10^7.) See Henderson (1913) for a classic discussion of the fortuitous conditions on Earth. See Dickerson (1978), Dobzhansky et al. (1977, Ch. 11), Folsome (1979), and Schopf (1978) for accounts of the origin of life on Earth.

Few biochemists with whom I have discussed extraterrestrial life agree with me that some form of cellular control besides DNA, RNA, and protein is possible. If they are correct, extraterrestrial life is even less likely because of the narrow ranges of ionic concentrations, temperature, and pH in which nucleic acids and proteins could originate and function.

20. It is also possible that vertebrates came onto land to exploit a new food source, insects. See Dobzhansky et al. (1977, Ch. 13) and Valentine (1978) for accounts of vertebrate evolution.

21. In general a species needs color vision only if its food or the members of the species are colored. For most mammals it is advantageous to pack the retina with more sensitive rods than the color-detecting cones.

Cartmill (1974) has suggested a different set of selection pressures leading to arborial primate adaptations.

22. The sequence of events described in this paragraph is largely conjectural, but any other sequence is just as unlikely to be duplicated on another planet. I am reluctant to describe human evolution in detail, because after only fifty years of research the conclusions are still subject to rapid revision. (See for example Johanson and White, 1979.) The fossil evidence for a progressively upright stance lies in the pelvis becoming more bowl-shaped, to support the viscera. Also the attachment of the neck to the head moves from the rear to beneath the skull, as if the face remained forward-looking while the backbone swung into a vertical position beneath it. See Dobzhansky et al. (1977, Ch. 14), Leakey and Lewin (1977, esp. Ch. 3), and Washburn (1978) for recent reviews of human evolution.

23. Simpson (1964, Ch. 13) was apparently the first to suggest the uniqueness of man. See also Dobzhansky (1972, 1973, Ch. 3). Shklovskii and Sagan (1966, Ch. 29) and Sagan (1972) present a different type of calculation of the number of interplanetary visits per year. The latter authors estimate that the total number of visits to *all* planets in this galaxy would be one-tenth the average survival time in years of societies capable of launching such a project, whether or not those societies are composed of humanlike forms of intelligent life. Pessimists estimate that our own space-age technology will end within 100 years, when (as the realists tell us) we run out of conventional energy and other resources. If 100 years is a typical survival time then there should be a total of ten voyages per year, by all forms of intelligence, to all

sorts of interesting places in our galaxy. Only a tiny fraction of voyages would be made to Earth by humanlike beings. The probability increases with more hopeful estimates of survival times of technological societies.

4.BORN AGAIN: THE REVIVAL OF SCIENCE IN THE RENAISSANCE

1. I assume the reader would rather not have to read about Claude Duret (died 1611), who described a tree in Scotland whose leaves turn into fish when they fall into water, and birds when they fall upon land. Nor need we linger over Father Kircher (1601–1680), who claimed that when a certain orchid touched the ground it produced birds and little men. (See Osborn, 1929 pp. 162–163.)

2. See Kearney (1964) for a sampling of views on the causes of the scientific renaissance. I leave it as an exercise for the reader to decide whether the four prerequisites for science discussed at the end of Chapter 2 were fulfilled in the Renaissance.

3. Copernicus expelled Aristotle's conception of the universe from science, but not quite from the mind. Dante's *Inferno* and *Paradiso* and Milton's *Paradise Lost,* all based on Aristotelian concepts, have left us with an indelible idea that Hell is within the Earth and Heaven above. Milton certainly accepted the Copernican view (he was acquainted with Galileo), but the Aristotelian scheme was better suited to his artistic needs.

The final triumph of reason over dogma came with Isaac Newton's (1642–1726) Theory of Universal Gravitation, which showed that the planets were not moved by God, but by the same force that caused apples to fall on Earth. See Koestler (1959) and Koyré (1957) for histories of Renaissance astronomy. For the Catholic reaction see White (1896, vol. 1, Ch. 3). Protestants were no less zealous in condemning the new astronomy, although they relied on Scripture rather than Aristotle for justification. Luther, who denounced the Schoolmen as "locusts, caterpillars, frogs and lice" and Aristotle as a "prince of darkness, horrid imposter, public and professed liar, beast and twice execrable," was nonetheless critical of the "upstart astrologer," Copernicus (Clodd, 1897, p. 87; White, 1896, vol. 1, p. 126). We are justly appalled by the viciousness of the Holy Inquisition, but often forget that Calvin was guilty of similar atrocities. One of his victims was Michael Servetus (1511–1553), burned alive for criticizing him. Servetus, incidentally, proposed the circulation of blood through the lungs, contradicting Galen's doctrine that blood passes from the right to the left ventricle directly through very fine pores. (See Hall, 1970, pp. 105–107).

The year 1543 saw the publication not only of *De Revolutionibus* but also *De Humani Corporis Fabrica,* by Andreas Vesalius (1514–1564). Just as Copernicus's work overthrew the authority of Aristotle, Vesalius's book overthrew the equal authority of Galen. Vesalius's careful drawings based on dissections of human corpses exposed the many errors which Galen and his followers had committed because of religious prohibitions against autopsies. Even when previous anatomists had seen the discrepancies between Galen and reality they often preferred to attribute them to their inability to see as well as Galen, or to the degeneration of the human body since the heroic age of Galen. Leonardo da Vinci (1452–1519) was a notable exception, but his anatomical drawings were not published until the nineteenth century. (See Singer, 1957 and Hall, 1956, pp. 34–50.)

4. The quotations are from Montaigne's *Essays* II. 12 (1580), Bacon's *Novum Organum* I. 63 (1620), and Gilbert's "Preface" to *De Magnete* (1600). This reaction against Aristotle was followed by a calmer judgment. In 1629 Descartes credited Aristotle's syllogisms as suitable "practice for the wits of youth" (see *Rules for the Direction of Mind II*). In 1651 William Harvey confessed that "the authority of Aristotle has always such weight with me that I never think of differing from him inconsiderately" ("Introduction" to *Anatomical Exercises on the Generation of Animals*).

5. It is interesting to compare Pascal's fear of infinity with the attitude of the Epicureans described in Chapter 2.

6. Harvey's remark is especially ironic considering Bacon's influence on the writing style of the Royal Society of London and thus on the English language. The Royal Society, founded in 1662 as a channel for concise scientific communication, largely adopted Bacon's prose as a model for scientific writing, and abandoned the flowery Elizabethan of his contemporaries. In contrast, the constitution of the first scientific society, the Academia dei Lincei of Rome, proclaims that "it will not neglect the ornaments of elegant literature and philosophy, which like graceful garnets, adorn the whole body of science. . ." (Durant and Durant, 1961, p. 584).

7. Bowen (1963), Eiseley (1973), and Farrington (1949) are among those who have written of Bacon's life and work. Blake et al. (1960, Ch. 3) present a lucid summary of Bacon's method.

8. *Discourse on Method* was the first European work on philosophy not written in Latin. It set the style for French philosophical writing, just as Bacon's *Advancement of Learning* had done in England.

9. For the life and work of Descartes see Gillispie (1971, vol. 4), Pearl (1977), C. U. M. Smith (1976, Ch. 15), and Vrooman (1970).

10. No one seems to have noticed a similar idea in Aristotle's *On the Motion of Animals,* Ch. 7: "The movements of animals may be compared with those of automatic puppets, which are set going on the occasion of a tiny movement; the levers are released, and strike the twisted strings against one another. . ." (See also *On the Generation of Animals* II. 1.) As far as I know there are no other descriptions of these puppets, which suggest a higher degree of technical sophistication than the ancient Greeks are usually credited with.

11. For a history of the development of experimentation see Crombie (1953) and Thorndike (1923–1958). See the reprint of Roger Bacon's *Opus Majus* (1962, vol. 2, Part 6) for his advocacy of experimentation.

12. Redi's work on the generation of insects is widely cited and quoted, but Redi himself has been neglected by English-speaking biographers. I have had to rely on brief biographies in the *Enciclopedia Italiana* (1949, vol. 28) and in Gillispie (1975, vol. 11).

13. Descartes obviously means "deduction." This is either a typographical error in the original or, as Blake et al. (1960, p. 103) suggest, Descartes considered one form of induction to be deduction.

14. Readers interested in further information on the development of scientific method may begin with Laudan (1968). See Popper (1959, pp. 31–32) and Reichen-

bach (1938, pp. 5–7) for the distinction between the creation and the testing of theories. I don't care for Reichenbach's use of the terms "justification" and "discovery." I agree with Popper (1972, Ch. 7) that one can never justify a theory, and I don't believe that theories have any objective existence which can be discovered like a buried treasure. Feyerabend (1970, 1975) rejects not only a methodology for creating theories but also a methodology for testing them. In fact, he sees no difference between the creation and the testing of theories. For the pedagogical difficulties which can result from confusing idealized methods of testing theories with the idiosyncrasies of creation, see Brush (1974).

15. The Darwin quotation is from Barlow (1958, pp. 119, 141). In Darwin's defense I should mention that the term "Baconian" was used so loosely in Darwin's time that not even Bacon would have recognized it. Elsewhere Darwin seems to have admitted that he began with a theory when he remarked how "odd it is that anyone should not see that all observations must be for or against some view if it is to be of any service." Later Darwin wrote: "I have often said and thought that the process of scientific discovery was identical with everyday thought, only with more care—" (F. Darwin and Seward, 1903, vol. 1, pp. 195, 216). Ruse (1975c) argues that it is an oversimplification to say that Darwin used either induction or deduction exclusively.

16. The best antidote to shame regarding falsified theories is Popper (1972, Ch. 7). For the original statement of falsifiability as the criterion of demarcation, see Popper (1959, pp. 40–42). Magee (1973) presents a concise introduction to Popper's philosophy. Testimony to Popper's influence on scientists may be found in Schilpp (1974).

Any attempt to falsify a theory will be based on some other theory which may be false. Evolution was once "falsified" by Lord Kelvin's proof that the sun would have cooled too rapidly to have allowed the hundreds of millions of years needed for evolution. Kelvin, of course, did not know that the sun is powered by nuclear energy (Burchfield, 1974, 1975, pp. 70–86). At that time evolution was a falsifiable theory, but I believe we are now justified in calling it a fact. By "fact" I mean a direct observation, or a conclusion that follows directly from observation. One cannot witness the origin of natural species in one's own lifetime, but this is not required in the modern conception of evolution, as defined in my "Introduction." More gradual degrees of evolution have been observed many times.

17. To understand induction as Darwin did, see Blake et al. (1960), Ellegard (1957), Hull (1973a, Ch. 2, 1973b), Ruse (1975a, 1979a), and writings on or by Francis Bacon, William Whewell, J. F. W. Herschel, and John Stuart Mill.

18. See Piaget (1954) or Gruber and Vonèche (1977, Ch. 20).

19. A similar criticism applies to any method, philosophy, or religion which claims to have a monopoly on truth. What argument is there for or against a system of thought which admits of no external criteria of judgment?

20. These comments also apply to mathematics, which is a system of deductions from axioms.

5. The Genesis of Evolutionism: The French Phase

1. The Enlightenment came at an opportune time to influence the Founding Fathers in America. Those of us who were nursed on patriotic myths often fail to appreciate that the "American" ideas of liberty, justice, and equality were inspired as much by the deistic or atheistic Enlightenment as by Christianity. The American debt to French thought is reflected in the Declaration of Independence, which Jefferson based on "the laws of nature and nature's God." Note also the influence of Descartes in the deduction of the American case from "self-evident" truths.

2. For a history of the Great Chain of Being see Lovejoy (1936). For histories of the impact of geology and paleontology on evolutionism see Bowler (1976a), Gillispie (1951), Greene (1959, Ch. 4), and Haber (1959a, b, c). See Bowler (1974a) and Roger (1963) for background to Enlightenment evolutionism. For Trembley see Baker (1952), Gillispie (1976, vol. 13), and Vartarian (1953).

3. For more information on Linnaeus see Gillispie (1973, vol. 8) and Hagberg (1953). See Farber (1972) and Lyon (1976) for Buffon's rejection of the Linnaean system. Buffon is traditionally included with Montesquieu, Rousseau, and Voltaire as one of the brightest lights of the Enlightenment. His major contribution was the forty-four-volume best seller, *Histoire naturelle.* Incidentally, as early as 1753 Buffon suggested that species change with the environment. He suggested that one species might be transformed into another, but almost in the same ink he denied that possibility. Samuel Butler, seeking to prove that Charles Darwin had made a poor counterfeit of the theories of Buffon, Erasmus Darwin, and Lamarck, claimed that Buffon's denials were only to avoid censure by the church. Clodd (1897, p. 110), Osborn (1929, p. 188), Eiseley (1958, pp. 39–45), and many others have accepted Butler's conjecture. It is true that Buffon had previously had to recant a contradiction of Genesis (Fellows and Milliken, 1972, pp. 82–85), and that Enlightenment writers often made an ironically absurd denial of a proposition in order to support the proposition. However, I am persuaded by Bowler (1973), Fellows and Milliken (1972, Ch. 7), Lovejoy (1959a), Roger (1962, p. xxiii, 1963, p. 577), and Wilkie (1959) that Buffon's denials were sincere in the case of evolution. It is possible, however, that many biologists before Darwin were as confused as Butler was, and became evolutionists because they thought Buffon had been. For Butler's claims see Barlow (1958, pp. 167–219) and Willey (1960).

Another Frenchman often erroneously mentioned as an early evolutionist is Benoît de Maillet (1656–1738), who proposed in 1748 that flying fish turned into birds, sea lions turned into lions, and mermaids and mermen turned into humans. Really. For a charitable review of de Maillet see Eiseley (1958, pp. 29–35).

The problem of identifying early evolutionists is complicated because the word "evolution" was until after Darwin an embryological term, referring especially to the theory that the organism unfolds from a preformed state during development (Bowler, 1975; Gould, 1977, Ch. 3; T. H. Huxley, 1896, Ch. 6.) The French often used the word *transformisme* where we would now use "evolution."

4. For biographies of Maupertuis see Gillispie (1974, vol. 9), Glass (1959b), and Lovejoy (1904). Callot (1965, Ch. 4) and Roger (1963, pp. 468–487) give a good introduction to his work.

5. From Jefferson's *Notes on Virginia,* Query VI, written in 1781. The context of this quotation is Jefferson's defense of the honor of American fauna against Buffon's slander that they were generally smaller than their European counterparts. Jefferson offered the bones of mammoths as evidence, and cited Indian legends that the mammoth and other large species still survived beyond the frontier.

6. For biographies of Diderot see Fellows (1977), Gillispie (1971, vol. 4), and A. M. Wilson (1972). For slightly different translations of the selections by Diderot see Crocker (1966). Callto (1965, Ch. 6), Crocker (1959), and Roger (1963, pp. 585–682) also discuss Diderot's biological ideas.

7. Translated from *Ouevres* (1951), pp. 840–841).

8. See also such passages as "Species are merely some tendency toward a common end which is proper to them. . ." in *Entretien entre D'Alembert et Diderot* and *La Rêve de D'Alembert.* These were written in 1769 but not published until some sixty-five years later.

9. See *City of God* XII. 25 for Augustine's unquestioning belief in Jacob's story. Hippocrates also accepted the inheritance of acquired character *(On Airs, Waters and Places* 14; *On the Sacred Disease),* but Aristotle rejected his arguments *(History of Animals* VII. 6; *Generation of Animals* I. 17, 18). For the early history of this venerable theory see Zirkle (1946).

10. Lamarck seldom credits his predecessors, but we can see in the Great Chain of Being the influence of Leibniz, Maupertuis, and Diderot, which Lamarck probably got through Buffon. Buffon may also have been the inspiration for Lamarck's rejection of the young, catastrophic Earth of Genesis (Burkhardt, 1977, p. 111). Lamarck's suggestion that the Earth was millions of centuries old in fact went further than Buffon, who may have been reluctant to offend the church a second time. From experiments based on the rates of cooling of metal spheres, Buffon had estimated that the Earth took approximately 75,000 years to cool to a temperature permitting life, which was reached some 40,000 years ago. Buffon's division of this period into seven epochs was the first in an unending attempt to rationalize Genesis and geology by letting a "day" be arbitrarily long. (See Fellows and Milliken, 1972, Ch. 3 and Greene, 1959, pp. 73–76 for Buffon's geological work.)

11. H. G. Cannon (1959, pp. 18–19) claims that Lamarckism applies equally well to plants, and that Lamarck never suggested that new organs arise. To read what Lamarck really said on these subjects see Part II, Ch. 5 of *Philosophie zoologique.* See also Burkhardt (1977, pp. 168, 177–178).

12. Historians, eager to say something nice about the pathetic Lamarck, have often stated that Lamarck's was the first scientific theory of evolution. However, Maupertuis seems to have had the first scientific theory, although one may quibble about the term "scientific" in either case.

For Lamarck's life and work I have relied especially on the excellent study by Burkhardt (1977). I have also profited from Elliot's biography in his 1963 translation of *Philosophie zoologique.* Other useful sources are Barthélemy-Madaule (1979), Gillispie (1959, 1975, vol. 7, pp. 584–594), Hodge (1971), Mayr (1972a), and Wilkie (1959). See Packard (1901, pp. 319–324) for another translation of the selection by Lamarck. Some readers may also be interested in the book by H. G. Cannon (1959), which is apparently an attempt to even the score against anti-Lamarckians by introducing numerous pro-Lamarckian distortions.

13. For the French reception of Darwinism see Farley (1974, 1977, p. 42) and Glick (1972, pp. 117–167). One exception to the general reluctance of Frenchmen to embrace evolutionism was Charles V. Naudin (1815–1899), who published in 1852 a theory of evolution by natural selection. If we take him literally, however, the natural selection envisioned by Naudin was the actual selection of the species which a conscious Nature desired to propagate. It was not the survival of the fittest. See Osborne (1929, p. 298) for the relevant portion of Naudin's paper.

14. For Cuvier's life and anti-Lamarckism see Burkhardt (1977, pp. 191–201), Coleman (1964), and Gillispie (1971, vol. 3).

Four other men of the late eighteenth century are often mentioned as evolutionists. Beginning around 1770 James Burnet, Lord Monboddo (1714–1799) argued for the kinship of men and apes, and even suggested that the orangutan was just a human who lacked the advantages of an English upbringing. A similar idea had been proposed by Rousseau and Buffon at the height of enthusiasm for the "noble savage." There is no hint, however, that either species evolved from the other. See the selection by Monboddo in McCown and Kennedy (1972, pp. 74–80) and discussions by Greene (1959, pp. 208–218) and Lovejoy (1904, 1948, pp. 45–54).

Johann Gottfried von Herder (1744–1803) wrote passages in *Ideen zur Philosophie der Geschichte der Menschheit* (1784–1785) which have occasionally been interpreted as suggesting evolution by natural selection. However, see Lovejoy (1959c).

Immanuel Kant (1724–1804) authored a number of passages which appear evolutionist to modern readers. See for example Section 80 of *Critique of Judgment.* Lovejoy (1959b) once again shows that there is less here than meets the eye.

Johann Wolfgang von Goethe (1749–1832) is also often said to have been an evolutionist as early as 1796. (See, for example, the citation by Lovejoy, 1959b, p. 205, fn. 34.) Certainly Goethe was as brilliant a scientist as he was a poet, and his evidence that flowers develop from leaves, and skulls from vertebrae was an important contribution to evolutionism. However, like Fothergill (1952, p. 81) and Magnus (1949, pp. 116–119), I find nothing in Goethe's writings clearly suggesting evolution. It is possible, however, that he supported the ideas of E. Geoffroy St. Hilaire.

15. The same idea has occurred to Gregory (1980). See Caws (1969), Coler (1963), Ghiselin (1952), Goldstein and Goldstein (1978), Koestler (1964), Rothenberg (1979), Taylor and Barron (1963), and Yukawa (1973), on the process of creativity.

16. See Gregory (1972, Ch. 9) for this and other aspects of illusions. One dramatic illustration of the role of learning in vision is the case of S. B., described by Gregory (pp. 194–199). After being cured of blindness S. B. had to learn to see objects, such as a bus, by first touching them. In addition to learning, there may also be genetic reasons for cultural differences in perception. (See Robinson, 1972, pp. 109–113.) It is difficult to understand why in any culture there should be trouble in perceiving photographs and illusions like the Necker cube, because the brain never receives three-dimensional information directly. The retina is essentially a two-dimensional projection screen.

17. See Popper and Eccles (1977) for the present knowledge (and more) regarding the interaction of brain with mind and both with themselves. The case of Sultan is cited by Koestler (1964, p. 574, 1978, p. 134).

6. THE GENESIS OF EVOLUTIONISM: THE BRITISH PHASE

1.The quotation by Shelley is from Grabo (1930, p. 30), whose third and fourth chapters should be consulted for Darwin's influence on Shelley's *Queen Mab* and *Prometheus Unbound.* See also Hassler (1973) and Logan (1936) for Darwin, the poet. See King-Hele (1977, Ch. 12) for Darwin's influence on Wordsworth and Coleridge. Perhaps Darwin's greatest legacy is *Frankenstein,* which was inspired by Byron's and Shelley's discussion of Darwin's ideas. (See the "Introduction" of Mary Shelley's *Frankenstein.*) Darwin is now neglected in texts and anthologies of English poetry, but fortunately not by biographers. See especially the thorough biography by King-Hele (1977) and the entertaining one by Pearson (1930). Most biographies depend heavily on the unreliable book by Seward (1804) and on Charles Darwin's tribute to his grandfather in Krause (1879). Boswell's *Life of Samuel Johnson* (1791) omits Darwin, but is an invaluable portrait of his times.

2. See Pearson (1930) and the bibliography in King-Hele (1977) for accounts of the Lunar Society and its members. Boswell raises three objections to Priestley's opinions in the *Life of Samuel Johnson,* in a footnote following Johnson's letter to Dr. Brocklesby dated August 29, 1783. Darwin's writings sound deistic, but Coleridge wrote that during a visit in 1796 Darwin tried to sway him to atheism, and confessed that he had never read a single page in religion. (Griggs, 1933, vol. 1, p. 39, 1956, vol. 1, p. 99). See McKendrick (1973) for Josiah Wedgwood.

3. An American edition of *Zoonomia* is available in the Readex Microprint Series of Early American Imprints (Evans Nos. 30312 and 32017). Dean (1906) has found a letter dated 1791 in which Darwin mentions "another work [*Zoonomia?*], which has lain by me nearly 20 years." This may indicate that Darwin was an evolutionist as early as the 1770s.

4. See Garfinkle (1955) for the political and religious climate of Darwin's evolutionism.

5. There is no evidence that Lamarck knew of Darwin's ideas. See Burkhardt (1977, p. 225, fn. 22). Charles Darwin was apparently the first to note the similarity of Lamarck's and his grandfather's theories. Charles Darwin's copy of *Zoonomia* bears the following notation in the margin beside the passage on the beak of birds: "Lamarck concisely forestalled by my grandfather" (quoted in King-Hele, 1977, p. 310). See also the second footnote in the "Historical Sketch" of the *Origin of Species,* and Charles Darwin's letter to T. H. Huxley, in F. Darwin (1901, vol. 1, p. 125). J. Harrison (1971) gives a thorough analysis of Darwin's views.

6. The acceptance of evolution confined within species is similar to the position of many present creationists who accept evolution confined within "kinds" (see Ch. 1). Thus we who consider Wells, Blumenbach, Prichard, and Lawrence evolutionists are in the odd position of also having to consider many antievolutionists to be evolutionists! We may be right.

See Wells (1971, 1973a) and Erickson (1975) for arguments that Wells and others were not evolutionists. See F. Darwin and Seward (1903, vol. 1, pp. 43–46) and p. lv. of the 1973 reprint of Prichard (1826) for evidence that Prichard was not an evolutionist. See Darlington (1959, 1961) for extravagant claims on behalf of Lawrence's evolutionism.

7. In Wells (1818, pp. vii–lxi). This *"Memoir,"* which often reads like a deathbed confession, is the only source of information on Wells's life that I know of. Shyrock (1944) suggests that Wells believed in the evolution of species.

8. The quotation by Darwin is from F. Darwin and Seward (1903, vol. 1, p. 187). See Barrett (1977, vol. 2, p. 32) for Darwin's public acknowledgment of Matthew's priority. See also the "Historical Sketch" in the *Origin of Species*. For the life and work of Matthew see Wells (1973b), on which my account is largely based. Additional details may be gleaned from Matthew's cordial letters to Darwin (de Beer, 1959). Gammage (1969, p. 70) mentions Matthew as a delegate to the Chartist Convention in London in 1839.

9. The quotation by Matthew will be found in Wells (1973b, p. 256). How poorly equipped Matthew was to develop his theory is evident from his letters to Darwin (de Beer, 1959).

10. Thus, contrary to a common assumption, Lyell's uniformitarianism was not essential to the development of evolutionism. Uniformitarianism has the advantage of providing ample time for gradual evolution, but catastrophism was more suited to Matthew's emphasis on the effects of environmental changes. See Eiseley (1958, pp. 127, 128) and Gillispie (1959, p. 266). While Lyell was not essential to evolutionism, Darwin was undoubtedly sincere when he wrote: "I always feel as if my books come half out of Lyell's brain, and that I never acknowledge this sufficiently" (F. Darwin and Seward, 1903, vol. 2, p. 117). Those interested in the arguments for catastrophism will find them, unimproved after almost two centuries, in some of the creationist literature cited in Chapter 1. See also W. F. Cannon (1960) and J. R. Moore (1970).

11. Darlington (1959, 1961) and others have charged that Charles Darwin got most of his ideas from his grandfather. See, however, Ghiselin (1976). For Darwin's early impressions of Lamarck, see Egerton (1976). Eiseley's (1979) charge that Darwin deliberately stole the idea of natural selection from Edward Blyth (1810–1873) has been completely refuted by Gould (1979), Gruber (1979), and Schwartz (1974). See also Beddall (1972, 1973). McKinney (1972, pp. 150–151) also points out that A. R. Wallace read Blyth's papers but saw nothing in them to suggest natural selection. See Limoges (1970, pp. 101–116) for evidence that Darwin did not plagiarize from Matthew, Wells, or Lawrence.

12. For Chambers, see Gillispie (1951, 1971, vol. 3), Hodge (1972), Lovejoy (1959d), Millhauser (1959), and Ruse (1979a, Ch. 5). The first edition of *Vestiges* was reprinted in 1969. For Darwin's failure to persuade his colleagues see Hull et al. (1978, p. 721). See also T. H. Huxley's essay "On the Reception of the 'Origin of Species' " in F. Darwin (1901, vol. 1). Weismann's comment is quoted by C. U. M. Smith (1976, pp. 232, 234). See Chapter 18 in Smith's book for an introduction to *Naturphilosophie*.

13. Quotations by Wordsworth are from "Preface" to the *Lyrical Ballads, Lines Written in Early Spring,* and *Prelude* III, ll. 60–63. For the relationship of science with Wordsworth's poetry see the "Preface" to the *Lyrical Ballads,* Bush (1950, Ch. 4), and Evans (1964). For Tennyson see Buckley (1960), Bush (1950, Ch. 5), and Ross (1973). Millhauser (1959, pp. 156–157) suggests that Tennyson was influenced by Chambers. Huxley's statement about Tennyson shows his ignorance of Erasmus Darwin.

14. For other Victorian poems reflecting evolutionism and nature's fall from

grace see Tennyson's *By an Evolutionist,* Robert Browning's *Paracelsus,* and Arnold's *In Harmony with Nature.* For other views on the role of the *zeitgeist* in science see Boring (1950, 1961).

7. DARWIN AND WALLACE: EVOLUTIONARY CONVERGENCE

1. Biologists still accept Darwin's proposal of 1837 that the ancestral marsupials colonized Australia via a land bridge at a time when there were few other mammals to compete with them. Elsewhere in the world most of the marsupials were later displaced by the more successful placental mammals. Australian marsupials were spared by being on an island (de Beer, 1963, pp. 92–93).

It will be apparent in the selections for this chapter that the convergence of Wallace and Darwin was not exact. The individuality of scientists is almost always preserved even when they hit upon basically identical theories (Stent, 1978, Ch. 5). See Merton (1973, Chs. 16, 17) for a general discussion of convergent creation of theories.

2. For Darwin's impressions of his father see his *Autobiography* (preferably the unexpurgated version edited by his granddaughter Lady Nora Barlow, 1958, esp. pp. 28–42), and pp. 356–357 of volume 2 of the *Life and Letters of Charles Darwin,* edited by his son, Francis Darwin in 1901. See also Himmelfarb (1962, pp. 8–12).

The standard biographies of Darwin are by Bradford (1926), Chancellor (1973), R. Moore (1954), Sears (1950), Stevens (1978), Ward (1927), West (1938), and Wichler (1961). See also the family reminiscences by Darwin's granddaughter, Gwen Raverat (1952), and Stone's biographical novel (1980).

3. See Wallace's autobiography (1905) and the biographies by George (1964), McKinney (1972), and Williams-Ellis (1966). Wallace's *Letters and Reminiscences* were compiled by Marchant (1916).

4. For Darwin's comments on his education see Barlow (1958, pp. 27, 28, 45, 46). See also his comments on Butler's school in the second collection of his letters, edited by Francis Darwin and A. C. Seward (1903, vol. 2, pp. 441, 442). On Darwin's intellect and passion for collecting see Barlow (1958, pp. 22–23, 28), F. Darwin (1901, vol. 2, p. 355), and F. Darwin and Seward (1903, vol. 1, pp. 3–5).

5. Quotations in this paragraph are from Barlow (1958, pp. 46–51) and F. Darwin and Seward (1903, vol. 1, p. 7). See West (1938, p. 60) for Dr. Duncan.

6. For Henslow's influence on Darwin see Barlow (1958, pp. 64–67, 1967) and F. Darwin (1901, vol. 1, pp. 160–164). See S. Smith (1960, p. 397) for de Beer's suggestion that Darwin met Lyell in June, 1831. For Darwin's field trip with Sedgwick, see Barlow (1958, pp. 52, 60, 68–70) and Barrett (1974). Sedgwick, a clergyman, later contributed several hostile reviews of his former student's *Origin of Species* (Hull, 1973a, pp. 155–170). For Sedgwick's life and letters see Clark and Hughes (1890) and Gillispie (1975, vol. 12).

Darwin's comment on the effect of Herschel's book is quoted from Barlow (1958, pp. 67–68). For more on Herschel's influence see Ruse (1975a, 1979a). Egerton (1970a) suggests that Humboldt's influence was even more profound than Darwin suggests.

7. See Wallace (1905, vol. 1, p. 77) for his denial of any religious impulse. See

Kottler (1974) for a discussion of his interest in spiritualism and Engels (1940, Ch. 10) for a devastating and witty criticism of it. Wallace's interest in spiritualism makes an interesting contrast with Darwin's materialism. In 1838 Darwin wrote the following note to himself: "Thought (or desires more properly) being hereditary it is difficult to imagine it anything but structure of brain hereditary, analogy points out to this.—love of the deity effect of organization, oh you materialist!. . .Why is thought being a secretion of brain, more wonderful than gravity a property of matter?" (Notebook C, p. 166, Quoted from Gruber and Barrett, 1974, pp. 450–451.) See also F. Darwin (1901, vol. 1, p. 280).

8. For Henslow's letter and the events leading up to Darwin's voyage, see Barlow (1946, 1958, pp. 71–72) and F. Darwin (1901, vol. 1, Ch. 5).

9. Darwin's primary role as companion, rather than naturalist, is discussed by Burstyn (1975) and Gruber (1969). For biographies of Fitz-Roy see Gillispie (1972, vol. 5) and Mellersh (1968). For evidence of Darwin's goodwill toward Fitz-Roy, see the letters written to him in 1836 and 1843. (F. Darwin, 1901, vol. 1, pp. 240–242, 299–300). This casts doubt upon Gould's (1977, Ch. 2) suggestion that Darwin became an evolutionist to spite the devout Fitz-Roy.

After the publication of the *Origin of Species* in 1859, Fitz-Roy's insistence on the literal Genesis got the better of his lingering sanity. At the Huxley-Wilberforce debate he paraded the Bible about, and subsequently attacked Darwin in the press. As always, Darwin remained above the fray, but quipped in a letter, "It is a pity Fitz-Roy did not add his theory of the extinction of *Mastodon,* etc., from the door of the Ark being made too small" (F. Darwin and Seward, 1903, vol. 1, p. 219). Fitz-Roy took his own life in 1865.

10. Darwin's *Voyage of the Beagle* is widely available in the Natural History Library Edition of 1962. See Barlow (1934; 1946) and Herbert (1980) for Darwin's *Diary,* letters and field notes from that period. Darwin also published several books based on research conducted on the voyage; these are listed in Darwin (1901, vol. 2, pp. 533–541). See also Darling (1960), Dibner (1964), Gruber and Gruber (1962), Keynes (1979), Moorehead (1969) and Thomson (1975) for descriptions of the ship and the journey. Ralling (1979) has compiled selections from Darwin's own words in connection with the BBC TV/Time-Life Series of seven films entitled "The Voyage of Charles Darwin."

11. An 1877 letter by Darwin is consistent with the conclusion that he was not an evolutionist until his return to England. "When I was on board the *Beagle* I believed in the permanence of species, but, as far as I can remember, vague doubts occasionally flitted across my mind" (F. Darwin and Seward, 1903, vol. 1, p. 367).

12. The quoted passage is from F. Darwin (1901, vol. 1, p. 164). Regarding the theory of coral reefs see Barlow (1958, p. 98). In his *Autobiography* Darwin confessed to an irresistible urge to theorize on every subject (Barlow, 1958, p. 141). See also a comment to the same effect by Francis Darwin (1901, vol. 1, p. 126). Ghiselin (1969) argues that Darwin usually began with a hypothesis, rather than induction, in accordance with the hypothetico-deductive method. See also Herbert (1977) for Darwin as theorist.

13. For Lyell's life and work see Bailey (1962), Gillispie (1973, vol. 8), Lyell (1970), and L. G. Wilson (1972). Rudwick (1971) discusses Lyell's influence on Darwin. See Barlow (1946, p. 111) for the "castles in the air." Himmelfarb (1962, p. 110) also

emphasizes Darwin's predominating interest in geology. As S. Smith (1960, p. 396) points out, Darwin's cramped quarters aboard the *Beagle* would have forced him to pack biological specimens away for shipment even if he had been inclined to study them immediately. Darwin's reluctance to consider evolutionism may also have been due, in part, to his having read Lyell's devastating attack on Lamarckism in 1832, when he received the second volume of *Principles of Geology* (Barlow, 1934, p. 435, fn. 22).

14. The quotations are from McKinney (1969, 1972, pp. 9, 11). Wallace was one of the few naturalists with a favorable view of the popular *Vestiges*. Wallace also defended evolutionism with the arguments of Lawrence and Prichard that all human races descended from a single race.

H. W. Bates is now famous as the discoverer of Batesian mimicry: the resemblance to a noxious, conspicuous species (such as the monarch butterfly) by a palatable species (such as the viceroy). See Gillispie (1970, vol. 1) and Woodcock (1969) for a biography of Bates. See Beddall (1969) for the journey of Bates and Wallace.

15. See George (1964, pp. 30–31, 304–305) and Beddall (1969) for Wallace's journey and contributions.

16. For the evolution of Darwin's religious beliefs see Barlow (1958, pp. 85–96), F. Darwin (1901, vol. 1, Ch. 8; vol. 2, pp. 105–106, 412), Gillespie (1979, Ch. 8), Himmelfarb (1962, p. 159), and Mandelbaum (1958). Darwin states that he remained a "theist" even while writing the *Origin of Species*. That is, he believed in a "first Cause having an intelligence in some degree analogous to that of man." However, see Manier (1978, pp. 195–196). It is now often erroneously stated that Darwin was a deist: one who believes in an abstract god who governs the universe only through natural law. Certainly Darwin knew the difference between theism and deism. Darwin's reference to "the Creator" in the last lines of the second and later editions of the *Origin*, and elsewhere, are not hypocritical. Natural selection gradually reinforced Darwin's doubts about the existence of God by neutralizing the argument that only an intelligent being could have designed living things. By age sixty-seven Darwin adopted T. H. Huxley's convenient term "agnostic."

17. For Freudian interpretations of Darwin see especially Greenacre (1963) and references cited by Barlow (1958, pp. 240–243) and Colp (1977).

18. Quotations are from Barlow (1958, pp. 97, 231–234) and F. Darwin and Seward (1903, vol. 1, p. 29). See Litchfield (1915) for Emma Darwin's letters.

19. Darwin was aware of the futility of proposing evolution without providing a mechanism for it (Barlow, 1958, p. 118). Gillespie (1979) and Gillispie (1951) provide a thorough description of the creationist context in which Darwin worked. Lovejoy (1959d) points out that most of the evidence for evolution was known by 1830, and Mayr (1972b) discusses the reluctance of Darwin's contemporaries to accept the evidence before the *Origin of Species*. For accounts of scientists' reluctance to accept new theories, see Barnes (1972) and Mauskopf (1978). An ironic illustration of scientists' devotion to their world view occurred in the Spokane Flood controversy of the 1920s, when loyal Lyellians refused to accept the geological evidence of a cataclysmic flood in Washington State (Baker, 1978).

20. This illustration of how the creationist "paradigm" was challenged by new observations and then replaced by a new paradigm may be an example of T. S. Kuhn's (1970; 1974; 1978) proposed general structure of scientific revolutions.

However, Ghiselin (1971), Greene (1971), Mayr (1972b) and Ruse (1970; 1971a) do not think so.

Darwin presents a lucid description of the enigma of the Galápagos species in *Voyage of the Beagle*, chapter 17. See Lack (1961) for a modern description.

For the scientific context in which Darwin worked see Bowler (1976a), Egerton (1968), Greene (1959), Gillispie (1951), Kinch (1980), Mandelbaum (1957), Manier (1978), Mayr (1972b), Rudwick (1976) and Ruse (1975c, 1979a).

21. William Paley's *Natural Theology* (1802) was one of the most influential books of its time. Darwin practically memorized it (Barlow, 1958, pp. 59, 87). See Bowler (1977) and Limoges (1970, pp. 31–47) for the contributions of natural theology to Darwinism. It appears that Patrick Matthew was never able to see natural selection as an alternative to design (de Beer, 1959, pp. 40–41).

22. It is likely that Matthew was also inspired by Malthus, at least indirectly. There is a Malthusian ring to his statement that "the extreme fecundity of nature . . . has . . . . a prolific power much beyond . . . what is necessary to fill up the vacancies caused by senile decay."

23. See Russell (1935, pp. 72–73) for the quotation. Marx was the first to note the resemblance of natural selection to laissez-faire economics (Gruber and Barrett, 1974, p. 71). In Engels's words, it is "the most amazing rubbish" to see only economic motives in scientific theories (quoted in Young, 1973, p. 395). Yet Marvin Harris (1968, pp. 114–116) persists in that belief. This question is thoroughly debated by Freeman et al. (1974). Grinnell (1969) has objective evidence that economic analogies did play a role in Darwin's thinking.

The Reverend Malthus is apt to impress modern readers as cruel, because of his opposing the Poor Laws and urging his parishioners not to feed their starving neighbors. Malthus realized that giving food to the poor without increasing the total supply would only make it more scarce and drive up the price. (There is a modern parallel in assisting the poor in paying fuel bills without controlling prices.) Malthus considered starvation a lesser evil than contraception. Matthew, Wallace, and probably Darwin saw an alternative to Malthus's dismal principle in a fairer distribution of resources among Britons. This is difficult to prove for Darwin except by reading between the lines of scattered passages such as this written in May 1838: "Educate all classes, avoid the contamination of castes. improve the women. (double influence) & mankind must improve—." See F. Darwin (1901, vol. 2, p. 356), Durant (1979), Gruber and Barrett (1974, p. 453), McKinney (1972, pp. 4–5), R. Smith (1972), and Wallace (1905, vol. 2, Ch. 35) for the political opinions of Darwin and Wallace.

Young (1969, 1971) has described how evolutionism and social policies were simultaneously influenced by Malthus. See also Bonar (1966), Bowler (1976b), Flew (1978, Ch. 2), Gale (1972), James (1979), Levin (1966), and Petersen (1979) for the life and influence of Malthus. The second *Essay on Population* (1803) is available in a modern edition (Himmelfarb, 1960). See also Burrow (1966), S. F. Cannon (1978), Cowles (1937), J. F. C. Harrison (1971), Himmelfarb (1968), Houghton (1957), Knoepflmacher and Tennyson (1978), Manier (1978), Ruse (1975d), Somervell (1929), and Young (1973) for the social context in which Darwin and Wallace worked.

See Lyell's journals on the species question (L. G. Wilson, 1970) and the second volume of *Principles of Geology* for his appreciation of the biological implications of Malthus. Erasmus Darwin seems also to have been affected by Malthus:

From Hunger's arm the shafts of Death are hurl'd;
And one great Slaughter-house the warring world!
Canto V, 11. 65–66, *The Temple of Nature* (1803)

24. Darwin's notebooks on transmutation of species, B through E, have been published by de Beer et al. (1960–1967). Gruber and Barrett (1974) present the M and N notebooks on "Man, Mind and Materialism," as well as portions of the other notebooks. Also valuable is the notebook in which Darwin recorded his readings (Vorzimmer, 1977). For reviews of the revolution in Darwin studies see Greene (1975) and Kohn (1975, Ch. 7). Among the important recent interpretations are those by Grinnell (1969), Gruber and Barrett (1974), Herbert (1968, 1974, 1977), Himmelfarb (1962), Kohn (1975), Kottler (1978), Limoges (1970), Mayr (1977), Ruse (1975c, 1979a), Schweber (1977), and S. Smith (1960). Much as I admire these studies I must call attention to the tendency to rely too heavily upon the notebooks, as if they contained a complete record of Darwin's thoughts.

25. This three-year whirlwind is described in Barlow (1958, pp. 82–85), Colp (1980), and F. Darwin (1901, vol. 1, pp. 243–269). For a discussion of the Glen Roy paper see Rudwick (1974). See Manier (1978, pp. 89–96) regarding Darwin's reading of Wordsworth at this time.

26. This passage appears in the pocket notebook Darwin kept on the voyage (Barlow, 1946, p. 247). Barlow believed that the passage was written on the Galápagos, which would mean that Darwin was thinking of evolution as early as September or October 1835. However, Gruber and Gruber (1962), Himmelfarb (1962, pp. 463–464), and S. Smith (1960) show that it was interpolated later. See Kottler (1978) for a different interpretation of the role of "Darwin's finches." See Kohn (1975, Ch. 3) for a detailed analysis of the influence on Darwin of other biogeographical findings. See also Sulloway (1979).

27. The last quotation is from Darwin's *Diary,* quoted by S. Smith (1960, p. 393). Incidentally, my use of the word "evolution" in connection with the notebooks is an anachronism. Darwin seldom used the word until the last edition of the *Origin of Species,* published in 1872.

For evidence that Darwin's conversion to transmutation occurred in March 1837, see Gruber and Barrett (1974, p. 135), Herbert (1974), Limoges (1970, p. 11), and S. Smith (1960). In a private letter written in 1877, Darwin made the inexplicable claim that he "did not become convinced that species were mutable until . . . two or three years had elapsed" since he had begun his notebooks. (F. Darwin and Seward, 1903, vol. 1, p. 367).

28. The quoted passage is from Barlow (1958, p. 119). We have already seen in chapter 4 that Darwin did not work on true Baconian principles, although apparently he did attempt to do so. He read the *History of the Inductive Sciences* by his former teacher William Whewell soon after it appeared in 1837. Darwin's reading notebooks (Vorzimmer, 1977) show that he read extensively in philosophy of science, evidently in search of the "correct" approach to creating his theory. See Ellegard (1957), Hull (1973b), Manier (1978), Ruse (1975a, 1979a), and Thagard (1977) for the influence of Whewell and other philosophers on Darwin.

Elsewhere (Notebook D, p. 117) Darwin suggested that induction was not used to the exclusion of deduction: "The line of argument often pursued throughout my theory is to establish a point as a probability by induction, & to apply it as hypothesis to other points & see whether it will solve them." However, in a letter to Lyell in 1859 Darwin omitted induction altogether, saying that his method was that of "inventing a theory and seeing how many classes of facts the theory would explain" (F. Darwin, 1901, vol. 2, p. 37). Ghiselin (1969) argues that Darwin pioneered in the hypothetico-deductive approach. See Caplan (1979), Flew (1978), Gillespie (1979, Ch. 3), and Ruse (1975c) for further discussion of Darwin's scientific method. Kleiner (1979) argues that Darwin departed from a rigorous method, though not to the extent advocated by Feyerabend (1970, 1975).

For two examples of the "printed enquiries" circulated in 1839, see Gruber and Barrett (1974, pp. 423–425) and Vorzimmer (1969b).

For a discussion of Darwin's ideas on monads see Gruber and Barrett (1974, Ch. 7). Other Darwin scholars have identified various other stages of theory in the notebooks. See Grinnell (1969, 1974) and Kohn (1975, Ch 4, 5).

29. The persecution note was written in May 1838 (Gruber and Barrett, 1974, p. 450). The date of this note is given by Vorzimmer, (1969a.) Darwin's justified fear is discussed by Gruber and Barrett (1974, Ch. 2).

See Barlow (1967, p. 124) for Darwin's letter to Henslow. The hints of evolutionism in *Journal of Researches* survive in *Voyage of the Beagle*, on p. 328 of the Natural History Library edition. See F. Darwin (1901, vol. 1, pp. 268, 269, 271) for letters to Lyell and Fox in which Darwin disguised his interest in evolution. William Darwin Fox, Charles's second cousin, was a country clergyman and amateur naturalist (F. Darwin, 1901, vol. 1, p. 147). Even when the *Origin of Species* was published Darwin expected Fox to reject the theory, and he was uncertain how Lyell would react. This latter uncertainty may seem strange, considering the close friendship of Darwin and Lyell and the latter's outspoken opposition to evolutionism in his *Principles*. However, T. H. Huxley believed that Lyell was personally inclined toward evolutionism even while he argued against it in his book (F. Darwin, 1901, vol. 1, pp. 544–547). It may be relevant to note that Lyell had been trained as a lawyer. Darwin was relieved when Lyell came out in favor of his theory, but complained bitterly when Lyell persisted in referring to it as a species of Lamarckism. See Bartholomew (1973), F. Darwin (1901, vol. 2, pp. 198–199), and L. G. Wilson (1971).

30. This and the following passages by Darwin are from Barlow (1958, pp. 119–121). Darwin also emphasized the importance of artificial selection in letters to Lyell in 1858 (F. Darwin, 1901, vol. 1, p. 474) and to Wallace in 1859 (F. Darwin and Seward, 1903, vol. 1, p. 118). It would have been odd for Darwin not to have looked to artificial selection as a model: his uncle, Josiah Wedgwood, was a leading sheep breeder, and Darwin belonged to a family of noted pigeon fanciers. Kohn (1975, pp. 188–207), Limoges (1970, pp. 75–76, 99), and Ruse (1979a, pp. 170–171) suspect Darwin of a faulty memory in this regard because the few notebook references to artificial selection prior to the Malthusian insight emphasize the *differences* between artificial selection and any natural process of selection he could then imagine. This, I believe, is an example of overreliance on the notebooks. All that can reasonably be deduced from the notebooks is what Darwin has already told us: that before reading Malthus he was unable to understand how selection was applied in nature. As Mayr (1977, p. 325) has observed, there was little for him to note regarding artificial selection, because it was providing no clues. The undisputed fact that Darwin spent

so much time studying artificial selection can only mean that he expected to find some form of selection as the mechanism of evolution. Ruse (1975b) and Vorzimmer (1969b) discuss the role of artificial selection in the development of Darwinism.

31. de Beer (1963, p. 100) and Gruber and Barrett (1974) doubt the importance of Malthus in Darwin's realization of natural selection because the notebooks prior to the Malthusian reading contain passages which we now interpret as selectionist. For example, C61 considers "whether species may not be made by a little more vigour being given to the chance offspring who have any slight peculiarity of structure. (hence seals take victorious seals, hence deer victorious deer, hence males armed & pugnacious all orders; cocks all war-like)" (I suspect that another reason for doubting the significance of Malthus is that the discovery of the Malthus pages, D134, 135, after they had been given up as lost, turned out to be anticlimactic. These pages do not exactly cry out "Eureka!") Gruber suggests that the concept of natural selection was fermenting in Darwin's brain before 28 September 1838, and that Malthus merely crystallized it. This is in keeping with Gruber's major thesis that all theories result from a process of slow development. The importance of reading Malthus may actually have been to give Darwin the first glimpse of struggle for survival among members of the same species, thus changing his focus from the simultaneous modification of all members of the species to change in the number of members modified. However, C61 quoted above makes this interpretation doubtful. For various interpretations of the role of Malthus see Bowler (1976b), Gale (1972), Herbert (1968, Ch. 4, 1971), Kohn (1975, Ch. 6), Mayr (1977), Ospovat (1979), and Vorzimmer (1969a).

32. The 1842 pencil Sketch and the 1844 Essay were published by Francis Darwin in 1909. See also Darwin and Wallace (1958). A draft and outline of the 1842 Sketch were found among old papers under the steps at Darwin's house at Down. According to Vorzimmer (1975), who has transcribed them, they date from 1839.

33. "Columbus and his egg: after the return of Columbus from his successful voyage of discovery he was invited to a banquet by Cardinal Mendoza. A shallow courtier present, impatient of the honours paid to Columbus, abruptly asked him whether he thought that in case he had not discovered the Indies, there were not other men in Spain who would have been capable of the enterprise. To this Columbus made no immediate reply, but taking an egg, invited the company to make it stand on end. Everyone attempted it, but in vain. Whereupon he struck it upon the table so as to break the end and left it standing on the broken part; illustrating in this simple manner that when he had once shown the way to the New World nothing was easier than to follow it." From *The Oxford Companion to English Literature*, 4th ed., p. 184.

Elsewhere Darwin says, it took him fifteen years to see the meaning and cause of divergence (F. Darwin, 1901, vol. 2, p. 211). Browne (1980) believes the insight occurred in 1857. It is evident from the selection in this chapter that Wallace immediately saw the solution to divergence.

34. See F. Darwin (1901, vol. 1, pp. 377–379) for instructions for publishing the 1844 essay. Darwin revealed his theory to Hooker in early 1844 (F. Darwin and Seward, 1903, vol. 1, pp. 40, 41; McKinney, 1972, p. 112). For information about Hooker see Allan (1967), Gillispie (1972, vol. 6), L. Huxley (1918), and Turrill (1963). Darwin hinted to others that he was considering evolution but apparently

spoke only to Hooker about natural selection prior to 1856. See McKinney (1972, pp. 108–110). Ruse (1979a, p. 184) states that Hooker reacted to the essay by suggesting that Darwin get out of the clouds with some real biology—hence the barnacle study. Darwin's doubts about the value of that study are quoted in Barlow (1958, p. 118). See F. Darwin (1901, vol. 1, pp. 314–319) for a more positive view.

35. For theories about Darwin's delay see Ghiselin (1969, pp. 47–48), Gould (1977, Ch. 1), Gruber and Barrett (1974, pp. 26–27), and Ruse (1979a, pp. 184–188). For Darwin's opinion of *Vestiges* see F. Darwin (1901, vol. 1, pp. 301–302). For the effect on Darwin of attacks on the author of *Vestiges* see Egerton (1970b).

36. Wallace's paper (reprinted in Brackman, 1980, pp. 311–325) moved Lyell to begin his own notebook on the species question (L. G. Wilson, 1970). See Beddall (1972) for the effect of Wallace's paper on Lyell and Darwin. Stauffer published part of Darwin's intended big book in 1975. See also Stauffer (1959).

One of the ironies of this episode is that Wallace's law was inspired by Lyell's uniformitarianism (Wallace, 1905, vol. 1, pp. 354–355). The date when Lyell first heard Darwin's theory is given by McKinney (1972, pp. 111–112). See Chapter 4 of that work for a discussion of Wallace's 1855 paper. Limoges (1970, p. 17) and others have pointed out that Darwin's "Law of the Succession of Types," as well as statements by others, anticipated Wallace's law. See the letters to Lyell and Hooker in which Darwin considered publishing a short sketch. (F. Darwin, 1901, vol. 1, pp. 426–430). Darwin was cautious in writing to Wallace that he, too, had been considering evolution, and that he thought highly of Wallace's paper. "Though agreeing with you on your conclusions in the paper, I believe I go much further than you; but it is too long a subject to enter on my speculative notions" (Marchant, 1916, pp. 107–108; George, 1964, pp. 56–57).

37. Quoted from Wallace (1905, vol. 1, pp. 361–363). McKinney provides a useful collection of this and three similar accounts by Wallace. (See McKinney, 1972, pp. 160–163, and also pp. 80–81, fn. 1 for other sources.) See McKinney (1972, Ch. 6 and App. 4) and Young (1969) for the role of Malthus in Wallace's thinking. See McKinney (1972, Ch. 8) for the date and circumstances surrounding Wallace's creation of the theory.

McKinney argues convincingly that Wallace was not actually at Ternate when he conceived of natural selection, but on the island of Gilolo, now Halmahera. McKinney is less convincing in arguing that Wallace deliberately lied about the location so that some of the romance of historic Ternate would rub off on his theory. It seems just as plausible that Ternate was given only as Wallace's permanent address, since Gilolo had no regular communication with the rest of the world.

38. For Darwin's letters to Lyell and Hooker regarding the Wallace MS, see Darwin (1901, vol. 1, pp. 472–487). See also Beddall (1968). Brackman (1980) and McKinney (1972, chap. 8) paint a dismal picture of Darwin's behavior in this episode.

Asa Gray (1810–1888) became the foremost Darwinian in America after the publication of the *Origin of Species*. See Dupree (1959), Gillispie (1972, vol. 5) and Gray's *Darwiniana*, reprinted in 1963.

39. See, for examples, F. Darwin (1901, vol. 1, p. 501; vol. 2, pp. 271–272), F. Darwin and Seward (1903, vol. 1, p. 119) and Marchant (1916, p. 131). Note also Wallace's statement that "the one great result which I claim for my paper of 1858 is that it compelled Darwin to write and publish his *Origin of Species* without further

delay" (Wallace, 1905, vol. 1, p. 363). See Beddall (1968) and Vorzimmer (1970, Ch. 8) for the relationship between Darwin and Wallace.

40. See Bates and Humphrey (1956) and Hyman (1963) for samplings of Darwin's later works. Darwin's comment on the *Origin* is from F. Darwin (1901, vol. 2, pp. 215–216). The serious student should consult the facsimile of the first edition of the *Origin of Species* and the variorum edition of Peckham. A less demanding version has been prepared by Leakey (1979). Hodge (1977) and Ruse (1979a, Ch. 7) analyze the *Origin*. See Durant (1979), R. Smith (1972), and the previously cited biographies for Wallace's later work.

Thomas Henry Huxley (1825–1895) is another whom I regret having to ignore in this chapter, because his most important role as Darwin's "bulldog" came after the *Origin* was published. Those who wish to experience true eloquence in scientific exposition should sample Huxley's *Darwiniana* (1896) and *Lay Sermons, Addresses and Reviews* (1871). See also the ever-popular *On a Piece of Chalk* (1967). For biographies of Huxley see Ashforth (1969), Bibby (1959, 1972), L. Huxley (1900, 1969), Irvine (1955), Paradis (1978), and Peterson (1932).

41. Wallace (1905, vol. 1, pp. 114–116) came to essentially the same conclusions regarding the foundations of his and Darwin's creativity.

42. Notes on the selection:

Himmelfarb (1962, pp. 471–472, fn. 2) suggests that the date of 1839 given for the pencil Sketch is simply an error. However, Darwin gave the same date to Wallace shortly after the Linnean Society meeting. (F. Darwin, 1901, vol. 1, p. 502). Vorzimmer (1975) suggests that it refers to the year in which the Sketch was first outlined.

See F. Darwin (1901, vol. 1, pp. 477–482) for the complete letter to Gray.

Note Lyell's and Hooker's observation that the theory is a "deduction," and Wallace's similar admission.

De Candolle, Augustin-Pyramus (1778–1841). Swiss. Like his friend Lamarck, he switched from medicine to botany.

Herbert, William (1778–1847). Served in British House of Commons. Clergyman and naturalist specializing in botany and taxonomy. In the "Historical Sketch" of the *Origin* Darwin credits him with questioning the absolute distinction between varieties and species in 1837.

Owen, Richard (1804–1892). Leading comparative anatomist of his day. Wavered between claiming priority for Darwin's theory and attacking it as an ally of Bishop Wilberforce.

natura non facit saltum. Literally, nature does not make a jump. This aphorism of Linnaeus was given new significance by Lyell and Darwin.

Note the similarity of Darwin's and Wallace's examples of the multiplication of birds. Just such coincidences have been the basis of charges of plagiarism against Darwin.

Within three decades after Wallace asserted the indestructability of the passenger pigeon the species was extinct.

Bowler (1976b, c) has drawn attention to an important difference between the contributions of Darwin and Wallace. Darwin emphasized the struggle among individuals of a species, while Wallace emphasized the struggle among established varieties within a species.

43. Ruse (1979a) argues that Darwin also attempted to follow the Newtonian

approach, as advocated by Whewell and Herschel. By Darwin's time, however, axioms were thought of more as laws to be discovered rather than intuitions to be invented. Darwin perceived natural selection as a natural law of evolution.

44. Darwin borrowed the phrase "survival of the fittest" from Herbert Spencer (1820–1903) on the advice of Wallace (F. Darwin and Seward, 1903, vol. 1, p. 270). It is clear in the *Origin of Species,* but not in Darwin's Linnean papers, that survival meant not only survival of the individual but also success in leaving progeny.

It is interesting to recall Matthew's statement that natural selection is "an axiom, requiring only to be pointed out to be admitted by unprejudiced minds of sufficient grasp." Wallace (1905, vol. 1, p. 361) also referred to natural selection as "self-evident." However, it is unlikely that either Matthew or Wallace were aware of the circularity of "survival of the fittest."

Many evolutionists and philosophers of evolution have justifiably complained of the tiresome regularity with which "survival of the fittest" is discovered to be a tautology. Haldane (1935) may have been the first, followed by Barker (1969), Delbrück (1949), Eden (1967), Harris (1975), Koestler (1978, Part III), Macbeth (1971, pp. 47–50), Manser (1965), Popper (1972, pp. 241–242, and in Schilpp, 1974, p. 137), Smart (1963, p. 59), (von Bertalanffy, 1960, p. 89), Waddington (1957, p. 64), and probably many others. R. H. Peters (1976, 1978) states that evolutionary theory is tautological in a somewhat different sense. See Caplan (1977), Castrodega (1977), Ferguson (1976), and Stebbins (1977 for discussion.

I should point out that among population geneticists fitness no longer has the commonsense meaning it had in Darwin's time. Fitness is now applied to groups sharing a genotype rather than to individuals. There are various modern definitions, but that of Dobzhansky et al. (1977, p. 101) is one of the most straightforward. "The Darwinian fitness, also called the selective or adaptive value, usually symbolized as w, is a relative rather than an absolute measure. If the carriers of a certain genotype transmit their genes to the next generation at a rate we may denote as unity ($w_1 = 1$), the carriers of another genotype in the same population may pass their genes at a lower or higher rate, $w_2 = 1 - s$ or $1 + s$. The value of s is the selection coefficient."

"Survival of the fittest" is explicitly circular by this definition.

Woodger (1937) attempted to show biologists how to use an axiomatic approach. However, Woodger and modern philosophers of science no longer use the term "axiom" in exactly the same way as Newton. Rather, they speak of an axiomatic system as a minimum set of statements required to deduce a theory. See Ruse (1973) and Williams (1970) for recent applications of formal axiomatization to biology. (However, see Caplan's [1978a] and Hull's [1969] criticisms of some aspects of this approach.) I have considered trying to avoid confusion by using some word other than axiom for "survival of the fittest," but alternatives such as assumption, postulate, and premise do not carry the appropriate flavor of intuitive conviction.

Williams (1970, 1973) has also proposed that "survival of the fittest" be taken as an axiom. From this and other axioms she formally deduced a pseudo-Darwinian theory of evolution. However, she still feels compelled to avoid circularity, which she manages to do only by leaving fitness undefined in the formal axiom. The problem with this tactic is that her deductions are equally valid if "unfitness" or "luck" or any other undefined term is substituted for "fitness." One then has a logically valid theory of evolution based on the "survival of the unfit" or the "survival of the lucky."

Williams justifies leaving fitness undefined by correctly noting that every theory includes terms which are not defined *within the theory*. However, in Darwin's original theory fitness retained the meaning which was already well established. This is one reason why Williams's theory is only pseudo-Darwinian. In fact it could also be called pseudo-Lamarckian, for there is nothing in Williams's axioms which specifies how adaptations are acquired and inherited. The axiomatic approach is valuable in revealing logical gaps in a theory and suggesting new axioms. Too often, however, philosophers are deluded into thinking they can recreate a theory according to the latest fashion in scientific methodology. They often do not appreciate that theories evolve in the same haphazard way as, for example, the ostrich. No doubt a committee of philosophers could design a large Australian bird which would be prettier than the ostrich. But biologists should not mistake it for a real ostrich, and they might even wonder whether the pseudo-ostrich would survive in the real world.

45. Barker (1969), Ruse (1973, pp. 37–41), Wasserman (1978), and Williams (1973) are among those who have noted the two aspects of natural selection.

46. Popper, himself, considers Darwinism an untestable theory (Schilpp, 1974, vol. 1, pp. 133–143).

47. Some defenders of natural selection have argued that circularity can be avoided by defining fitness in terms of "adaptation," "improved design," "adaptive complexity," "relative adaptation," and so on (Domning, 1978; Gould, 1977, Ch. 4; Lewontin, 1978; Maynard Smith, 1969). They generally avoid defining what they mean by such terms, but I suspect it has something to do with survival. Incredibly, Dobzhansky et al. (1977, p. 506) accuse those who claim natural selection is circular of equating fitness and adaptation. Other would-be defenders of natural selection have argued that the circularity is removed because fitness means only a greater probability of surviving, not a guarantee of surviving (Ghiselin, 1969, p. 64; Hull, 1969; Mills and Beatty, 1979; Ruse, 1971b; Scriven, 1959). Of course the probabilistic aspect of survival is obvious in the Linnean papers and the *Origin of Species*. However, "survival of those who have a greater probability of surviving" is still circular.

48. Darwin's quotation is from later editions of the *Origin of Species*, Chapter 6, in the section on "Utilitarian Doctrine." Ghiselin (1969, Ch. 3) and Gillespie (1979, Ch. 4) cite this and other supposed tests of natural selection given by Darwin. However, most of them are tests of evolution, not natural selection. Those that could potentially falsify "survival of the fittest" are, in practice, saved by the same kind of ad-hoc assumptions discussed above. Von Bertalanffy (1960, pp. 87–92) discusses the ability of natural selection to make difficulties go away.

It is no good arguing that such cases as self-toxicity would disappear if only we knew enough (Domning, 1978; Hull, 1974, p. 68). We can never know if we know enough. Further knowledge might indeed show that it is good for a plant to poison itself, but still more knowledge could reverse that conclusion.

49. Birch and Ehrlich (1967), Ehrlich and Holm (1962), Olson (1960), von Bertalanffy (1969), and Waddington (1957) are among the eminent biologists who have suggested that there might be a better theory of evolution if only one would look. Black (1978), Grassé (1977), Ho and Saunders (1979), Koestler (1967, and in Koestler and Smythies, 1969), Popper (1972, Ch. 7), Riedl (1979), Saunders and Ho (1976), Stanley (1975), and Wolsky and Wolsky (1976) are among the many who have attempted to replace or supplement "survival of the fittest." Lest anyone think that

the present theory is entirely satisfactory, Maynard Smith (1977) describes many questions about evolution which remain unanswered by the presently accepted theory. Raup (1977) has shown that a purely random model of survival, rather than one based on natural selection, can explain the prevalence of species in the fossil record. See also Gould (1978).

8. DARWINISM IS DEAD: LONG LIVE NEO-DARWINISM

1. Among histories of genetics are those by Dunn (1951, 1965), Jacob (1973), Robinson (1979), Stubbe (1972), and Sturtevant (1965). Useful collections of classic papers in genetics have been compiled by Carlson (1967), J. A. Moore (1972), J. A. Peters (1959), and Voeller (1968).

2. See F. Darwin and Seward (1903, vol. 1, p. 310) for a description of Darwin's concept of pangenesis. Darwin's original manuscript on pangenesis is transcribed by Olby (1963). For the date of the conception of pangenesis see F. Darwin (1901, vol. 2, p. 255). The fact that pangenesis originated so early disproves the common assertion that Darwin proposed it to answer criticisms of the *Origin of Species*. For discussion see Bowler (1974b), Geison (1969), Ghiselin (1969, pp. 181–186), Kohn (1975, p. 159), and Vorzimmer (1963). See Ghiselin (1975) for the possible roots of Darwin's theory. Darwin's statement on Hippocrates is in F. Darwin (1901, vol. 2, p. 265). See also the selection by Maupertuis in Chapter 6 for another version of pangenesis. For a history of the idea of pangenesis see Zirkle (1946).

3. Darwin admitted to Francis Galton in 1875 that "every year I come to attribute more and more to [use and disuse during the life of the individual]" (F. Darwin and Seward, 1903, vol. 1, p. 360). This is apparent in comparing the various editions of the *Origin*, and from Darwin's letters and *Autobiography* (See Barlow, 1958, p. 89). However, Ghiselin (1969, p. 180) and Vorzimmer (1970, Ch. 5) argue that this was only a slight shift in emphasis.

4. Quoted from C. Darwin (1905, vol. 2, p. 338). See Darden (1976) for a discussion of Darwin's use of these "facts." For a history of some of these ideas of heredity see Zirkle (1951a). See Stubbe (1972, Ch. 7) for a summary of the genetic information available to Darwin.

5. Galton's paper on pangenesis and Darwin's reply are reprinted in J. A. Moore, (1972, pp. 9–25). For an account of Galton's stirp theory see Dunn (1965, pp. 37–39). See also Cowan (1972). For Galton's biography see Forrest (1974), Galton (1908), Gillispie (1972, vol. 5), and Pearson (1914–1930). Lysenkoists in Russia in the 1950s and early 1960s tried Galton's experiment on chickens and reported successful transfer of plumage color. However, their work could not be replicated by Kosin and Kato (1963) or by Lowe et al. (1963).

6. See Coleman (1965) and Stubbe (1972, Ch. 8) for brief accounts of advances in cell biology in the nineteenth century. Matthias Jacob Schleiden (1804–1881) first practiced law, failed at suicide, then turned to botany. He was instrumental in getting Carl Zeiss (1816–1888) started. Schleiden's proposal that all plant tissues consist of cells was extended to animals by Teodor Schwann (1810–1882). Carl Wilhelm von Nägeli (1817–1891) studied botany under Schleiden. Rudolph Ludwig Virchow

(1821–1902) applied cell biology to medicine, and was also active in politics and anthropology.

7. The most thorough biography of Weismann, by Gaupp (1917), is not available in English. Short biographies in English are in Gillispie (1976, vol. 14), Petrunkevich (1963), and Stubbe (1972, pp. 252–260). See also Churchill (1968). For the 1885 paper as well as others on heredity and against Lamarckism see Weismann (1889). Additional lectures on evolution are in Weismann (1904).

8. For more on Nägeli see Gillispie (1974, vol. 9). The standard biography of Mendel is by Iltis (1932). See also Gillispie (1974, vol. 9) and Iltis (1951). Portugal and Cohen (1977, pp. 109–114) and Stubbe (1972, pp. 126–129) summarize some of the facts of Mendel's life recently brought to light by Krizenecky (1965). Sootin (1959) has written a fictionalized biography of Mendel. At age twenty-seven Mendel wrote an autobiographical sketch which is reprinted by Crew (1966, pp. 18–19) and Iltis (1954).

9. For the historical background to Mendel's work see Olby (1966), Roberts (1929), Zirkle (1951b), and the previously cited histories of genetics. Mendel first reported his experiments in two sessions of the Brünn Natural History Society in 1865, and the paper was published the following year. The paper was first translated by William Bateson (1909), and an improved version appeared in Stern and Sherwood (1966). Both translations are frequently included in anthologies.

10. In fact Mendel obtained ratios closer to 3 : 1 than is now considered likely for statistical reasons. This aroused Fisher's (1936) suspicion that Mendel had "cooked" his data. However, see Sturtevant (1965, pp. 13–16) and Wright (1966).

11. Curiously, Galton told Darwin in 1875 that a 1 : 2 : 1 ratio of black : gray : white would be expected in the offspring of hybrids having one black and one white gemmule (Olby, 1965). Perhaps Galton did not know of dominance, and Darwin lacked the mathematical insight to see how Galton's suggestion could explain his 3 : 1 ratio.

Since the early 1900s it has been known that many traits do tend to associate, because their genes are linked on the same chromosome. Fisher (1936) doubted that Mendel had actually done all the experiments he described because of the seeming impossibility of finding seven independently assorting traits in a species with only seven pairs of chromosomes. However, Novitski and Blixt (1977) show that some of the traits Mendel studied are indeed linked, but very weakly. Thus Mendel was not dishonest, but certainly blessed with luck.

12. My conclusion that Mendel was showing how new species could arise from a single hybrid is directly contrary to the thesis of Brannigan (1979) and Olby (1979). They argue that those who "rediscovered" Mendel in 1900 actually misinterpreted this point to bolster their own position that mutation, rather than natural selection, is the major cause of evolution. Correns did, indeed, point to this passage to support the mutationist position, but his interpretation was not mistaken (Stern and Sherwood, 1966, p. 129).

It may appear that Mendel's discussion, near the end of his paper, of how a hybrid can be transformed into a new species supports the argument of Brannigan and Olby. However this passage relates to artificial selection, not what could reasonably happen in nature.

Mendel was not himself antiselectionist, as a letter to Nägeli implies: "[T]he naturally occurring hybridizations in Hieracium [hawkweed] should be ascribed to temporary disturbances, which, if they become permanent, would finally result in the disappearances of the species involved, while one or another of the more happily organized progeny, better adapted to the prevailing telluric and cosmic conditions, might take up the struggle for existence successfully and continue it for a long stretch of time, until finally the same fate overtook it."

13. For Nägeli's response to Mendel's paper see Iltis (1932, pp. 191–192). Mendel's letters to Nägeli are translated in *Genetics* 35 Part II (1950), pp. 1–29, and in Stern and Sherwood (1966).

Vorzimmer has found references to Mendel in Darwin's library, but Darwin apparently missed them. On the question why and whether Mendel was ignored, see Brannigan (1979), Gasking (1959), Glass (1953), Olby (1979), Olby and Gautry (1968), and Weinstein (1977). On the general question of prematurity or delayed recognition in science, see Garfield (1980). For Wallace's view of Mendelism see George (1964, pp. 77–80) and Wallace (1905, vol. 2, pp. 212–213).

14. That genetics was invented in 1900, not rediscovered, has been insisted upon by Brannigan (1979) and Olby (1979), and previously implied by many others who noted the absence of any reference to hereditary particles in Mendel's paper. The papers announcing the "rediscovery" are reprinted in the issue of *Genetics* cited in the previous note, and in Stern and Sherwood (1966). For an account of the "rediscovery" see Roberts (1929) and Zirkle (1964).

The international character of science at the turn of the century is illustrated by the "rediscoverers" of Mendel: a Dutchman, a German, an Austrian, a Frenchman, and an Englishman.

In his "rediscovery" paper Correns made the important observation that not all traits show dominance and assort independently.

Neither Galton nor Weismann, by the way, had much to say about Mendel (Crombie, 1963, pp. 529–533, 597–603; De Marrais, 1974, p. 146).

15. On the evolution of De Vries's ideas see G. E. Allen (1969), Bowler (1978), Darden (1976), and Heimans (1962). For translations of his two books see De Vries (1909–1910; 1910). For a biography of De Vries see Gillispie (1976, vol. 14). The "mutations" in evening primrose turned out to be caused by the odd mode of reproduction in that species, rather than by genetic mutations in the modern sense.

16. For histories of the Mendelain-biometrician controversy see Cock (1973), Mackenzie and Barnes (1979), Norton (1973, 1975), and Provine (1971). For Bateson's life and work see Bateson (1928) and Gillispie (1970, vol. 1). Galton's role is described by Cowan (1972), De Marrais (1974), Froggatt and Nevin (1971a, b), and Swinburne (1965).

On the work of Morgan and his associates see G. E. Allen (1968, 1978, 1979a, b) and Shine and Wrobel (1976). The chromosome theory of heredity was summarized by Morgan et al. (1915). Examples of premature obituaries for natural selection are Kellogg (1907) and Morgan (1916).

17. For a review of the role of mathematical population genetics in neo-Darwinism see Provine (1978). For a summary of R. A. Fisher's contributions see Fisher (1930). His daughter has written his biography (Box, 1978). Sewall Wright is now Emeritus Professor of the University of Wisconsin and of the University of Chicago. See Wright (1967) for a summary of his early contributions. The most detailed

biography of Haldane is by Clark (1968). See also Dronamraju (1968) and Werskey (1971).

18. Naomi Haldane Mitchison (1897–) is a novelist. Readers of *The Double Helix* may recall her as J. D. Watson's hostess, and the person to whom that book is dedicated.

19. Some of Haldane's popular writings were collected in books published in 1928, 1933, 1938, 1940, 1947, and 1958.

20. See Werskey's (1978) collective biography of Haldane and other Marxist scientists of the thirties. See also Haldane (1939) and his introduction to Engels's *Dialectics of Nature* (1940).

21. The orthodox view may be found in the now-classical writings of Theodosius Dobzhansky, E. B. Ford, Julian Huxley, Ernst Mayr, H. J. Muller, George Gaylord Simpson, and G. Ledyard Stebbins. This is not to say that they all speak with one voice. For a divergent history of the synthesis of evolution and genetics see Mayr and Provine (1980), who trace the synthesis primarily to Theodosius Dobzhansky.

22. On the oversimplication of population genetics see Lewontin (1970) and Wadington (1969, pp. 95–97). See Harris (1975) on spontaneity as an axiom. Another objection to the idea of chance mutations is that no one really understands what chance is. See Hardy et al. (1973, Part II by Harvie) and Koestler (1972) for some of the unexpected ways order can assert itself over chance.

To compensate for my shameful hurrying over molecular genetics see Judson (1979), Olby (1974), Portugal and Cohen (1978), and Stent (1971). I also recommend Watson's *Double Helix* (1968), not as history but as a revolutionary's account of a scientific revolution.

23. See Kimura (1979) for a relatively simple description of the neutral theory. On the genetic similarity of men and chimps see Cherry et al. (1978), King and Wilson (1975), and Yunis et al. (1980). On man as an immature ape see Gould (1977, Ch. 7, 8).

24. I first proposed these criteria in Harris (1975). Compare Frank (1957, pp. 348–360), Kuhn (1977, Ch. 13), and Turchin (1977, pp. 295–297). Kuhn's five criteria—accuracy, consistency, broadness of scope, simplicity, and fruitfulness—are essentially the same as mine if we equate accuracy and consistency with being canonical, and broadness of scope and simplicity with being neat.

25. I am grateful to Dr. Paul Roman for the quotation by Dirac. For the role of aesthetics in physics see Chandrasekhar (1979) and Wechsler (1978).

26. For additional discussion of the role of aesthetics in Darwin's thought see the chapter by Gruber in Wechsler (1978). See Stent (1978, Ch. 5) for more on style in science.

9. MODERN TIMES: MARXISM, LYSENKOISM, AND SOCIOBIOLOGY

1. For this interpretation I have relied especially on the 1940 translation of Engels's *Dialectics of Nature* and the 1939 edition of his *Anti-Dühring*. Also useful have been Graham (1971), Haldane (1939), Heilbroner (1980), Popper (1965, Ch. 15, 1966), Zirkle (1959), and the articles on Marx and Engels in Gillispie (1978, vol. 15).

2. For an introduction to the vast literature on "social Darwinism" see the references cited by Young (1973, p. 424, fn. 228). See Greene (1977) for an analysis of Darwin's own attitude toward "social Darwinism."

3. Quoted from Young (1973, p. 385, fn. 121). On Marx's guarded enthusiasm for Darwinism see Ball (1979) and Colp (1974). The latter article and many others must be revised in light of the discovery that Marx *did not* ask to dedicate part of *Capital* to Darwin. See Colp and Fay (1979), Fay (1978), and Feuer (1975, 1976, 1978).

4. See Gould (1980a, Ch. 17) Eldredge and Gould (1977) and Ridley (1980). Gould's and Eldredge's theory is referred to as the theory of punctuated equilibrium. Note that the brief periods of evolution are many thousands of years long.

5. For Marx's failure as a prophet see Popper (1966, Ch. 20). It should be noted that Marxists are less interested in making falsifiable predictions about the future than in analyzing the contradictions of the present.

6. From a *Pravda* news article of 1927, quoted by Zhores Medvedev (1969, p. 11). My account of Lysenkoism depends heavily on Medvedev's book. See also Graham (1971, Ch. 6), J. Huxley (1949), Joravsky (1970), Lindegren (1966), Medvedev (1978), Mikulak (1967, 1970), and Zirkle (1949, 1956), as well as the article on Lysenko in the *Great Soviet Encyclopedia*, vol. 15, Macmillan, New York, 1977. See Lewontin and Levins (1976) for a stimulating account of Lysenkoism from a Marxist perspective.

7. On the introduction of Marxism into Soviet science see Graham (1971, pp. 58–59) and Joravsky (1961, 1970, Ch. 8). Prezent also showed Lysenko the supposed relevance of Darwinism (Medvedev, 1969, p. 17), and explained to him the fallacies of Mendelism (Graham, 1971, p. 269).

8. Medvedev (1970) and Popovsky (1979) show that the government of the USSR has still not learned many of the lessons of Lysenkoism. In 1969 after Popovsky tried to publish a biography of Vavilov he was forbidden to publish anything at all for two years.

9. Medvedev (1969, p. 168). See Graham (1971, pp. 219–237) and Jaravsky (1970, Ch. 7) for patient treatments of Lysenko's theories.

10. See Gaissinovitch (1980) and Joravsky (1959, 1961, Ch. 9) regarding Soviet Lamarckism before Lysenko. See Koestler (1971) for a sympathetic treatment of Kammerer and his work, but see also Gould's (1972) review of this book. For histories of neo-Lamarckism see Fothergill (1952, pp. 251–274, 368–370) and Pfeifer (1965).

11. For more on Michurin see Gillispie (1978, vol. 15) and Joravsky (1970, pp. 40–54).

12. Lenin (1970, p. 249). For the various uses of materialism by Marx, Engels, and Lenin see Kernig (1973, vol. 5).

13. According to Lewontin and Levins (1976) some radical Maoists still accept this rationale of Lysenko. See their paper for further criticism of Lysenko's argument that Mendelism is antimaterialist.

14. Regarding public demonstrations against Wilson see Beckwith and Lange (1978), Currier (1976), Wade (1976), and the *New York Times,* 16 February 1978. It should be noted that the violent protests against Wilson have been denounced as counterproductive by many of Wilson's critics (Beckwith and Lange, 1978).

I am grateful to Professor Wilson for sending me the material on which this biography is based. This includes a preprint of an article to appear in *McGraw-Hill*

Scientists and Engineers, the text of a speech delivered at the University of Alabama Sesquicentennial Celebration, and *Current Biography* for October 1979 (40 (10): 39–42).

15. So many books and articles are being written about sociobiology that a comprehensive bibliography would soon be out of date. For a sampling of diverse views see Barlow and Silverberg (1978), Caplan (1978b), Clutton-Brock and Harvey (1978), Gregory et al. (1978), Hunt (1980), Montagu (1980), Ruse (1979b), Sahlins (1976), and Suppe and Asquith (1977).

16. On facial expressions see Darwin's *The Expression of the Emotions in Man and Animals* and Hass (1970).

17. The quotation by Marcus Aurelius is from *Meditations* VI. 54. Darwin wrote to Wallace in 1868 that "Natural Selection cannot effect what is not good for the individual, including in that term a social community" (F. Darwin and Seward, 1903, vol. 1, p. 294). See also *Origin of Species,* Ch. 6, "On Utilitarian Doctrine. . ."

18. See Wilson (1975a, pp. 415–418) and Oster and Wilson (1978, Ch. 3) for more rigorous applications of kin selection to social insects.

19. On Popper see Schilpp (1974, vol. 1, pp. 133–143). Lewontin (1977a) and Sociobiology Study Group (1976, 1977) are among those who argue that sociobiology is not falsifiable. See Gould (1980b) and Ruse (1979b, Ch. 6) for discussions of the falsifiability of sociobiology. See Oster and Wilson (1978, p. 103) for examples of falsifiable and falsified theories of sociobiology.

20. For the full quotation see the selection by Lysenko. See Beach (1978) for a criticism of Wilson and others for transferring terms, especially "homosexuality," across species. The Sociobiology Study Group (1976, 1977) also points out that Wilson's use of the term "slavery" to describe the captivity of one species of any by another is inappropriate, for human slavery involves members of the same species. "Domestication" would better fit the ants. However, the use of "slavery" to describe what ants do goes back at least to the *Origin of Species.* See Wilson (1975a, pp. 242–243) and Sahlins (1976, pp. 7–16) on the error of equating animal aggression with human warfare. For further discussion of Barash's study of "rape" in ducks see *Science* 201:280–282 (1978).

21. For information on Science for the People see Greeley and Tafler (1979), Henig (1979), Lewontin (1979), and Walsh (1976). The views endorsed by one or more Marxists are expressed in Allen et al. (1975), Alper et al. (1976), Lewontin (1977a, 1977b), and Sociobiology Study Group (1976, 1977). See also Marvin Harris (1979, Ch. 5) for criticism of sociobiology from a Marxist perspective. For Gould's, Lewontin's and Levins' application of Marxism see Eldredge and Gould (1977) and Lewontin and Levins (1976).

22. See Wilson (1978a, pp. 198–201, 208–217, 230) for definition and discussion of scientific materialism and Marxism.

23. Numerous human fossils have been found with arrowheads imbedded, tomahawk marks on the skull, and other signs of mayhem. See for examples Pfeiffer (1977, pp. 246–247) and Zimmerman and Whitten (1980). There is indisputable evidence of warfare among pre-Columbian Indians of meso-America, and among North American Indians such as the Iroquois and Algonquins prior to white settlement. See the Book of Joshua in the Old Testament for other examples of war and genocide among stateless peoples.

The Malthusian Principle is another form of "biological determinism" unacceptable to many Marxists (Bookchin, 1977, Vandermeer, 1977.) In the People's Republic of China birth control was frowned upon at one time as Malthusian. (Ding Chen, 1980).

24. Wilson (1975a, pp. 298, 299, 592, 594) defines a role as "a pattern of behavior that appears repeatedly in different societies belonging to the same species . . . that has an effect on other members of the society." Polyethism is "division of labor" or "the differentiation of behavior among categories of individuals within the society, especially age and sex classes and castes." References cited by Wilson in the selection are not listed in this bibliography.

See Wilson (1975b; 1976) for rebuttal to some of the charges made here.

For further discussion of Wilson's ideas on homosexuality see Adkins (1980, pp. 401–403). She notes that the twin study cited by Wilson as evidence for a genetic contribution to homosexuality is now rejected by Kallmann himself. But see Wilson (1978a, p. 151) for additional evidence.

25. Homozygotes are individuals with two identical genes for a trait, one on each chromosome of a pair. Heterozygotes have different genes on each chromosome of a pair.

26. For a philosophical defense of intolerance see Wolff, et al. (1965). For Stalin's quotation see Joravsky (1970, p. 150). See also Feyerabend (1978) and Seaton (1980) on Marxism and tolerance.

27. See Currier (1976) and Wade (1976) for relations between Lewontin and Wilson.

28. Wilson (1975c) has warned against the naturalistic fallacy. See also Caplan (1978b, Part III), Flew (1967a, b), Hudson (1969), Munson (1971, Part 3) and Taylor (1975, pp. 175–207). See Paul (1981) for Marx's racism.

29. The analogy of natural and social evolution is developed by Cavalli-Sforza (1971), Cavalli-Sforza and Feldman (1981) and Lumsden and Wilson (1980; 1981).

Bibliography

Adkins, E. K. 1980. Genes, hormones, sex and gender. In *Sociobiology: beyond nature/ nurture?*, ed. G. W. Barlow and J. Silverberg, pp. 385–415. New York: Praeger.

Allan, M. 1967. *The Hookers of Kew, 1785–1911.* London: Joseph.

Allen, E. et al. 1975. Against "sociobiology." New York Review of Books, Nov. 13, pp. 182, 184–186.

Allen, G. E. 1968. Thomas Hunt Morgan and the problem of natural selection. J. Hist. Biol. 1:113–139.

———. 1969. Hugo de Vries and the reception of the "mutation theory." J. Hist. Biol. 2:55–87.

———. 1978. *Life science in the twentieth century.* New York: Cambridge Univ. Press.

———. 1979a. *Thomas Hunt Morgan: the man and his science.* Princeton, N.J.: Princeton Univ. Press.

———. 1979b. Naturalists and experimentalists: The genotype and the phenotype. In *Studies in history of biology*, vol. 3, ed. W. Coleman and C. Limoges, pp. 179–209. Baltimore: Johns Hopkins Univ. Press.

Allen, L. H. 1967. *Bryan and Darrow at Dayton: The record and documents of the "Bible-evolution trial."* New York: Russell & Russell.

Alper, J. et al. 1976. The implications of sociobiology. Science 192:424–427. (Reprinted in Caplan, 1978b.)

Ann Arbor Science for the People Editorial Collective, ed. 1977. *Biology as a social weapon.* Minneapolis: Burgess.

Anonymous. 1967. *Did man get here by evolution or by creation?* New York: Watch Tower Bible and Tract Soc. of New York.

Anonymous. 1970. *Evolution: Science falsely so-called.* 18th ed. Toronto: International Christian Crusade.

Appleman, P., ed. 1970. *Darwin.* New York: Norton.

Aristotle. *History of Animals*, trans D. W. Thompson in numerous editions. Trans. A. L. Peck in Loeb Classical Library. Cambridge: Harvard Univ. Press.

———. *Parts of Animals*, trans. A. L. Peck in Loeb Classical Library. Cambridge: Harvard Univ. Press.

Ashforth, A. 1969. *Thomas Henry Huxley.* New York: Twayne.

Augustine. *The City of God*, trans. M. Dods.

Aulie, R. P. 1972. The doctrine of special creation. Am. Biol. Teacher 34:191–200, 261–268, 281.

Ayala, F. J. and Dobzhansky, T., eds. 1974. *Studies in the philosophy of biology: Reduction and related problems.* Berkeley: Univ. of California Press.

Bacon, F. *Novum Organum.*

Bacon, R. 1962. *Opus Majus.* New York: Russell & Russell.

Bailey, E. 1962. *Charles Lyell.* Garden City, N.Y.: Doubleday.

Baker, J. R. 1952. *Abraham Trembley of Geneva: Scientist and philosopher 1710–1784.* London: Edward Arnold.

Baker, V. R. 1978. The Spokane Flood controversy and the Martian outflow channels. Science 202:1249–1256.

Bakker, R. T. 1975. Dinosaur renaissance. Sci. Am. 232 (Apr.):58–78.

Ball, T. 1979. Marx and Darwin: A reconsideration. Political Theory 7:469–483.

Barash, D. P. 1977a. Sociobiology of rape in mallards *(Anas platyrhynchos):* Responses of the mated male. Science 197:788–789.

———. 1977b. *Sociobiology and behavior.* New York: Elsevier.

———. 1980. Predictive sociobiology: mate selection in damselfishes and brood defense in white-crowned sparrows. In *Sociobiology: beyond nature/nurture?*, ed. G. W. Barlow and J. Silverberg, Ch. 8. New York: Praeger.

Barker, A. D. 1969. An approach to the theory of natural selection. Philosophy 44: 271–290.

Barlow, G. W. 1980. The development of sociobiology: a biologist's perspective. In *Sociobiology: beyond nature/nurture?*, ed. G. W. Barlow and J. Silverberg, Ch. 1. New York: Praeger.

Barlow, G. W. and Sivlerberg, J., eds. 1980. *Sociobiology: beyond nature/nurture?* New York: Praeger.

Barlow, N. 1934. *Charles Darwin's diary of the voyage of H.M.S. "Beagle."* New York: Macmillan.

———, ed. 1946. *Charles Darwin and the voyage of the Beagle.* New York: Philosophical Library.

———, ed. 1958. *The autobiography of Charles Darwin, 1809–1882.* New York: Norton.

———, ed. 1967. *Darwin and Henslow: the growth of an idea; letters 1831–1860.* London: John Murray.

Barnes, S. B. 1972. On the reception of scientific beliefs. In *Sociology of science*, ed. B. Barnes, pp. 269–291. New York: Penguin.

Barrett, P. H. 1974. The Sedgwick-Darwin tour of North Wales. Am. Phil. Soc. Proc. 118:146–164.

———, ed. 1977. *The collected papers of Charles Darwin.* Chicago: Univ. of Chicago Press.

Barthélemy-Madaule, M. 1979. *Lamarck ou le mythe du précurseur.* Paris: Editions du Seuil.

Bartholomew, M. 1973. Lyell and evolution: an account of Lyell's response to the prospect of an evolutionary ancestry for man. Brit. J. Hist. Sci. 6:261–303.

Bartlett, C. J. et al. 1977. Religious leaders' views on the theory of evolution. In *A Compendium of information on the theory of evolution and the evolution-creationism controversy*, ed. J. P. Lightner, pp. 55–63. Reston, Va.: National Association of Biology Teachers.

Bates, M. and Humphrey, P. S., eds. 1956. *The Darwin reader.* New York: Scribner's.

Bateson: B. 1928. *William Bateson, naturalist.* Cambridge, England: Cambridge Univ. Press.

Bateson, W. 1909. *Mendel's principles of heredity: a defence.* Cambridge, England: Cambridge Univ. Press.

Beach, F. A. 1978. Sociobiology and interspecific comparisons of behavior. In *Sociobiology and human nature,* ed. M. S. Gregory, A. Silvers and D. Sutch, Ch 6. San Francisco: Jossey-Bass.

Beck, W. S. 1961. *Modern science and the nature of life.* Garden City, N.Y.: Doubleday (Anchor).

Beckner, M. 1959. *The biological way of thought.* New York: Columbia Univ. Press.

Beckwith, J. and Lange, B. 1978. AAAS: sociobiology on the run. Science for the People Mar./Apr., pp. 38–39.

Beddall, B. G. 1968. Wallace, Darwin and natural selection: a study in the development of ideas and attitudes. J. Hist. Biol. 1:261–323.

———. ed. 1969. *Wallace and Bates in the tropics: an introduction to the theory of natural selection.* New York: Macmillan.

———. 1972. Wallace, Darwin and Edward Blyth: further notes on the development of evolution theory. J. Hist. Biol. 5:153–158.

———. 1973. "Notes for Mr. Darwin": letters to Charles Darwin from Edward Blyth at Calcutta: a study in the process of discovery. J. Hist. Biol. 6:69–95.

Bell, C. 1833. The hand, its mechanism and vital endowments . . . (Bridgewater Treatise 4. Excerpt in *Science before Darwin,* ed. H. M. Jones and I. B. Cohen. London: Andre Deutsch. 1963.)

Bell, P. R., ed. 1959. *Darwin's biological work.* Cambridge, England: Cambridge Univ. Press.

Bennett, J. H., ed. 1973. *Collected papers of R. A. Fisher.* Adelaide, Scotland: University of Adelaide.

Bermant, C. and Weitzman, M. 1979. *Ebla: a revelation in archeology.* New York: Times Books.

Bibby, C. 1959. *T. H. Huxley: scientist, humanist and educator.* New York: Horizon.

———. 1972. *Scientist extraordinary: the life and scientific work of Thomas Henry Huxley, 1820–1895.* Oxford: Pergamon.

Birch, L. C. and Ehrlich, P. R. 1967. Evolutionary history and population biology. Nature 214:349–352.

Black, S. 1978. On the thermodynamics of evolution. Pers. Biol. Med. 21:348–356.

Blake, R. M., Ducasse, C. J. and Madden, E. H. 1960. *Theories of scientific method: the Renaissance through the nineteenth century.* Seattle: Univ. of Washington Press.

Bohannon, L. 1975. Shakespeare in the bush. In *Ants, indians and little dinosaurs,* ed. A. Ternes, pp. 203–216. New York: Scribner's.

Bonar, J. 1966. *Malthus and his work.* New York: A. M. Kelley.

Bookchin, M. 1977. Ecology, society, and the myth of biological determinism. In *Biology as a social weapon,* ed. Ann Arbor Science for the People Editoral Collective, pp. 123–129. Minneapolis: Burgess.

Boring, E. G. 1950. Great men and scientific progress. Am. Phil. Soc. Proc. 94:339–351.

———. 1961. The dual role of the Zeitgeist in scientific creativity. In *The validation of scientific theories,* ed. P. G. Frank, pp. 187–211. New York: Collier.

Bowen, C. D. 1963. *Francis Bacon: the temper of a man.* Boston: Little, Brown.

Bowler, P. J. 1973. Bonnet and Buffon: theories of generation and the problem of species. J. Hist. Biol. 6:259–281.

———. 1974a. Evolutionism in the Enlightenment. Hist. of Science 12:159–183.

———. 1974b. Darwin's concepts of variation. J. Hist. Med. Allied Sci. 29:196–212.

———. 1975. The changing meaning of "evolution." J. Hist. Ideas 36:95–114.

———. 1976a. *Fossils and progress: paleontology and the idea of progressive evolution in the nineteenth century*. New York: Science History Publications.

———. 1976b. Malthus, Darwin, and the concept of struggle. J. Hist. Ideas 37:631–650.

———. 1976c. Alfred Russell Wallace's concepts of variation. J. Hist. Med. Allied Sci. 31:17–29.

———. 1977. Darwinism and the argument from design: suggestions for a reevaluation. J. Hist. Biol. 10:29–43.

———. 1978. Hugo De Vries and Thomas Hunt Morgan: the mutation theory and the spirit of Darwinism. Annals of Sci. 35:55–73.

Box, J. F. 1978. *R. A. Fisher: the life of a scientist*. New York: Wiley.

Brackman, A. C. 1980. *A delicate arrangement: the strange case of Charles Darwin and Alfred Russel Wallace*. New York: Times Books.

Bradford, G. 1926. *Darwin*. New York: Houghton Mifflin.

Brandon, S. G. F. 1963. Creation legends of the ancient Near East. London: Hodder & Stoughton.

Brannigan, A. 1979. Reification of Mendel. Social Studies of Sci. 9:423–454.

Breck, A. D. and Yourgrau, W., eds. 1972. *Biology, history, and natural philosophy*. New York: Plenum.

Brown, P. 1967. *Augustine of Hippo*. Berkeley: Univ. of California Press.

Browne, J. 1980. Darwin's botanical arithmetic and the "principle of divergence," 1854–1856. J. Hist. Biol. 13:53–89.

Brush, S. G. 1974. Should the history of science be rated X? Science 183:1164–1172.

Bube, R. H. 1971. *The human quest: a new look at science and the Christian faith*. Waco, Tex.: World Books.

Buckley, J. H. 1960. Doubt and faith in Tennyson's *In Memoriam*. In *Tennyson: the growth of a poet*. Cambridge: Harvard Univ. Press.

Burchfield, J. D. 1974. Darwin and the dilemma of geological time. Isis 65:300–321.

———. 1975. *Lord Kelvin and the age of the Earth*. New York: Science History Publications.

Burkhardt, R. W., Jr. 1977. *The spirit of system: Lamarck and evolutionary biology*. Cambridge: Harvard Univ. Press.

Burnet, J. 1957. *Early Greek philosophy*. 4th ed. New York: Meridian.

Burrow, J. W. 1966. *Evolution and society: a study in Victorian social theory*. Cambridge, England: Cambridge Univ. Press.

Burstyn, H. L. 1975. If Darwin was not the Beagle's naturalist, why was he on board? Brit. J. Hist. Sci. 8:62–69.

Bush, D. 1950. *Science and English Poetry*. New York: Oxford Univ. Press.

Buttrick, G. A., ed. 1952. *The interpreter's Bible*. New York: Abingdon.

Cadden, J. J. and Brostowin, P. R. 1964. *Science and literature: a reader*. Boston: D. C. Heath.

Callaghen, C. A. 1980. Evolution and creationist arguments. Am. Biol. Teacher 42: 422–427.

Callot, E. 1965. *La philosophie de la vie en XVIIIe siècle.* Paris: Marcel Rivière et cie.

Cannon, H. G. 1959. *Lamarck and modern genetics.* Westport, Conn.: Greenwood.

Cannon, S. F. 1978. *Science and culture: the early Victorian period.* New York: Science History Publications.

Cannon, W. F. 1960. The uniformitarian-catastrophist debate. Isis 51:38–55.

Caplan, A. L. 1977. Tautology, circularity and biological theory. (Letter.) Am. Naturalist 111:390–393.

———. 1978a. Testability, falsifiability, and the synthetic theory of evolution. Erkenntnis 13:261–278.

———. 1978b. *The sociobiology debate.* New York: Harper & Row.

———. 1979. Darwinism and deductivist models of theory structure. Studies in Hist. and Phil. of Sci. 10:341–353.

Carlson, E. A., ed. 1967. *Modern biology: its conceptual foundations.* New York: Braziller.

Carnegie, A. 1900. *The gospel of wealth and other essays.* (Excerpt in Appleman, 1970.)

Cartmill, M. 1974. Rethinking primate origins. Science 184:436–443.

Castrodega, C. 1977. Tautologies, beliefs, and empirical knowledge in biology. (Letter.) Am. Naturalist 111:393–394.

Caute, D. 1978. *The great fear: the anti-Communist purge under Truman and Eisenhower.* New York: Simon & Schuster.

Cavalli-Sforza, L. L. 1971. Similarities and dissimilarities of sociocultural and biological evolution. In *Mathematics in the archeological and historical sciences,* ed. F. R. Hodson, D. G. Kendall and P. Tautu, pp. 535–541. Edinburgh: Edinburgh Univ. Press.

Cavalli-Sforza, L. L. and Feldman, M. W. 1981. *A theory of cultural evolution: cultural transmission.* Princeton, N.J.: Princeton Univ. Press.

Caws, P. 1969. The structure of discovery. Science 166:1375–1380.

Chambers, R. 1969. *Vestiges of the natural history of creation.* New York: Humanities Press.

Chancellor, J. 1973. *Charles Darwin.* New York: Taplinger.

Chandrasekhar, A. 1979. Beauty and the quest for beauty in science. Physics Today 32 (July):25–30.

Cherry, L. M., Case, S. M. and Wilson, A. C. 1978. Frog perspective on the morphological difference between humans and chimpanzees. Science 200:209–211.

Chroust, A. H. 1973. *Aristotle: new facts on his life and on some of his lost works.* Notre Dame, Ind.: Univ. of Notre Dame Press.

Churchill, F. B. 1968. August Weismann and a break from tradition. J. Hist. Biol. 1:91–112.

Clagett, M. 1955. *Greek science in antiquity.* New York: Collier.

Clark, J. W. and Hughes, T. M. 1890. *The life and letters of the Reverend Adam Sedgwick.* Cambridge, England: Cambridge Univ. Press.

Clark, R. W. 1968. *JBS: the life and work of J B S Haldane.* New York: Coward-McCann.

Clodd, E. 1897. *Pioneers of evolution: from Thales to Huxley: with an intermediate chapter on the causes of arrest of the movement.* New York: Arno.

Cloud, P. 1977. "Scientific creationism": a new Inquisition brewing? Humanist 37 (Jan./Feb.).

Clutton-Brock, T. H. and Harvey, P. H., eds. 1978. *Readings in sociobiology.* San Francisco: Freeman.

Cock, A. G. 1973. William Bateson, Mendelism and biometry. J. Hist. Biol. 6:1–36.

Cole, F. C. 1959. A witness at the Scopes trial. Sci. Am. 200 (Jan.):121–130.

Cole, S. G. 1931. *The history of fundamentalism.* New York: R. R. Smith.

Coleman, W. 1964. *Georges Cuvier, zoologist: a study in the history of evolution theory.* Cambridge: Harvard Univ. Press.

———. 1965. Cell, nucleus and inheritance: an historical study. Am. Phil. Soc. Proc. 109:124–158.

Coler, M. A., ed. 1963. *Essays on creativity in the sciences.* New York: New York Univ. Press.

Colp, R., Jr. 1974. The contacts between Karl Marx and Charles Darwin. J. Hist. Ideas 35:329–338.

———. 1977. *To be an invalid: the illness of Charles Darwin.* Chicago: Univ. of Chicago Press.

———. 1980. "I was born to be a naturalist": Charles Darwin's 1838 notes about himself. J. Hist. Med. Allied Sci. 35:8–39.

Colp, R., Jr. and Fay, M. A. 1979. Independent scientific discoveries and the "Darwin-Marx" letter. J. Hist. Ideas 40: 479.

Condon, E. U. 1969. *Scientific study of unidentified flying objects.* New York: Bantam.

Cowan, R. S. 1972. Francis Galton's contributions to genetics. J. Hist. Biol. 5:389–412.

Cowles, T. 1937. Malthus, Darwin and Bagehot: a study in the transference of a concept. Isis 26:341–348.

Cramer, J. A. 1971. General evolution and the second law of thermodynamics. J. Amer. Scientific Affiliation 23:20–21.

Crew, F. A. E. 1966. *The foundations of genetics.* New York: Pergamon.

Crocker, L. G. 1959. Diderot and eighteenth century French transformism. In *Forerunners of Darwin: 1745–1859*, ed. B. Glass, O. Temkin and W. L. Straus, Jr., pp. 114–143. Baltimore: Johns Hopkins Univ. Press.

———, ed. (Trans. D. Coltman.) 1966. *Diderot's selected writings.* New York: Macmillan.

Crombie, A. C. 1953. *Robert Grosseteste and the origins of experimental science, 1100–1700.* Oxford: Oxford Univ. Press.

———. 1959. *Medieval and early modern science.* Garden City, N.Y.: Doubleday.

———, ed. 1963. *Scientific change: historical studies in the intellectual, social and technical conditions for scientific discovery and technical invention, from antiquity to the present.* New York: Basic Books.

Culliton, B. J. 1975. XYY: Harvard researcher under fire stops newborn screening. Science 188:1284–1285.

Currier, R. 1976. Sociobiology: the new heresy. Human Behavior, Nov., pp. 16–22.

Darden, L. 1976. Reasoning in scientific change: Charles Darwin, Hugo De Vries, and the discovery of segregation. Studies in Hist. and Phil. of Sci. 7:127–169.

———. 1977. William Bateson and the promise of Mendelism. J. Hist. Biol. 10:87–106.

Darling, L. 1960. The *Beagle:* a search for a lost ship. Natural History 69 (May):48–59.

Darlington, C. D. 1959. The origins of Darwinism. Sci. Am. 200 (May):60–66.

———. 1961. *Darwin's place in history.* New York: Macmillan.

Darwin, C. 1859. *The origin of species.* Cambridge: Harvard Univ. Press. (Reprint of the first edition, 1964. Numerous other editions.)

———. (Ed. R. E. Leakey.) 1979. *The illustrated origin of species.* New York: Farrar, Straus & Giroux.

———. (Ed. M. Peckham.) 1959. *The origin of species: a variorum text.* Philadelphia: Univ. of Pennsylvania Press.

———. 1905. *The variation of animals and plants under domestication.* New York: Appleton.

———. (Ed. L. Engel.) 1962. *The voyage of the Beagle.* Garden City. N.Y.: Doubleday.

———. 1965. *The expression of the emotions in man and animals.* Chicago: Univ. of Chicago Press.

Darwin, C. and Wallace, A. R. 1958. *Evolution by natural selection.* Cambridge, England: Cambridge Univ. Press.

Darwin, E. 1794, 1796. *Zoonomia: or the laws of organic life.* (Many editions. American editions available in Readex Microprint Series of Early American Imprints, Evans nos. 30312 and 32017.)

Darwin, E. 1803. *The temple of nature; or, the origin of society: a poem, with philosophical notes.* London: J. Johnson. (Facsimile reprint 1973, Menston: Scolar Press.)

Darwin, F. 1901. *The life and letters of Charles Darwin.* New York: Appleton.

———, ed. 1909. *The foundations of the origin of species; two essays written in 1842 and 1844.* Cambridge, England: Cambridge Univ. Press.

Darwin, F. and Seward, A. C., eds. 1903. *More letters of Charles Darwin.* New York: Appleton.

Dasa, D. 1978. Exploding the big bang theory. Back to the God Head: The Magazine of the Hare Krishna Movement 13 (no. 7):27.

Dean, B. 1906. Two letters of Dr. Darwin: the early date of his evolutional writings. Science 23:986–987.

de Beer, G. 1959. Some unpublished letters of Charles Darwin. Notes and Records of the Royal Soc. of London 14:12–66.

———. 1963. *Charles Darwin: evolution by natural selection.* Garden City, N.Y.: Doubleday.

de Beer, G. et al., eds. 1960–1967. Darwin's notebooks on transmutation of species. Bull. Brit. Museum (Nat. Hist.), Hist. Series 2:27–200; 3:129–176.

de Camp, L. S. 1968. *The great monkey trial.* Garden City, N.Y.: Doubleday.

———. 1969. The end of the monkey war. Sci. Am. 220 (Feb.):15–21.

Delbrück, M. 1949. A physicist looks at biology. Trans. Conn. Acad. Arts and Sci. 38:173–190. (Reprinted in *Phage and the origins of molecular biology,* ed. J. Cairns, G. S. Stent and J. D. Watson, pp. 9–22. [1966.] Cold Spring Harbor, N.Y.: Cold Spring Harbor Laboratory).

Delgado, J. M. R. 1969. *Physical control of the mind.* New York: Harper & Row.

De Marrais, R. 1974. The double-edged effect of Sir Francis Galton: a search for the motives of the biometrician-Mendelian debate. J. Hist. Biol. 7:141–174.

Descartes, R. 1967. (Trans. E. S. Haldane and G. R. T. Ross.) *The philosophical works of Descartes.* New York: Cambridge Univ. Press.

D'Espagnat, B. 1979. The quantum theory and reality. Sci. Am. 241 (Nov.):158–181.

DeVries, H. 1909–1910. *Mutation theory.* Chicago: Open Court.

———. 1910. *Intracellular pangenesis.* Chicago: Open Court.

Dibner, B. 1964. *Darwin of the Beagle.* New York: Blaisdell.

Dickerson, R. E. 1972. The structure and history of an ancient protein. Sci. Am. 226 (Apr.):58–72.

———. 1978. Chemical evolution and the origin of life. Sci. Am. 239 (Sept.):70–86.

Diderot, D. 1951. *Oeuvres.* Paris: Gallimard.

———. 1754. *Penseés sur l'interprétation de la nature.* (Reprinted in *Chefs d'oeuvres.* Paris: La Renaissance du Livre.)

Ding Chen. 1980. The economic development of China. Sci. Am. 243 (Sept.):152–165.

Diogenes Laertius. 1950. *Lives of eminent philosophers.* Cambridge: Harvard Univ. Press.

Dobzhansky, T. 1972. Darwinian evolution and the problem of extraterrestrial life. Pers. Biol. Med. 15:157–175.

———. 1973. *Genetic diversity and human equality.* New York: Basic Books.

Dobzhansky, T., Ayala, F., Stebbins, G. L. and Valentine, J. W. 1977. *Evolution.* San Francisco: Freeman.

Dobzhansky, T. and Pavlovsky, O. 1971. Experimentally created incipient species of *Drosophila.* Nature 230:289–292.

Domning, D. P. 1978. On the falsifiability of natural selection. Systematic Zool. 27:346–347.

Dronamraju, K. R., ed. 1968. *Haldane and modern biology.* Baltimore: Johns Hopkins Univ. Press.

Dunn, L. C., ed. 1951. *Genetics in the 20th century: essays on the progress of genetics during its first 50 years.* New York: Macmillan.

———. 1965. *A short story of genetics.* New York: McGraw-Hill.

Dupree, A. H. 1959. *Asa Gray, 1810–1888.* Cambridge: Harvard Univ. Press.

Durant, J. R. 1979. Scientific naturalism and social reform in the thought of Alfred Russel Wallace. Brit. J. Hist. Sci. 12:31–58.

Durant, W. 1950. *The age of faith.* New York: Simon & Schuster.

———. 1966. *The life of Greece.* New York: Simon & Schuster.

Durant, W. and Durant, A. 1961. *The age of reason begins.* New York: Simon & Schuster.

Eden, M. 1967. Inadequacies of neo-Darwinian evolution as a scientific theory. In *Mathematical challenges to the neo-Darwinian interpretation of evolution,* ed. P. S. Moorehead and M. M. Kaplan, pp. 5–19. Philadelphia: Wistar Institute Press.

Egerton, F. N. 1968. Studies in animal populations from Lamarck to Darwin. J. Hist. Biol. 1:225–259.

———. 1970a. Humboldt, Darwin, and population. J. Hist. Biol. 3:325–360.

———. 1970b. Refutation and conjecture: Darwin's response to Sedgwick's attack on Chambers. Studies in Hist. and Phil. of Sci. 1:176–183.

———. 1976. Darwin's early reading of Lamarck. Isis 67:452–456.

Ehrlich, P. R. and Holm, R. W. 1962. Patterns and populations. Science 137:652–657.

Einstein, A. et al. 1923. *The principle of relativity.* New York: Dover.

Eiseley, L. 1958. *Darwin's century.* New York: Doubleday.

————. 1973. *The man who saw through time.* New York: Scribner's.

————. 1979. *Darwin and the mysterious Mr. X.* New York: Dutton.

Eldredge, N. and Gould, S. J. 1977. Punctuated equilibria: the tempo and mode of evolution reconsidered. Paleobiology 3:115–151.

Ellegard, A. 1957. The Darwinian theory and nineteenth-century philosophers of science. J. Hist. Ideas 18:362–393.

————. 1958. *Darwin and the general reader.* Gothenburg, Sweden: Gothenburg University.

Engels, F. 1939. *Herr Eugen Dühring's revolution in science (anti-Dühring).* New York: International Publishers.

————. 1940. *Dialectics of nature.* New York: International Publishers.

————. 1969. *Ludwig Feuerbach and the end of classical German philosophy.* Moscow: Progress Publishers.

Erickson, P. A. 1975. Anthropology and evolution: a comment on Wells. Isis 66:96–97.

Evans, B. I. 1964. Wordsworth and science. In *Science and literature: a reader,* ed. J. J. Cadden and P. R. Brostowin, pp. 126–136. Boston: D. C. Heath.

Farber, P. L. 1972. Buffon and the concept of species. J. Hist. Biol. 5:259–284.

Farley, J. 1974. The initial reaction of French biologists to Darwin's *Origin of Species.* J. Hist. Biol. 7:275–300.

————. 1977. *The spontaneous generation controversy from Descartes to Oparin.* Baltimore: Johns Hopkins Univ. Press.

Farrington, B. 1949. *Francis Bacon: philosopher of industrial science.* New York: Schuman.

————. 1966. *Science and politics in the ancient world.* New York: Barnes & Noble.

————. 1967. *The faith of Epicurus.* London: Weidenfeld & Nicolson.

Fay, M. A. 1978. Did Marx offer to dedicate *Capital* to Darwin? J. Hist. Ideas 39:133–146.

Fellows, O. E. 1977. *Diderot.* Boston: Twayne.

Fellows, O. E. and Milliken, S. F. 1972. *Buffon.* New York: Twayne.

Ferguson, A. J. 1976. Can evolutionary theory predict? Amer. Naturalist 110:1101–1104.

Feuer, L. S. 1975. Is the "Darwin-Marx correspondence" authentic? Annals of Sci. 32:1–12.

————. 1976. Of the Darwin-Marx correspondence. Annals of Sci. 33:383–394.

————. 1978. The case of the "Darwin-Marx" letter: a study in socio-literary detection. Encounter (Oct.): 62–78.

Feyerabend, P. K. 1970. Against method: outline of an anarchistic theory of knowledge. In *Analyses of theories and methods of physics and psychology,* ed. M. Radner and S. Winokur, pp. 17–130. Minneapolis: Univ. of Minnesota Press.

————. 1975. *Against method.* London: New Left Books.

————. 1978. *Science in a free society.* London: New Left Books.

Finegan, J. 1964. *Handbook of Biblical chronology: principles of time reckoning in the ancient world and problems of chronology in the Bible.* Princeton, N.J.: Princeton Univ. Press.

Fisher, R. A. 1930. *The genetical theory of natural selection.* Oxford: Clarendon Press. (2nd rev. ed. 1958, New York: Dover.)

————. 1936. Has Mendel's work been rediscovered? Annals of Sci. 1:115–137. (Reprinted in Stern and Sherwood, 1966.)

Flew, A. G. N. 1967a. *Evolutionary ethics.* New York: St. Martin's.

————. 1967b. From is to ought. In *New studies in ethics,* ed. W. Hudson, pp. 31–51. New York: St. Martin's.

————. 1978. *A rational animal.* New York: Clarendon.

Folsome, C. E. 1979. *The origin of life: a warm little pond.* San Francisco: Freeman.

Forrest, D. W. 1974. *Francis Galton: the life and work of a Victorian genius.* New York: Taplinger.

Fothergill, P. 1952. *Historical aspects of organic evolution.* London: Hollis & Carter.

Frank, P. 1957. *Philosophy of science.* Englewood Cliffs, N.J.: Prentice-Hall.

Frank, P. G., ed. 1961. *The validation of scientific theories.* New York: Collier.

Frazer, J. G. 1918. *Folk-lore in the Old Testament.* New York: Macmillan.

————. 1967. *Creation and evolution in primitive cosmogonies.* Freeport, N.Y.: Books for Libraries Press.

Frederick II. 1943. *The art of falconry: being the De arte renandieum avibus of Frederick II of Hohenstaufen.* Stanford, Cal.: Stanford Univ. Press.

Freeman, D. et al. 1974. The evolutionary theories of Charles Darwin and Herbert Spencer. Current Anthropology 15: 211–237.

Freeman, K. 1956. *Ancilla to the pre-Socratic philosophers: a complete translation of the fragments in Diels, Fragmente der Vorsokratiker.* Cambridge: Harvard Univ. Press.

Freund, P. 1965. *Myths of creation.* New York: Washington Square Press.

Froggat, P. and Nevin, N. C. 1971a. Galton's "law of ancestral heredity": its influence on the early development of human genetics. Hist. Sci. 10:1–27.

Froggatt, P. and Nevin, N. C. 1971b. The "law of ancestral heredity" and the Mendelian-ancestrian controversy in England, 1889–1906. J. Med. Genetics 8 (Mar.):1–36.

Furniss, N. F. 1963. *The fundamentalist controversy, 1918–1931.* Hamden, Conn.: Archon.

Gaissinovitch, A. E. 1980. The origins of Soviet genetics and the struggle with Lamarckism, 1922–1929. J. Hist. Biol. 13:1–51.

Gale, B. G. 1972. Darwin and the concept of a struggle for existence: a study in the extrascientific origins of scientific ideas. Isis 63:321–344.

Galton, F. 1908. *Memories of my life.* London: Methuen.

Gammage, R. G. 1969. *History of the Chartist movement, 1837–1854.* New York: Augustus M. Kelley.

Garfield, E. 1980. Premature discovery or delayed recognition—why? Current Contents, Life Sci. 23 (21):5–10.

Garfinkle, N. 1955. Science and religion in England, 1790–1800: the critical response to the work of Erasmus Darwin. J. Hist. Ideas 16:376–388.

Gasking, E. B. 1959. Why was Mendel's work ignored? J. Hist. Ideas 20:60–84.

Gaupp, E. 1917. *August Weismann: sein Lieben und sein Werk.* Jena: G. Fischer.

Geison, G. L. 1969. Darwin and heredity: the evolution of his hypothesis of pangenesis. J. Hist. Med. and Allied Sci. 24:375–411.

George, W. 1964. *Biologist philosopher: a study of the life and writings of Alfred Russel Wallace.* New York: Abelard-Schuman.

Ghiselin, B. 1952. *The creative process: a symposium.* Berkeley: Univ. of California Press.

Ghiselin, M. T. 1969. *The triumph of the Darwinian method.* Berkeley: Univ. of California Press.

———. 1971. The individual in the Darwinian revolution. New Lit. Hist. 3:113–134.

———. 1975. The rationale of pangenesis. Genetics 79 (suppl.):47–57.

———. 1976. Two Darwins: history versus criticism. J. Hist. Biol. 9:121–132.

Gillespie, N. C. 1979. *Charles Darwin and the problem of creation.* Chicago: Univ. of Chicago Press.

Gillispie, G. C. 1951. *Genesis and geology.* New York: Harper Torchbooks.

———. 1959. Lamarck and Darwin in the history of science. In *Forerunners of Darwin: 1745–1859*, ed. B. Glass, O. Temkin and W. L. Straus, Jr., pp. 265–291. Baltimore: Johns Hopkins Univ. Press.

———. ed. 1970–1980. *Dictionary of scientific biography.* New York: Scribner's.

Ginger, R. 1958. *Six days or forever?* Boston: Beacon.

Gish, D. T. 1973. Creation, evolution, and the historical evidence. Am. Biol. Teacher 35:132–140.

———. 1975. A decade of creationist research. Creation Research Soc. Quart. 12 (June):34–46.

———. 1976. Cracks in the neo-Darwinian Jericho, Part 1. Impact Series no. 42, Institute for Creation Research, San Diego, Cal.

———. 1978. *Evolution? The fossils say no!* San Diego: Creation-life.

Glass, B. 1953. The long neglect of a scientific discovery: Mendel's laws of inheritance. In *Studies in intellectual history*, pp. 148–160. Baltimore: Johns Hopkins Univ. Press.

———. 1959a. The germination of the idea of biological species. In *Forerunners of Darwin: 1745–1859*, ed. B. Glass, O. Temkin and W. L. Straus, Jr., pp. 30–48. Baltimore: Johns Hopkins Univ. Press.

———. 1959b. Maupertuis, pioneer of genetics and evolution. In *Forerunners of Darwin: 1745–1859*, ed. B. Glass, O. Temkin and W. L. Straus, Jr., pp. 51–83. Baltimore: Johns Hopkins Univ. Press.

———. 1959c. Heredity and variation in the eighteenth century concept of the species. In *Forerunners of Darwin: 1745–1859*, ed. B. Glass, O. Temkin and W. L. Straus, Jr., pp. 144–172. Baltimore: Johns Hopkins Univ. Press.

Glass, B., Temkin, O. and Straus, W. L., Jr., eds. 1959. *Forerunners of Darwin: 1745–1859.* Baltimore: Johns Hopkins Univ. Press.

Glick, T. F., ed. 1972. *The comparative reception of Darwinism.* Austin: Univ. of Texas Press.

Goldstein, M. and Goldstein, I. 1978. *How we know: an exploration of the scientific process.* New York: Plenum.

Goran, M. 1978. *The modern myth: ancient astronauts and UFOs.* Cranbury, N.J.: Barnes.

Gould, S. J. 1972. Zealous advocates. Science 176:623–625.

———. 1977. *Ever since Darwin.* New York: Norton.

———. 1978. Generality and uniqueness in the history of life: an exploration with random models. BioSci. 28:277–281.

———. 1979. Darwin vindicated! N.Y. Rev. of Books, Aug. 16.

————. 1980a. *The panda's thumb.* New York: Norton.

————. 1980b. Sociobiology and the theory of natural selection. In *Sociobiology: beyond nature/nurture?*, ed. G. W. Barlow and J. Silverberg, Ch. 10. New York: Praeger.

Grabiner, J. V. and Miller, P. D. 1974. Effects of the Scopes trial. Science 185:832–837. (See also Science 187:389–390.)

Grabo, C. 1930. *A Newton among poets: Shelley's use of science in Prometheus Unbound.* Chapel Hill: Univ. of North Carolina Press.

Graham, L. R. 1971. *Science and philosophy in the Soviet Union.* New York: Knopf.

Grant, E., ed. 1974. *A source book in medieval science.* Cambridge: Harvard Univ. Press.

Grassé, P. P. 1977. *Evolution of living organisms: evidence for a new theory of transformation.* New York: Academic Press.

Graves, R. and Patai, R. 1964. *Hebrew myths: the book of Genesis.* Garden City, N.Y.: Doubleday.

Gray, A. 1963. *Darwiniana: essays and reviews pertaining to Darwinism,* ed. A. H. Dupree. Cambridge: Belknap Press of Harvard Univ. Press.

Grayeff, F. 1974. *Aristotle and his school.* New York: Barnes & Noble.

Grebstein, S. N., ed. 1960. *Monkey trial: the state of Tennessee vs John Thomas Scopes.* Boston: Houghton Mifflin.

Greeley, K. and Tafler, S. 1979. History of Science for the People: a ten year perspective. Science for the People Jan./Feb. (Reprinted in *Science and liberation,* ed. R. Arditti, P. Brennan and S. Cavrak, pp. 369–382. [1980] Boston: South End Press.)

Greenacre, P. 1963. *The quest for the father: a study of the Darwin-Butler controversy as a contribution to the understanding of the creative individual.* New York: International Universities Press.

Greene, J. C. 1959. *The death of Adam: evolution and its impact on Western thought.* Ames: Iowa State Univ. Press.

————. 1971. The Kuhnian paradigm and the Darwinian revolution in natural history. In *Perspectives in the history of science and technology,* ed. D. H. D. Roller, pp. 3–25. Norman: Univ. of Oklahoma Press.

————. 1975. Reflections on the progress of Darwin studies. J. Hist. Biol. 8:243–273.

————. 1977. Darwin as a social evolutionist. J. Hist. Biol. 10:1–27.

Gregory, M. S., Silvers, A. and Sutch, D., eds. 1978. *Sociobiology and human nature.* San Francisco: Jossey-Bass.

Gregory, R. L. 1972. *Eye and brain: the psychology of seeing.* 2nd ed. New York: McGraw-Hill.

————. 1980. Perceptions as hypotheses. Phil. Trans. Roy. Soc. London B 290:181–197.

Grene, M. 1963. *A portrait of Aristotle.* Chicago: Univ. of Chicago Press.

————. 1976. Aristotle and modern biology. In *Topics in the philosophy of biology,* ed. M. Grene and E. Mendelsohn, pp. 3–36. Boston: Reidel.

Grene, M. and Mendelsohn, E., eds. 1976. *Topics in the philosophy of biology.* Boston: Reidel.

Griggs, E. L., ed. 1933. *Unpublished letters of Samuel Taylor Coleridge.* New Haven, Conn.: Yale Univ. Press.

————., ed. 1956. *Collected letters of Samuel Taylor Coleridge.* Oxford: Clarendon.

Grinnell, G. J. 1969. The Darwin case: a computer analysis of scientific creativity. Ph.D. diss., Univ. of California, Berkeley.

———. 1974. The rise and fall of Darwin's first theory of transmutation. J. Hist. Biol. 7:259–273.

Grmek, M. D. 1972. A survey of the mechanical interpretations of life from Greek atomists to the followers of Descartes. In *Biology, history, and natural philosophy,* ed. A. D. Breck and W. Yourgrau, pp. 181–195. New York: Plenum.

Gruber, H. E. 1978. Darwin's "tree of nature" and other images of wide scope. In *On aesthetics in science,* ed. J. Wechsler, pp. 121–140. Cambridge, Mass.: MIT Press.

———. 1979. The origin of the Origin of Species. New York *Times* Book Review, 22 July, pp. 7, 16.

Gruber, H. E. and Barrett, P. H. 1974. *Darwin on man: a psychological study of scientific creativity. Together with Darwin's early and unpublished notebooks, transcribed and annotated by Paul H. Barrett.* New York: Dutton.

Gruber, H. E. and Gruber, V. 1962 The eye of reason: Darwin's development during the *Beagle* voyage. Isis 53:186–200.

Gruber H. E. and Vonèche, J.J., eds. 1977. *The essential Piaget: an interpretive reference and guide.* New York: Basic Books.

Gruber, J. W. 1969. Who was the Beagle's naturalist? Brit. J. Hist. Sci. 4:266–282.

Grünbaum, A. 1955. Modern science and refutation of the paradoxes of Zeno. Scientific Monthly 81:234–239.

Guerlac, H. 1961. Science during the French Revolution. In *The validation of scientific theories,* ed. P. G. Frank, pp. 159–176. New York: Collier.

Guthrie, F. B. A. 1962. *A history of Greek philosophy.* Vol. 1. *The earlier presocratics and the Pythagorians.* New York: Cambridge Univ. Press.

Haber, F. C. 1959a. Fossils and early cosmology. In *Forerunners of Darwin: 1745–1859,* ed. B. Glass, O. Temkin and W. L. Straus, Jr., pp. 3–29. Baltimore: Johns Hopkins Univ. Press.

———. 1959b. Fossils and the idea of process of time in natural history. In *Forerunners of Darwin: 1745–1859,* ed. B. Glass, O. Temkin and W L. Straus, Jr., pp. 222–261. Baltimore: Johns Hopkins Univ. Press.

———. 1959c. *The age of the world: Moses to Darwin.* Baltimore: Johns Hopkins Univ. Press.

Hagberg, K. 1953. *Carl Linnaeus.* New York: Dutton.

Haldane, J. B. S. 1928. *Possible worlds, and other papers.* New York: Harper & Bros.

———. 1933. *Science and human life.* New York: Harper & Bros.

———. 1935. Darwinism under revision. Rationalist Ann. 19–29.

———. 1938. *Heredity and politics.* London: Allen & Unwin.

———. 1939. *The Marxist philosophy and the sciences.* New York: Random House.

———. 1940. *Adventures of a biologist.* New York: Harper & Bros.

———. 1947. *Science advances.* London: Allen & Unwin.

———. 1955. Population genetics. New Biol. 18:34–51.

———. 1958. *The unity and diversity of life.* Delhi, India: Ministry of Information and Broadcasting.

———. 1966. *The causes of evolution.* Ithaca, N.Y.: Cornell Univ. Press. (Reprint of 1932 ed.)

Hall, A. R. 1956. *The scientific revolution: 1500–1800.* Boston: Beacon.

Hall, T. S., ed. 1970. *A source book in animal biology.* Cambridge: Harvard Univ. Press.

Hamilton, W. D. 1964. The genetical theory of social behaviour. I, II. J. Theoret. Biol. 7:1–52.

Hardy, A., Harvie, R. and Koestler, A. 1973. *The challenge of chance.* New York: Random House.

Harris, C. L. 1975. An axiomatic interpretation of the neo-Darwinian theory of evolution. Pers. Biol. Med. 18(2):179–184.

Harris, M. 1968. *The rise of anthropological theory.* London: Routledge & Kegan Paul.

———. 1979. *Cultural materialism: the struggle for a science of culture.* New York: Random House.

Harrison, J. 1971. Erasmus Darwin's view of evolution. J. Hist. Ideas 32:247–264.

Harrison, J. F. C. 1971. *The early Victorians, 1823–51.* London: Weidenfeld & Nicolson.

Hass, H. 1970. *The human animal.* New York: Delta.

Hassler, D. M. 1973. *Erasmus Darwin.* New York: Twayne.

Heidel, A. 1949. *The Gilgamesh Epic and the Old Testament parallels.* 2nd ed. Chicago: Univ. of Chicago Press.

———. 1951. *The Babylonian Genesis.* 2nd ed. Chicago: Univ. of Chicago Press.

Heilbroner, R. L. 1980. *Marxism: for and against.* New York: Norton.

Heimans, J. 1962. Hugo De Vries and the gene concept. Am. Naturalist 96:93–104.

Henderson, L. J. 1913. *The fitness of the environment.* Boston: Beacon.

Henig, R. M. 1979. Science for the People: revolution's evolution. BioSci. 29:341–344. (See also BioSci. 29: 509.)

Herbert, S. 1968. The logic of Darwin's discovery. Ph.D. diss., Brandeis Univ.

———. 1971. Darwin, Malthus, and selection. J. Hist. Biol. 4:209–217.

———. 1974. The place of man in the development of Darwin's theory of transmutation. I. To July 1837. J. Hist. Biol. 7:217–258.

———. 1977. The place of man in the development of Darwin's theory of transmutation. II. J. Hist. Biol. 10:155–227.

———. 1980. *The red notebook of Charles Darwin.* Ithaca, N.Y.: Cornell Univ. Press.

Himmelfarb, G., ed. 1960. *On population.* New York: Modern Library.

———. 1962. *Darwin and the Darwinian revolution.* New York: Norton.

———. 1968. *Victorian minds.* New York: Knopf.

Ho, M. W. and Saunders, P. T. 1979. Beyond neo-Darwinism: an epigenetic approach to evolution. J. Theoret. Biol. 78:573–591.

Hodge, M. J. S. 1971. Lamarck's science of living bodies. Brit. J. Hist. Sci. 5:323–352.

———. 1972. The universal gestation of nature: Chambers' *Vestiges* and *Explanations.* J. Hist. Biol. 5:127–151.

———. 1977. The structure and strategy of Darwin's "long argument." Brit. J. Hist. Sci. 10:237–246.

Holton, G. and Blanpied, W., eds. 1976. *Science and its public.* Boston: Reidel.

Horton, R. 1973. African traditional thought and Western science. In *Africa and change,* ed. C. M. Turnbull, pp. 454–519. New York: Knopf.

Houghton, W. E. 1957. *The Victorian frame of mind: 1830–1870.* New Haven, Conn.: Yale Univ. Press.

Hudson, W. D., ed. 1969. *The is/ought question: a collection of papers on the central problem in moral philosophy.* New York: St. Martin's.

Hull, D. L. 1969. What philosophy of biology is not. J. Hist. Biol. 2:241–268.

———. 1973a. *Darwin and his critics.* Cambridge: Harvard Univ. Press.

———. 1973b. Charles Darwin and nineteenth-century philosophies of science. In *Foundations of scientific method: the nineteenth century,* ed. R. N. Giere and R. S. Westfall, pp. 115–132. Bloomington: Indiana Univ. Press.

———. 1974. *The philosophy of the biological sciences.* Englewood Cliffs, N. J.: Prentice-Hall.

Hull, D. L., Tessner, P. D. and Diamond, A. M. 1978. Planck's principle. Science 202:717–723.

Hunt, J. H. 1980. *Selected readings in sociobiology.* New York: McGraw-Hill.

Hutchins, R. M., ed. 1952. *Great books of the Western world.* 54 vols. Chicago: Encyclopaedia Britannica.

Huxley, J. 1949. *Heredity East and West: Lysenko and world science.* New York: Schuman.

Huxley, L., ed. 1900. *Life and letters of T. H. Huxley.* New York: Appleton.

———. 1918. *Life and letters of Sir Joseph Dalton Hooker.* London: Murray.

———. 1969. *Thomas Henry Huxley: a character sketch.* Freeport, N.Y.: Books for Libraries Press.

Huxley, T. H. 1871. *Lay sermons, addresses, and reviews.* New York: Appleton.

———. 1896. *Darwiniana.* New York: Appleton.

———. 1967. *On a piece of chalk.* New York: Scribner's.

Hyman, S. E., ed. 1963. *Darwin for today: the essence of his works.* New York: Viking.

Iltis, H. 1932. *The life of Gregor Mendel.* New York: Norton.

———. 1951. Gregor Mendel's life and heritage. In *Genetics in the 20th century,* ed. L. C. Dunn, Ch. 2. New York: Macmillan.

———. 1954. Gregor Mendel's autobiography. J. Hered. 45:231–234.

Irvine, W. 1955. *Apes, angels and Victorians: the story of Darwin, Huxley and evolution.* New York: McGraw-Hill.

Jacob, F. 1973. *The logic of life: a history of heredity.* New York: Vintage.

James, P. 1979. *Population Malthus: his life and times.* London: Routledge & Kegan Paul.

Johanson, D. C. and White, T. D. 1979. A systematic assessment of early African hominids. Science 203:321–330.

Joravsky, D. 1959. Soviet Marxism and biology before Lysenko. J. Hist. Ideas 20:85–104.

———. 1961. *Soviet Marxism and natural science 1917–1932.* New York: Columbia Univ. Press.

———. 1970. *The Lysenko affair.* Cambridge: Harvard Univ. Press.

Judson, H. F. 1979. *The eighth day of creation: the makers of the revolution in biology.* New York: Simon & Schuster.

Kearney, H. 1964. *Origins of the scientific revolution.* London: Longmans.

Kellogg, V. L. 1907. *Darwinism today.* New York: Henry Holt.

Kennedy, G., ed. 1957. *Evolution and religion: the conflict between science and theology in modern America.* Boston: D. C. Heath.

Kerkut, G. A. 1960. *Implications of evolution.* New York: Pergamon.

Kernig, C. D., ed. 1972–1973. *Marxism, Communism and Western society: a comparative encyclopaedia.* New York: Herder & Herder.

Keynes, R. D., ed. 1979. *The Beagle record: selections from the original pictorial records and written accounts of the voyage of H.M.S. Beagle.* New York: Cambridge Univ. Press.

Kimura, M. 1979. The neutral theory of molecular evolution. Sci. Am. 241 (Nov.):98–126.

Kinch, M. P. 1980. Geographical distribution and the origin of life: the development of early nineteenth century British explanations. J. Hist. Biol. 13:91–119.

King, M.-C. and Wilson, A. C. 1975. Evolution at two levels in humans and chimpanzees. Science 188:107–116.

King-Hele, D., ed. 1968. *The essential writings of Erasmus Darwin.* St. Albans, England: MacGibbon & Kee.

———. 1977. *Doctor of revolution: the life and genius of Erasmus Darwin.* London: Faber & Faber.

Kleiner, S. A. 1979. Feyerabend, Galileo and Darwin: how to make the best out of what you have or think you can get. Studies in Hist. and Phil. of Sci. 10:285–309.

Knoepflmacher, G. P. and Tennyson, G. B., eds. 1978. *Nature and the Victorian imagination.* Berkeley: Univ. of California Press.

Koestler, A. 1959. *The sleepwalkers.* New York: Macmillan.

———. 1964. *The act of creation.* New York: Macmillan.

———. 1967. *The ghost in the machine.* New York: Macmillan.

———. 1971. *The case of the midwife toad.* New York: Random House.

———. 1972. *The roots of coincidence.* London: Hutchinson.

———. 1978. *Janus: a summing up.* New York: Random House.

Koestler, A. and Smythies, J. R., eds. 1969. *Beyond reductionism.* New York: Macmillan.

Kofahl, R. E. 1976. (Letter.) Sci. Am. 234 (May): 6, 8.

Kohn, E. D. 1975. Charles Darwin's path to natural selection. Ph.D. diss., Univ. of Massachusetts, Amherst.

Kosin, I. L. and Kato, M. 1963. A failure to induce heritable changes in four generations of the white leghorn chicken by inter- and intra-specific blood transfusion. Genetical Res. 4:221–239.

Kottler, M. J. 1974. Alfred Russel Wallace, the origin of man, and spiritualism. Isis 65:144–192.

———. 1978. Charles Darwin's biological species concept and theory of geographic speciation: the transmutation notebooks. Annals of Sci. 35:275–297.

Koyré, A. 1957. *From the closed world to the infinite universe.* New York: Harper & Bros.

Krause, E. 1879. *Erasmus Darwin. With a preliminary notice by Charles Darwin.* London: Murray. (Reprinted 1971, Westmead, England: Gregg International.

Krizenecky, H. 1965. *Fundamenta genetica.* Prague: Czechoslovak Academy of Sciences.

Kuhn, T. S. 1970. *The structure of scientific revolutions.* Rev. ed. Chicago: Univ. of Chicago Press.

———. 1974. Second thoughts on paradigms. In *The structure of scientific theories,* ed. F. Suppe, pp. 459–482. Urbana: Univ. of Illinois Press.

————. 1977. *The essential tension: selected studies in scientific tradition and change.* Chicago: Univ. of Chicago Press.

Lack, D. 1961. *Darwin's finches.* New York: Harper & Bros.

La Fay, H. 1978. Ebla: splendor of an unknown empire. Nat. Geog. 154: 730–759.

Lamarck, J. B. P. A. de M. de 1963. (Trans. H. Elliot.) *Zoological philosophy.* New York: Hafner. (Originally published 1914, New York: Macmillan.)

Lambridis, H. 1976. *Empedocles: a philosophical investigation.* University: Univ. of Alabama Press.

Laudan, L. 1968. Theories of scientific method from Plato to Mach: a bibliographical review. Hist. Sci. 7:1–63.

Leakey, R. E., ed. 1979. *The illustrated origin of species.* New York: Farrar, Strauss & Giroux.

Leakey, R. E. and Lewin, R. 1977. *Origins.* New York: Dutton.

LeClercq, F. S. 1977. The Constitution and creationism. Am. Biol. Teacher 36:139–145.

Legge, F. 1964. *Forerunners and rivals of Christianity.* New Hyde Park, N.Y.: University Books.

Lenin, V. I. 1970. *Materialism and empirio-criticism.* Moscow: Progress Publishers.

Levin, D. A. 1979. The nature of plant species. Science 204:381–384.

Levin, S. M. 1966. Malthus and the idea of progress. J. Hist. Ideas 27:92–108.

Lewontin, R. C. 1968. The concept of evolution. In *International Encyclopedia of the Social Sciences.* vol. 5, ed. D. L. Sills, pp. 202–210. New York: Macmillan and The Free Press.

————. 1969. The bases of conflict in biological explanation. J. Hist. Biol. 2:35–45.

————. 1970. On the irrelevance of genes. In *Towards a theoretical biology,* vol. 3, ed. C. H. Waddington, pp. 63–72. Chicago: Aldine.

————. 1977a. Sociobiology: a caricature of Darwinism. In *Proceedings of the 1976 biennial meeting of the Philosophy of Science Association,* vol. 2, ed. F. Suppe and P. D. Asquith, pp. 22–31. East Lansing: Philosophy of Science Assoc., Michigan State Univ.

————. 1977b. Biological determinism as a social weapon. In *Science as a social weapon,* ed. Ann Arbor Science for the People Editorial Collective, pp. 6–18. Minneapolis: Burgess.

————. 1978. Adaptation. Sci. Am. 239 (Sept.): 212–230.

————. 1979. (Letter.) BioSci. 29:509.

Lewontin, R. C. and Levins, R. 1976. The problem of Lysenkoism. In *The radicalization of science,* ed. H. Rose and S. Rose, Ch. 2. London: Macmillan.

Lightner, J. P. 1975. Tennessee "Genesis law" ruled unconstitutional. Nat. Assoc. Biol. Teachers News and Views 19 (Apr.): 2.

Lightner, J. P., ed. 1977. *A compendium of information on the theory of evolution and the evolution-creationism controversy.* Reston, Va.: National Association of Biology Teachers.

Limoges, C. 1970. *La sélection naturelle: étude sur la première constitution d'un concept (1837–1859).* Paris: Presses Universitaires de France.

Lindberg, D., ed. 1979. *Science in the Middle Ages.* Chicago: Univ. of Chicago Press.

Lindegren, C. C. 1966. *Cold war in biology.* Ann Arbor, Mich.: Planarian Press.

Lippman, W. 1928. *American inquisitors.* New York: Macmillan.

Litchfield, H., ed. 1915. *Emma Darwin: a century of family letters.* London: Murray.

Lloyd, G. E. R. 1968. *Aristotle: the growth and structure of his thought.* New York: Cambridge Univ. Press.

———. 1973. *Greek science after Aristotle.* New York: Norton.

Logan, J. V. 1936. *The poetry and aesthetics of Erasmus Darwin.* Princeton, N.J.: Princeton Univ. Press.

Lovejoy, A. O. 1904. Some eighteenth century evolutionists. Pop. Sci. Monthly 65:238–251, 323–340.

———. 1936. *The great chain of being.* Cambridge: Harvard Univ. Press.

———. 1948. *Essays in the history of ideas.* Baltimore: Johns Hopkins Univ. Press.

———. 1959a. Buffon and the problem of species. In *Forerunners of Darwin: 1745–1859,* ed. B. Glass, O. Temkin and W. L. Straus, Jr., pp. 84–113. Baltimore: Johns Hopkins Univ. Press.

———. 1959b. Kant and evolution. In *Forerunners of Darwin: 1745–1859,* ed. B. Glass, O. Temkin and W. L. Straus, Jr., pp. 173–206. Baltimore: Johns Hopkins Univ. Press.

———. 1959c. Herder: progressionism without transformism. In *Forerunners of Darwin: 1745–1859,* ed. B. Glass, O. Temkin and W. L. Straus, Jr., pp. 207–221. Baltimore: Johns Hopkins Univ. Press.

———. 1959d. The argument for organic evolution before the *Origin of Species,* 1830–1858. In *Forerunners of Darwin: 1745–1859,* ed. B. Glass, O. Temkin and W. L. Straus, Jr., pp. 356–414. Baltimore: Johns Hopkins Univ. Press.

Lowe, P. C., Carson, J. R. and King, S. C. 1963. Effect of blood transfusions on plumage color in chickens. J. Heredity 54:17–22.

Lubenow, M. L. 1978. Does a proper interpretation of scripture require a recent creation? Impact Series no. 65, Institute for Creation Research, San Diego, Cal.

Lucretius. *De rerum natura (On the nature of things).*

Lumsden, C. J. and Wilson, E. O. 1980. Translation of epigenetic rules of individual behavior into ethnographic patterns. Proc. Nat. Acad. Sci. 77:4382–4386.

Lumsden, C. J. and Wilson, E. O. 1981. *Genes, mind, and culture: the coevolutionary process.* Cambridge: Harvard Univ. Press.

Lyell, C. 1830–1832. *Principles of geology.* London: Murray. (Reprinted 1969, New York: Johnson Reprint Corp.)

Lyell, K. 1970. *Life, letters and journals of Sir Charles Lyell, Bart.* Westmead, England: Gregg International.

Lyon, J. 1976. The "initial discourse" to Buffon's *Histoire Naturelle:* the first complete English translation. J. Hist. Biol. 9:133–181.

Lysenko, T. 1948. *The science of biology today.* New York: International Publishers.

Macbeth, N. 1971. *Darwin retried.* New York: Dell.

MacCulloch, C. J. A., ed. 1931. *Mythology of all races.* Boston: Marshall Jones.

Mackenzie, D. and Barnes, B. 1979. Scientific judgment: the biometry-Mendelism controversy. In *Natural order: historical studies of scientific culture,* ed. B. Barnes and S. Shapin, pp. 191–210. Hollywood, Cal.: Sage.

Magee, B. 1973. *Karl Popper.* New York: Viking.

Magnus, R. 1949. *Goethe as scientist.* New York: Schuman.

Mandelbaum, M. 1957. The scientific background of evolutionary theory in biology. J. Hist. Ideas 18:342–361.

———. 1958. Darwin's religious views. J. Hist. Ideas 19:363–378.

Manier, E. 1978. *The young Darwin and his cultural circle.* Dordrecht, Holland: Reidel.

Manser, A. R. 1965. The concept of evolution. Philosophy 40:18–34.

Marchant, J., ed. 1916. *Alfred Russel Wallace: letters and reminiscences.* New York: Harper & Bros. (Reprinted 1975, New York: Arno.)

Marx, J. L. 1978. Warm-blooded dinosaurs: evidence pro and con. Science 199:1424–1426.

Marx, K. 1979. (Trans. S. K. Padover.) *The letters of Karl Marx.* Englewood Cliffs, N.J.: Prentice-Hall.

Matthew, P. 1831. *On naval timber and arboriculture.* . . London: Longman, Rees, Orne, Brown & Green.

Maupertuis, P.-L. M. de. 1745. *Vénus physique.* (Xerox reprints available from New York: Clearwater. Trans. *[The earthly Venus]* S. B. Boas, 1966. New York: Johnson Reprint.)

Mauskopf, S. H., ed. 1978. *The reception of unconventional science.* New York: Praeger.

Mayer, W. V. 1973. Evolution and the law. Am. Biol. Teacher 35:144–145, 162.

Maynard Smith, J. 1969. The status of neo-Darwinism. In *Towards a theoretical biology,* vol. 2, ed. C. H. Waddington, pp. 82–89. Chicago: Aldine.

———. 1977. The limitations of evolution theory. In *The encyclopaedia of ignorance,* ed. R. Duncan and M. Weston-Smith, pp. 235–242. New York: Pergamon.

Mayr, E. 1972a. Lamarck revisited. J. Hist. Biol. 5:55–94.

———. 1972b. The nature of the Darwinian revolution. Science 176:981–989.

———.1976. *Evolution and the diversity of life: selected essays.* Cambridge: Belknap Press of Harvard Univ. Press.

———. 1977. Darwin and natural selection. Am. Sci. 65:321–327.

———. 1978. Evolution. Sci. Am. 239 (Sept.):46–55.

Mayr, E. and Provine, W. B., eds. 1980. *Perspectives on the unification of biology.* Cambridge, Mass.: Harvard Univ. Press.

McCown, T. D. and Kennedy, K. A. R., eds. 1972. *Climbing man's family tree: a collection of major writings on human phylogeny, 1699–1971.* Englewood Cliffs, N.J.: Prentice-Hall.

McKendrick, N. 1973. The role of science in the Industrial Revolution: a study of Josiah Wedgwood as a scientist and industrial chemist. In *Changing perspectives in the history of science,* ed. M. Teich and R. Young, Ch. 17. Boston: Reidel.

McKinney, H. L. 1969. Wallace's earliest observations on evolution: 28 December 1845. Isis 60:370–373.

———. 1972. *Wallace and natural selection.* New Haven, Conn.: Yale Univ. Press.

McWilliams, C. 1950. *Witch hunt: the revival of heresy.* Boston: Little, Brown.

Medvedev, Z. A. 1969. *The rise and fall of T. D. Lysenko.* New York: Columbia Univ. Press.

———. 1971. *The Medvedev papers.* New York: St. Martin's.

———. 1978. *Soviet science.* New York: Norton.

Mellersh, H. E. L. 1968. *FitzRoy of the Beagle.* London: Rupert Hart-Davis.

Mendel, G. 1866. Versuche über Pflanzen-Hybriden. Verh. naturforsch. Verein Brünn 4:3–47. (English translation: Experiments on plant hybrids. Trans. W.

Bateson. 1901. J. Roy. Horticultural Society. Trans. E. R. Sherwood. 1966. In *The origin of genetics: a Mendel source book,* ed. C. Stern and E. R. Sherwood. San Francisco: Freeman.)

Menzel, D. H. and Taves, E. H. 1977. *The UFO enigma.* New York: Doubleday.

Merton, R. K. 1973. *The sociology of science.* Chicago: Univ. of Chicago Press.

Metzger, W. P. 1955. Darwinism and the new regime. In *The development of academic freedom in the United States,* ed. W. P. Metzger and R. Hofstadter, Ch. 7. New York: Columbia Univ. Press.

Mikulak, M. W. 1967. Trofim Denisovich Lysenko. In *Soviet leaders,* ed. G. W. Simmonds, pp. 248–259. New York: Crowell.

———. 1970. Darwinism, Soviet genetics, and Marxism. J. Hist. Ideas 31:359–376.

Millar, R. 1972. *The Piltdown men.* New York: Ballantine.

Millhauser, M. 1959. *Just before Darwin: Robert Chambers and "Vestiges."* Middletown, Conn.: Wesleyan Univ. Press.

Mills, S. K. and Beatty, J. H. 1979. The propensity interpretation of fitness. Phil. Sci. 46:263–286.

Montagu, A., ed. 1980. *Sociobiology examined.* New York: Oxford Univ. Press.

Moore, J. A. 1972. *Readings in heredity and development.* London: Oxford Univ. Press.

———. 1974. Creationism in California. Daedalus 103:173–189.

———. 1975. On giving equal time to the teaching of evolution and creation. Pers. Biol. Med. 18:405–417.

Moore, J. N. 1973. Evolution, creation and the scientific method. Am. Biol. Teacher 35 (Jan.):23–27.

———. 1977. The impact of evolution on the social sciences. Impact Series no. 52, Institute for Creation Research, San Diego, Cal.

Moore, J. R. 1970. Charles Lydell and the Noachian deluge. J. Am. Scientific Affiliation 22:107–115.

———. 1975. Evolutionary theory and Christian faith: a bibliographical guide to the post-Darwin controversies. Christ. Sch. Rev. 4:211–230.

Moore, R. 1954. *Charles Darwin.* New York: Knopf.

Moorehead, A. 1969. *Darwin and the Beagle.* New York: Harper & Row.

More, L. T. 1925. *The dogma of evolution.* Princeton, N.J.: Princeton Univ. Press.

Morgan, T. H. 1916. *A critique of the theory of evolution.* Princeton, N.J.: Princeton Univ. Press.

Morgan, T. H., Sturtevant, A. H., Muller, H. J. and Bridges, C. B. 1915. *The mechanisms of Mendelian heredity.* New York: Henry Holt.

Morris, H. M., ed. 1974. *Scientific creationism (public school edition).* San Diego: Creation-Life.

———. 1976. Entropy and open systems. Impact Series no. 40, Institute for Creation Research, San Diego, Cal.

———. 1977a. The religion of evolutionary humanism and the public schools. Impact Series no. 51, Institute for Creation Research, San Diego, Cal.

———. 1977b. *The scientific case for creation.* San Diego: Creation-Life.

Munson, R., ed. 1971. *Man and nature.* New York: Dell (Delta).

Needham, J. 1969. *The grand titration: science and society in East and West.* Toronto: Univ. of Toronto Press.

Nelkin, D. 1976a. Science or scripture: the politics of "equal time." In *Science and its public,* ed. G. Holton and W. A. Blanpied, pp. 209–227. Boston: Reidel.

———. 1976b. The science-textbook controversies. Sci. Am. 234 (Apr.):33–39.

———. 1977a. *Science textbook controversies and the politics of equal time.* Cambridge, Mass.: MIT Press.

———. 1977b. Creation vs. evolution: the politics of science education. In *The social production of scientific knowledge,* ed. E. Mendelsohn, pp. 265–288. Dordrecht, Holland: Reidel.

Newell, N. D. 1974. Evolution under attack. Nat. Hist. 83 (Apr.):32–39.

Nordenskiold, E. 1929. *The history of biology.* London: Kegan Paul, Trench, Trubner.

Northrup, F. S. C. 1950. *The meeting of East and West.* New York: Macmillan.

Norton, B. J. 1973. The biometric defense of Darwinism. J. Hist. Biol. 6:283–316.

———. 1975. Biology and philosophy: the methodological foundations of biometry. J. Hist. Biol. 8:85–93.

Novitski, E. and Blixt, S. 1977. Mendel, linkage and synteny. BioSci. 28:34–35.

Odhiambo, T. R. 1967. East Africa: science for development. Science 158:876–881.

Olby, R. C. 1963. Charles Darwin's manuscript of pangenesis. Brit. J. Hist. Sci. 1:251–263.

———. 1965. Francis Galton's derivation of Mendelian ratios in 1875. Heredity 20:636–638.

———. 1966. *Origins of Mendelism.* New York: Schocken.

———. 1974. *The path to the double helix.* Seattle: Univ. of Washington Press.

———. 1979. Mendel no Mendelian? Hist. of Sci. 17:53–72.

Olby, R. C. and Gautry, P. 1968. Eleven references to Mendel before 1900. Annals of Sci. 24:7–20.

Olson, E. C. 1960. Morphology, paleontology, and evolution. In *Evolution after Darwin,* vol. 1, ed. S. Tax, pp. 523–545. Chicago: Univ. of Chicago Press.

Osborn, H. F. 1929. *From the Greeks to Darwin.* New York: Scribner's.

Ospovat, D. 1979. Darwin after Malthus. J. Hist. Biol. 12:211–230.

Oster, G. F. and Wilson, E. O. 1978. *Caste and ecology in the social insects.* Princeton, N.J.: Princeton Univ. Press.

Ostrom, J. H. 1978. A new look at dinosaurs. Nat. Geog. 154 (Aug.):152–185.

Packard, A. S. 1901. *Lamarck: the founder of evolution. His life and work.* New York: Longmans, Green. (Reprinted 1980, New York: Arno.)

Paine, T. 1794. *The age of reason: being an investigation of true and fabulous theology.* New York: Willey.

Paley, W. 1802. *Natural theology: or evidences of the existence and attributes of the Deity collected from the appearances of nature.* London: T. Tegg. (Excerpt in *Science before Darwin,* ed. H. M. Jones and I. B. Cohen, pp. 15–36. [1963.] London: Andre Deutsch.)

Paradis, J. G. 1978. *T. H. Huxley: man's place in nature.* Lincoln: Univ. of Nebraska Press.

Parker, G. 1978. Nature's challenge to evolutionary theory. Impact Series no. 64, Institute for Creation Research, San Diego, Cal.

Paul, D. 1981. "In the interests of civilization": Marxist views of race and culture in the nineteenth century. J. Hist. Ideas 42:115–138.

Pearl, L. 1977. *Descartes.* Boston: Twayne.

Pearson, H. 1930. *Doctor Darwin*. New York: Walker.

Pearson, K., ed. 1914–1930. *The life, letters and labours of Francis Galton*. Cambridge, England: Cambridge Univ. Press.

Peters, F. E. 1968. *Aristotle and the Arabs*. New York: New York Univ. Press.

Peters, J. A., ed. 1959. *Classic papers in genetics*. Englewood Cliffs, N.J.: Prentice-Hall.

Peters, R. H. 1976. Tautology in evolution and ecology. Am. Naturalist 110:1–12.

———. 1978. Predictable problems with tautology in evolution and ecology. Am. Naturalist 112:759–762.

Petersen, W. 1979. *Malthus*. Cambridge: Harvard Univ. Press.

Peterson, H. 1932. *Huxley, prophet of science*. London: Longmans, Green.

Petitot, L. H. 1966. *The life and spirit of Thomas Aquinas*. Chicago: Priory Press.

Petrunkevitch, A. 1963. August Weismann: personal reminiscences. J. Hist. Med. Allied Sci. 18:20–35.

Pfeifer, E. J. 1965. The genesis of American neo-Lamarckism. Isis 56:156–167.

Pfeiffer, J. E. 1977. *The emergence of society*. New York: McGraw-Hill.

Piaget, J. 1954. *The construction of reality in the child*. New York: Basic Books.

Pilbeam, D. and Gould, S. J. 1974. Size and scaling in human evolution. Science 186:892–901.

Plato. *Timaeus*. (Many editions, including B. Jowett trans., in *Great Books of the Western World*, vol. 7, ed. R. M. Hutchins. [1952.] Chicago: Encyclopaedia Britannica.)

Plutarch. *The lives of the noble Grecians and Romans*.

Pollard, W. G. 1979. The prevalence of Earthlike planets. Am. Sci. 67:653–659.

Popovsky, M. 1979. *Manipulated science: the crisis of science and scientists in the Soviet Union today*. New York: Doubleday.

Popper, K. R. 1959. *The logic of scientific discovery*. New York: Harper & Row.

———. 1965. *Conjectures and refutations*. New York: Harper Torchbooks.

———. 1966. *The open society and its enemies*. Vol. 2. *Hegel and Marx*. Princeton, N.J.: Princeton Univ. Press.

———. 1972. *Objective knowledge: an evolutionary approach*. New York: Oxford Univ. Press.

Popper, K. R. and Eccles, J. C. 1977. *The self and its brain*. New York: Springer International.

Portatié, E. 1960. *A guide to the thought of Saint Augustine*. Chicago: Henry Regnery.

Portugal, F. H. and Cohen, J. S. 1977. *A century of DNA*. Cambridge, Mass.: MIT Press.

Prichard, J. C. 1973. *Researches into the physical history of man*. Chicago: Univ. of Chicago Press.

Prigogine, I. 1973. Can thermodynamics explain biological order? Impact of Sci. on Soc. 23:159–179.

Provine, W. B. 1971. *The origins of theoretical population genetics*. Chicago: Univ. of Chicago Press.

———. 1978. The role of mathematical population geneticists in the evolutionary synthesis of the 1930s and 1940s. In *Studies in the History of Biology*, vol. 2, ed. W. Coleman and C. Limoges, pp. 167–192. Baltimore: Johns Hopkins Univ. Press.

Radl, E. 1930. *The history of biological theories*. London: Oxford Univ. Press.

Ralling, C., ed. 1979. *The voyage of Charles Darwin*. New York: Mayflower Books.

Randall, J. H., Jr. 1960. *Aristotle*. New York: Columbia Univ. Press.

Rashdall, H. 1936. *The universities of Europe in the Middle Ages*. Oxford: Oxford Univ. Press.

Raup, D. M. 1977. Probabilistic models in evolutionary paleobiology. Am. Sci. 65:50–57.

Raverat, G. 1952. *Period piece*. New York: Norton.

Redi, F. 1909. (Trans. M. Bigelow.) *Experiments on the generation of insects*. Chicago: Open Court.

Reichenbach, H. 1938. *Experience and prediction*. Chicago: Univ. of Chicago Press.

Rensch, B. 1971. *Biophilosophy*. New York: Columbia Univ. Press.

Ridley, M. 1980. Evolution and gaps in the fossil record. Nature 286:444–445.

Riedl, R. 1979. *Order in living organisms: a systems analysis of evolution*. New York: Wiley.

Roberts, H. F. 1929. *Plant hybridization before Mendel*. Princeton, N.J.: Princeton Univ. Press.

Robinson, G. 1979. *A prelude to genetics. Theories of a material substance of heredity: Darwin to Weismann*. Lawrence, Kansas: Coronado Press.

Robinson, J. O. 1972. *The psychology of visual illusion*. London: Hutchinson Univ. Library.

Roger, J. 1962. *Buffon: les époques de la nature, edition critique*. Paris: Editions du Museum.

———. 1963. *Les sciences de la vie dans la pensée française du XVIIIᵉ siècle*. Paris: Armand Colin.

Roosevelt, T. 1913, Biological analogies in history. In *History as literature*, vol. 26 of *The works of Theodore Roosevelt*, pp. 39–93. Port Washington, N.Y.: Kennikat Press.

Ross, R. H. 1973. *Alfred, Lord Tennyson "In Memoriam"; an authoritative text, backgrounds and sources of criticism*. New York: Norton.

Rothenberg, A. 1979. *The emerging goddess: the creative process in art, science, and other fields*. Chicago: Univ. of Chicago Press.

Rudwick, M. J. S. 1971. Uniformity and progression. In *Perspectives in the history of science and technology*, ed. D. H. D. Roller, pp. 209–237. Norman: Univ. of Oklahoma Press.

———. 1974. Darwin and Glen Roy: a "great failure" in scientific method? Studies in Hist. and Phil. of Sci. 5:97–185.

———. 1976. *The meaning of fossils: episodes in the history of palaeontology*. 2nd ed. New York: Science History Publications.

Ruse, M. 1970. The revolution in biology. Theoria 36:1–22.

———. 1971a. Two biological revolutions. Dialectica 25:17–38.

———. 1971b. Natural selection in *The Origin of Species*. Studies in Hist. and Phil. of Sci. 1:311–351.

———. 1973. *The philosophy of biology*. London: Hutchinson University Library.

———. 1975a. Darwin's debt to philosophy: an examination of the influence of the philosophical ideas of John F. W. Herschel and William Whewell on the development of Charles Darwin's theory of evolution. Studies in Hist. and Phil. of Sci. 6:159–181.

———. 1975b. Charles Darwin and artificial selection. J. Hist. Ideas 36:339–350.

————. 1975c. Charles Darwin's theory of evolution: an analysis. J. Hist. Biol. 8:219–241.

————. 1975d. The relationship between science and religion in Britain, 1830–1870. Church Hist. 44:505–522.

————. 1979a. *The Darwinian revolution.* Chicago: Univ. of Chicago Press.

————. 1979b. *Sociobiology: sense or nonsense?* Hingham, Mass.: Reidel.

Russell, B. 1935. *Religion and science.* New York: Oxford Univ. Press.

Russett, C. E. 1976. *Darwin in America: the intellectual response 1865–1912.* San Francisco: Freeman.

Sagan, C. 1972. UFO's: the extraterrestrial and other hypotheses. In *UFO's: a scientific debate,* ed. C. Sagan and T. Page, pp. 265–275, New York: Norton.

————. 1977. *The dragons of Eden.* New York: Ballantine.

Sagan, C. and T. Page, eds. 1972. *UFO's: a scientific debate.* New York: Norton.

Sagan, C. et al. 1978. *Murmurs of the Earth.* New York: Random House.

Sahlins, M. D. 1976. *The use and abuse of biology.* Ann Arbor: Univ. of Michigan Press.

Salzman, F. 1979. Sociobiology: the controversy continues. Science for the People Mar/Apr., pp. 20–27.

Sarton, G. 1927–1948. *Introduction to the history of science.* Baltimore: Williams & Wilkins.

————. 1952. *A history of science.* Vol. 1. *Ancient science through the Golden Age of Greece.* Cambridge: Harvard Univ. Press.

————. 1959. *A history of science.* Vol. 2. *Hellenistic science and culture in the last three centuries B.C.* New York: Wiley.

Saunders, P. T. and Ho, M. W. 1976. On the increase of complexity in evolution. J. Theoret. Biol. 63:375–384.

Schilpp, P. A., ed. 1974. *The philosophy of Karl Popper.* Lasalle, Ill.: Open Court.

Schopf, J. W. 1975. Precambrian paleobiology: problems and perspectives. Ann Rev. Earth and Planetary Sci. 3.

————. 1978. The evolution of the earliest cells. Sci. Am. 239 (Sept.):110–138.

Schwartz, J. S. 1974. Charles Darwin's debt to Malthus and Edward Blyth. J. Hist. Biol. 7:301–318.

Schweber, S. S. 1977. The origin of *The Origin* revisited. J. Hist. Biol. 10:229–316.

Scopes, J. T. and Presley, J. 1967. *Center of the storm.* New York: Holt, Rinehart & Winston.

Scriven, M. 1959. Explanation and prediction in evolution theory. Science 130:477–482.

Sears, P. B. 1950. *Charles Darwin: the naturalist as a cultural force.* New York: Scribner's.

Seaton, J. 1980. Dialectics: freedom of speech and thought. J. Hist. Ideas 4:283–289.

Seward, A. 1804. *Memoirs of the life of Dr. Darwin.* Philadelphia: Classic Press.

Shine, I. and Wrobel, S. 1976. *Thomas Hunt Morgan: pioneer of genetics.* Lexington: Univ. Press of Kentucky.

Shklovskii, I. S. and Sagan, C. 1966. *Intelligent life in the universe.* San Francisco: Holden-Day.

Shyrock, R. H. 1944. The strange case of Wells' theory of natural selection. In *Studies and essays in the history of science and learning offered in homage to George Sarton,* ed. M. F. A. Montagu, pp. 197–207. Reprinted 1977, New York: Arno.

Simon, M. A. 1971. *The matter of life: philosophical problems of biology.* New Haven, Conn.: Yale Univ. Press.

Simons, E. L. 1972. *Primate evolution.* New York: Macmillan.

Simpson, G. G. 1964. *This view of life: the world of an evolutionist.* New York: Harcourt, Brace & World.

Singer, C. 1957. *A short history of anatomy and physiology from the Greeks to Harvey.* New York: Dover.

Sirks, M. J. and Zirkle, C. 1964. *The evolution of biology.* New York: Ronald.

Siu, R. G. H. 1957. *The Tao of science: an essay on Western knowledge and Eastern wisdom.* Cambridge: MIT Press.

Smart, J. J. C. 1963. *Philosophy and scientific realism.* New York: Humanities Press.

Smith, C. U. M. 1976. *The problem of life: an essay on the origins of biological thought.* New York: Wiley.

Smith, N. K., ed. 1935. *Hume's dialogue concerning natural religion.* New York: Oxford Univ. Press.

Smith, R. 1972. Alfred Russel Wallace: philosophy of nature and man. Brit. J. Hist. Sci. 6:177–199.

Smith, S. 1960. The origin of "The Origin." Advancement of Sci. 16:391–401.

Sociobiology Study Group. 1976. Sociobiology: another biological determinism. BioSci. 26: 182, 184–190.

———. 1977. Sociobiology: a new biological determinism. In *Biology as a social weapon,* ed. Ann Arbor Science for the People Editorial Collective, pp. 133–149. Minneapolis: Burgess.

Solzhenitsyn, A. 1973. *The Gulag Archipelago I–II.* New York: Harper & Row.

Somervell, D. C. 1929. *English thought in the nineteenth century.* London: Methuen.

Sootin, H. 1959. *Gregor Mendel: father of the science of genetics.* New York: Vanguard.

Stahl, W. H. 1962. *Roman science.* Madison: Univ. of Wisconsin Press.

Stanley, S. M. 1975. A theory of evolution above the species level. Proc. Nat. Acad. Sci. 72:646–650.

Stauffer, R. C. 1959. "On the Origin of Species"; an unpublished version. Science 130:1449–1452.

———. ed. 1975. *Charles Darwin's natural selection. Being the second part of his big species book written from 1856 to 1858.* New York: Cambridge Univ. Press.

Stebbins, G. L. 1973. The evolution of design. Am. Biol. Teacher 35:57–61.

———. 1977. In defense of evolution: tautology or theory? (Letter.) Am. Naturalist 111:386–390.

Stent, G. S. 1971. *Molecular genetics.* San Francisco: Freeman.

———. 1978. *Paradoxes of progress.* San Francisco: Freeman.

Stern, C. and Sherwood, E. R., eds. 1966. *The origin of genetics: a Mendel source book.* San Francisco: Freeman.

Stevens, L. R. 1978. *Charles Darwin.* Boston: Twayne.

Stiefel, T. 1977. The heresy of science: a twelfth-century conceptual revolution. Isis 68:347–362.

Stone, I. 1980. *The origin: a biographical novel of Charles Darwin.* Garden City, N.Y.: Doubleday.

Strickberger, M. W. 1973. Evolution and religion. BioSci. 23:417–421.

Strong, R. 1976. *The space gods revealed.* New York: Harper & Row.

Stubbe, H. 1972. *History of genetics*. Cambridge, Mass.: MIT Press.

Sturtevant, A. H. 1965. *A history of genetics*. New York: Harper & Row.

Sulloway, F. J. 1979. Geographic isolation in Darwin's thinking: the vicissitudes of a crucial idea. In *Studies in history of biology*, vol. 3, ed. W. Coleman and C. Limoges, pp. 23–65. Baltimore: Johns Hopkins Univ. Press.

Suppe, F. and Asquith, P. D., eds. 1977. *Proceedings of the 1976 biennial meeting of the Philosophy of Science Association*, vol. 2. East Lansing: Philosophy of Science Assoc., Michigan State Univ.

Swinburne, R. G. 1965. Galton's law: formulation and development. Annals of Sci. 21:15–31.

Tarski, A. 1969. Truth and proof. Sci. Am. 220 (June):63–77.

Taton, R., ed. 1963. *Ancient and medieval science: from the beginning to 1450*. New York: Basic Books.

Taylor, C. W. and Barron, F., eds. 1963. *Scientific creativity: its recognition and development*. New York: Wiley.

Taylor, P. W. 1975. *Principles of ethics: an introduction*. Encino, Cal.: Dickenson.

Temkin, O. 1959. The idea of descent in post-Romantic German biology: 1848–1858. In *Forerunners of Darwin: 1745–1859*, ed. B. Glass, O. Temkin and W. L. Straus, Jr., pp. 323–355. Baltimore: Johns Hopkins Univ. Press.

Thagard, P. 1977. Darwin and Whewell. Studies in Hist. and Phil. of Sci. 8:353–356.

Thomas, R. D. K. and Olsen, E. C., eds. 1978. A cold look at the warm-blooded dinosaurs. N.Y.: Praeger.

Thomas Aquinas. *Summa theologica*. (Trans. Fathers of the English Dominican Province.)

Thomson, K. S. 1975. H.M.S. *Beagle*, 1820–1870. Am. Sci. 63:664–672.

Thorndike, L. 1923–1958. *History of magic and experimental science*. New York: Macmillan.

Torrey, H. B. and Felin, F. 1937. Was Aristotle an evolutionist? Quart. Rev. Biol. 12:1–18.

Turchin, V. F. 1977. *The phenomenon of science*. New York: Columbia Univ. Press.

Turrill, W. B. 1963. *Joseph Dalton Hooker*. London: Nelson.

Valentine, J. W. 1978. The evolution of multicellular plants and animals. Sci. Am. 239 (Sept.):140–158.

van de Fliert, J. R. 1969. Fundamentalism and the fundamentals of geology. J. of the Am. Scientific Affiliation 21:69–81.

Vandermeer, J. H. 1977. Ecological determinism. In *Biology as a social weapon*, ed. Ann Arbor Science for the People Editorial Collective, pp. 108–122. Minneapolis: Burgess.

Vanderpool, H. Y., ed. 1973. *Darwin and Darwinism: revolutionary insights concerning man, nature, religion and society*. Lexington, Mass.: D. C. Heath.

Vartarian, A. 1953. Trembley's polyp, La Mettrie and eighteenth century French materialism. J. Hist. Ideas 11:259–286.

Veith, I. 1960. Creation and evolution in the Far East. In *Evolution after Darwin*, vol. 3, ed. S. Tax and C. Callender, pp. 1–17. Chicago: Univ. of Chicago Press.

Voeller, B. R. 1968. *The chromosome theory of inheritance*. New York: Appleton-Century-Crofts.

von Bertalanffy, L. 1960. *Problems of life*. New York: Harper Torchbooks.

———. 1969. Chance or law. In *Beyond reductionism,* ed. A. Koestler and J. R. Smythies, pp. 56–84. New York: Macmillan.

Vorzimmer, P. 1963. Charles Darwin and blending inheritance. Isis 54:371–390.

———. 1968. Darwin and Mendel. the historical connection. Isis 59:77–82.

———. 1969a. Darwin, Malthus and the theory of natural selection. J. Hist. Ideas 30:527–542.

———. 1969b. Darwin's *Questions about the breeding of animals* (1839). J. Hist. Biol. 2:269–281.

———. 1970. *Charles Darwin: the years of controversy. The Origin of Species and its critics, 1859–1882.* Philadelphia: Temple Univ. Prss.

———. 1975. An early Darwin manuscript: the "Outline and draft of 1839." J. Hist. Biol. 8:191–217.

———. 1977. The Darwin reading notebooks (1838–1860). J. Hist. Biol. 10:107–153.

Vrooman, J. R. 1970. *René Descartes.* New York: Putnam's.

Waddington, C. H. 1957. *The strategy of the genes.* London: Allen & Unwin.

———, ed. 1969. *Towards a theoretical biology,* vol. 2. Chicago: Aldine.

Wade, N. 1972. Creationists and evolutionists: confrontation in California. Science 178:724–729.

———. 1976. Sociobiology: troubled birth for new discipline. Science 191:1151–1155.

Wallace, A. R. 1905. *My life: a record of events and opinions.* New York: Dodd, Mead.

Walsh, J. 1976. Science for the People: comes the revolution. Science 191:1033–1035.

Ward, H. 1927. *Charles Darwin and the theory of evolution.* Indianapolis: Bobbs-Merrill.

Washburn, S. L. 1978. The evolution of man. Sci. Am. 239 (Sept.):194–208.

Wasserman, G. D. 1978. Testability of the role of natural selection within theories of population genetics and evolution. Brit. J. Phil. Sci. 29:223–242.

Watson, J. D. 1968. *The double helix.* New York: New American Library (Signet).

Wechsler, J., ed. 1978. *On aesthetics in science.* Cambridge, Mass.: MIT Press.

Weinstein, A. 1977. How unknown was Mendel's paper? J. Hist. Biol. 10:341–364.

Weismann, A. 1889. On heredity. In *Essays upon heredity and kindred biological problems,* ed. E. B. Poulton, S. Schonland and A. E. Shipley, pp. 69–105. Oxford: Clarendon.

———. 1904. *The evolution theory.* London: Edward Arnold.

Wells, K. D. 1971. Sir William Lawrence (1783–1867): a study of pre-Darwinian ideas on heredity and variation. J. Hist. Biol. 4:319–361.

———. 1973a. William Charles Wells and the races of man. Isis 64:215–225.

———. 1973b. The historical context of natural selection: the case of Patrick Matthew. J. Hist. Biol. 6:225–258.

Wells, W. C. 1818. Two essays: one upon single vision with two eyes; the other on dew. A letter to the Right Hon. Lloyd, Lord Kenyon, and an account of a female of the white race of mankind, part of whose skin resembles that of a negro; with some observations on the causes of the differences in colour and form between the white and negro races of men. London: A. Constable.

Werskey, P. G. 1971. Haldane and Huxley: the first appraisals. J. Hist. Biol. 4:171–183.

————. 1978. *The visible college: the collective biography of British scientific socialists of the 1930s.* New York: Holt, Rinehart & Winston.

West, G. 1938. *Charles Darwin: a portrait.* New Haven, Conn.: Yale Univ. Press.

White, A. D. 1896. *History of the warfare of science with theology in Christendom.* New York: Appleton. (Reprinted 1960, New York: Dover.)

Whittaker, R. H. and Feeny, P. P. 1971. Allelochemics: chemical interactions between species. Science 171:757–770.

Wichler, G. 1961. *Charles Darwin.* New York: Pergamon.

Wicken, J. S. 1979. Entropy and evolution: a philosophic review. Pers. Biol. Med. 22:285–300.

Wilkie, J. S. 1959. Buffon, Lamarck and Darwin: the originality of Darwin's theory of evolution. In *Darwin's biological work,* ed. P. R. Bell, pp. 262–307. Cambridge, England: Cambridge Univ. Press.

Willey, B. 1960. *Darwin and Butler: two versions of evolution.* New York: Harcourt, Brace.

Williams, G. C. 1966. *Adaptation and natural selection.* Princeton, N.J.: Princeton Univ. Press.

Williams, M. B. 1970. Deducing the consequences of evolution: a mathematical model. J. Theoret. Biol. 29:343–385.

————. 1973. The logical status of natural selection and other evolutionary controversies. In *The methodological unity of science,* ed. M. Bunge, pp. 84–102. Dordrecht, Holland: Reidel.

Williams-Ellis, A. 1966. *Darwin's moon: a biography of Alfred Russel Wallace.* London: Blackie.

Willis, D. C. 1972. *Horror and science fiction films: a checklist.* Metuchen, N.J.: Scarecrow Press.

Wilson, A. M. 1972. *Diderot.* New York: Oxford Univ. Press.

Wilson, E. O. 1971. *The insect societies.* Cambridge: Belknap Press of Harvard Univ. Press.

————. 1975a. *Sociobiology: the new synthesis.* Cambridge: Belknap Press of Harvard Univ. Press.

————. 1975b. For sociobiology. (Letter.) New York Rev. of Books, Dec. 11.

————. 1975c. Human decency is animal. New York Times Magazine, Oct. 12.

————. 1976. Academic vigilantism and the political significance of sociobiology. BioSci. 26:183–190.

————. 1978a. *On human nature.* Cambridge: Harvard Univ. Press.

————. 1978b. Introduction: what is sociobiology? In *Sociobiology and human nature,* ed. M. S. Gregory, A. Silvers and D. Sutch, pp. 1–12. San Francisco, Jossey-Bass.

Wilson, L. G., ed. 1970. *Sir Charles Lyell's scientific journals on the species question.* New Haven, Conn.: Yale Univ. Press.

————. 1971. Sir Charles Lyell and the species question. Am. Sci. 59:43–55.

————. 1972. *Charles Lyell: the years to 1841: the revolution in geology.* New Haven, Conn.: Yale Univ. Press.

Wolff, R. P., Moore, B., Jr., and Marcuse, H. 1965. *Critique of pure tolerance.* Boston: Beacon.

Wolsky, M. de I. and Wolsky, A. 1976. *The mechanism of evolution: a new look at old ideas.* Basel: S. Karger.

Woodcock, G. 1969. *Henry Walter Bates: naturalist of the Amazons.* New York: Barnes & Noble.

Woodger, J. H. 1937. *Axiomatic method in biology.* Cambridge, England: Cambridge Univ. Press.

Wright, S. 1966. Mendel's ratios. In *The origins of genetics: a Mendel source book,* ed. C. Stern and E. R. Sherwood, pp. 173–179. San Francisco: Freeman.

———. 1967. The foundations of population genetics. In *Heritage from Mendel,* ed. R. A. Brink and E. D. Styles, pp. 245–263. Madison: Univ. of Wisconsin Press.

Young, R. M. 1969. Malthus and the evolutionists: the common context of biological and social theory. Past and Present 43:109–145.

———. 1971. Evolutionary biology and ideology: then and now. Sci. Studies 1:177–206.

———. 1973. The historiographic and ideological contexts of the nineteenth-century debate on man's place in nature. In *Changing perspectives in the history of science,* ed. M. Teich and R. M. Young, pp. 344–438. Boston: Reidel.

Yukawa, H. 1973. *Creativity and intuition.* New York: Kodausha International.

Yunis, J. J., Sawyer, J. R. and Dunham. K. 1980. The striking resemblance of high-resolution G-banded chromosomes of man and chimpanzee. Science 208:1145–1148.

Zimmerman, L. J. and Whitten, R. G. 1980. Prehistoric bones tell a grim tale of Indian v. Indian. Smithsonian 11 (Sept.):100–108.

Zirkle, C. 1941. Natural selection before the *"Origin of Species."* Am. Phil. Soc. Proc. 84:71–123.

———. 1946. The early history of the idea of inheritance of acquired characters and of pangenesis. Am. Phil. Soc. Trans. 35:91–152.

———. 1949. *Death of a science in Russia.* Philadelphia: Univ. of Pennsylvania Press.

———. 1951a. The knowledge of heredity before 1900. In *Genetics in the 20th century,* ed. L. C. Dunn, Ch. 3. New York: Macmillan.

———. 1951b. Gregor Mendel and his precursors. Isis 42:97–104.

———. 1956. L'affaire Lysenko. J. of Heredity 47:47–57.

———. 1959. *Evolution, Marxian biology, and the social scene.* Philadelphia: Univ. of Pennsylvania Press.

———. 1964. Some oddities in the delayed discovery of Mendelism. J. of Heredity 55:65–72.

Index